TRAP SHOOTING SECRETS
"What they won't tell you...this book will!"

"**Trap Shooting Secrets**"
Printed in the United States of America.
Published by James Russell Publishing
780 Diogenes Drive, Reno, NV 89512

"**Trap Shooting Secrets**"
Written by James Russell © 1997, 1998, 1999, 2000.
Illustrations by James Russell, Phone:
First Printed Edition © 1997
ISBN No. 0-916367-06-1
Second Printed Edition © 1997
ISBN No. 0-916367-09-6
Third Revised Printing © February 1998 and June 1999.
Fourth Revised Printing January 2000 (no ISBN change).
ISBN No. 0-916367-09-6

This book can be purchased from:

Any major bookstore via special order. Or you may order direct from the following:

➢ **Pinnell's Competitive Components**, Inc., P.O. Box 3703, Central Point, OR 97502 (541)-664-4994.
➢ **Shotgun Sports Magazine**, P.O. Box 6810, Auburn, CA 95604 (800)-676-8920, (916)-889-9106.
➢ **Clay Shooting Magazine**, Thruxton Down House, Thruxton Down, Andover, Hampshire, England SP11 8PR Phone: (01264-889533).
➢ **Scribani Rossi Olympic Shooting School**, GPO Box 1390, Sydney, Australia NSW-1043
➢ Phone: +61(0)295552728.
➢ Amazon.com, Barnes & Noble, Borders Books, Waldens Books, Books-A-Million, Chapters (Canada), Varsity Books, your local bookstore.
➢ Check our ad in the **ATA** - Amateur Trapshooting Association's **Trap & Field Magazine** P.O. Box 567 Indianapolis, Indiana 46206. Look us up on the Internet. Search via book titles or by James Russell Publishing or use search word; trap shooting. We are also linked on the major trap shooting sites.
➢ Visit our Website: http://www.powernet.net/~scrnplay for free trapshooting lessons and where to find professionals who give lessons (some are listed in this book).

Printed in the USA by

MORRIS PUBLISHING

3212 East Highway 30 • Kearney, NE 68847 • 1-800-650-7888

SPECIAL THANKS TO
The Psalms of David in the Bible.

DEDICATED TO
Those who avail the distressed and filleth minds with good things.

A THOUGHT TO PONDER
"There are 800 promises in the Bible God will fulfil for you." Have you read them?

A SPECIAL DEDICATION OF THANKS
To all mothers of trapshooters supporting us in our endeavors with unfailing love.
Whether here now or there in peace, we gently bow.
To this cause we dedicate in their honor.

TABLE OF CONTENTS

CONSUMER NOTICE

The products mentioned in this book are not endorsements product reviews and evaluations by the author or publisher, but are used solely for information, reference, and examples. Liability and consequential or incidental damages, expressed or implied, or the use or misuse of such products lies solely with the manufacturer and / or with the consumer. Sold or distributed as information only.

COMPANY LISTINGS

Addresses for companies listed herein, may change. If this occurs, most can be found on the Internet and in the shotgun magazines or at your public library. If you find an address is no longer valid, please feel free to write and let us know.

SUCCESS HAS A PRICE

"Fortune's expensive smile is earned."   Emily Dickinson

If you deem the price of this book is costly, contemplate the expense of shooting improperly! Calculate the cost of thousands of shells expended, practice session fees at $3 - 3.50 per round of 25 targets, tournament entry and option fees, gun modifications. It all adds up to more money spent than you wish to recall. For less than the cost of a half-case of ammo and lower than shooting one tournament, 'Trap Shooting Secrets' will place you years ahead of those who don't read the book, who are likely practicing the same mistakes over-and-over again. Moreover, if 'Trap Shooting Secrets' does its job, increasing your scores (I guarantee it will) then just one win will pay for the book many times over for years to come. Consider it an investment. Pay a little now or a lot later. Any book that can save money but also make you money... is truly an asset to be valued. Any doubts? Let the results speak for themselves!

WHY YOU NEED THIS BOOK

"Some people make things happen - some watch things happen - while others wonder what has happened."

Could there be a better way? I decided to explore what the successful trapshooters were doing differently. Did they know something I didn't? Would new information and education lead to higher achievement? So I watched what the pros were doing, spoke with them to gain insight into the real truth, and examined the laws of physics, including the mental and visual aspects of the game.

As I began to sort out what I had learned and apply what really needed to be done, I found my scores took a huge leap forward. I even began to earn money in trapshooting with the options, a little at first, but more as time progressed...more than I thought I ever would! 'Trap Shooting Secrets' will help you avoid the costly mistakes everybody else makes! Picture yourself breaking away from the competition!

But let's make sure we balance your expectations with a realistic attitude. 'Trap Shooting Secrets' will not provide you 'instant success' making you into a "Superstar All-American" shooter overnight but rather concentrate on teaching you how to be extremely well-known and respected in your own backyard. Walking is one step away from falling, yet children keep at it until walking becomes second nature. Before you can run you need to learn how to walk and that means walking in all the right places before you begin running to all the wrong places. You'll acquire the ability to isolate the trivial, and focus on the vital knowledge required to properly concentrate on what you need, as I lay out each step you must complete. You will see results, this I can guarantee.

And yes, trapshooting really is a system with some very specific rules chiseled in stone. Ignore the rules and the years will painfully wither away leaving you with few tangible results to show for your efforts. Others may not put a label on these 'secret rules' or even realize they are using them, but they still use them. You will too! And success will come to you. You'll be evaluating what went right vs. what went wrong, so you'll detect your mistakes and build on your achievements. But beware, a little knowledge can be dangerous to your competition! It can also be dangerous to yourself. As there is so much information here, you should digest it slowly. Attempting to assimilate too much information too rapidly results in futility. Take it easy, one step at a time. Perfect each phase, then move on to the next. Some suggestions you've likely heard before, but don't be hasty to ignore or skip the chapter, as you may not be aware of the 'reasoning' behind the technique.

The first goal of 'Trap Shooting Secrets' is to teach you how to shoot targets with accuracy and understanding, and secondly, to help you make money as quickly as possible. I believe once you start earning money, that in and of itself will be powerful persuasion to keep shooting. After all, shooting is fun, that's why you got into this crazy sport in the first place, and if you can pay for your fees and components from your winnings, even a portion of your costs - that's an achievement! Lack of knowledge is why most trapshooters ultimately fail. 'Trap Shooting Secrets' will give you the success you deserve. It will enable you to complete a comprehensive 'Action Plan' to motivate, identify and select your goals, using a timeline that is both realistic and practical. Take yourself to whatever level of accomplishment you desire: local, regional, national, international. The information is here, all you have to do is use it. 'Trap Shooting Secrets' will pull it all together for you and drastically transform the way you shoot, starting immediately! You will have a clear understanding of what you need to do, and undo. This small effort will produce the results that have eluded you for so long. How successful do you want to be?

A NOTE FROM THE AUTHOR
"Try to reason about trapshooting and you will lose your reason."

There is, by design, intentional replication within the text to facilitate memory retention of essential information. The vast and difficult subjects were isolated, broken down and fragmented into localized domains to expose and resolve complications inflicting deficiencies on the shooter. This required isolating and separating underlying complexities of the game into mini-chapters. Some repetition was unavoidable and necessary to tie the innumerable knots and untangle the sails as technical sum and substance involuntarily, although naturally, overlap each other. Writing this book was arduous as a myriad of technical factors interwove to combine into one: mind, spirit, body, moods, physics, mechanics, aeronautics, psychology, physiology, ergonomics, etceteras. Blending these complex elements with ever-changing environmental variations into a simplified, easy to read interpretation, ending with an efficient and usable textbook was distillingly challenging, though at times I considered impossible to abridge. No surprise there are few trapshooting technical books. Overall, I believe, I have accomplished the goal of identifying the critical stumbling blocks, exposing technique fault factors, and ultimately tying-up the beast.

Please keep in mind this book focuses primarily on handicap shooting - any yardage beyond the 16 yard line. Howbeit, I have attended to particular pointers for shooting singles for those poor apparitions of necessity who thrive on the sixteen... wandering spirits of shotgunners who haven't yet discovered the heavenly wonders of handicap shooting.

SATISFACTION GUARANTEED !
Happiness ain't a thing in itself—it's only a contrast with something that ain't pleasant. Mark Twain

Books do not traditionally attach a warrantee or guarantee. They are sold 'as is' on a buyer beware basis. 'Trap Shooting Secrets' is the lone exception. It is fully guaranteed for thirty-days from date of purchase to your complete satisfaction or your money will be refunded. There are only two customary requirements, which is reasonable and fair. If you are not satisfied with this book we ask that it be returned in salable condition along with your sales receipt indicating where the book was purchased and the cost of purchase. Make sure the book is packaged so it does not become damaged in shipment. This money back guarantee is a "no questions asked" return for refund of the purchase price. Send a *letter* with your sales receipt to: James Russell, P.O. Box 10121, Eugene, OR 97440. Your satisfaction is guaranteed! Please, if you do wish to return the book for a refund, do not send it to the retailer as they may not be authorized or equipped to handle returns. Send a letter first requesting return instructions. Do not return the book. Give the book a chance to increase your scores. You should see positive results within 30-days, but this of course will depend on your shooting proficiency level at the time of purchase. If you are new to trapshooting, it may require more time to reach high scores.

STRANGE BUT TRUE
"Everybody knows nothing until they learn."

The advice you read here may sound strange, even to the experienced shooter, but it is all true and verified by 'professional' clay target shooters. Thousands of shooters have found great success from the information in this book. If it all appears strange to you it is likely you need this book all the more to raise your scores. The book is endorsed by professional shooters, the first book to gain such a recognition in the history of trap shooting!

HOW TO INTERPRET TEXT
"I'm not confused, just well informed."

1. If confusion or conflicting theorems arise, recall that 'Trap Shooting Secrets' primarily focuses on ATA or DTL handicap trapshooting and Olympic Trap, not singles, doubles, skeet or sporting clays. Crossing these boundaries often leads to misinterpretation and bafflement. Many tips may apply, but not all.
2. Don't rush through the book or perplexity will descend upon you without compassion or conscience. Trapshooting is easy, though the interpretation for the reasons why is not.
3. This is only one point of view on the game, not an absolute. It's written to stimulate ideas to enhance your own creativity and talent. Consider it an "idea bank" to withdraw inspiration and solutions as needed to resolve shooting difficulties.
4. Try the tips and suggestions and if they work for you, fine. If not, just continue on to the next chapter. What doesn't work for you now may very well produce strong results next season or two years from now.
5. To fully comprehend the entire text will necessitate multiple readings over a period of extended time, for some of what you read today may not be thoroughly understood in the present but will take on increasing importance in the future. A subtitle may appear inconsequential when read at your current skill level and equivalent knowledge yet retain valuable interpolations as you become more sensitized and finely tuned as your shooting improves. Keep this book in your car with your gun so you can easily refer to it when needed. You'll be glad you did.

KNOWLEDGE IS POWERFUL
"Call on God, but row away from the rocks."

How important it is to have accurate information! Everyone has a story to tell, giving advice, aid, and oftentimes discomfort, whether intentional or not, but frequently harmful. Friends don't give friends bad advice, still the road to hell is paved with good intentions. Confusion and 'mind-clutter' sets in quickly, compounding the agonizing distress most shooters experience. Therewith the old verbiage, *"Why did I miss that target?"* sets in *deep,* relying more on realities of luck than true skill. Many shooters have gone through the mill experimenting with thousands of shells to individually discern slow progress. I've listened to wing shooters, shooting since childhood and skeet, sporting clay and trapshooters who are worthy shooters, though not professional. All had much to say, yet could not accurately explain how to become a great shot. For most, we march into a dead end.

The road to enlightenment is long and difficult. It is perilous and costly to shoot tournaments without a solid foundation of skill. Everyone believes they can pick up a shotgun and learn to shoot it, but this is not true. Everyone can drive a car though few can win a stock car race never mind the Indy 500. With this fact firmly established, shotgunning is no exemption. Of course, eventually you will catch on and shoot well, but how long will it take? How many thousands of dollars are you willing to spend? It is the goal of 'Trap Shooting Secrets' to vastly accelerate the learning curve and save you a bundle of money; thousands of dollars! The book will pay for itself many times over. And of notable value, when you need help, it's right here waiting for you to turn the page to find the answer. In fact, the better you get the more valuable this book will be to you!

At some point in your shooting career you will fall into a nasty tailspin and commence blaming the loads, the gun, the puller, the squad, the sun and then some. Don't blame God for making the tiger, thank him for not giving him wings! Many are mistaken, few are blameworthy. Brush away the cobwebs in your mind, the uncertainty is you! The problem is me, not the gun. A finer gun will still exclusively be as worthy as the shooter. A pro could break 100s straight with a well-fitted field gun! So save yourself a ton of money. The gun you now have may very well be the ticket to success. And you can forget about fiddling with shotshell patterns. Once you pattern your gun you will behold it is to a large degree not adjustable except for choke size. Shot patterns are three-dimensional, requiring multi-camera high-speed strobe photography to reveal their true configurations. The optimum way to fill time is to waste it. It's a superfluous expenditure of time and money to experiment with reloads in trapshooting. What will you do if you prepare to shootoff and run out of your unrivaled favored shells? You'll lose the shootoff, that's certainly a high probability. Use factory shells in a shootoff or use reloads with factory components. You can't substitute shells and be a consistent winner. More on this later.

You have heard, *"You must go on the line with confidence."* In contrast, you will gain little if you go on station awash with conviction. Others and I have tried it... it doesn't work in and of itself. Confidence without skill can't effectively coexist. Skill and polished technique build self-assurance and confidence. This takes time to master, since success is a journey, not a destination. However, Trap Shooting Secrets will vastly accelerate the learning curve. And talking about curves? Did you know you missed the target because you are never shooting a straight-away? The odds of getting a straight-away target, remarkably, is near impossibility. And I'm talking about the trap set in the #2 hole where traditionally seemingly straight targets are produced. The effect is the same no matter if the trap is set in the #3 hole. When the A.T.A. recommended a rule change in 1995, shooters missed targets when traps were moved from the #2 to the #3 hole. Why? You must ascertain immediately how to shoot circles, not straight lines (something you probably never heard of before, right?). You'll understand the concept and absolutely prove to yourself these strange, yet consequential realities exist. Managing these curves will increase your scores, as no matter what hole the trap is set to, there are no straight-away targets. The lone anomaly: you'll see a true straight target when the trap machine is locked into a non-oscillating mode and even then, eddy currents and wind may likely deviate the target's trajectory, enough so you'll miss the target!

Don't expect a price won't be paid to increase your scores. The highest price is looking for the easy way and setting up a mental block refusing to try new things. You must be willing to learn and be enthusiastic to acquire fresh techniques that will, at first, feel uncomfortable. Bear in mind, you'll be experimenting with changing foot stances, altering gun mount, swing approach, visual focus, etc. It will feel awkward and you may not always see instant results. Never judge a style simply because you tried it a few times and found it didn't work, or you felt uncomfortable with it. That is taking the easy way out. Ask any guitarist how hard it was to twist, bend and distort his wrists to play a 'bar' chord. He'll tell you how physically and mentally painful it was to learn, but now bar chords are a vital feature of music and he couldn't play without them.

The finest techniques are always the most difficult to master! But they pay high rewards to those who persevere. When you try a new concept or method don't calculate the number of broken targets, that is prejudging and it is a fatal error. Trying a new style or form will always induce lost targets! Ask yourself if the approach makes sense. If it makes perfect sense then, by golly, work on it and the targets will break. Yes, scores do drop, frequently to embarrassing levels, when resolving bad habits or testing new technique. This is to be expected as you search for the right moves, stance, call, etc. You can't make an omelet without breaking eggs. You won't find opportunities to improvement if you're not looking for them! There isn't a shooter alive that would not trade a temporary reduction in scores to reach a higher score. The discouragement is the high scores arrive later with patience. Mark Twain sums it up, *"What, then, is the true Gospel of consistency? Change. Who is the really consistent man? The man who changes. Since change is the law of his being, he cannot be consistent if he stuck in a rut."*

When someone shows you a sound, solid, proven skill don't say; *"I can't shoot that way."* Yes you can! You have to break bad habits no matter how uncomfortable it may at first feel. Suddenly, with practice and time, it all comes together, your scores match your previous ability, then surpass it with remarkable speed and agility. If you're not willing to learn the right way, you're wasting time, money and opportunity for advancement. Well begun is half done. A good beginning almost assures success. Shooting may be fun, but I assure you the joy will vaporize as you keep losing events to those who have 'open minds' and have 'worked' to overcome bad habits. Shooting is like playing a instrument, you need instruction to master the basics or you'll never make it to Las Vegas.

The point of view taken here is; numerous different paths lead to the goal of good shooting, *Trap Shooting Secrets* is one path. Try your hand with these tips and you will be a better shooter. Every chapter is a step up the ladder toward improving accuracy and precision. With each chapter you should stop for a while and learn where you are, what you are doing, and why, before climbing any higher. Take it slowly. This is not a crash course. Learn each chapter thoroughly before going on to the next. When you are learning a skill, a lot of practice by itself is not enough. Practice should be spread over a considerable period of time for learning to be successful. It takes time to develop a skill! You'll discern this fact likewise applies to playing musical instruments, woodworking, masonry, mechanics, etc. You've heard it before, neglect not the gift that is in thee. Be amenable to change attitudes and put in a little elbow grease. Myth as metaphor. You must give up certain myths and time-honored beliefs to take charge of your goals. Shooting and winning is no different than any other aspect of your life. It requires you take the responsibility to make it happen. Proficiency will not materialize out of thin air. You should develop a plan of action, then act upon it. Many folks are very sincere about their shooting, though are not committed to making excellence materialize. Sincerity is an attitude, commitment is an action. Sincerity without action doesn't make anything happen.

I have spoken with champion All-American shooters. What do these professionals have we don't have? Real leaders are ordinary people with extraordinary determination! Read on and discover the inside secrets to enlighten your awareness of the realities of the game, and hopefully, obliterate myth from reality. There is voluminous information in this book. Don't overload yourself with analysis paralysis (information overload). Assimilating all in one month will raise confusion. The book is meant to be a guide, a road map and a troubleshooter. A valuable reference to fall back on when things seem to fall apart. **Keep this book in your vehicle**, bring it to practice and competitive shoots. This way you'll have instant access to information you may need, when you want it! *"Trap Shooting Secrets"* can't help you if it's collecting dust on your bookshelf while you're shooting wishing you had brought it with you - particularly in competitive events. Remember too, that it's not, *"My way or hit the highway."* Read, grasp the sensibilities, practice these tips to incorporate into your own form and style of shooting. **Keep this book by your side, and you'll shoot respectable scores wherever you go, in any weather, day or night**.

SOUND ADVICE
"Any port in a storm."

A teacher is more than two books. Find a coach, a shooter you respect who cares, because you won't learn much if you know the instructor doesn't care and is solely teaching for the money. Insure the advice and instructions are validated by certification, reputation or positive results. Keep in mind, in the history of sports some of the best coaches in the world were never licensed to teach. Teamwork divides the effort and multiplies the effect. A good coach will teach technique broken down into easily remembered segments. It's all to do with the training; you can do a lot if you're properly trained. Buy a trap gun and insure it fits you, so as the gun meets the shoulder and face a repeatable sight picture will form. Practice with dedication and a purpose. Don't shoot another gun. It will devastate your scores as each gun shoots with a altered point of impact (POI), [See Fig. 1-2 and Managing Point of Impact to understand basic POI]. Every gun also swings, points, weighs and feels differently. Shooters should spend more time studying and shooting targets than playing with reload recipes, choke tubes, and other gizmos. Discover, question, learn, search, find. If no instructor is available? Use books, magazines, videotapes. But let us not forget a tried and true fact of life; experience is the greatest teacher and teaches more effectively than books or school. Many veteran shooters agree, as I hear them preach this often to shooters seeking advice.

A respected veteran in Medford, Oregon once told me, *"Jim, try everything. When you're tired of listening to all the bullheaded clowns who claim to know all things, just call, keep your head down and your eye on the target. This is the secret of winning."* Makes a lot of sense to me! But does it work? It does. Interviews with professional shooters in magazine articles proclaim the same logic repeatedly. What they don't always say is how to apply what you are supposed to do. That's the hard part since everyone is so unique -- how can they explain the details? Trap Shooting Secrets tries to bridge that gap. Often, professionals really don't know what they are doing to reach such high levels of proficiency. They do so well because shooting is an unconscious phenomena, which makes explaining 'how to do it' very difficult. This book delves into the inner workings and secrets, explaining not just by exposition and dialog (talk) but by 'doing'. For when you initiate the practice tips within these chapters, the die will be cast to begin the innermost journey towards higher levels of expertise. Overall, the ideas within contain momentous criteria, so take it in slowly, one step at a time.

With all the information in this book it will be near impossible to apply each and every technique all at one time so assimilate each tip one by one over a long period of time. Don't let this new knowledge make you too mechanical. In an effort to perform like a machine you will create excessive tension and produce errors. Take it easy. It will all come together in due time. Consider this your freshman year in college... you have three more years to go, you will see remarkable results the slower you progress. Haste makes waste. The tortoise did beat the hare!

CHAPTER 1

FINDING THE SHOTGUN THAT'S RIGHT FOR YOU
"Nobody's sweetheart is ugly."

You may already have the suitable gun! Shotgun fit is not an in-depth subject of deliberation, so visit a stockfitter to ensure the gun you use fits, from the comb to the recoil pad, and is well balanced. A flat butt-plate recoil pad allows the gun to mount higher on your shoulder so you're looking at target in the center of your eye which increases target visibility (so will a high comb and sight rib). Others prefer a curved pad to help mount the gun consistently. You'll find stockfitters at registered shoots. If you can't find a stockfitter, contact:
Bernie Henry, P.O. Box 512, Shady Cove, OR 97539 (503)-878-2480.
Recoil-less Engineering 9 Fox Oaks Court, Sacramento, CA 95831 (916)391-1242.
Or for a custom built stock contact: Murray's Gunshop, 14720 NE Sandy Blvd., Portland, OR 97230
800-459-3503. Or Reinhart Fajen, Inc., Rt. 1, Box 214A-H, Lincoln, MO 65338 (816)-548-2215 ask for their catalog which is chock-full of technical information. Also, see; 'Flinching and Recoil Reduction' for stock-modified recoil shock absorbers.

It is rare, if not impossible, to pick up a factory produced gun off a dealer shelf and discover it fits you perfectly. Guns are made to fit the 'average' person - - 5'10" tall at 180 lbs. Everyone requires the gun be fitted to their unique physical dimensions. If at all possible, try to buy a gun that has a moveable comb, variable length of pull, alterable butt-plate to adjust height and cant, recoil reduction device, a high or adjustable sight rib. The latter is optional, though will come in handy later as you fine-tune your POI. Here you will defend your bank account by not having to spend a fortune to add these items later. You can readily purchase a good used gun with all the gizmos attached. If you can't find one, go to a major registered shoot and visit 'vendor's row'. This is to say a field gun is <u>not</u> your perfect gun for trapshooting because it isn't a trap gun. They shoot flat and they don't fit. However, modifications can be made to transform it into a trap gun. The stock will need modification to trap specifications, a full choke barrel or removable choke, a high vented rib to reduce visual distortion by heat waves. A high sight rib can raise point of impact (gun will shoot higher than point of aim a few inches), head position and eye alignment is vertically enhanced. It can be expensive to convert a field gun to trap specifications, and you may still be dissatisfied with its performance. Spend good money the first time around and the gun will reward you with abundant years of high performance. If you wish to excel in trap, buy a gun specifically designed and configured for the trap game.

GUN SELECTION - MINIMUM FEATURES
"Men have become the tools of their tools." Henry David Thoreau

Here's a brief run down as what you ideally should look for: Seek a barrel in the 30" to 34" inch range, 12 gauge over and under or single barrel, removable chokes, duel sight beads on rib. The 32" barrel has been used successfully in trap for years in Europe and the Olympics games. The gun is slightly lighter in weight and swings a tad quicker for double target events, but not too quickly. Your first gun for versatile shooting should be an over & under (O&U) with 30" or 32" barrels, preferably internally chrome lined for longevity. Ideally, a combo would be a good choice if you can afford the cost. The O&U (or combo) may be the first and last gun you need to buy as the O&U gun can shoot trap and doubles games all with the same stock. Notwithstanding, if you've been shooting a 34" barrel gun for a lengthy time, don't buy anything less than a 32" or you'll have an additional learning curve to tackle, with the expense of firing thousands of shells to become acclimated to the gun -- an expensive and unnecessary proposition. A gun with a 30" barrel with a quality choke (such as Briley, Rhino and Seminole) will shoot as well and throw just as tight patterns as a 34" barrel at any yardage. The longer barrel primarily cedes a deep (longer) sighting plane, and that's it. The difference between 30" and 34" barrel in weight, balance and ballistic performance is so minor it's not worth mentioning. Yes, you do need duel sight beads, significantly so at handicap yardage where accuracy becomes ever more critical. No beads = mismounting gun and a loss of consistency and precision. Looking down a barrel without sights is like rolling a bowling ball without lane markers or throwing a baseball blindfolded. Reference points are required. Two beads are superior to one. The O&U gun has the advantage of two guns in one, whereas if one firing mechanism were to fail you could continue to shoot the alternate barrel. It's a good starting gun to own. See: Trap Gun Features. See Fig. 11-10 to see proper eye and rib alignment.

IDEAL FEATURES
"Life is easy with proper tools."

Ideal features include all of the above in 'Minimum Features' plus adjustable comb to raise or lower comb height and pitch; adjustable stock for fitting length of pull; variable butt-plate for canting butt to shoulder, toe-in and / or toe-out, drop of heel to enhance eye / barrel alignment; recoil reduction device, preferably one allowing the butt-plate plate to compress, giving the gun a Howitzer retraction effect, channeling and absorbing substantial shock waves - - you can shoot it all day without soreness. Definitely get one! An adjustable sight rib to adjust point of impact is good when learning and earning your way to the 27 yard line. The reasoning is the rib setting can be set at minimum POI as the novice shooter requires a flatter shooting gun to visualize the sight bead / target relationship. This shooter also tends to shoot slow. As experience builds, speed timing increases, and handicap yardage increases the rib can be raised to lower the barrel below the target increasing point of impact so the shotstring rises to the target. See Fig. 1-2. Then once you positively know what POI setting works foremost for you, then you can order a fine custom-built gun knowing exactly what point of impact you want. Excellent gun fit = good balance with enhanced pointability, so add a barrel or stock weight, if necessary, to shift gun weight between the hands. It will help you swing to the target with ease, increasing accuracy thus raising scores.

The high rib gun has many benefits as the rib is set high above the barrel. See Fig. 1-1. This permits you to see the target quicker, dampens distorting heat waves that can cloud a target's visible clarity, your head is more erect so you can see the target rise from the traphouse without the barrel blocking your view (which also dampens head-lifting when calling for the target). It is proven a high rib gun is more accurate at handicap distances because a raised rib and comb creates a true sighting plane as the eye is at the same level of the rib. There is less slanting of the field of view with your head erect than with a low rib gun, where your face is down on the comb yet your head and eyes are tilted sideways.

If you have a long neck, the high rib gun will fit you better than a low rib gun. Once point of impact, sight beads, comb or rib have been adjusted, don't tinker with it. The exemption to this rule is when you're punched yardage beyond 23 yards you may want to forge fine-tuned adjustments as your shooting speed (timing) has likewise increased. A rising shotstring is desirable the faster you shoot targets and as distance to target increases. If your gun's rib won't adjust? Don't sweat it. Just study the required leads and the new timing factors involved. These features, when adjustable as mentioned, have advantages of making sure the gun fits you, and continues to fit in the event you gain or lose weight, as alterations are easily made. Moreover, a O&U gun will bestow the benefit of shooting doubles events at registered shoots, whereas a single barrel gun will require you shoot another gun - which requires an additional learning curve. Thankfully, the learning curve is not as great switching to the doubles game, as trap and doubles are two entirely unique games... each requires differing techniques. Plus, you won't need to Easter Egg hunt for hulls or be subjected to the dreaded 'hull thief'.

TOO MANY GUNS
"The road to excess leads to the palace of ruin."

Never underestimate the benefits of shooting only one gun. It is an edge many shooters envy. Many top shooters shoot one gun for all sports with the adjustable features available today. Reliability is important, as excessive gun malfunctions and misfires are penalized as lost targets in registered events. Again, the O&U gun takes the lead over the autoloader shotgun. The autoloader requires unblemished cleaning and often jams and parts wear out and fail. Reliability is increasing, still I doubt they will ever attain the reliability to fire as consistently as the break-open gun. They will always be susceptible to jamming, high maintenance, and painstaking disassembly to clean a gun which becomes a nuisance over time. Even if the gas gun does fail to cycle due to clogged ports, you can always fire one shot in trap, but not so in doubles or sporting clays events. You are stuck with only one choke size with an automatic when shooting at two targets, which can be compensated to a degree by shell selection. Plus you'll have to pick up hulls as they fling to the ground even with a shell catcher. Furthermore, gas guns are longer in length, 3 1/2" due to the receiver dimensions, which can be an advantage to produce a longer sighting plane, nevertheless may be a disadvantage to others regarding gun fit.

The greatest indisputable advantage of the gas gun is its inherent recoil reducing qualities. The stocks on semi-autos are easy to shim up and down for minimal adjustment for fitting the gun. The downside is semi-auto triggers usually require a good tune-up with a gunsmith. Some claim a single barrel gun is easier to point with, but this is a matter of opinion, not fact. Try telling the Europeans to switch to single barrel; they use O&U for virtually everything and it's no secret the games they disport are more formidable than us stateside folks dare to play. Owning too many guns will disserve you. One gun capable of firing two shells is sufficient or a single barrel gun for trap and one O&U for doubles. Any more guns and you're inviting trouble, as most shooters can't persevere the complexity of multiple learning curves. Stop the violins. It just doesn't work. If you treasure guns as a collector, that's okay. Just don't expect to shoot them all, anytime, anywhere, in heavy competition.

The O&U gun is reliable and easy to maintain firing two shells with no mechanical delay or shell shuttling as with a pump or autoloader gun. Jams and misfires are rare. If you do experience misfires or hang-fire, suspect hulls are worn out, the primers set too deep when reloading, or air pocket in powder charge due to insufficient wad seating pressure. The gun will enable you to play doubles, sporting clays, skeet, and continental trap with dependability. Later, as you progress, you may yearn to purchase an expensive single barrel trap gun after you are fully aware of what you want and need. To spend big bucks for an expensive gun when learning is not advisable for most shooters as the first gun you buy will likely not be your last. Expensive guns do not guarantee you will hit targets. Spend your money on a gun that fits you, shoots straight, and is reliable, and you will have a gun that is a beast to contend with in competition. Leave well enough alone. If your gun shoots tolerably well, your efforts to improve the situation by buying a new and costly gun may make things worse. Uncountable shooters with expensive guns have lost events to accurate economical trap guns. It's not the gun, it's the shooter! The key element is not price but how well the gun is balanced, and how snugly it fits for proper eye/rib alignment.

A trap gun has unique dimensions over a field or sporting clays gun. Typical trap dimensions are 1 3/8" drop at comb (distance from sight line to front section of comb), 14 1/8" length-of-pull (stock length), with a 1 degree pitch down. There are other dimensions to consider, pitch, grip swell, etc. The gun should fit you in each of these dimensions and which is why you should buy a gun with adjustments. There is nothing absolute in gun dimensions, owing to people and shooting styles differ, so strict textbook measurements are not critical; however, the gun has to fit you. Very few shooters can shoot consistent correctly with a gun that does not fit. Simply buying your buddy's old gun or procuring one off a dealer's rack just won't cut it. A suitable place is 'Vendor's Row' at registered shoots. New and used trap guns are already configured or can be fitted with the essential constituents within hours, and you can try out the gun on the spot. For those looking for variety, contact: Shotgun News, P.O. Box 669, Hastings, NE 68902 (402) 463-4589 or; Gun List, 700 E. State St., Iola, WI 54990 (715) 445-2214. Visit gun clubs, as members always have trap guns to sell.

TRAP GUN MANUFACTURERS
"All that glitters is not gold."

Which are the finest trap guns? Tough question, as there are certainly so many fine models to choose. One must furthermore consider the shooter's skill, body dimensions and personal preferences to determine which gun is superlative. It is advisable to try as many guns as possible before you commit. One will stand out above the others. Often, your best advice will come from a professional gun fitter, shooting coach or pro shooter.

Aim Inc., (410)-329-680. Maker of Silver Seitz trap gun.
Berretta U.S.A., 17601 Beretta Drive, Accokeek, MD 20607, (301) 283-2191.
Browning, Route 1, One Browning Place, Morgan, UT 84050, (800) 333-3288.
Cole Arms, 2225 Pinehurst, McMinnville, OR 97128, (503)-472-8539.
Du Pont / Krieghoff, P. O. Box 3528, Vero Beach, FL 32964-3528, (800)-735-4867, and Alan Rhone, PO Box K-80, Wrexham, United Kingdom LL13 0ZH Tel: +44(0)1978-780-390 new, repairs, alterations, comb conversions.
Ithaca Acquisition Corporation, 891 Route 34B, King Ferry, New York, 13081, (315)-364-7182.
Kreighoff International, PO Box 549, Ottsville, PA 18942, (215)-847-5173.
Ljutic Industries, Inc. 732 N. 16th Ave. Suite 22, P.O. Box 2117, Yakima, WA 98907, (509) 248-0476.
Perazzi USA, 207 S. Shamrock Ave., Monrovia, CA 91016, (818)-303-0068.
Remington Arms, 14 Hoesler Ave. Ilion, NY 13357, (315)-895-7791.
Winchester Repeating Arms., 275 Winchester Ave., P.O. Box 30-300, New Haven, CT 06511, (203) 789-5000.

Cast Off is bending the stock to the right when viewing from the rear of the gun. It would be away from the face on a right hand shooter and toward the face on a left-hand shooter. Cast On bends the stock to the left, toward the face on a right hand shooter, away from the face on a left-hand shooter. The reason for cast is to align the shooter's eye squarely over the sight rib. If you can do this, then the cast is set correctly. Before you bend a stock or set cast check the gun's POI first. If you are shooting to the left or right of your aim point then cast needs adjusting, or the sight rib or barrel may be bent. What is important; is the gun shooting where you aim? It must do this first before it can shoot where you are looking. If the gun shoots accurately, half the battle is won. This may appear elementary though you would be shocked to learn just how many guns out there don't fit their owners. Rest assured the superior shooters have a gun that fits like a fine glove. Everyone's facial configuration and shooting form is different, but guns are mass produced replicas. Does your gun fit? Odds are it doesn't.

Ask shooters to try their guns. Most will oblige. After assaying a myriad of distinct guns, you may be befuddled or be lucky enough to sniff out the right gun for you. Try to buy a light weight gun -- 8 pounds or less. A heavy gun will tire you in long competitive shoots. I started with a Browning Citori® O&U trap gun with all the adjustable features and Invector Plus® chokes, and I wasn't sorry I did. It's a hard hitting monster, reliable as dependable can be. The Remington 90-T® is a virtuous single-shot shotgun, though the price is higher. Browning's BT - 100® is a meritorious single barrel gun and we all know the BT - 99 was and is no bungler on the trapfield. It's time-tested, winning many championship shoots. The BT-100 has superior features over the BT-99. Have fun selecting your gun. Try them all. You can't shoot a new gun at most dealers, so where do you go to try them out? Registered shoots have gun dealers and here you can take them out to the practice trap and shoot em'up. Your local gun club is a good place to start. A <u>new</u> shooter should not spend thousands of dollars just to try out the sport, by reason of new shooters often are reshuffling technique, constantly searching for the proper means and methods. This is no time to spend a fortune on expensive guns or costly modifications to a gun. Buy a trap gun, yes. Nevertheless, save the bells and whistles for last when you know what you <u>need</u> in a gun. They say the differences between men and boys is the price of their toys - not so in trapshooting - marksmanship wins!

SAVING MONEY
"Who will not save a penny, shall never have many."

All sports cost money -- especially those with prize money at stake. Trapshooting is costly, nonetheless, there are approaches to reduce costs. Reloading shotshells can save money, as ammunition is the foremost financial drain for the shooter. In my opinion, the most economical, reliable, lightweight, progressive shotshell loader is Hornady's Apex Auto. This loader has many real-world features for the money. Two of Hornady's greatest advantages are its light weight and the ability to remove a defective shell from a loading station with ease, yet continue loading. It has narrow dimensions to easily mount in small spaces. It crimps shotshells to factory prescription, a very nice press. Hornady Manufacturing, Co., P. O. Box 1848, Grand Island, Nebraska 68802 Phone: 800-338-3220. Ask for a catalog and dealer in your area as purchasing direct from Hornady will not be discounted. Ponsness / Warren, P.O. Box 8, Rathdrum, ID 83858 800-732-0706 is esteemed by many as the Mercedes Benz of loaders. In contrast, the cost is higher and the loader's dimensions are larger, not as convenient for anyone who travels with a reloader in a trailer or motor home. Midway, 5875 W. Van Horn Tavern Rd., Columbia, MO 65203 (800)-243-3220 builds a portable stand that easily mounts any reloader in small confines and disassembles for storage. Hornady and Midway is a fine combination if space-saving is essential, more so for those who travel in RV's as storage space comes at a premium. Another reloader to check out; Spolar Enterprises, 17376 Filbert St., Fontana, CA 92335, (800)-227-9667.

You can manufacture economical practice shooting ammunition by downloading. This is simple. If you have been practice shooting with standard 1 1/8 oz. shot, simply step the shot size down to 1 oz. and lower the powder charge volume to <u>identically match the velocity</u> of the 1 1/8 oz shotshell you normally use. Here you will save on shot and powder costs. Wear safety glasses when reloading. It only requires one unfortunate accident or mistake to sacrifice your eyesight forever.

You'll save even more money using reclaimed lead instead of new shot. You can trim costs further by using a powder that costs less for a given load. Of course, saving money on shotshell components has a penalty of not providing the optimum target load. Propellants, soft shot and aftermarket wads often fail to match performance with factory new shells. Keep in mind aftermarket components, especially wads, are not identical to Original Equipment Manufactures (OEM) specifications. If they were identical, the component would infringe the manufactures patent, something we all know the OEM's would never allow. It's generally okay to use aftermarket components for practice, but switch back to OEM ingredients when shooting registered targets and other meaningful competitive games (better still, use new ammunition). And as a safety reminder, always follow the specified component recipe when reloading. Keep your reloads close to factory velocity specifications. You don't want to alter shotstring velocity. Doing so will throw timing off, then later, returning to factory spec loads will induce missed targets. Practice with what you shoot with. [**Note:** Shot velocity itself is not a culprit once you become acclimated to the perceived lead sight picture and timing. Lead, sight picture and timing problems arise when you change shells with wide variations in velocity. In all things, consistency is desired.]

If money is less of a concern, then always reload with factory shotshell components. This way you'll never blame the shotshell for a missed target and be better concentrated on aiming, technique, etc. New shells have a shot velocity tolerance of plus or minus 75 feet per second (acceptable industry standard deviations, yet the best quality shells hold this deviation down to 25 f.p.s. in constant temperature). Any load deviating under or over 100 to 150 f.p.s may likely initiate serious timing problems. Some shooters will not reload a hull fired more than twice, claiming friction drag scuffing of the hull's interior and crimp weakness change shot velocity and patterns. The velocity shift is too minor to measure under actual trapshooting conditions on a twice-fired reloaded hull and is likely within the 75 f.p.s. tolerance, although no one can reasonably argue against using high quality components in like-new condition. The key is crimp quality. If the crimp is weak, patterns tighten due to poor combustion, producing a loss of shot velocity; furthermore, point of impact may shift - two combinations deadly to accuracy. A shell delivering 1,150 f.p.s. versus a 1,200 f.p.s. shell is not a 50 f.p.s. change in velocity at 40 yards. It is approximately 20 f.p.s.. That's too small of a variance for leads to be concerned with. All things being equal, what makes for speed is the size of the shot, as 7 1/2's will reach the target sooner than light 8s, with tighter patterns and more energy to punch the target.

Another means to save money that holds credence when practicing is to shadow fire. When a practice squad is short, ask if you can stand on a station and track their targets, though you won't fire at the targets. You'll practice mounting the gun, track, and dry fire when others are shooting. When your turn comes to shoot, they simply skip you. You'll save money on shells and trap fees. You'll require a supportive squad to permit this, as it can be disruptive. If it's a fun-shoot there shouldn't be a problem. Most shooters are persnickety and won't allow it, however, keep asking others until you get a station. Dry firing is good training to mount the gun consistently, practice gun hold points, eye placement and focus, track the target and maintain trigger control. Use a snap cap to save wear and tear on your firing pin. You won't know if you hit or miss the target beyond all reasonable doubt, still the shadow-firing practice session will certainly be efficient and lead you to increased proficiency.

You can manufacture your own chilled lead shot. There are risks to consider: exposure to poisonous lead fumes, spatter burns, etc. If you would like to produce lead shot contact: J. F. Littleton, 275 Pinedale Ave., Oroville, CA 95966 (916)-533-6084. Selling the shot could recover your costs.

Other means of saving money attending distant registered shoots is to buddy up on motel rooms, use a $40 tent to camp free on site if weather permits. Don't shoot the singles if you'll merely win a trophy. Shoot the handicap event playing the 25 / 50 options and the Calcutta. Shooting singles can be fun, though expensive. The money is in handicap. You can burn a lot of cash trying to master 16 yard singles shooting while earning yardage in handicap. Each time you switch back and forth from your newly earned yardage, it's a new learning curve and more money spent in practice. Though singles is often regarded as just a warm-up for the handicap, a method you could use is to shoot the practice trap for warm-up and play only the handicap events. When you finally get punched back to the 27 yard line, then all you need learn is shooting the 27 and 16's. Otherwise, be prepared to smoke a bundle of cash. Developing accuracy and good eye / hand coordination at the lowest possible cost can be had by using a air rifle on a swinging target (see: Eye Exercises).

RELOAD MANIA
"The privilege of absurdity is a disease unconquered, from the sublime to the ridiculous is but a step."

Reloading is enjoyable and saves money, too. Experimenting with various combinations of powders, wads, primers, hulls and shot sizes is amusing but dangerous to your scores, as it sets up psychological distractions ensuing inconsistent shooting. Each load has unique ballistic characteristics and the combinations are inexhaustible. You can freely get caught up in reload mania and fail to focus on what is genuinely important, your shooting. No matter what you do with reloads, always reload to a specific velocity, say 1200 feet per second which matches a 3 dram handicap powder charge of 1 1/8 oz. lead shot factory loads. Whatever the major ammunition companies are manufacturing try to stay with the velocity they use for a specific load. The reason being getting into a shootoff and not having to compose mental and physical adjustments to your shooting. Less velocity will require advanced lead on hard angle targets and a quarter angle target could slip away through the time zone. (Note: when I say lead, I am referencing barrel swing and follow through, but for simple and practical reasons lead will be referred to as simple forward allowance measured as sight bead relationship to target).

Increased velocity requires less lead. Using different ammo is a recipe for fluctuating and ruinous scores. Experiment on the practice range, not at a registered shoot. If you reload, you know undercharging a shell is more apt to happen than overcharging due to conservative powder bushing size and density. In tournament shooting, if the wad leaves the muzzle on a dud load and you miss the target, it's scored as lost. An undercharged shell will most always cause a miss by shooting behind the bird. By shooting 3 dram loads, an undercharged shell would likely maintain sufficient velocity to equal a 2 3/4 dram load, yet still maintain velocity to break the target. Formula: 3-drams produce high combustion heat + high chamber pressure (8,000 + p.s.i.) to insure uniform flame propagation and burn = velocity consistency. Top shooters don't use reloads in tournaments for they have too much at stake to risk reload-originated malfunctions.

If you crave instant gratification, load a 3-dram 1 oz. shot load and watch your scores increase. The velocity will approach 1275 f.p.s., which requires little to no lead to the target. You could become a big fish in a little town quickly with this load shooting the singles' event. Step onto the handicap event and pray you never get into a prolonged shootoff, or be programmed to haul a few cases of your special reloads wherever you go. The golden rule: if the big four -- Winchester, Remington, ACTIV and Federal -- produce it, and its <u>widely available</u>, shoot it. If not, don't. Then again, if you don't mind carting cases of shells, do shoot with any reload recipe you desire. Just be mindful of the vexatious risk of competing in a shootoff, then running dry of shells. Be aware a 1 oz. load's effective pattern is distinctly 26 to 27 inches, whereas a 1 1/8 oz. load's pattern is 30 inches, over 12% larger. At long yardage handicap distances the 1oz. load (51 less pellets with #8, and 44 less pellets with #7 1/2 shot) can make your game difficult as you must increase accuracy over and beyond your competitor who may be using 1 1/8 oz loads (461 pellets with #8 shot, 394 pellets with #7 1/2 shot). If and until the rules change, use the maximum amount of shot and dram powder charge permitted. Power is an asset at any yardage! You should always be nose-to-nose and toe-to-toe with whomever you may be competing with.

The prime reasons for shooters switching to 1oz. loads are reduced reloading costs, low recoil, high velocity. The latter is where benefit and risk coincide. Some shooters are using 1oz. shot reloading recipes powered at or near 3-dram to increase velocity to practically omit lead on targets. Scores do improve to a point, in contrast in the long haul with all things considered - pattern diameter, pellet count, and long yardage distance - using readily available factory produced 3-dram 1 1/8 oz loads of consistent velocity is wiser for the better.

When reloading don't be overly concerned using 'wad pressure' to seat wads. The wad should not be under severe pressure when seating into the hull. You seat the wad gently to remove air over the powder charge and that is all. Placing excess pressure on a wad will plainly crush the cushion post sections, tilt wad out of alignment, deform the shot cup ultimately to reduce power, disrupt shot patterns and is suspected of bursting barrels. Forcing wads could, though rarely, permit an overcharge of lead shot, as wad compresses to make room can burst a tightly choked barrel. When seating the wad in a reloader, you should be able to turn the hull with slight drag felt when the wad insertion ram is fully depressed and the wad fully seated. If the hull won't turn, the wad is being deformed from over-pressure. Remember, a crushed deformed sideways-cocked wad will throw wild shotstrings. Once a wad's compression section is flexed, its ability to absorb shock is greatly diminished, causing increased deformation of lead pellets and permitting combustion gas blow-by, equaling velocity reduction. This will cause many missed targets, especially hard left and right angles and some quarter-angling targets where speed is critical to lead the target. A properly seated wad insures a tight crimp and energetic clean combustion. Certainly, always follow ammo manufacturers published reloading recipes.

Another issue sloppy reloaders experience is squad rejection. No one likes to shoot with someone who double charges shells, has frequent misfires and gun action jams. It disrupts everyone to the extent no one wants to shoot with the person. Stay with factory recommended shotshell components and you'll have few mishaps. If you undercharge shells, fix your reloader or switch powders to those that properly flow through charge bushings. If you still have problems, fashion a 'wad popper'. This is simply a cut-in-half empty hull with a live primer. Establish no spilt gunpowder is in the chamber of the gun, insert the wad popper, aim into the field, pull the trigger, the wad is gone. This uniquely works with guns that are not autoloaders. The wad popper will clear the wad quickly so as not to overly disturb the squad and put you back into the game without having to locate a ramrod.

Stay with factory components when reloading, especially if you use reloads in registered shoots. Shoot with quality and you'll know why you're hitting or missing targets. Remove as much guesswork and mystery as you can from your game. You should never be suspicious of missing a target due to a shotshell component. If you miss, it was your fault. Take responsibility. Don't blame the loads, unless your reloads are total garbage. Convert the loads back to factory specifications with factory components. Don't let reload mania destroy your scores. Trying endless reload combinations will particularly drive you up the walls and you may never find the perfect load for all situations. And if you do find it, will it guarantee you run 100 straight? Of course not. Let the factory ballistic engineers, mechanical engineers, plastic and chemical engineers, and aeronautical engineers do the research and testing they get paid for, as you keep collecting money and prizes from playing options and winning tournaments. A good rule of thumb: Shoot what the pros shoot. Read that again!

When you do reload, use hard shot 3% to 5% antimony (or hardened shot via alternative lead processing similar to case hardening; i.e., Diamond® brand shot) content for low pellet deformation and tight patterns. Consider 8% antimony shot is harder, but less lead content = reduced down-range energy. Use factory wads, primers, powder charges to maintain velocity to reproduce, as closely as possible, factory loads you plan to shoot. Substitute cheaper components at your own risk. The use of rapid or slow burning powders is your choice. Accelerated powders are easy to recognize as the hull requires less powder for a given velocity. The controversies are endless as to fast vs. slow burning powders relating to felt recoil and patterns. That's why pattern boards and chronographs were invented. Use them to closely resemble the factory load. And be ever mindful never to exceed published loading data regarding chamber pressure. Stick with factory recommendations for consistent overall results and convenience. It can take several lifetimes to find the 'best' reload for a single gun and it would certainly be ready for the scrap heap before all possible combinations were tried.

There is a great freedom in using reloads parroting factory loads. You can attend any shoot without having to lug cases of shells with you. Without further ado buy new shells at the shoot and go to work. You will have mastered the shell you shoot with complete conviction in its performance during the shoot and in the shootoff. A no-nonsense approach to shotgunning will benefit you more than reload wizards could imagine. After all, factory shells are winning the competition shoots. Why? Because they work!

Choose your ammunition and stick with it unless something better comes along and is widely available for purchase at every gun club. It is true some gun barrels seem to enjoy any load over others, moreover, it is not what most shooters think it to be. They believe it's the pattern that is most affected, but in reality it is the point of impact! Ever try a box of unfamiliar shells and miss more targets than usual? Two factors are at play here: velocity changes and alteration of point of impact. The pattern diameter is usually not a predicament when missing targets. Be primed to face a learning curve when changing ammunition. If you keep trying different loads searching for that magic bullet you may never get it right. For each load you'll have to reshape your timing and sight pictures... a heavy penalty to pay. The goal is: *"No hang-ups on ammunition."* It's just one more snare to divert your mind away from the business of smoking targets. Don't focus on the mechanical aspects, focus on state of mind. When it comes to ammo, be confident in factory loads and you'll never have to doubt your ammo's competency. Shooters often overly concern themselves with ammo and chokes more than carefully watching the target. Keep this in mind, when shot velocity falls point of impact drops as much as 4" at 40 yards for both 8 and 7 1/2 shot. This is another reason why you need to maintain velocity of the shells you normally reload, including purchasing new shells. If you shoot 3 dram loads, don't switch to light or extra light shells... be consistent.

AMMO THE PROS SHOOT
"If the camel once gets his nose in the tent, his body will follow."

I am a stubborn advocate of factory-produced ammunition. Money shooters use quality shells. Of course these shooters and industry reps obtain shells free to promote the product, but notice how consistently they still shoot and win! Again, it's the shooter's skill, not solely the gun or ammo which makes a professional shoot well. Notice when pros get into a shootoff they have no concern of running out of their pet reloads. I've seen way too many shooters lose because they had to buy new shells in a shootoff and consequently were not familiar with how they shot. If you shoot reloads, be prepared to run out of ammo and blow the game. Try it sometime... seeing is believing. Use your reloads for practice, then shootoff with a friend who is a good shot. Place a side bet of $1 to put a touch of pressure on you both. Now buy a new box of factory ammo and shoot it out. Your mind will instantly blur when you miss a target. You'll go to pieces trying to figure out what is wrong, wondering where the shotstring is going, and the recoil may be harsher. The odds are you will lose the shootoff. If not, you were intensely lucky or a seriously talented athlete to be congratulated. Most of us aren't so gifted.

Everyone uses different shells for different reasons. The superlative shell for you is the one that breaks the most targets. It could be an Activ, Winchester AA, Remington, Fiocci, or Federal Gold Medal. I would be mindful to consider one of the major names in the industry: Winchester AA, Remington and Federal Gold Medal. Why? Because no matter where you go these shells are normally available in quantity at every gun club. I found most shooters can easily switch between AA or Gold Medal without much difficulty, though there can be 'point of impact' differences as is experienced when changing to any brand of ammo. My personal preference is Gold Medal (plastic or paper hull) as they appear to have a harder hit with less perceived recoil. In addition, the plastic hull crimps with a unique swirl pattern, center-locking the crimp tightly for reliable combustion / velocity performance. Reloaded shell-crimps don't relax and unwind in storage or in transit, spilling shot pellets. The reload life of the hull is impressive. Many shooters use the Gold Medal 'paper hull' for registered shoots. This shell is regarded highly by shooters for consistent pattern / performance. They fire once and toss away as paper hull reload life is naturally limited. Let's not derail the train; it's the shooter, not the shell, that wins tournaments. For brochures call or write;
Activ 1000 Zigor Rd., P.O. Box 339, Kearneysville, WV 25430 (304)-725-0451.
Federal Cartridge Co., Anoka, Minnesota 55303 (612)-323-2300.
Fiocchi USA, 5030 Fremont Road, Ozark, MO 65721 (800)-721-2666.
Olin / Winchester, 427 North Shamrock, East Alton, IL 62024 (618)-258-2000.
Remington Arms Co., 1011 Centre Rd.,Delle Donne Corp. Ctr., Wilmington, DE 19805 (302)-993-8547.

Regardless of your choice of shell manufacturer, including your reloads, use shells that are the most consistent for you. Don't keep switching from 7.5 shot to 8.5 shot, 9 shot, then back to 8 shot at different yardage's. At first you will believe you are improving your chances of winning, and you may win, but in the long run switching too often can mutate your shooting style, deviate pattern form and densities and alter your timing, POI and sight picture, resulting in inconsistent shooting and lost targets. *"I wish I had used my number eight and one halve shot at sixteen yard singles. Darn, I had to use seven and one halves and that's why I scored badly."* How often have you heard similar declarations? At most, pick two shells and no more. That's all you need. Use #8 at 16 to 20 - 23 yards, then switch to 7.5 from 24 to 27 yards. Keep it simple.

If you use light 2 3/4 dram #8's for 16 yard and then switch to 3 dram #8 or # 7 1/2 loads at handicap, again, your timing may be off mark. If you have to use lights, then you should modify your gun as recoil is presumably influencing you to switch to a lighter load shell. Ultra-lights loads are unreliable at 27 yard, so why bother with them? Get a recoil reducer and send your shot on its merry way with as much energy your gun can muster. Don't expect it will be easier on you to use ultra super light loads then eventually transition to heavy loads as you gain handicap wins. All it will do is set you back months and months when you eventually do switch loads. That is expensive not to mention the frustration and anguish you will experience of trying to acclimate yourself to the higher velocity handicap load.

To make life even less complex, shooting lead 1 1/8 oz, #8 shot, on all yardage's is not a bad idea at all. More and more 27 yard shooters are winning with 8's. If you look at a Federal shotshell box, it tells you how much pellet impact energy 7.5 and 8's have at 40 yards distance. The 7.5's have 1.1 foot pounds, and 8's have .09 ft-lbs. That is merely a .2 difference. The 8's have 461 pellets and the 7.5's have 394. The 8's have 67 more pellets each, wielding <u>almost</u> as much force as the 7.5 shot. Although 7.5's tend to pattern tighter, travel faster and will hit harder, 67 more 8's is an advantage worthy of consideration. However, at 20 yards distance 7.5's have 2.1 impact energy and 8's have 1.8. At 30 yards 7.5's have 1.5 and 8's have 1.3. It's a close race to the finish, yet one should consider it always requires more than one pellet to reliably break a target, so cumulatively #7 1/2 shot has more walloping energy to deliver. To find which shot size is right for you, pattern your gun inspecting point of impact, flyers and effective pattern core density. Customarily the highest density pattern wins; however, don't be misled by pattern details, as you must <u>verify</u> if the two-dimensional pattern board results actually do faithfully and responsibly shatter the targets. Breaking the most targets is the final decisive factor. Huge holes can exist in a perfect pattern imprint. A quality choke, hard #7 1/2 or #8 shot, plus OEM factory reload components or new ammo usually gets the job done. Bear in mind shot sizes are sometimes mixed due to improper sizing during packaging. If this is the case, you should screen the shot or use #7 1/2 shot, not the #8's. The 'Golden Rule' still applies: Use high antimony magnum #7 1/2 shot 3 dram loads beyond the 23 yard line.

When you buy lead shot, don't use chilled shot. This is soft lead even if the shot bag claims it is 'hard shot' or 'extra hard shot'. Look for shot containing at least 5% antimony. Antimony is a metallic element having four allotropic forms, the most common of which is a hard crystalline material. It is used in a wide variety of alloys, especially to 'harden' lead shot to reduce deformations of pellets. Using cheap shot in registered shoots is tossing good money at a worthless investment. Deformed pellets will 'fly' randomly away from the shotstring. Pellets become deformed when the shotshell is first fired, slamming the wad into the pellets. It's called 'set-back' as pellets crush backwards upon each other. The pellets again are crushed and become dented when forced into the barrel forcing cone, squeezed and crushed again in the barrel choke, and set-back one more time slam-hammered exiting the muzzle. Look at a fired wad and witness both the cup and petals of the wad are dented. Antimony reduces pellet deformation, thereby reducing pellets straying from the string. The ultimate pellet would be hard, employing dimples on the exterior as a golf ball. These dimples are very aerodynamic. Shot manufactures could produce them, though it would be a costly manufacturing process.

RELOADING COMPONENTS
Ballistic Products Inc., 20015 75th Ave N., Corcoran, MN 55340, (612)-494-9227.
Best Buy Shooting Supply, Route 2, Box 26 - M, Chattaroy, WA 99003, (509)-238-6165.
Brownell's, 200 South Front Street, Montezuma, Iowa 50171-1000, (515)-623-5401 - gun parts, tools, etc.
Gamaliel Shooting Supply Inc., 1525 Ft. Run Road, P.O. Box 156, Gamaliel, Kentucky 42140, (800)-356-6230.
Hornady Manufacturing, 3625 Old Potash Hwy., P.O. Box 1848, Grand Island, NE 68802, (800)-338-3220 (Primarily sells reloader).
Larry's Shooting Headquarters, 224 3rd Avenue-South, Nampa, Idaho 83651 (208)-467-9201.
Mary's Guns & Reloading, 826 7th St., P.O.Box 695, Havre, MT 59501 (406)-265-9506.
Precision Reloading, Inc., P. O. Box 122, Stafford Springs, CT 06076, (800)-223-0900.
*Pinnell's Competitive Components, Inc., P.O. Box 3703, Central Point, OR 97502 (541)-664-4994.
Reloading Specialties, P. O. Box 1130, Pine Island, MN 55963 (507)-356-8500 (Shot, wads).
Taracorp Industries, 1200 16th St., Granite City, IL 62040 (618)-451-4400 (Shot).
*Southwest Shooter's Supply, P.O. Box 9987, Phoenix, Arizona 85068 (602)-943-8595
*Southwest has many interesting catalog items for the shotgunner and is included for this reason though they do not specialize in reloading supplies. Pinnell's sells clothing and reloading components, etc.

COMPETITION TRAPSHOOTING ASSOCIATIONS
"The right time is right now!"

Without fanfare, these are the North American continent trapshooting associations regulating competition tournaments in most every city, town and province. You must be a member to shoot the A.T.A. & P.I.T.A. heats, but you can readily join upon arrival at the tournament. Membership fee is approximately $12 for the year. To keep abreast of the organizations listed, see subchapter; 'Shotgun Sports Magazines' which report shoot results, etc.

Amateur Trapshooting Association (A.T.A.) 601 W. National Rd., Vandalia, OH 45377 (513-898-4638)
Pacific International Trapshooting Association (P.I.T.A.) P.O.Box 9217 Brooks, OR 97305 (503)-792-3622.

CLAY TARGET SHOOTING FOUNDATIONS
National Shooting Sports Foundation, 11 Mile Hill Rd., Newton, CT 06470
Quickshots,USA Shooting, One Olympic Plaza, Colorado Springs, CO 80909 (719)-578-4670
Women's Shooting Sports Foundation, 1505 Hwy. 6 South, Suite 103, Houston, TX 77077 (713)-548-9907.

USA Shooting (listed above) is the national governing body for Olympic shooting. They train and select teams to represent the United States at the World Cups, World Shooting Championships, Pan American, International and Olympic games. They also have training development centers for young shooters with Olympic dreams. So don't be shy to contact this fine organization. Many shooters train in their own hometowns with USA coaches, while others relocate into their resident program in Colorado. Anyone can obtain membership and compete in sponsored events. USA Shooting is for all shooters, regardless of skill level, pistol, rifle or shotgun. The Olympics, long dominated by males, now has women of all ages on the Olympic teams. Members receive discounts on shooting team merchandise. Yes, you can join and become a member. Give them a call.

Each state and Canadian province has their own Trapshooting Associations, too numerous to list here. Contact your local gun club for information. If they can't help you, simply attend a registered shoot by contacting the P.I.T.A. or the A.T.A. and I'm certain they will lead you in the right direction. Trapshooting is a 'hidden sport' peculiarly unknown by the general public at large. Usually you won't see advertisements in the newspapers or on TV, although one day this may change, and should! However, once you do join this 'elite' class of shooters, you'll discover most every city, town, county and province conducts registered shoots within easy driving distance. It's really a huge sport! I hope you will attend a shoot for it's one of the best experiences of fun and accomplishment, wrapped into multiple fantastic events you won't forget. Come join us!

CHAPTER 2

PROVING YOUR SHOTGUN IS COMPETENT
"To err is human, to really screw up you need a expensive gun."

Countless shooters are constantly on the lookout for the gun that will increase their hits and scores. A new broom sweeps clean doesn't apply to shotguns. Stop blaming your gun. Stop looking for a new gun. There are things in life that are expensive: getting married, divorce, and changing guns. Once you have a gun that fits and feels comfortable, it is right for you. You don't need a Perrazzi, Krieghoff or Lutjic. These are fine guns, no doubt about it, but do they come with a guarantee you will run 100 straight? Of course not. They are just fine guns. Like all shotguns they will do the same thing as an economical gun, toss shot out of the barrel. If prestige is your goal and you want to look like a pro, go ahead, spend thousands of dollars. If you wish to break targets, get your mind off of the gun and into your technique. If you can afford a prized gun, do as your heart desires, but don't envision a price tag to be a solution to missing targets. What appears to be of great value may be quite worthless. Don't judge a book by its cover. Likewise, don't judge a gun's merit by its price tag. An expensive gun that does not come even close to fitting you, is too heavy or too light, is not comfortable or balanced for your physical dimensions is worthless on the trap line. The gun must fit.

A worker may be the hammer's master, but the hammer still prevails for it knows exactly how it is meant to be handled, while the user can only have an approximate idea. If the gun fits and is reliable, it is the right gun for you. To prove this to yourself, and to anyone else who may disagree, place your gun in a solid vice, set up a target on a pole at any reasonable distance of your choosing (or draw a bulls-eye on a pattern board) and pull the trigger. The shot will break the target every time! Now you know your shotgun, as all are, is a precision instrument designed to shoot consistently wherever it is pointed. The gun won't lie to you. It won't shoot inconsistently. It will always shoot straight as long as the gun is not seriously defective with a bent barrel, sight rib, or a loose stock. Since the gun is precise the exclusive variable is you. The gun will shoot to whatever you point at, and it will do so repeatedly without flaw.

Never, ever, blame your gun for missed targets, particularly when it shoots straight and is not defective. If you do you are defeating yourself, as your subconscious mind will never allow you to shoot well because 'it' doesn't like your gun. Learn to like your gun. Tell yourself, *"This gun is accurate, it fits, it shoots solid, hits targets hard, and the gun is perfect for me."* You must pioneer trusting dependence in your equipment before you win self-confidence in your game. Someday, when you have polished your shooting talent, you may want an expensive gun for prestige, or whatever. Go ahead and buy it: however, be forewarned your scores may suffer for a spell. If you are a Top Gun shooter you'll be able to make the conversion more palatable than when you were not as accomplished. Again, this reinforces the contention it is not the gun, but the shooter who shoots well.

You will meet many a gun collector in the shooting sports. From their armory they often switch from gun-to-gun trying to find the premium gun for 16-yard, and the optimum for variable handicap yardage. The pros exclusively use one gun for singles and handicap. The primary gun swap is customarily feasible when playing doubles, although many pros still use their O&U or autoloader, which is a wise move. With shotguns less is more. One gun for all games develops and maintains skill, familiarity, and consistency. If you don't consider this as true, try changing guns with a friend and witness the devastation to your scores! The sound of *"Lost"* rings in the ears. Buy a trap gun designed to play trap and doubles. If you must have two guns, assure they fit and are suitably designed for the games you project to play.

Generally speaking, no two guns are alike and no one gun can play all the shotgun sport games: trap, doubles, skeet and sporting clays. Buy a gun designed for the sport you plan to play the most. If you prefer to play all the games, your trap gun may do just fine since this is the gun you positively know and understand, specifically if your gun fires two successive shells, has adjustable features with barrels no longer than 30". Like a marriage partner, you know your babe intimately better than someone who has two wives. The O & U (or single barrel break open breech) is more reliable with less breakdowns due to less moving parts, easy to clean, and expends more pellet energy to the target. The autoloaders expend energy to cycle the receiver, and they are not reliable for most shooters unless kept meticulously clean. The pros use both types of guns. Take your pick. The key is to formulate trust in the gun you shoot. Buy a new gun plainly if the gun you now own is inaccurate or unreliable. You must have faith in your equipment, for confidence is fragile and emotion is recurrently moody - -especially when bad scores arrive. The obstacle is your disposition, not the gun. Buying a new gun is a total mistake if the new gun still does not fit you! Perhaps you should peruse your old gun, insuring it fits. Maybe that is why you feel you need a new gun? If for no other reason you just want a new gun, then go for it, as long as you can live with the price and bear the frustration and expense of tackling the new learning curve. Life is too short not to have fun. Paul Roberts (Clay Shooting 9-95 issue/ Yardley) coined the affliction of trading guns too often as a case of *"Ballistic Thrombosis."* People believe guns win matches, but it's the shooter not the gun!

BE LEERY OF GIZMOS
"You can't fit a round peg in a square hole, lest it rattles."

The moment scores fall, shooters rarely fail to buy something, anything, to correct the problem. The gizmo market is full of doohickey thingamajig gadgets all designed to increase scores. It can be carnival trying them out, but it is costly experimentation serving to misdirect your mind away from the target only to focus back onto the gun. Observe the machines professionals shoot and you won't see innumerous thingamabobs hanging on the gun. You will find the basics: internal barrel work, external barrel porting, adjustable stocks and combs, a high or adjustable rib, removable choke tubes and recoil reduction device. These alterations are basic, and of these the less the better! Anything more and all you will have is an expensive heavy gun you can't shoot well. Gizmos will not increase your scores...only you can do that. You can save a pile of money by buying a new or used shotgun with all these features inherited. If you don't, then be fixed to spend some cash, at the very least, a recoil reducing adjustable comb and adjustable butt-plate recoil pad combination. Minimally, this will soften the jolt of recoil which leads to head-lifting and flinching and warrant the gun fits you properly. This is all you necessarily require on your gun. Anything more is icing on the cake, which may not improve your scores at all. However, since the trap game is 90% mind over matter, if it makes you feel good and builds confidence knowing all these gizmos are helping you hit more targets, then who is to say it is wrong? Even a stopped clock is right twice a day! If you consider modifying guns amusement, then have a ball. Just don't get caught up in a pitfall believing you must have these items or you'll never be a good shooter. This is not so. Remember, the gun will shoot straight... all you have to do is aim it properly and it will break the target. Enough said.

MOUNTING THE GUN
"Don't close the barn door after the horse runs away."

First, verify the gun is unloaded, safety is on and no obstructions are around you. You may accidentally bump into objects, or worse, someone walks into the area hitting them with the gun barrel. You will have your eyes closed in some of the gun mounting / unmounting exercises.

When you mount the gun you should see a perfect figure-eight with the sight beads, the muzzle-end bead on the rib sitting on top of the first bead. See Fig. 10-3. If you don't see the figure-eight, adjustments are required to ensure the gun fits you and the point of impact is correct. If you see rib between the beads, the comb is too high. If you see solely one bead at end of barrel the comb is too low. If the height of the heel is incorrect, you'll have a tendency to bend your neck downward and lift your head when firing. Your thumb should be close to 1 to 1 1/2" from your nose. The gun must, I repeat and heavily emphasize the word must, fit you if you wish to shoot well. You will forever be a poorly inconsistent shooter if the gun does not fit and the POI is incorrect. You may even believe the gun you have fits and requires no adjustments. Are you a stock fitter? Never assume you don't require adjustments, as you probably do, and when you do have your gun properly fitted your scores will increase...that I can assure you. If you are overweight, have a long neck, are a left-handed shooter missing angle targets, and recoil is kicking you, it's time to consult a stockbender. Consider a gun with a high rib (see; Ideal Features). It is astonishing to observe so many shooters spending money in tournaments yet have never had their gun fitted. This is throwing good money into the furnace. To be competitive your equipment must be on equal ground with your competition. To shoot accurately and win events your gun must be fitted. No exceptions!

Everyone mounts their gun differently. It doesn't matter how you mount the gun as long as it is comfortable for you, it is consistently mounted perfectly each time you do, and it does not obstruct your ability to swing the gun accurately without binding muscles or applying adverse muscular pressure to your spine. I suggest viewing some video tapes on gun mounting or take a lesson from a stock fitter who is a skillful trapshooter. Comfort, ease of mounting and consistency is the key to a good gun mount routine. One smooth circular motion to the shoulder leaves little room for error. It is quick, requires limited strength and is comfortable. Compare this method to others and you'll see the light. See Fig. 11-13. Keep in mind when mounting the gun you don't have to keep checking the figure-eight once the mounting process is perfected. You want your eyes focused out into the trapfield, not on the barrel. You'll know when the gun isn't mounted properly, as you can feel it is not right.

Many shooters fail to practice gun mounting, reasoning it is not significant. They have a false, yet incredible conviction shooting parameters -- tracking, aiming, pulling the trigger -- after calling for the target takes priority. How wrong can wrong be? Correct setup of which proper gun mounting is a component, is the solid foundation to build consistent broken targets and success. See Fig. 2-1 'Setup Chart' to instantly determine why targets are missed. Trapshooting is a series of finely honed dexterity. Gun mount is critical. An improperly mounted gun will always shoot off course. It's a high probability why you missed a target...the gun wasn't shouldered properly. Watch closely when the pros shoot. The mount and setup process at first glance appears inconsequential, yet is an intricate, highly polished, defined procedure. The next time you see a pro shoot focus in on their setup.

What is most critical when mounting the gun? Verify you feel the pressure of your cheek on the comb of the gun -- every time you mount the gun -- and this pressure remains constant when swinging the gun. You should feel the gun is part of you not an item you are suitably holding in your hands. You and the gun must become one. Keeping your face down on the comb sounds easy and basic, yet targets are lost because the shooter's cheek floated off the comb... often looking for the target. It's called, *"Playing Goose."* If you lift your head, you will shoot over the target, guaranteed. This is a severe enigma for shooters when the weather is foul, overcast, or the target gets the jump on you out of the house. The target appears small, and your mind is saying, *"I can't see the target,"* as you lift your head ever so slightly to peek, pull the trigger, and the target floats away unburned. Your eye is the rear sight of the barrel. If you lift your head the target flies away. Even shifting your eye in the wrong place with your head fully down on the comb will make your opponent smile. Remember, the gun will shoot where you look and aim. If you're not looking at the target, the scorekeeper will sing, *"Lost."*

Practice mounting the gun and dry-firing at targets. Ask a squad at your local gun club if you can join them though you won't be firing. You just want to practice mounting the gun on every target, track and dry-fire them. That one session alone will grant you 100 gun mounts, 100 foot stance checks, 100 eye /hand coordination moves, and 100 lessons of trigger pull discipline. You'll be exhausted, but you'll build stamina, toning the muscles required in trapshooting. You are using muscles no other exercise can simulate. There is no substitution. Examine your setup and maintain your usual gun mount speed. Even 50 of the above is better than none, and it's free practice.

Now for the test. Mount your gun as you normally would and dismount. Now close your eyes and mount your gun, then open your eye (s). Do you see your line of sight facing directly down the center of the rib? Do you see the sight beads perfectly stacked in a figure-8 pattern? Did you see this without moving the gun, your head or your arm? This is the ultimate test of knowing you have mastered gun mount technique. Don't overlook this, as it is critical. Try it again. Each time must be perfect. If it is not perfect, then you should practice mounting the gun so your brain can train your muscles to repeat the action consistently. Closing your eyes will provide you the ability to recognize immediately if the gun is mounted properly, or not even, before you open your eyes. Now you are getting it right! Shooting is much more than just seeing, it's a feel, a presence of mind, a sense of precision. Do this right now and you will be making your first contact with your subconscious mind. When you get it right, you will know it's right, even when your eyes are closed! If you still can't mount the gun smoothly without fidgeting or adjusting the gun, you have a serious gun fit problem. The gun must fit or your low scores will drive you into fits. Don't shoot a gun that does not fit you, as you will wholly be wasting your time and money and eventually your scores will become so frustrating you may even quit the sport. Now practice mounting your gun until you get it right. Don't forget to close your eyes and practice swinging the gun smoothly. Do you feel your shoulders shrugging? You shouldn't be. Is the grip on your gun firm but not tight? Can you swing the gun along an imaginary target's curved flight path with your eyes closed? Remember, targets bend in flight and do not travel in straight lines.

PROPER GUN GRIP
"The only certainty is there is nothing certain."

Don't hold the gun with a ironclad grip. A soft yet firmly held grip to the gun's forearm is best. The hand and arm relaxed so a smooth swing can take place. Swing easy, hit hard. Tense muscles harvest jerky muzzle motion. Relax, relax, relax is the rule here. Try twisting your hand so your index finger is directly pointing under the barrel. See Fig. 2-5. This twisted wrist, locks the gun solidly as the elbow and acts as a brace so the gun doesn't sag or drop when calling for the target. It restrains wavering barrel movements, creating a solid supportive foundation to swing to the target. To comprehend the reasoning, watch a few targets fly and randomly point your finger at the target as a gunslinger would quick-draw. Notice how natural it is to point. An outstretched finger assists your natural pointing ability directly to and at the target. If you can't physically twist your hand all the way (with practice you can) you likely can shift it enough so your index finger resides along the side of the forearm in line with the barrel. It's not as accurate, but it'll get you closer to the target than merely gripping the forearm without a purpose. It requires unusual muscle stretching exercise to eventually grow comfortable, though the end-results are impressive. No pain, no gain. Wear a glove on forearm grip only, never the trigger-finger unless you are trying to resolve a flinch problem. A shooting glove can give you positive control of the gun, just as a driving glove helps control a vehicle or golf club. The glove prevents hand repositioning and slippage from perspiring skin and gun oils. Hold the gun with a sense of authority in your hands. You and the gun are one.

GUN SWING TECHNIQUE
"Change your mind, change your world."

Gun swing is a smooth, precise, symphonic composition of motions that needs to perform in harmony. The foundation of proper gun swing is a proper foot stance and gun mount (setup). If you perform the first two correctly, the swing will naturally be correct. See Fig. 11-6. **Example:** If shoes are worn-out, your balance is affected as you pivot your body to swing the gun. This is like trying to shoot while standing in a rowboat. If your foot stance is incorrect, too flexible or too ridged, the swing will waver off course or fail to flow into the target... usually shooting over the top of the target. Use a light hand grip on the gun's forearm so the gun will swing freely. Your hand is the extension to the target. A light grip increases smooth and easy swing control. Many missed targets are from too much muscle in the swing. Pivot by the hips to control lateral motion and use your arm to control vertical motion, don't push the gun around with your arm alone. It is important to have an effective 'swing attitude' to concentrate on. After taking your stance, fix your attention on the following; 1) Mechanics of the swing. This is something you should be practicing at home, not on the trap line, however, for a beginner it is okay, for now... remind yourself to swing properly. 2) Don't over concentrate to the point of immobilizing your mind and body. Loosen up, relax and learn to stay relaxed with proper relaxation technique. Control your breathing rate. Don't hold the gun tightly in your arms after firing. 3) Begin your swing the moment you have determined the proper angle of the target, not when you see the bird leave the traphouse. This is so you will follow and properly track the target without jerky coarse correction movements due to surprise factors. 4) Be smooth yet aggressive keeping your eye on the target constantly. Don't look back at the sights or barrel as the muzzle will stop and you'll shoot behind the target. 5) Unload your mind during the swing by keeping your eye on the target with intense visual energy. 6) Any motion producing a weight shift from one foot to another is undesirable producing instability and erratic gun swing. Now you know why proper foot stance is so important. It forms the direction of power. We all know the direction you want the gun to go...towards the target! Aligning your body's weight to be equally dispersed on both feet, to pivot by the hips, powers your swing to the target. This weight should be in the middle of your feet, not shifting from toe to heel. Your foundation should be rock solid. Power and control comes from the pivot of the upper body and hips, not the arm. Proper foot placement directs the power of the swing. All is at risk without capable shoes. 7) Remember, hand grip is your connection with the gun. To grip effectively, your forearm hand should apply a light, pleasantly consistent pressure in concert with hip pivoting while your trigger hand is holding on tightly. Using one or the other by themselves won't cut it. Try these when you practice. But don't keep reminding yourself, as you do not want to develop a habit of cluttering your mind with these thoughts; instead, it should become second nature without further effort. Good shots require good swing attitudes. In the course of the learning phase (which never really ends) be aware of subtle changes in swing and all other shooting techniques. Especially the days when you are shooting well... remember what you were doing right and write it down for future evaluation and recall. Every great mistake has a halfway moment, a split second when it can be recalled and remedied.

Let the center field stake be your friend. Watch the missed targets that fly near the stake and note if the targets are falling short of overshooting. This determines the speed of the targets. Also, you can use the mid-point between the traphouse and field stake to focus your eyes on the ground when shooting low flying targets in a tail wind. It's a little trick to force you to pre-focus your eyes low and to drop the gun hold down where it belongs. Try it.

Know how to play each shot. Each post requires a slightly differing eye and gun hold and zone. Find these and you'll find the golden key to hitting those targets hard, one-by-one. It's formulating a plan. Do you have a plan on each post and on each target? If not, start developing one.

When you swing the gun, even way back on the 27-yard line, you must use a swing to the target or you will "push" the gun with the forearm and that will spell L-O-S-T T-A-R-G-E-T. Your arms and body turn together like a robot would. This maintains the swing arc dynamics, allowing the gun to follow the true path of the target smoothly. If the arm and hand swing independent of the body, the gun will be pulled off line to the target, usually on the outside line of the target which results in shooting over the top. Keep the gun on the inside line of the target, meaning under the target at all times. If you are shooting over the top of targets, especially the hard angles on post #1 and #5, keep the gun extra low because these targets drop as they fly. They appear to be rising but they are falling along the arc flight path due to gravity and velocity drop. Shotstring will also drop, as most people are not going to shoot these hard angles right out of the house. So, now you know the secrets of hitting these hard angles... keep the gun low in the swing. Now, you can't keep the gun low if you're pushing the muzzle. Try it and you'll see you can't do it consistently. Body English is king on the trapfield.

There are many variances of gun grip, swing, posture, etc. Develop a formula that works for you, and if it does not work, no matter how comfortable it may feel to you... get rid of it! Copy elements the pros use and work them into your form and you'll find a combination that works for you. It all boils down to experimentation. Hard work is more than ample substitute for lack of talent as long as it is performed intelligently with a purpose. You can work hard with no focus or plan and sweat for nothing. Learn how to practice with the intent on learning a new technique and embed it into your mind.

DISMOUNTING THE GUN
"He who rides the tiger can never dismount."

We hardly read or hear of dismounting the shotgun. Why? Because shooters just don't consider it critical; however, it is essential to dismount the gun for multiple reasons. I for one had a difficult time trying to maintain my strength and energy level at prolonged practice sessions and registered shoots. My back would ache. My mind was no longer 100% focused on the targets. As a result, I would tumble into a black hole, wildly missing targets. It became so bad at the P.I.T.A. Grand in Salem, Oregon I considered selling my gun and even quitting trapshooting! I then spoke with a stockfitter and he told me a thing that was so obvious I could slap myself. *"Put the gun down to dispose weight, don't hold the gun in your arms all day long."* It was good advice. Often in competition shoots we are so keyed up in concentration we forget to dismount the gun to allow our muscles a rest between shots. Find a technique that works for you, but dismount the gun fully. Often, muscle strain can create a flinch. Get comfortable as soon as you can after shooting the target.

Another very important tip is to totally dismount the gun whenever you call for a target, see an obvious fast or slow pull, no target, or a broken target emerge from the traphouse. Don't keep the gun on your shoulder and call for another target as the setup is ruined. Some shooters dismount the gun, break open the action and start over again. Whatever you normally do just prior to your turn of shooting is where you should return to when dismounting your gun. You may not think it important to dismount during interruptions, but it is. Some won't do it on account of the fear of disrupting the rhythm of the squad. If you are shooting with a squad timing itself to the speed of a rapid-fire machine gun that scorns gun dismounts, then move from that squad or educate them. These shooters are unprofessional and just playing games, shooting for festivity only with no real intent of becoming proficient trapshooters or winning. [Fun = breaking targets, performing to maximum ability, pushing the envelope of performance and enjoying the accomplishment.] If you don't think winning is fun, try losing. Regardless of conditions, you have the right to dismount the gun; therefore, do so to insure the setup is repeated each and every time. If you speed up with a machine-gun squad, you'll be rushed to mount the gun rapidly and you'll get sloppy and miss targets. Maintain your own timing, play your own game, downshift if necessary so your setup will be smooth and unhurried. In time, the setup phase comes second nature. Watch the pros' timing and assimilate it. Maintain self-control. Don't shoot like a machine, a creature of nonintellectual habit. You still have to pay attention to each target. Get lazy, targets will escape.

Again, as mounting the gun, close your eyes and dismount the gun all the way back to the starting point with the gun action open and at rest in your arms. Open your eyes. You should find yourself at rest, but your gaze out into the distance as if staring at a traphouse. Your body should be in good posture with feet secure. Now close your eyes and mount the gun. Imagine a target left the house and swing to it. This is your first lesson in visualizing targets with your 'mind's eye'. Now try it with your eyes open. Can you see the target? Did you see it break? Do it again and again. Practice this. You have just learned how to mount, dismount, and break a target that did not exist. It is this same visualization pros use just before they call for the target. When you learn to mount your gun perfectly and visualize your performance, you are on the road to high scores.

Here's a tip for you... stay in the gun after you pull that trigger and stay there until the target breaks. Otherwise you will lift your head right before you pull the trigger and shoot over the top. Keep your cheek solid to the comb during the swing and after the gun fires and when you see the target break, then dismount. Another tip... dismount *slowly*. The faster you dismount your gun from your cheek, the higher the probability you will develop the bad habit of head-lifting. Believe me, your unconscious mind will actually begin the dismount process before you even contemplate doing it and that is when the head lifts. It's the mind's reaction to recoil. Stay in control of the gun at all times. Get the idea? And if you think that by holding the gun tight to the cheek it won't happen, you will be surprised to learn, the harder you hold down, the worse head-lifting becomes. Most shooters don't even realize they are lifting their heads, and if you tell them they will likely cuss at you in their denial. That's how insidious the habit is. When you stay in the gun, it cures head-lifting, especially if you are using a moving gun technique.

CHAPTER 3
BASIC SHOOTING

THE SETUP
"Accomplishments always come by surprise."

Simply mounting a gun, calling for the target and chasing it down is not all it seems. The setup is simply a reliable, repeatable routine of foot stance, gun mount, gun hold, eye focus, mind-set, and calling for the target. It never changes once it is perfected, except gun hold point during windy conditions; otherwise, all other variables remain consistent. If you are missing targets, it is likelier something went wrong in the setup phase than it did when you pulled the trigger. This must be reinforced in your mind. Trapshooting is learning a strict combination of routines that should not vacillate once perfected. The setup is heavily based on psychology -- the atmosphere and mood, including others around you. That's why professionals shoot with professionals. It's not loyalty of friendship. They are competing against each other. It's the setup! The setup phase begins even before the day you shoot. What you eat can ruin a good night's sleep for the following day. See Fig. 11-7, Fig.11-11 and Fig. 11-12 for very basic gun holds. Advanced gun holds are explored in the *"Precision Shooting"* book. See the back of this book for details. You may order the book from most any major bookstore or direct from publisher.

The moment you wake up, the setup begins to take hold. Keeping a calm mind is important for some, where activity is beneficial to others. Whatever clears the cobwebs from your mind is right for you. The setup then extends to the squad selection process and station posting. Haven't you observed shooters at tournaments change squads and request specific posts? This 'squad building,' too, is part of their setup routine. It would be ideal not to develop hang-ups or become too dependent as to who you must shoot with, for they may not show up for the shoot, pre-squad without you, and you'll have to hoof it alone. I notice many local gun club groups squad with each other. That's fine, but is it wise? It can become a serious detriment to a shooter who will not shoot, or is leery of shooting with a strange squad. It's a psychological crippling injury to blame poor scores on other shooters. Try to build a squad, or shoot a short squad if you feel you must. Though no one can deny the advantages of shooting with known consistent shooters performing on the same level as oneself, it too can be a disadvantage if you travel a lot, attending tournaments out of state. You'll have to shoot with unknowns.

Determine to shoot with any squad and on any post as this will force you to focus on your technique, not your surroundings. Be flexible and you will earn more friends as you shoot with diversified squads. Of course it is a definite advantage to shoot with a familiar squad, especially when shooters 'groove shoot' intent to hit the targets within the same time and place (zone or spot shooting). The basic rhythm of the squad helps. Nobody treasures shooting with someone who fires chronic dud loads, gun jams, misfires, etc. Squad selection has advantages, though ultimately, it is your technique and how you handle events going on around you (your attitude) that ultimately determines your scores. The next phase of the setup is mental preparation. Your emotions, moods, and thoughts must be swept aside to focus on the game factors. Preparation technique depends on your personality profile, however, realize the disadvantage of emotions is they lead us astray! They are intense mental states of mind that arise subjectively rather than through conscious effort.

Take a stroll along the trap houses noting how the traps are set. Are the trap house and trap stations square to each other? If they are out of alignment it will cause you to miss targets if you don't compensate for traphouse misalignment. How about the background scene? Is the target destined to fly into the shade and emerge into sunlight? Will it pass by a bank of yellow flowers on a distant rise, cross before trees then enter a blue or gray sky? Are the targets flying straight, fast, slow? Is the wind blowing and from which direction? Where is the sun? Will it be in your face or behind you? All these small details are important. It's all part of the setup. Depending on conditions, you may have to alter some of your shooting variables (not technique) to compensate for these conditions. You may have to break the target sooner or later in its flight path or be more aware of wind forcing targets to suppress, rise or change direction suddenly. The flowers in the distant field of view may obscure the target, inducing a background blur forming an optical anomaly of the target traveling faster than it really is. This phase of the setup requires time and experience to learn.

The most important factor to remember is... keep your head down on the comb and keep your eye squarely behind the sights and on the target. Don't concentrate on the variables too much. Just know they exist and compensate as best you can, but never take your eye off the target. Yes, it is possible to swear you kept your head down when tracking a target passing by clear or confusing backgrounds and still miss cleanly. The cause is your eye lifting away from the sighting focus to the background, or lagging the target. It is not enough to just keep your head down on the comb. Your eye is the rear sight of the gun - - look away or look in the wrong spot for a split second and you'll discover why you missed. Locking your eye onto the sights, then looking to the traphouse before you call for the target is part of the setup. What happens here is: 1) Your eye is on the target, but the gun is too far behind so the sight picture was not correct when you pulled the trigger. Speeding up your swing to the target will help eliminate this problem if lazy eye or muscular fatigue sets in. 2) You failed to acquire the target at the moment it left the traphouse. You can't have the gun barrel dragging behind the target and your eye on the target. Both your eye and gun barrel should lock onto the target as quickly as possible. 3) You likely anticipated a target and it surprised you by going in the opposite direction. 4) Your swing to the target slowed down not placing proper lead. 5) You failed to lock onto the target's true trajectory. 6) A mini-flinch occurred pulling the trigger or jerking the barrel erratically. To ascertain this, mount your gun, then shift your eyes horizontally to the extreme left away from the sights, call for the target and you will see an exaggerated scene of what I'm describing as you try to play catch-up. (See, 'Flinching' and 'Snap Shooting' for more on trigger control and missing targets).

The next phase of the setup is your station pose and foot stance (both mean the same in this section for simplicity. See Fig. 11-6 for explanation). Adopt a tried and proven trapshooting foot stance. Don't stand like a skeet, sporting clays shooter or field hunter; the stance is not technically suited for trapshooting competition because the balance is wrong and lacks repeatable precision. You don't want any weight shifting to upset your gun's swing to the target. Balance is absolute. Equal weight distribution to the center of both feet is required, not on the toe and not on the heel, right in the middle, equally distributed. If you can't do this, at least distribute weight on the heels. Whatever your stance may be, it has to be comfortable and must be repeated over and over and over again without error. A new stance will become comfortable, but is often awkward when learning it. Some shooters stand erect, bend their knee, push their bodies forward, then call for the target. Notice many fail to stop their body's forward motion! Here they have a gun in motion calling for the target (called a moving gun technique). That's generally a unsound policy by reason it can't be repeated as the gun barrel is in motion. If you shoot like this, then strive to reach a comfort zone you can reliably feel and freeze right there, then call for the target. Better still, purge this inclement habit, acquiring the traditional trapshooting stance. Any trapshooting videotape will demonstrate the traditional side-stance fundamentals. Grip the gun forearm snugly, not with a ironclad grip.

Don't release your finger grip on firing. It's a bad habit, break it. You lose control of the gun right when you need it the most. It's a flinch reaction. Dispose of it. How? By wearing a glove. Breaking old habits demands resolve, as it is always toilsome to convince oneself, *"When in Rome, do as the Roman's do."* If your setup is not consistent then your shooting will be solemnly discrepant. This includes foot position/stance (see Fig. 11-6). Learn the right way to shoot trap through understanding the proper fundamentals. There is a precise manner to grip a bowling ball, golf club, baseball, football, basketball. All have been calculated, tried, tested, and proven as giant footprints in cement. Deviate from these holds and your scores will fall or never rise to excellence. You can develop your own style, but first start at the foundation level before you build. Learn to stand correctly, then branch off. You can't break the rules until you fully understand the discipline of the rules! Unfortunately, most people refuse to start over again. It's like teaching an old dog new tricks. If you want to be a good trapshooter, then start practicing the fundamentals of proper foot positioning and good posture stance. Of course, it's uncomfortable and your scores will be embarrassing, though this is the penalty to pay to excel.

The next phase of the setup is mounting the gun consistently in the same place every time. It requires two sights on the rib to stack into a figure-eight pattern to verify proper eye alignment with the barrel. A single sight won't cut the mustard until you become a very experienced shooter. If you don't have two sights, then install one. The center bead is to insure a proper gun mount and prevent visual cross-firing. Without the center bead the eye / rib alignment can easily deviate from a straight sight plane when swinging the gun to the target. The gun can move away from your eye which is the rear sight. The center bead verifies if the gun is mounted properly as they stack into a figure-eight when looking down the rib. Trapshooting is a game of precision and accuracy, it is not spontaneous and reactive as wing shooting. Using a field gun for trapshooting is like using a hammer to install glass windows... it doesn't make sense. To learn gun mount correctly, close your eyes and shoulder the gun, open your eyes. Your master eye should be looking right down the center of the sight rib without any movement to correct alignment. Practice this until you get it right. If it doesn't work, then your gun doesn't fit you. You should never be fidgeting with the gun once it is mounted. If you fidget, the gun doesn't fit -- too heavy for the shooter or out of balance, etc. It is highly likely you have a worthless gun mount technique. You would be thunderstruck to see tournament shooters with horrendous gun mounting conventions -- nasty habits they will not change, even for the better. The pros get it right. Observe and learn from them. If you are mounting the gun "your way" it's probably not the right way. If it feels comfortable you may have become acclimated to a bad habit. Are you certain you don't have this problem, too? How often do you practice gun mounting? If you don't practice how then can you determine if you are mounting the gun properly? Have someone video tape you as you shoot, you may be surprised to discover you are one of 'them,' having gun mounting problems and you didn't even know it.

Correct gun mount is mechanical and physical. The gun should be mechanically designed to fit you. This includes comb height, cast (on or off), stock length of pull (One inch or two finger width between thumb and nose), recoil pad / sight line pitch cant (zero, negative, positive), recoil pad shape, rib height and duel sights, drop at heel (distance of sight line to rear of stock). Field guns lack these features. Many trap guns don't have these features when purchased off a dealers rack. Often you'll need to install devices to effect the adjustments. If you just buy any gun thinking you can practice your way to perfection, you're exclusively wasting time and money. The gun must fit properly. If the gun doesn't fit, expect to be kicked like a mule, leading to flinch difficulty, discomfort, etc. Once the gun fits, it can then be mounted perfectly each and every time, retaining comfort, balance, and accuracy. Remember, an improperly mounted gun creates an incorrect sight picture and missed targets. Is your gun custom fitted? Are you sure it fits you? If you purchased the gun without modifications it probably doesn't fit you! Don't deceive yourself believing it fits when it doesn't. It's a proven fact guns off the shelf are not fitted, although you could get lucky, it's highly unlikely. If the gun fits, targets you'll hit. If the stock is of the proper length, your cheek will meet slightly forward of the midpoint between heel and comb. A slip-on pad can be used to increase the length of pull or install butt-plate spacers. This will, of course, alter the balance of the gun. If you don't have an adjustable sight rib, you can change the point of impact by removing the butt-plate and placing a spacer or washer on the heel or toe. To raise POI lower the forward portion of an adjustable comb, or sliding the butt-plate up or down, or try corrective POI chokes, etc. See a stock fitter to obtain precise adjustments.

Now that your gun fits, and you acquired the proper foot positions and stance posture for shooting trap, (Fig. 11-6) it's time to zero-in on the last phase of the set up. Before it is your turn to shoot, check your foot position and look where you intend to break the target. This isn't anticipating what target angle you will receive, but knowing where you will smash that target no matter what angle emerges. It's setting up your mind to visually break the target, a form of positive thinking. It wipes out the mystery of the surprise factor because you are prepared for any angle, owing to deliberating the angles. You'll be surprised when the target gets the jump on you if you were not expecting that hard right or left quartering target. Why? You didn't remind yourself the target could go there and had no plan to break it. Planning is critical. You must have a plan on each station, as each station requires its own set of rules. Know where you are! You can't plan to shoot a hard right at station #1 because it doesn't exist. The same with station #5 no hard left exist. So study your basic angles at each station and, once you know them, formulate a plan of mental preparedness to attack them... and do this each time you shoot! Remember, a round of trap isn't 25 targets, it is only one target... one at a time. This is why the setup is so important because one error leads to lost target(s) and the trophy or option money vaporizes. Live and learn.

Another phase of the setup sporadically mentioned is nerves. Nervousness is normal, though be aware it destroys the setup. Nervousness stimulates glands to secrete hormones which sensitize the central nervous system, causing voluntary and involuntary motor nerve muscle contractions, including the eye's iris and lens. Being aware of this fact should place thoughts in your mind like, *"Okay, it's no problem, I've done it thousands of times before and if I setup properly I'll break the target."* Then shoulder your gun and break the target! Easier said than done; nerves can be controlled to a certain extent. You know the feeling when you run all four stations and now you are on station #5 with all those hard rights just waiting to humiliate you. You hit one. Good, four more to go. The tension builds. Again you hit one, and three more to go. More tension. Do you know how to break that tension? It's very easy. Tell yourself: *"There aren't 25 targets, just one target, only one!"* The sooner you convince yourself there is only one target the finer trapshooter you will be. It's an exclusive method to arrest anxiety attacks of counting. *"Oh, no, only five targets left and I'll have 100 straight!"* Dissolve those dreadful thoughts out of your mind. Each target you hit is history. It's gone and you can't bring it back. You can't unscramble an egg. Who cares about the last 99 targets? There really is only one target! It's just a target, too, there is nothing special or magical about it. You should put no more importance into that last target than you did with all the others. Once you feel these last target(s) are 'something special' they will likely be missed as you divert your mind from the setup and the business of shooting. Same is true with your first target. This is very important psychology, so take heed.

The setup must become mechanical. You have heard it said and seen high gun shooters shoot, "like a machine." This is true. Their setup is so patented they resemble machinery. It is compulsory to learn, too, to become so mechanical all trusting is in your technique. Then you have arrived at a lofty place in your shooting career. Remember this... when you find you have your setup under control, there is one more thing to remember, and this is timing. Not timing the shot, but the speed which you mount the gun, etc., should never change. If you miss targets, recall your timing. I'd bet it accelerated or slowed down. Why? Likely due to squad timing. The other shooters are probably shooting too fast and your subconscious mind recognizes the acceleration and causes you to speed up. I know you have experienced this before, everyone has and is susceptible to it. Be aware of yourself when shooting. Maintain your own game at your own speed to your propensity. Don't get caught up in swift squad rhythms, accelerating faster and faster. The effective means to avoid this situation is to be the squad leader. You have the opportunity to reset the tempo when you change stations. At least you will acquire a break as the others crave to machinegun their way into the Hall of Fame. A proficient squad leader will maintain an even keel pace. The squad is a symphony requiring orchestration. The squad leader is the conductor. A detrimental squad leader is a vigorous one who inclines to rush the squad to push the day behind him. This brings to mind when shooters are speeding up the rhythm, perchance they missed targets and are now shooting for tomfoolery to rid frustrations. Don't get caught up in someone else's game!

For those who regard setup is little more than hogwash, take this test. Try calling for the target with another call. Instead of the customary *"Pull"* say *"Down"* or anything wildly differing than routine. Also transition the tone of voice from low to high. Now run them all and I bet you can't! Try standing in a different position than you normally do. Try mounting the gun at a different speed or changing gun grip. Do it on all 25 targets, not just one or two. This will silence any critic that setup is frivolous. I bet scores go to the birds.

JUST SAY PULL?
"Speech is power."

The game begins with the call of "Pull." Any vowel will do: A, E, I, O, U. Everyone has their own unique touch, though how you call for the target can mean missed targets. Watch closely the loud callers and you'll notice the tip of their gun barrel dances. Some calls are so severe, I've seen barrels dance in circles and figure eight patterns, some even go so far as to begin chasing a target that has not even appeared yet. Are you doing the same thing? You may and not realize it. Ask someone to observe and report results. The louder you call, the more your cheek muscles move and your face will induce barrel ballet. It's a clear disadvantage to have an improperly moving gun when the target emerges because your eye and mind must expend corrective calculation to compensate for incorrect visual acquisition of the target, and, the gun must follow the eye, never the eye trailing the gun. Have you ever found you missed a target because you didn't track it properly? It may very well be your gun is in motion and you're following the wrong track. Ask someone to watch you call and monitor barrel movement. If it moves, it's time to experiment with a new call. The vowels are recommended since the sound can be made without cheek movement. If you like saying *"pull"* try saying *"ull"* as face muscles are not activated. The sound should originate from the diaphragm just as a singer sings. The call is louder and it will save your vocal chords. Don't force a call by inducing chest or stomach muscles to heave. Call with little external muscular movement. Take a deep breath before calling. It does three things. First, it supplies a surge of oxygen to your eyes, opening the pupil, making your eyes more alert. Second, it allows a large volume of air to pass by the vocal chords, making for a loud call without muscular movement that can move your gun. Third, you'll receive fewer fast and slow pulls. You will promptly learn the small and often ignored improvements, helping you smack those extra targets that randomly get away. The setup before calling for the bird is more important than the actual act of shooting. Your call is the last-chance phase of the setup. Blow it here and targets will slip away. Practice your calling style. Don't get into any hang-ups if others say, *"You sound funny."* Just tell them, *"I yell because I care."* Keep experimenting with a call you feel comfortable with, has a loud tone to minimize erroneous pulls, and of most importance, the barrel stays motionless. Remember to use the vowels or a combination thereof. A short, loud call may result in less frequency of slow and fast pulls. A loud aggressive call, all the way to target, sets up a 'tone' in ears, blocking out distractions. However you call, as long as the gun doesn't move, and the call can be easily heard, retains an element of aggressive attack and authority, your call is okay. Experiment with call tone, volume, duration, determination. Words and sounds induce emotions, for good or bad. A specific call can trigger deep levels of concentration you never knew existed. A change could be for the better.

A word of caution. In the game of trapshooting the most insignificant concerns are ultimately the most significant. The game is so fickle the slightest noise, feeling or mood variant can cause you lost targets. The reasons for this sensitivity is the game is 90% psychological in nature. Subtle changes in your call can trigger the subconscious it is experiencing a new learning curve, a technique it is unfamiliar with which results in lost targets. When I mention to "play your own game" I really mean play your own game all of the time, every time. Modify your call and targets will be lost. So, be aware of the 'Pall Parrot' manifestation. You start out calling for targets as usual, then unconsciously, your call changes and you don't even know it has! To observe this in action watch a friend in a heated shootoff competition. You may surprise yourself to hear his call tone or volume level change because someone on the squad (or pure self-induced aggression) has influenced him by his own call flair. I've seen it time and time again with the same results... lost targets! Investigate to determine if this is affecting you too. Now that you are aware of it, you should be able to recognize deviations. Consistency pays rewards.

GUNPOWDER MANUFACTURERS
The following companies publish reloading recipe data.
Alliant Techsystems, (formerly Hercules Powder), Smokeless Powder Group, 200 Valley Road, Ste. 305, Mt. Arlington, NJ 07856 (800)-276-9337 maker of Red Dot®.
Hodgdon Powder, 6231 Robinson, Shawnee Mission, KS 66202 (913)-362-9455 maker of Clays® powder.
IMR, 1080 Military Turnpike, Plattsburgh, NY 12901 maker of Hi-Skor® 700-X powder.
Kaltron-Pettibone / Ammunition Unit, SF-41330 Vihtavouori, Finland (800)-683-0464 makers of VihtaVouri Oy.
Winchester/Olin, (800)-526-0015 maker of the Double AA® shotshell and powders.

Everyone asks which gunpowder is superlative? They're all good. Principally, a pattern board decides which powder patterns best in your gun. There's no getting around it. This does not center entirely on two-dimensional printed pattern proportions, as of paramount importance point of impact must be checked. Here are a few principal requirements that make a gun ballistically accurate; 1) the inbred accuracy of the barrel, 2) performance of the shotshell, primarily velocity and velocity consistency as velocity changes POI and patterns, 3) reasonably consistent point of impact at all temperature ranges, 4) choke size with true concentricity, 5) gunpowder that flows smoothly into the hull for uniform powder charges, 6) ammo quality, shot hardness, wad performance, 7) shooting ability. Still and all, performance is the true determining ingredient... the powder breaking the most targets is the best powder money can buy!

CHOKE TUBES AND SHOT
"Learning what you can't do is more important than knowing what you can do."

More importantly, is the choke! The proper choke will usually get the job done as well or better than experimenting with endless shotshell loading recipes. A full, light full, or improved modified choke can be used from the 27 yard line all the way down to the 16. The tighter the choke, the longer in length the shotstring will be and the tighter the pattern radii. A long shotstring is desirable as you can place more forward lead on a target with less chances of missing, assuming the shotstring is not thin or too long. Soft shot produces a longer unstable shotstring due to pellet deformation, so use hard shot with high antimony content. A full choke with #7 1/2 or #8 shot is preferred for long yardage handicap. A light full or improved modified with #8 shot is great for mid-yardage and even long yardage. A modified or improved modified choke using #8 1/2 shot is okay to use at the 16 yard line. Some shooters prefer to shoot 'dust' #9 shot in singles 16 yard line, but if a target gets the jump on you odds are you'll miss the long shot with #9's. There are two sizes I use: #8 or # 7 ½. I will shoot the larger size 7 1/2's for any target at any yardage in any weather conditions. My reasoning follows, 1) If you place the sight bead where it should be, you will break the target. 2) 7 1/2 shot contains a higher level of energy per pellet and one pellet could slice a chip off the target, especially when shooting moisture laden targets in high humidity areas. 3.)

Pellet deflection -- a target's curved surfaces can deflect high speed projectiles, use 7 1/2 shot, 3 dram loads. **4)** Don't complicate the game. Make life simple.

When purchasing shot, buy quality shot. There are some companies who sell screened reclaimed shot which appears to be new shot as there is no indication on the bag of its contents. Screened reclaimed shot is simply shot mined from the field, cascaded over a vibrating screen -- hopefully separated via shot size -- and bagged. The danger is small stones can be found in the bag which may scratch your barrel. The shot is often whitish in appearance (oxidized), pellets are dented or out of round, and little or no graphite lubricant is applied. Insure when you buy reclaimed shot it is at least remelted, sized, and lubed. This can be used for practice shooting even though the antimony average level may be below 5%. For quality shooting, insist on magnum hard shot which is lead shot with at least, 5% antimony. Don't use soft chilled shot for competition. Even if the shot bag says XXXX HARD shot, look for the logo stating at least, 5% antimony. If antimony or the word 'magnum' isn't imprinted on the bag, it is not hard shot! The antimony hardens the lead shot to prevent pellet deformation when the shell is initially fired, squeezed through the forcing cone and choke, then kick-slammed out the barrel. They tend to retain their spherical shape producing tighter patterns. Deformed pellets will surely fly off course. You would be amazed to discover how many shooters who use reloads in competition don't realize they are shooting soft chilled or reclaimed shot.

The shot manufacturers / reclaimers should clearly identify on their shot bags exactly what the buyer is buying. Find a reputable shot manufacturer and stick with them. It may cost more to shoot quality, but it costs even more to replace a barrel and lose tournaments. Another important factor to consider about shot is if you look closely you may notice the #7 1/2's have #8 shot sprinkled throughout. It's a problem with the processing / screening operation failing to size the shot. When #8 shot is packaged you may similarly find #9 shot intermixed. In some cases all three sizes are found. This is another good reason to use 7 1/2 shot for handicap yardage as #8's will damage the target. If you use #8 shot be assured these #9 infiltrators will never break the target. You can re-screen the shot yourself if you obtain a defective bag, or return it for replacement. Have you checked your shot bags for proper sizing? Could very well be why you are missing targets. Keep in mind #7 1/2 shot will hit the target harder and arrive sooner than #8's due to high momentum and resistance to atmospheric friction. The best shells to buy? Snag those special Grand American shells all major ammo manufactures develop just for the Vandalia Grand. They are a tad faster than standard production. A smidgen over 3-drams equivalent of energy is used (still allowed at the Grand so it's technically legal) with extra hard spherical shot. They are finer shells, still how much better 'score-wise' one really doesn't know until tried. New shells = Higher quality shot than you can buy for reloads.

Defining which choke or shot to use is like catching a falling dagger. Everyone has their own opinion and this is to be respected. My advice is to try them all and whatever works for you, works for you. However, the key to discovery is experimentation and noting actual performance... not emphasized on a two-dimension pattern board, but how the choke and shot breaks targets. The ideal is to break targets into a cloud of smoke, not slicy chips or chunky breaks (see, A Tid-Bit About Pattern Misconceptions). Your scores will tell you more than any pattern board, chronograph or theories. To simplify life, a light-full or full choke with #8 shot 3-dram load will take you where you want to go, from the 16 all the way to the back fence. It is to your advantage to purchase a replacement choke from a reputable specialty choke manufacturer. As of this writing I am using Briley's extended, black oxide-coated, ported tubes with extra full, full or light full in my Browning O & U trap gun. For this gun, they throw consistent tight patterns. The big three choke manufactures -- Rhino, Briley and Seminole -- specialize in chokes, and they expend a great deal of effort to insure true constriction dimensions are retained, including elongation / concentric tolerances. The nice thing is, they work as advertised. You can expect 20% improvement in dense even patterns over factory chokes (though this gap is closing due to OEM improvements). Rhino's competition series chokes are made of strong 17-4PH stainless steel (used in tips of sidewinder missiles). The smooth, hand-lapped finish reduces plastic wad fouling known to upset pattern quality. These chokes increase pattern density, allowing the shooter to opt for a more open choke without risking gaps in the pattern, thereby decreasing errors in aim to smoke more targets. Don't forget to lube choke threads. A good anti-seize lube is Break Free® Santa Ana, CA 92705 (714)-953-1900 and is a superb lubricant for all moving gun parts.

Before you buy any chokes, verify your gun shoots straight where you aim, or should aim with a high point of impact gun. It is not uncommon to find a new or old gun not shooting where you aim. Often, a corrective choke can be purchased to remedy the problem, though straightening the sight rib, stock or barrel is your better bet in the long run. Keep this in mind when buying any gun. Verify it shoots straight. Most manufacturers will correct the fault if you purchased the gun new within the warrantee period. Use a pattern board to determine barrel accuracy. What you are looking for is the point of impact relative to your point of aim. Don't get overturned if you find the pattern above the point of aim, a trap gun should shoot high. Look for patterns drifting left, right, or below your point of aim. Do this with a cold barrel, then with a hot barrel after shooting a round of trap. It is possible the POI can shift as the metal expands and you will at least want to know by how much. If you find your point of impact changes a lot when hot, then don't shoot with 'short squads' or known shooters who 'machine gun' in rapid succession in competition as the barrel will not have time to cool. The advantage of an O&U is you can alternate barrels to arrest overheating. Use a damp cloth to wipe barrels to keep them cool.

A full choke will produce approximately 65% to 75% pellets in a 30" circle at 40 yards. Improved modified 55% to 65%. Modified 45% to 55%. As you can discern, the full choke wins the race. You may think an extra-full choke would add more pellets into the pattern, but due to the crushing of the pellets as they are forced through the tight choke, deformed pellets are created which result in flyers. You may receive 50% to 68%. This may not be true with your gun. The exclusive means to verify is to test fire on a pattern board. A longer choke will deform less pellets no matter which constriction choke you use. The extended choke, which extends beyond the barrel, is proving its worth on the trapfield. Briley has the 'Excentrix' choke allowing you to correct POI at 40 yards up to 8" in any direction. The choke will even convert side-by-side shotguns for trapshooting, especially double trap (doubles shooting events). Here's a few manufactures who specialize in choke tubes.
Briley 1230 Lumpkin, Houston, TX 77043 (800)-331-5718.
Rhino Gun Cases, Inc., 4960 SW 52nd St., #408, Davie, FL 33314 (800)-226-3613.
Seminole Gunworks 3049 U.S. 1, Mims, FL 32754 (407)-383-8556.
Hastings, Box 224, Clay Center, KS 67432 (913)-632-3169.

There are more choke manufacturers which can be found in shotgun sports magazine advertisements. A quality choke is a trapshooter's best ally. Find the choke that works best for you, regardless what others may say since each gun is different. What works well for the other guy may not for you, even with identical guns!

CHOKE TUBE MAINTENANCE
The single most important barrel maintenance on a shotgun is the choke. It should be clean and free of plastic wad and powder carbonization. A fouled choke will throw wild shotstrings, modify the point of impact causing missed targets and induce a barrel explosion if obstructed with heavy carbonization. Many gun cleaning chemicals can be used with a brass or fiber bristle brush. A product I use is MPro-7™, the same cleaner the Air Force uses to clean F-16 fighter jet cannons. It produces no fumes and cleans the barrels of all guns, dissolving lead, copper, brass, carbon fouling. It quickly removes deeply baked carbonized plastic wad fouling from chokes, is non-flammable, emits no foul odors, easily cleans to bright mirror finish, is non-corrosive and non-reactive with any metal. Once you try MPro-7 you won't use anything else on your guns, and I mean all your guns, pistols, rifles and shotguns. This product is impressive and very economical. You need to try MPro-7 to believe how worthy it really is. Furthermore, they manufacture a unique bore patch that works like a magnetic sponge absorbing everything in its path without smearing. Contact: Windfalls Distributing, Inc., P. O. Box 54988, Phoenix, AZ 85078 (800) 937-4677. You can purchase Mpro-7 lube and cleaner from our web site or write to us for pricing. See the title page of this book. Be certain to lube the choke tube threads with anti-seize compound, BreakFree® works great. Extended knurled choke tubes still require tightening with a wrench despite claims finger-tight is sufficient. Heat, pressure and vibration will loosen the choke, fouling exposed threads; lead, plastic and powder deposits can cause cross-threading. A loose choke will snag wad and pellets, tossing bizarre patterns, producing point of impact

floatation. Do not over-tighten, simply snug is fine, but always use a wrench to snug. Over-tightening can deform concentricity warping patterns and relocating POI. Normally, chokes for lead shot use do not wear out, they become warped over time by dropping them on the ground, over-tightening, under-tightening, or stress cracking. If targets are slipping by, check the choke tube, pattern, and point of impact! A dirty barrel retains heat and will alter POI.

SHOOTING CIRCLES
"Though this be madness, yet there is method in it." Hamlet, by William Shakespeare

There's more than one way to break a target! Skepticism is a basic part of the mind. The skeptic is not he who doubts, but who investigates, as opposed to him who thinks without finding. Proof is required before you know for sure if what you think you are seeing is what you are really seeing. When learning new ideas we are bound to be skeptical, until proof is demonstrated. Even so, if the new wisdom conflicts with the existing mind-set, there is a proclivity to abate the new information. Historically, all new scientific discoveries were ridiculed by a skeptical public, so don't be timorous to try new techniques and ideas. Experimentation constructs an excellent trapshooter Now, let's shoot the circle.

When I first uncovered this mysterious illusion -- yet a solid law of physics enacted on the trapfield -- I was shocked. I told other experienced shooters about it and they adamantly declared, *"I'll believe it when I see it with my own eyes."* However, after proving it to them, they too were puzzled at the anomaly -- a true deviation from the rules. No 'Hot Shot' trapshooter openly spoke of it. Yet here it was, clear as daylight... an answer to why many targets are missed! No magic here; seeing is believing. Be prepared to alter your comprehension of target angles. When you finish reading this section you'll agree there is no such thing as a straight-away target, it just doesn't exist! Even the hard left and right targets are not running straight horizontally or vertically. They bend! Everything you see is an optical illusion, and you can't hit targets if you indeed don't know where they are. Have you ever wondered why you missed a straight-away, shook your head in disgust, vowing it would never happen again? We all have. Then you missed again, blaming the misperceived holes or 'doughnut' in the shot-pattern theory, or head lifting. Well, you can say good-bye to these missed targets as we explore the mystery of target angles. In Fig. 3-1 (A) you can see what most trapshooters see, target angles flying in straight lines. If you shoot tracking the target on these straight lines you are bound to miss targets, more than you should. For most shooters, angling targets are tough to hit, but the straight-away will get you more often than not, often by sheer surprise. You've seen it happen to others, and no doubt you've experienced it too. So what gives?

First, let's simplify matters and talk about basic target angles. A straight target is rising constantly on a sharp incline. Quarter angle targets do the same, but drift left or right on an oblique angle. Hard left and right angle targets do not rise as sharply as lateral motion is accelerated as gravity exerts negative forces on its ascent. This energy transfer causes angular motion acceleration, hence a speeding hard right or left target. The actual physical forces are slight, but the eye knows how fleeting those extreme angle targets truly are... they tend to whiz by in a blur. In Fig. 3-1 (C) the protractor reveals target angles varying between zero and 40° (approximate). Legal trap target angles in the #2 hole are generally 0 to 25 degrees. Close your eyes when practicing and imagine the protractor overlaid over the traphouse. Now open your eyes and you should see a narrow field of view and the expected maximum angle target you will receive. On stations #1 and 5 expect swift flying 40° angled targets. Stations # 2 and #4 have 30° and station #3 has 20° angled targets. Now you are visualizing breaking the targets, knowing where these angle targets will be when they emerge. You'll be prepared for them.

So now that you know the basic hard-angles a trap machine will throw, it's time to step into the distance factor. All targets will rise to an apex, then change direction and descend. See Fig. 3-1-(B). Many shooters wait for the target to peak to shoot, though hard angle targets' peak crests are not so visually pronounced. See Fig. 2-6 (B) and (C). However, you can only do this on a true straight-away or a slight quarter-angle target. The target appears to stop in midair when it changes direction, but it is still moving, and likely moving opposite where you perceive. The hard left and right angle target, you don't see a peak. So waiting for any target to peak is not a good idea. Distance has now already inflicted a huge disadvantage. It's hard to judge a target's true angle the further away it gets from the traphouse and your shot pattern opens up too wide and the shot loses velocity = a reduction of pellet energy to reach and break the target. Not to mention the shotstring elongates to as much as 15 feet. Shoot a straight rising target by putting your bead on it and it will not smoke. The target is quickly rising, remember? Your sight bead (on a flat shooting gun) must be placed on top or above the target. Of course, your eye should be looking at the top edge of the target; pull the trigger and it's history... sort of, or at least it should break, that is if it was truly a straight-away target. The shotstring, which at 40 yards is approximately 9 to 14 feet long should plow into the target. To shoot an angle target, your eye must be on the leading edge of the target, establish the proper lead. Pull the trigger and the target vanishes, sort of... that is, if it were truly a target traveling in a straight line. What most shooters see are straight lines. The target is moving to the left or right or rising or falling. No precise attention is made to identify the 'true flight path' of the target and it is here where missed targets are born. You will now learn the reasoning behind shooting fast instead of waiting for a target to apex or gain distance on you. Is it true targets positively do travel in arcs and not in straight lines?

Fig. 3-1 (C), (D) and (E) reveals targets do not travel in straight lines or tracks; they are curving like a bursting firework arcing into semi-circles. To indeed understand this illusion and reality, place your hands in a T-square configuration as shown in Fig. 3-3. Observe the targets and behold the curves are reality. Another method to fine tune your vision for judging true angles is to place a fine blade of grass or wire vertically, at arms length, in the center of the traphouse standing behind station #3 and watch for a straight-away. See Fig. 2-1- (F). It just doesn't happen, and it rarely occurs on any other station, regardless if the oscillating trap is set in the #2 or #3 hole. And if it does, it is so rare you'll break the target anyway. A straight target is easy to break, the missed straight-aways are in fact quarter angle targets, but you thought they were straight-aways! That's why you'll miss them. When you imprint in your mind no targets are straight, less decision making benefits as you'll expect all targets to be angle targets.

What we are looking for is the true acute angle of the targets using fixed reference points. An acute angle is the amount of deviation less than a quarter circle, less than 90°. Technically, a right angle is exactly 90° and obtuse angles are greater than 90° but less than 180°. For simplicity we will use a simple protractor held upright flat side down in hand using 90° as 0° for measuring acute angle reference. See Fig. 3-1- (C). This conversion makes it easy for interpretation purposes, to see for yourself targets are indeed curving. If you position the protractor vertically with 90° on top, you can measure the exact target angle. The trap machine is throwing targets randomly due to its oscillation motor. Hold the protractor (flat side down with 90° aligned with the center field post) and witness the machine tossing targets at various angles, and they are rarely straight -- once in a blue moon. At the top of the protractor, 90° indicates a true straight-away target flight path. What are the odds of the machine stopping at any particular angle, especially at 90 degrees? I wouldn't want to calculate the odds, never mind the enhanced complication of the odds of probabilities which perplex odds by thousands of combinations. Leave this to the mathematicians. Our concern is to recognize targets are not traveling in straight lines. So rule #1 is to realize what may appear to be a straight-away target is a mirage. Flush all thoughts out of mind you will receive a straight-away target and reprogram with, *"All targets are angle targets."* It's a true anomaly; the target travels in an arc. Law of gravity applies.

You call for the bird, it looks straight, you shoot and miss clean. You call another target, it looks like it's angling, you shoot and miss clean. *"Hmm, I don't know why I missed it."* Someone standing behind or beside you whispers you shot behind it. True, you did. You shot a phantom mirage-- a target that appeared to be where it wasn't. Take a look at the trap throwing targets, and I mean watch the targets' total flight path within the limits of the protractor. Notice how a straight-away bends away from the 90° mark. The quarter angle and hard left or right angle bends radically away from true center, and it doesn't travel in straight lines, but in curves. So, if you are tracking a target with your gun locked on like a freight train pinned to straight tracks, you can see how the curving target can be difficult to hit consistently. The smoothest route through any angle is the line with the longest radius, which will have the least curvature. In Fig. 2-2 (A) and (C) and Fig. 3-2 the shotstring is traversing the line of least possible radii. Canting the gun reduces the extreme angle in relation to both target and shotstring.

Intersecting the target at sharp right angles = lost targets or luck of the draw shooting as demonstrated in Fig 2-2 - (B), and Fig. 2-6 (A), (B) and (C). Canting the gun slightly using the bow technique takes full advantage of reducing these sharp angles, properly aligning shotstring to track with the target's curved angled flight path. And less muzzle movement is required to swing at severe angled targets. Since we are not shooting a missile with a missile, you can break targets without gun canting, but a slight cant should increase your accuracy. Regardless of the style of your shooting, you will at least recognize why targets are missed, as the targets are not traveling in straight lines but are constantly 'bending' away from the gun's sight beads. When you miss a target, determine if the target did indeed slip away due to its profiled bending behavior.

It is important to recognize the longer you wait to shoot a target the more severe the angle progresses. Holding your hands as shown in Fig. 3-3 will prove targets travel in arcs. It is one reason why in doubles the second target is harder to hit on account of distance having compounded its ever increasing curving angle as shown in Fig. 3-1 (C and E), Fig. 3-4 and Fig. 2-6 (B) and (C). When you shoot, you miss. The same with trap. Watch the target angle in the protractor and note how severe the angle becomes compared to the square of its distance. The angle becomes outrageously curvaceous. It is very hard to hit a curving target, one that is bending away from a straight shotstring. Watch the target until it falls to the ground, now look at the angles it has traversed. Get the picture? Learn to shoot circles, not straight targets. Many sporting clay shooters complain their hardest targets are quartering and looping angles. They would conquer them if they, too, did this test and realized the eye can truly be deceiving. The secret is to keep the muzzle on a proper angulation, 90° to the target at all times while tracking the clay. The eye and gun must follow the 'true' path of the target, not zigzag or haphazardly point without precision.

Since the target's angle increases dramatically with distance, it assuredly is reasonable to shoot swiftly before the angle has a chance to deviate from its minimal angle where it emerges from the traphouse. However, the magic is to recognize the angle in the first place and shoot at the proper point of aim at the target. Are you swinging to these targets believing they are traveling in straight lines? That may be why you are missing targets! You can't reliably shoot curves with a straight-arrow shotstring. This is the main reason why shooters discover the need to shoot quickly at targets. The longer you wait, the more pronounced the curve and the harder it is to smoke the target. You have less than 1 1/2 seconds to hit the target or risk losing it due to widening pattern, natural angle flight deviation, atmospheric eddy currents, shot velocity and energy reduction. The arcing is extremely severe when the target has traveled beyond its apex and is falling. But the arc still exists in the one-second timeframe.

Fig. 3-4 reveals the angles. Notice the angles are less severe closer in to the traphouse. Notice how divergent they are beyond this point. Now you know why professional trapshooters shoot quick, they don't have to worry much about targets angling away. Note in Fig. 2-6 (B) the straight or any angle target as in Fig 3-1 (C), (E) and (F) incessantly bends away from true center. If you can't shoot fast at this point in your game, try aiming your eye and the gun to the left forward face of any left quarter angle bird (aim to the right for a right quarter angle). You can do either on a true 90° straight-away target and still hit it. But since recognizing the angle is so important, here is how you do it.

First, visualize as you stand on station there are no straight-away targets. Researchers and sports medicine experts have long suspected, but now studies have proven, people who visualize objects experience enhanced brain signal activity in the area where visual processing occurs. The visual cortex of the brain is activated by mental images identical to visual perceptions. This is why visualizing breaking the target before shooting results in a broken target when you do shoot. Visualization also has a direct communication link with the subconscious mind which will, ultimately, perfect eye / hand coordination. Second, visualize the protractor superimposed over the traphouse, or two imaginary vertical walls on both sides of the traphouse. Third, use your gun barrel as a reference to determine which direction the target is angling. You will see a left-trending target rise alongside the left side of your barrel. A right angle target will emerge on the right side of your barrel. A true straight-away will rise under your barrel. Using the barrel as a focal point to judge proximity will increase your ability to instantly recognize the angle of the target. Even if you hold a low gun on the traphouse, you can still use the end of the gun barrel to judge proximity. Now how do you shoot these quarter angle targets once you recognize they are indeed angling? It's really easy.

A quarter angle target trending left requires you shoot to the left forward edge, not the face of the target. A quartering right target necessitates shooting to the right forward edge of the target. A straight-away can be smoked by touching the target, preferably by hitting it to the left or right depending on its angle. The primary reason you'll miss these targets hereafter will be misjudging the angle of the target. You may occasionally perform a miscalculated error, shooting to the left of a right angle target... something you've conceivably been doing all along anyway as a matter of redundant habit. Pay attention! Watch the target leave the traphouse to pass by your barrel. Don't use backgrounds or roof of traphouse as a reference point. It is worse than a crime; it is a mistake. They are unreliable and varied from club-to-club, station-to-station and traphouse-to-traphouse. It's wise to use a constant... the barrel.

So this brings an important gun retention point into mind. Your gun should not move vertically or side-to-side when you call for the target. If it does, your reference point and angle of attack will be annihilated. A steady gun is required. More so if you anticipate by beginning to move or swing the muzzle to the target before it emerges, as your eyes must see the target before the gun moves to the target. You'll miss targets if your eyes trail behind the gun. You want the gun to follow your eyes! Eye / hand coordination, not hand / eye coordination. There are a couple of debatable, though acceptable, pre-target release gun movements. One is rolling the gun barrel as you call for the target, pressing cheek down to comb to prevent head-lifting, that is, if you use a roll technique when shooting which most shooters do not employ. The other is a slight forward slow motion stab of the barrel towards the traphouse. Both are called moving gun techniques and are equally difficult to perfect. Fact is, no movement of the barrel is generally agreed upon as the proper technique, but in trapshooting rules are to be broken on an individual case-by-case basis. *"That fellow seems to me to possess but one idea, and that is a wrong one"* does not equitably apply to trapshooting. Whatever works consistently for you, works fine.

If you are still plagued with missing these targets, it's imperative to train your eye to recognize high-speed target angles emerging from trap houses. You may be shooting long (too slow) allowing the target to angle severely as distance increases. Remember, the angle increases the further from the traphouse... and it can be very oblique (slanting). If you shoot long, no doubt you will have to track your gun along a steep curve, not in a straight line, for consistent hits. It is too difficult to hit curves with a linear shotstring. However, the roll technique tracks curving targets naturally, though is difficult to master. Your best remedy is to get down to polishing brass tacks and start some serious practicing to shoot fast. A rolling stone gathers no moss. Hit those targets 20 - 30 feet from the traphouse and angles won't be much of a concern. However, to do this, read 'Practice Snap Shooting' section detailing how to practice expeditious shooting. Recall the longer you wait to shoot, the worse the angle, illusory mirage effects emerge, the shot pattern opens, shot energy decreases, and it distinctly spells, M-I-S-S-E-D T-A-R-G-E-T-S.

Waiting for the target to apex and sit still for a moment is an illusion...it appears to slow down, yet accelerates on descent. The target at its apex is changing direction and this is not a good time to shoot it. You will smoke most, but miss too many as the target relocates position. Here, holes in the shotstring will take advantage of you. Wind and eddy currents will complicate the dilemma. The target should be smoked when it is still rising so wind, breezes, thermal air currents, vertical and horizontal wind shear, low and high level air mass vorticity, and the angle of the target have a minimal effect. If you wait too long to shoot, you will always be an inconsistent shooter. Sometimes you're good, and other times it's, *"I can't hit anything today."* Then again, we are all inconsistent due to human error and mood change. Some days are better than others.

Another test you can employ to imprint into your mind there are very few real straight-away targets is to watch when they are setting a trap. How often do you see the target hitting the center field pole? It's most always to the left or right of the pole, and that's with the trap machine <u>locked</u>. Now pick up a protractor, convex side up, and look at angle 90° (zero angle). This is a straight-away target. Now look at all the lines left and right of 90°.

Those are angle targets. Now, still holding the protractor in hand, watch the trap machine oscillate left and right, throwing targets at random. How many did you see hitting the 90° zero angle flight path? Few indeed, if any! Place the protractor on the ground and spin a pencil. Place your bet money the pencil will point to zero angle. You'll surrender your paycheck. The odds of getting a true straight-away target are phenomenal. Consider all targets are angling targets and the straight-away you 'think you see as straight' is unmistakably drifting to the right or left. Now you'll be taking an extra hard look at the target's flight plan instead of routinely assuming it's a straight-away. The sleight-of-hand is determining which direction it is drifting. As a vague general rule:

Post #1. What appears straight is very likely angling to the left.
Post #2. What looks straight is most probably trending left or right. More repeatedly, left.
Post #3. What may be straight is quite prone to be oblique quartering left or right.
Post #4. What seems straight is most possibly drifting to the left or right. Most frequently, right.
Post #5. What could be straight is promising quartering to the right.

When you call for the target, never expect a straight-away. Prepare for the meanest angling target. Clear your mind of any straight-aways because: 1) Odds are it won't be straight. 2) A true straight target is easy to score a hit. It's the quartering angles that appear to be straight are truly troublesome and challenging. 3) You'll hit more targets. Pay attention to recognizing the true angle of the target as it emerges from the traphouse. At the least, if you are mentally prepared to expect an angle target, you'll fathom the secret in identifying these mystery targets when they appear. Trapshooting is challenging, as you'll never know where the target will fly or how it will behave in flight, still, knowing the odds should hand over a few extra dead targets to increase scores.

HEAD LIFTING & CANTING THE GUN
"For the last time, keep your head down."

The next time you witness a target flash by intact after pulling the trigger, suspect you lifted your head... even if you believe you didn't! You probably did and failed to sense it as 1/4" of lift = 10" error at 40 yards! There is a technique that virtually guarantees you can't lift your head when shooting. This does at first seem irrational, but there really is a plan to it. You gently shrug both shoulders to push the comb against your face when swinging the gun to the target. It works, though it takes some getting used to. Instead of holding the gun using your forearm and waist to move the gun barrel, tilt your body, as the Japanese do, a delicate and gentle 'bow'. It's a slight rolling of both your shoulders, placing a shallow 'cant' on the gun. Don't tilt your shoulders one side up, one side down. Keep shoulders level but bow slightly both shoulders from the hips as you simultaneously turn body toward target. If you are a right hand shooter, bow always to your right on both left and right targets. This system pushes the gun to your cheek and keeps it there, by virtue of your face being buried into the comb. The bowing motion reduces the impulse to overly push the gun's forearm to the target. Barrel movement is reduced and the bow motion cants the barrel to follow the natural arc of the target's flight trajectory. See Fig. 2-1 (A), (B) and (C). This technique will require grievous practice sessions and embarrassing scores before you get the hang of it. It is not easy to learn, and most shooters will give up long before seeing improvements... once bitten, twice shy! Nothing ventured, nothing gained. If you don't risk anything, you won't gain anything. It can take well beyond six months to acquire how to shoot this form, and few will persevere. Why bow slightly to cant the gun muzzle? It has the natural advantage of rolling into the target that is catapulted on a curved line of flight, less gun movement, keeps cheek tight to comb, induces lead, and is deadly accurate. It is so precise, this is why scores collapse when learning. The slightest room for error is penalized. It has a magical ability to allow the shooter to adapt to corrections in mid-flight, plus, you can truly discern the angles of each target clearly referenced to the barrel... even when the target is in flight! That's how tight the sight picture is. See Fig. 2-3 (A) and (B) and Fig. 2-4 (A) and (B) sight pictures.

The direction of the bow is identical for left and right targets. For straight-trending angle targets you still bow to raise your gun. Practice this and you will see it certainly works. Left hand shooters can use the same approach. The bow angle is tipped always to your left for both left and right targets. The distinct problem with this technique is the barrel will tend to roll on its side as you swing to a hard angle target. It's okay, as long as you are still looking down the sight plane accurately. A gun can shoot sideways, to a limit, depending on your point of impact setting. If the POI is high, canting the gun slightly on hard angle targets will automatically place some forward lead on the target. If POI is low or flat, canting the gun will have no effect on leads. A flat shooting shotgun can shoot accurately upside-down or on any off-centered angle. Canting a flat shooting gun will likely cause shoulder dipping, which is undesirable.

Muzzle canting is not as far-fetched as you may believe it to be. If you observe exemplary trapshooters very closely, you will see the muzzle cant slightly, bending, following the target's curved flight path. It happens quickly, but it does happen! The shooter may or may not consciously realize he is, in fact, canting but he is. You are likely doing it too! How is that? Because the target is traveling on an arc trajectory, the eye is tracking the target and your arm will naturally follow the curve if eye / hand coordination is correct. If it is not correct missed targets appear. The problem is when the eye is not on the target or the hand / muzzle is late, shooting behind as the target bends ever more away from the target / sight bead line up. Inconsistent timing compounds this problem ten-fold, giving rise to more opportunity for errors. By forcing a bit more cant on the gun, it helps you get on the target quicker, track the proper trajectory and lead the target. When you force a smidgen of cant, it reminds the brain it is shooting a bending target, not a straight line. It tightens the sight picture. Granted, when you track a target with your gun's muzzle, shooting as you normally do, you don't see much of an arc because the events happen so quickly. Recognition begins with awareness. If you really pay attention, you will begin to see these arcs, even when sighting down the sight rib. And when you begin to see them, you will lock-on to these targets with much increased accuracy.

Keep in mind, dipping the shoulders is not a recommended methodology of many instructors and they warn against it. Rolling the shoulders is not dipping! It's using 'Body English' a technique few are familiar with in trapshooting, yet used in all physical sports. This certainty is an intensely difficult system to master. Shooters tend to cock the shoulders out of alignment (one up, one down) instead of rolling both shoulders simultaneously from the hips, using a touch of Body English into the target. Many trapshooting instructors are unfamiliar with the technique, yet sporting clay shooters know they must cant their guns to hit arcing or looping targets. See Fig. 2-2 (A), and (C) and Fig. 2-6 (A), (B) and (C) - [Target angles - bottom view, canted]. It's definitely not for the average shooter who hasn't the determination to relearn all over again, but those who master it can see scores rise to higher levels. This rolling routine works best when hugging the gun close in to your face and shoulders and the roll is gentle, smooth, yet snappy quick. You surprisingly feel the gun in your arms, unlike other methods hence, more control of the gun, and you can say goodbye to head-lifting! More control can likewise impart rise to more errors. You can combine the bow technique with a slight traditional controlling drive of the forearm to reduce the bow angle if you prefer. It's not an easy style to learn, still the bottom line is, it works like a miracle. If you notice a shooting style that totally makes sense, yet it is hard to execute, simply resolve yourself to make it work! Where there's a will, there's a way. Dedication is the fuel allowing common people to attain uncommon results!

I DON'T WANT TO CANT THE GUN !
"Boney says he's hungry."

So you don't want to cant the gun? Fine, you don't have to if you don't want to, though you will do so naturally to a slight degree anyway as your muzzles will always flow with the eye, and the eye is following a arcing target. Trying canting on a few practice sessions will, at least, implant firmly into your mind how you can hit bending targets with increased reliability, feel the enhanced muzzle control of Body English, tighten sight pictures to a micron, plus improve deliberate precision and disciplined shooting. The key to learn this is to track the target slowly and deliberately, almost like rifle shooting. Later, the process can be accelerated. This revelation may be exactly what you needed to stop those few targets slipping away from you. The better shot you are, the more targets you will hit, until you start getting real good -- then always a target keeps slipping by here and there. It can be frustrating. Most of those targets you miss are mirages, bending away, and you're likely shooting behind. I believe if you try slight canting, you will see the target / bead relationship more clearly and pick up those extra lost targets. Regardless if you intentionally cant the gun or not, just learning how to recognize these mind-searing evading oblique angle targets should pick up your scores. Despite conventional wisdom, canting will increase accuracy. Increased precision = more broken targets!

CHAPTER 4

FLINCHING
"Emotions lead us to all the wrong places."

Surprisingly, a flinch can be what you don't think it is, and is not always what trapshooting books and magazine articles tell you it is. Make ready for an education. It is not perpetually caused by recoil, but from your internal time clock! We'll get to this later. First, what is a flinch? It's a nervous reaction materializing in a variety of forms. It can be as severe and obvious as a uncontrollable arm or neck muscle retraction or a subtle closing of the eyes when pulling the trigger or even the 'frozen in stone' effect of not pulling the trigger at all -- or at the wrong time. If you have a flinch, this chapter will do you wonders. But first, not all shooters have a flinch. Wrong! Everyone flinches! To say you don't is not recognizing you have a problem. It is preferable to recognize and correct a difficulty than outright renounce it. When the gun fires, a jolting recoil is sent into your shoulder, face, and brain. Your mind compensates with 'anticipation' of the forthcoming jolt by signaling the brain to twitch or tighten a muscle, somewhere on your body, usually close by where the gun is clobbering. Flinching is a prevalent reaction to stress. Some flinch less than others, yet everyone has one. Don't be flustered if someone says you are flinching. It is only one more hurdle in the game to manage. Who said trapshooting was easy?

You may rarely recognize a flinch when it occurs, except for vast flinches tripping a violent chain reaction in your nervous system causing a ferocious muscular reaction. I had a dilemma of randomly pulling the trigger when the proper bird to bead relationship did not exist. To control this flinch I keep my finger out of the trigger cage and slowly bring the trigger finger onto the trigger once I see the target. Some call this 'slap shooting,' but it worked for me, and others too. In fact, those who shoot release triggers are doing the same thing, instantaneously slapping the trigger outward, but with aggrandized costly remedy... a 12 pound set and 8 pound release pressure snaps your finger away from the trigger so there's no time for flinching. Compare this to a standard pull trigger set at a sensitive tension of 4 to 5 pounds or less. The same is true with faster shooting. See Fig. 4-3. Keep this important tip in mind ... with your finger off the trigger it helps you get deeper into the target (lead) for clean center hits, reducing short-shooting behind the target. There may be some controversy here. Should you slap shoot or slap with a release trigger? Slap shooting is inexpensive, no doubt about it. Traditional trigger control will be lost when slap shooting, still, with practice it can be deadly accurate, right on the money. The same is true with a release trigger, the learning curve is strenuous.

Remember, we are not shooting rifles and pistols, we are shooting shotguns spitting hundreds of pellets. If you pull the trigger as late as 1/4 second with a shotgun, you can still hit the target as long a proper lead and sight picture is maintained. Unlike a bullet, the shotstring is approximately nine feet long, 2 1/2 feet wide and very forgiving. It is more suitable to slapshoot or use a release trigger than quit the sport due to a uncontrollable flinch. Enough said. For shooters who ride the trigger, trigger tension is more important, and frequent trigger tune-ups are often neglected as trigger components wear. A crisp 4 to 5 pound trigger with minimum creep and fast lock time (hammer release and fall time) is desired. If you find yourself shooting behind targets, it's time for a trigger tune-up or: *"Don't fire until you see the whites of their eyes."* For custom triggers contact: Allem's Gun Craft 7937 Sigmond Rd., Zionville, PA 18092 (215)-679-9016. Allen Timney Gunsmith, 13524 Edgefield St., Cerritos, CA 90701 (310)-865-0181.

If you flinch, it must be dealt with. You can't ignore it, as it will not go away by itself. Most shooters don't even know why they flinch or how it suddenly comes upon them, takes control away, and forces them to do something they had no intention of doing. That's the misery of the flinch. However, there are cures. If flinching is causing you to pull the trigger at the wrong time or causing your arm to jerk the gun off target, or face is lifting away from the comb, I have good news for you... you are not alone and it is not incurable. Fig. 4-4 Flinch is Under Control chart is a quick reference to use if a flinch develops. For most shooters it will sooner or later.

First, I'll tell you how I managed to control flinching. Keeping my finger totally out of the trigger guard pointing my finger alongside the breech in the direction of the target I accomplish two things. 1) The flinch is gone. 2) I have my finger pointed down the side of the barrel which naturally points to the target. It took a bit of time to adjust to the method, but those uncontrolled flinches have gone with the wind. Before you begin changing techniques and spend money on gizmos, ensure the gun fits you properly. So basic, though significant. Visit a stockfitter. A poorly fitted gun will always rise up slamming into your cheek when it fires, causing a flinch. When you place your cheek on a comb and it kicks into your face you will always have a propensity to lift your face away when you shoot. It becomes an unconscious act; after a time you don't even know it's happening. Your cheek must be locked down snugly onto the comb at all times. If your head lifts, (cheek pressure on comb is reduced) just a tiny bit, you will miss targets, for your eye is the rear sight of the gun! If you find yourself missing targets, it's a good idea to remind yourself to keep your cheek down onto the comb. Proper cheek pressure does not mean pressing the cheek to the bone. You need some space for muscle to absorb shock. Firm pressure, not too much, not too little. Try firm yet thin high density padding on comb as a last resort for comfort. Multiple layers of soft thick padding will get you into trouble. In short time it'll compress and gradually ruin the setup. If you can't shoot without discomfort in face or shoulder, then it's time to stop bantering and take additional measures, predominately making sure the gun fits you.

Keep in mind shotgun shooting is not like rifle or pistol shooting. You don't squeeze-off the trigger! The rules are not interchangeable. Trap isn't silhouette shooting. The target is catapulting rapidly, your body / arm is in movement, shooting is instinctive, and shotstrings are wide and long. Slowly squeezing the trigger will cause anticipation of recoil developing a flinch. For severe flinchers, if you move to the target quick, get the sight picture, yank the trigger punctually you could flinch after you pulled the trigger. That's okay to flinch after the gun has fired, the shot charge has already left the barrel. Faster shooting cures many flinches. You want things to happen so expeditious you don't have time to flinch, or at the very least, beat the flinch at it's own game. To reduce recoil induced flinching is to deal with one prime root of the problem causing flinching... recoil. Though the laws of physics dictate recoil cannot be totally eliminated, its sharp jolt can be spread along a pressure curve over time. Buy a soft comb recoil absorbing device, allowing the butt to compress inward as the gun recoils. Your gun will mimic a Howitzer cannon as the gun moves rearward into a compression device. This is the premium recoil reduction recommendation I can give you, as they work profoundly well. You can shoot 3 dram handicap loads all day long and not feel any soreness to your face or shoulder, period. Some shooters may merely need padding or a soft comb on their gun to tenderize recoil. Shooting light 1 oz shot loads dramatically reduces recoil, but remember to maintain standard velocity ratings of factory ammunition if reloading so it won't throw your timing off. You'll shoot fine until you earn a prolonged shootoff and run out of shells, then you will miss targets when you have to buy 1 1/8 oz factory ammo; 1 oz loads have less pellets and smaller patterns too. Learn autosuggestion, telling yourself you do enjoy the recoil, backlash, and noise, flinching will dissolve, as long as the gun fits you! Fear of flinching compounds flinching.

Barrel porting acts as a muzzle brake, reducing felt recoil and muzzle jump, suppressing the comb striking your face. Gun barrel work has risks. There is no guarantee the work will increase performance and may even make an adequate gun inferior. Ported chokes and barrels are permitted in American trap, not in European bunker trap tournaments. Stroboscopic photography reveals barrel porting slightly reduces muzzle jump. When shooting 3-dram loads the effects are more pronounced and will reduce recoil to the face, which can cause flinching. It's more practical to buy a new gun with the ports than to pay later to see if it will work. A ported barrel will not guarantee you'll hit more targets, so some shooters feel porting is just a gimmick. Extended ported chokes will assist barrel porting, reducing felt recoil. Lifting your head off the comb, ever so slightly, will cause the gun to rise up and wallop your cheek. It's hard to convince someone who is recoil shy to press the cheek tighter against the comb, when it's the comb causing the jolt. Yet the reality is, the cheek must be in full contact with the comb or it will bite you. Observe others when they shoot and witness a multitude of shooters who have this basic problem and don't realize it. They play goose, lifting their heads and consequently missing targets. Maybe more of us should scream at them, *"Keep your head down!"* A good practice procedure is to place self-adhesive Velcro® on your cheek and the gun's comb. You'll know instantly if you are lifting your head or not. Even experienced shooters adamantly deny ever lifting their heads when they miss a target, but they do.

Often a simple trigger tune-up, wearing a glove on trigger hand, applying a bandage to reduce trigger finger sensitivity, or changing trigger shoes -- reducing recoil via shells or mechanical devices and padding can help control a flinch. For some shooters who have a severe flinch that unconditionally won't cease, a release trigger is the last recourse. They are a royal pain you-know-where and your wallet will scream for mercy. Release triggers are unreliable and can be hazardous, especially when first switching over. Try everything else first to manage flinching before you go to a release trigger. If all else fails, then buy one. If this doesn't work? Try specific earnest internalized thinking, even visit a hypnotist to force your subconscious mind to cease flinching. Seeing a hypnotist may be more appropriate than buying a release trigger. Shooting lighter dram loads won't guarantee a cure for flinching, as sensitivity will readjust and you'll be flinching again. But wait, before resorting to a release trigger, go one step further, as a release trigger does not warrant you will never flinch again...it's a remedy not a cure. Check your internal time clock. Let's explore the deeper level of what causes flinching.

TIMELY FLINCHING
"Time is intangible yet most confining."

Did you know flinching is caused by timing? It is the deep inner cause of flinching. A flinch is related to timing, as your brain reacts in anticipation of the recoil about to strike your face. So it is true with trigger timing. The quicker you identify the target, the faster you can shoot targets, and here is where the mature flinch begins and ends with experienced shooters. Everyone has a built-in time clock telling them when to break the target. When you disobey this internal clock, you can expect a flinch and at the very least many a missed target. Believe it or not, quite a few shooters have not discovered this internal clock even exists and prefer to break the target when they 'see' the target rise to its peak or ark of flight, or some other habitual location. At this point, their 'mind' has probably told them to pull the trigger two or more times, yet they refuse to shoot until the target 'looks right' and is in its proper position. Worse, they don't even know their subconscious mind told them to pull the trigger... they are not in tune with their internal time clock.

First, we have to recognize the time clock. There are two of them, internal and external. The internal time clock is a preset time that exists, yet waits to be discovered. You can't see or feel it until you do some testing. The external time clock is the most deceptive and devious of the two... it is your eyes! Shooters who let their eyes tell them when to shoot will always miss more targets than they deserve. Bear with me, as this is difficult material to communicate. To simplify matters, look at the shooter who waits for the target to reach its peak or beyond midpoint of travel, then shoots. He has numerous disadvantages working against him and will always be inconsistent. 1) Wind will easily drive the target off course. 2) Target angle increases dramatically to the square of its distance causing a rapidly widening target angle. He'll likely miss targets by shooting behind them. Sound familiar? 3) Shot pattern opens speedily in a cone-shaped form expanding radially. See Fig. 4-1. The shot folds back upon itself plowing into each other; flyers develop as pellets crash together and shot velocity dramatically decreases with distance. The ballistics of the shotstring are radical in nature and progressively worsen to the square of distance. Not a good place to be breaking targets. 4) Eye concentration deteriorates swiftly the longer you stare at a target. Vision sensory overload and fatigue (often unnoticed) sets in. Also, background objects come into view and induce the eye to focus and re-focus as target passes by these visual intrusions. What does this have to do with a flinch? A lot. The shooter's internal time clock is being violated.

Now look at a shooter who shoots quick. He's likely a superior shooter, hitting more targets, getting the job done swiftly. The four items as mentioned above are eliminated or greatly diminished. He doesn't shoot only with his eyes, fact is, his eyes identify the target, swing the gun to the target, fine tune the sight picture, but the internal time clock tells him it's time to pull the trigger. He's shooting so fast he has no time to flinch! There is no reason to flinch, since he is shooting within a zone, the natural time zone his mind has set to shoot. There is no anticipation or second guessing or delay. The target is shot quickly. These are subconscious subjects here and are not readily recognizable until some testing is done. The shooter who shoots long, waiting for the target to peak, cannot be convinced he is shooting out of phase with his internal time clock. Why? Because he has not discovered a time clock exists yet. He believes his natural time clock is where he is shooting. Not so. The brain is much faster than the eye can behold. The shooter who shoots a bit quicker rather than waiting for the target to peak is making contact with his internal time clock, but is not yet in synchronization with it. His mind probably already told him to shoot earlier. He's a finer shooter than the long shooter, though not as good as the pros. Fig 3-1 indicates where you should shoot the target for maximal effectiveness.

You have heard it time and again, trapshooting is 10% ability, 90% mental. It is. When you get into sync with your true inner time clock, your scores will rise dramatically. It becomes instinctive shooting where the subconscious mind take over. And this is where you want to be! You want things to happen so rapidly, you don't have time to think of anything but seeing the target. Remember, the moment you think, the eyes shift away from the target or lose focus! With the mind, a microsecond can be an eternity, a quarter second, forever! So for obvious reasons as mentioned earlier, shooting quick has advantages. It locks you into a lightening fast mind-set that gives the ability to shoot the target faster and more accurately than you could with thought processes alone. And it dissolves flinching! The testing process is grueling hardship, so be disposed to very discouraging scores and many, many, wildly missed targets. Be forewarned, you may be taunted by other shooters as your scores drop. They may tell you to not do it. Pay no heed, do of your own accord. If it makes sense, do it. You have heard it said, *"You'd be shooting fast, too, if you shot as much as he did."* That is a fabrication. Shooting rapidly does not arrive based on how much you shoot. There are many veteran shooters out there who have never learned to shoot fast or instinctively. To shoot quick, you have to <u>practice</u> shooting fast. In the process you will come into contact with your internal time clock, and lo and behold discover you can shoot faster, more accurately, and realize you were shooting out of phase with your mind all along.

INTERNAL TIME CLOCK TEST
"I do not like work even when someone else does it."   <small>Mark Twain</small>

The goal is twofold. You will recognize when your mind informs you to shoot and learn the zone where you should be shooting. This form of fast shooting is called 'zone shooting'. You shoot when you see the target in a specific zone (a point of distance away from the traphouse). Zone is the visual aspect, but the mental aspect is based on time, not a zone. You can break targets beyond the zone as long as your eye focus and target recognition has not delayed excessively after the target emerges, as distance is a trapshooter's worst enemy. The time clock begins the moment you see the target emerge from the house. I can't tell you when to shoot. I can't tell you how many tenths of a second your zone is. I can tell you my zone, at this time, is from 1 to 1 1/4 seconds. Most shooters will find theirs to be less than two seconds or perhaps one second or less. It's breakneck shooting! Let's try a few paces:

1. The moment the target emerges from the traphouse, shoot. Shoot as rapidly as you ever shot in your life. Try to break the target within one foot of the traphouse and you'll get a picture of how fast I'm asking you to shoot in this <u>test</u>. You won't break the target one foot from the traphouse, but you may break it within 15 feet or so. The point is not to break the target at this phase, but to accelerate your nervous system and reflexes. Shoot five shots and amaze yourself how awkward and uncomfortable it feels. Don't worry, you'll miss many targets.
2. Now slow back down to your usual shooting for a couple rounds, then speed up, but this time not as brisk as in step #1 above. About half-speed is okay. You'll be close to your new shooting and timing zone here, though you may not yet realize it. Keep your eye tuned and focused to see the target pass by the barrel so you can recognize the angle of the target leaving the traphouse. This is very important.
3. Keep repeating steps 1 and 2 above. Don't worry if you missed the target, or the target appears to be traveling too quickly for your ability. Concentrate on when you pulled the trigger. Recognize when your mind is telling you

to pull the trigger. Shoot fast so your eyes can't mislead you when to fire. You are looking for an instinctive impression or impulse, something in your mind making you pull the trigger when you do.

Attempt to establish communication with your inner time clock. It's there! You need to experiment to find it. You may not find it in your first few attempts. It can take hundreds of rounds to positively fine-tune it, though you should have roughly recognized it after a dozen tests are made. It will feel like, *"That's where I want to shoot, but it's too hard to do it."* Now you have found the inner time clock! You are now 'snap shooting'. Slow down a wee bit and you'll be in the sweet spot. You don't want to shoot at maximum speed, as exhaustion develops rapidly. By practicing snapshooting, it accelerates your nervous system so when you do slow down to normal speed, it decreases lazy eye syndrome. Now what? Good question. Should I practice this from now on? Or should I slowly attempt to increase my shooting speed? Take your pick. I'd recommend unhurried exertion to evade utter confusion, information overload and disappointment. This is the hardest, most demoralizing ego-deflating phase of trapshooting you will conceivably ever encounter... learning to shoot fast. It's like relearning the whole shebang over again. It takes time and exertion to master. At first, diminishing the target's streak zone- - or comet tail -- is overbearing until you train your eye to acquire and track the target instantly. Target acquisition is the key! It takes eye training. Looking at streaking targets is good eye training, so pull targets for other shooters so you can centralize your vision skills. After much exercise, the comet tails disappear and you will see a <u>clean</u> target emerge from the traphouse. Practice makes perfect here.

You may flinch when practicing shooting fast. This is not a flinch to be concerned with as it's not the same kind of flinch that is deeply imbedded in the mind. It is a self-induced flinch due to jarred nerves and a tired mind. It is not permanent, so don't worry about it. It goes away, never to return again, after you smooth out the wrinkles in the technique. Be easy on yourself at this phase of learning, it is terribly hard to do and you may feel you just don't have what it takes. You <u>can</u> do it. It's not a talent but an exercise... so genius ability is not required. For most, it is so difficult you'll likely curse the day you first picked up a shotgun to play trap! Be prepared for disappointment here, yet it makes sense... so make it happen! Watch shooters who shoot quick. It's no substitute for practice, but it can give you an idea of timing and zones. Notice how consistent they are! Even if the target leaves the zone, they still annihilate it. You'll be able to do this because the clock doesn't tick until the eye has seen the target properly. These are very subtle psychological influences that play immense roles in trapshooting. Ignore them at your own peril. If you don't discover your internal time clock and shoot in synchronization with it, you can expect losing competitions and flinching your way to bad scores. Remember, the longer you wait to shoot the harder it is to hit the target. Learn to be comfortable shooting quickly, it takes much practice, but is truly rewarding.

Once you have learned where your zone of shooting is, based on your internal time clock, you still must learn how to break targets when they leave the zone at further distances from the trap. Reason is some targets will slip by and you don't want to pull the trigger and miss just because of instinct. Know the zone; still, expect some targets will ever so often get the jump on you. Targets do this on account of not paying attention to seeing the bird leave the house, fatigue, eyes not focused properly, looking in the wrong spot, overly anticipating target angles, improperly holding the gun over the traphouse in a area which creates a blind spot, or receiving a fast or slow pull. To help cure this problem, hold the gun lower or right down on the far edge of the traphouse, because seeing the target and judging its angle is vitally important. See Fig. 4-2 - (A) and (B). Many shooters hold the gun too high over the traphouse so there is less gun movement to the target, but this can be a puzzle, as blind spots do occur even if you shoot with two eyes. Lower the gun a wee bit and note if it works for you. Keep lowering it until you find the right spot for you. Keep in mind you'll have to break old habits and that again requires an often painful learning curve. Notice in Fig. 4-2 - (B) the eye is always above the barrel of the gun in the zone where the most severe "angle" target will emerge. Never sight down the plane of the rib, move your eyes up to clearly see the target exit. Now practice shooting targets at different distances from the traphouse. Shoot in your natural inner time zone, but discipline yourself by purposely letting the target escape, chase and turn it into powder. Don't fall into a groove, be flexible, know how to break targets at any reasonable distance. First break the target in your zone, then just before the target peaks, then right when the target peaks. On angle targets you won't see a peak, so use varying distances. You are now learning discipline and trigger control to shape you into a finely tuned shooter.

FLINCHING AND RECOIL REDUCTION
"People flinch when you tell them they are."

Recoil is the act of the central nervous system springing back on the backward action of firing the gun. It often develops after a few thousand targets have been crunched. Then one day, you freeze and can't pull the trigger or you pull the trigger knowing you shouldn't have, or arm muscle spasm causes the gun to jerk violently. It's a shocking experience. A recoil flinch is a physical motion or an emotional withdrawal or retreat, shying away, as to evade something unpleasant or threatening. If you call for the target and you're not ready, split-second decision making and fear of missing develops a flinch. The root cause is a momentary psychological loss of courage. Flinch denotes a shrinking away from what is unpleasant or difficult, described as a faint-hearted retreat from a necessary undertaking. A quality padded shooting vest helps control flinching, and a vest obviously has superior gun mounting consistency -- qualities not to be ignored. If you are not shooting with a vest, you are at a major disadvantage and you can expect to miss innumerable targets. A vest 'locks the gun' into your shoulder, you can instantly identify if the gun is mismounted, the shoulder padding extends and retains length of pull, reduces recoil shock, flinching, enhances gun mount consistency, adds smooth freedom of movement. Professional shooters wear shooting vests not for appearance reasons, but for productive efficiency. Browning® makes excellent vests at a reasonable cost, (800) 333-3288. Here's a few more: Bob Allen Sportswear®, Box 477, Des Moines, IA 50302 (515)-283-2191. 10x Products®, 2915 LBJ Freeway, Suite 133, Dallas, TX 75234 (214)-243-4016. Flyer Sportswear, 224 3rd Ave., South, Nampa ID 83651 (208)-467-9201. Gamebore, Great Union Street, Hull, HU9 - 1AR, England. If you routinely shoot without a vest you'll perpetually agree to missed targets.

There are steps to reduce flinches due to recoil. Use lighter loads such as 1 1/8 shot, 2 3/4 dram. Buy a shooting vest with thick recoil absorption pads. Browning makes fine vests with a gel pad inserted on the inside. It's called the Reactor® and it'll take the hammer out of the jolt. You can buy this pad separately and sew it into your existing vest. A shooting vest subtly enhances positive self-image, self-esteem and builds confidence. It keeps you organized, comfortable and has spare shell pockets. Increased comfort with less disorder = better performance. Kick-Eeez® recoil pads attach to gun's butt-plate and are well respected recoil absorbers; P. O. Box 12767, Wichita, KS, 67277 (316) 721-9570. This pad has a low rebound factor and prevents the comb from rising into the cheek.

You can try a slow burning single-base powder, though be aware you may not feel a difference in recoil as increased powder charge is required to maintain a set velocity over a faster burning double-base powder. Reducing muzzle velocity by decreasing the weight of the shot charge is much more effective, so the invention of the 1oz. shot shell is upon us. The penalty is having approximately 64 pellets less in a 1oz. 7 1/2 shot load than a 1 1/8 oz load. On a near-missed target, it could mean the difference of winning or losing an event. The finest antidote is invest in a recoil reduction device allowing the butt-plate to recede into the stock. You can shoot 3 dram loads all day long and the flinch may finally be whipped into submission. Here's another tip. Internally tapered ammunition hulls use less powder yet generate high chamber pressures that can generate increased recoil. A straight wall hull uses a tad more powder to maintain velocity; however, I feel Federal Gold Medal hull with the Federal 12S3 wad has effective piston rings controlling gas leakage to prevent blown patterns and strong over-powder cushioning to diminish felt recoil. A tight choke builds higher chamber pressures to increase recoil. You may want to try a less constricted choke. Verify the gun's butt is mounted snugly to your shoulder, as weak contact with the toe or heel will engender the gun to kick like a mule. These are all things to experiment with to isolate what works best for you. Ultimately, recoil devices are a meritorious investment that work. Keep in mind recoil builds up over the years as sensitivity increases. If recoil is a problem you may want to consider a semi-auto as they are inherent recoil reduction machines. Getting beat up by recoil will surely bruise your scores.

Many shooters do not realize a high rib gun can reduce flinching. The high rib lowers the barrel bore line, diminishing recoil to the cheek. You don't need to have your head crouched down deeply to contact the comb with a high rib gun. Furthermore, most high rib guns have raised combs to further lower the barrel bore line, and the combs are often padded. The benefit is lower recoil and your field of view is less slanted. It's not good to be shooting targets when your field of view is slanted and recoil is slamming the comb up into your face. Recoil should travel straight back to the shoulder. Try a high rib gun and determine for yourself if it's your cup of tea. Of course, shooting a high rib gun is different than a low rib gun. It takes much practice to learn how to shoot one. They do have advantages, especially if you can change the point of impact. It helps you find exactly which point of impact you really need. When you speed up your shooting, you don't have to put as much lead on the target because the POI may already be set 100 % high, 3 to 12 inches above point of aim. When you shoot, the shotstring rises automatically to compensate for lead, especially for quarter angle targets and those appearing to be straight-aways. This is assuming you are shooting quickly at a rapidly rising target. Some guns are now coming with pistol grips. This too can be very helpful to a shooter suffering from recoil flinch. The hand absorbs and dampens recoil. A pistol grip makes good sense as it provides improved control over the gun than with a conventional stock. A palm swell reduces recoil through a firmer leveraged grip. When it comes to flinching, try everything you can to get rid of it, and never say never or quit. It must and can be conquered. I know a lot of shooters who flinch, yet do nothing to deal with the problem. Don't be one of them.

A gun with a 30" barrel will recoil less than a gun with 34" barrel. It is true a heavier gun will absorb recoil; further, there is another factor not always understood. The longer the barrel, velocity of the shot increases and this creates more reactive forces, intensifying recoil, especially with unported tight constriction chokes. A 30" doubles gun used for trap can be as heavy or heavier than a 34" single barrel gun. More weight = less recoil and flinching. Stock and comb shape can increase recoil if improperly fitted. The geometry of O&U guns reduce recoil. Back-boring reduces felt recoil and improves patterns, but not all guns can be safely bored. As you can fathom, there are no set solutions except installing a compressible stock recoil reduction device. Using low mass, low speed ammunition alters your timing, sight picture and point of impact resulting in relearning how to shoot the load. Not a good idea, when you consider how much time and money it already cost you to learn how to shoot at the proficiency level you have already obtained. A gun too heavy induces arm and back muscle fatigue and, soon to follow, mental listlessness. For help in reducing recoil and stock fitting, contact these companies:

G Squared, 5059 San Aquario Drive, San Diego, CA 92109 (619)274-2261.
Danuser Machine Co., 550 E. Third St., Fulton, MO 65251 (314)-642-2246.
Don's Carey Comb, 11430 Payette Heights Rd, Payette, ID 83667 (208)-642-1884.
Oregon Gun Works, 1015 Molalla Ave., Oregon City, OR 97045 (800)-398-5839.

If your cheek is getting slapped, it's a sure sign of an improperly fitted gun, defective shooting style or setup. If the stock's cast, height, shape or pitch is improper expect a beating. If your shoulder is getting slammed, it's often the stock length causing a problem or the toe of the butt (toe-in or toe-out & pitch) digging into your shoulder, which not only causes discomfort, but produces an unstable inaccuracy when swinging the gun. Pain and face slap create serious flinching and must be corrected. Gun fit is critical to reduce recoil effects, for even an improperly configured pistol grip or palm swell can prevent your hand from absorbing recoil and the comb rises to strike your face. Too much pitch will cause the comb to leap into your face.

EYE-DIVERSION FLINCH

In anticipation of the recoil, the shooter pulls the trigger and unconsciously closes his eyes or looks away from the target. It is said the cure is practice more, shoot more, but practice often only goes so far. The shooter should treat the cause of the flinch, not the symptoms. Again, it's a bad habit developed from shooting a gun that does not properly fit when first learning to shoot and has carried over through the years. I emphasize in Chapter 1 the importance of selecting the proper trap shotgun for this reason. The singular practical way to correct this score busting impulsion is to modify the gun so little recoil is generated. It's time to buy a recoil reducer that allows the gun to compress rearward. It's the most functional device to stop flinches, as the gun travels in a linear horizontal line, strikes the shoulder and compresses. Without this device, the gun travels back, deadens against the shoulder and the recoil energy lifts the gun upward, striking the shooter's cheek. This is a major disruption to the eyes, slamming them out of focus, ruining the setup for the next shot. Remember, it requires time to re-focus the eyes once they are jarred out of focus. Less recoil = better vision.

Another alteration to reduce recoil is barrel porting. It serves other purposes, primarily two things in trapshooting; 1) It vents combustion gasses upward and rearward to reduce recoil and muzzle jump. If the muzzle jumps backwards and upward, it may strike your shoulder and face. Rear facing ports reduce recoil and muzzle jump, increasing by canceling reactive forces. Adding extended ported chokes increases the effectiveness of porting, performing the same function as barrel porting but to a lesser degree, though combined, decreases felt recoil and muzzle rise considerably. 2) A side benefit of using ported barrels and chokes is purely physics relative to ballistics. High gas pressures dramatically accelerate when introduced to low atmospheric pressure. A barrel with no ports expels concentrated high pressure high velocity gasses through the muzzle with truly untamed violence. The high pressure wave-front clobbers the wad with a punishing hammer blow on exit, which deforms pellets to create flyers and bounces shot right out of the wad before it has a chance to find equilibrium. Choke porting vents these violent gasses, reducing the pressure shock wave to help alleviate pellet deformation and wad slamming. Keep in mind when having a barrel ported, oval ports have the edge over circular, as the latter have been found to eventually suffer migrating stress cracking. Laser or electrical discharge machining is advisable when porting as the process removes metal molecule by molecule without overheating the metal preventing stress-induced cracking. For barrel porting contact:
Ballistic Specialties, 100 Industrial Dr., Batesville, AR 72501 (800)-276-2550.
Kolar, 1925 Roosevelt Ave., Racine WI 53406 (800)-625-6527.
Lazer-Ports, 14145 Proctor Ave., Suite 3, City of Industry, CA 91746 (800)-833-2737.
Pro-Port Ltd., 41302 Executive Dr., Harrison Twp., MI 48045 (800)-469-7323.
Seminole Gunworks, 3049 US1, Mims, FL 32754 (407)-383-8556.
Shotgun Shop, 14145 Proctor #3, City of Industry, CA 91746 (800)-833-2737.
Stan Baker Barrels, 10,000 Lake City Way, Seattle, WA 98125 (206)-522-4575.
Tom Wilkinson, 5690 Bob Daniel Rd., Oxford, NC 27565 (919)-603-0167.
Top Line Porting, 12745 Ottawa Ave. So., Savage, MN 55378 (612)-895-0037.

The companies listed above do more than barrel porting. Shotgun Shop does everything you can desire to a shotgun: forcing cones, custom stocks, you name it. Other fine firms not compiled here are listed in shotgun sports magazines. To learn about barrel alterations from forcing cones to chokes read the, 'Shotgun Barrel Alteration Manual' from Tom Roster, 1190 Lynnewood Blvd., Klamath Falls, OR 97601 (541)-884-2974.

If you suffer from eye closing or looking away when the gun fires, use every recoil reduction means available to you, as you have likely become sensitized to recoil flinching. It's going to be an arduous habit to break without gun alterations. A good place to start is being aware you have a problem. Try forcing yourself to keep your eyes wide open when firing. If after prolonged practice it fails or sneaks its way back in occasionally, then modify the gun. If installing a recoil reducer is not feasible at this time, you may be better off shooting a lighter 1oz. 2 3/4 dram load, then later graduate back to heavier 1 1/8 oz. 3 dram loads once the difficulty is overcome. When switching to 1oz. loads remember not to reduce the shot velocity as it will throw off your timing. Installing a padded comb would be beneficial and inexpensive than barrel modification, such as backboring and lengthening forcing cones which are questionable related to cost versus substantial results. Be forewarned of excessive backboring. You may get less recoil but at a heavy price. If the bore is too large, you will get blown patterns as combustion gasses blow by the wad and mix with the pellets. Don't exceed .745 back-bore dimensions. Federal 12S3 wads employ piston rings to assist gas sealing, reducing blow-by and wad instability. Spending $1,000 on barrel modifications? Forget it. The Howitzer effect recoil reducer is a valuable investment. A gas autoloader would be viable option, still the reliability and cleaning chores should be equally considered. There is a peril to becoming accustomed to shooting 1oz. loads, even if they are factory loads. One day you will find yourself back at the handicap 24 to 27 yard line and you'll need every ounce of power and pellet working for you. You can get away with it at the 16 to 23 yard line, but targets will be lost due to the shell's inherent disadvantages at the aforementioned distances. Even with 3 dram 1 1/8 oz. shotshells, targets are missed at these distances. Why make the game harder than it already is? If you shoot 1oz. loads -- or any load for that matter at handicap yardage -- you had better learn to shoot very quickly as patterns expand dramatically to the square of distance. Until we are forced to shoot 1oz. loads, stay with 1 1/8 oz. in tournament shoots. When numbers are concerned, the hard facts of mathematics rule. Less pellets = reduced odds of breaking the target. The same is true with shot size. Less mass = reduced energy and distance traveled. Heavy shot + high power = increased odds of success.

Deal with the recoil instead of disabling yourself by using light loads. Why? Because in time you may redevelop the flinch with the lighter load, as long as the impediment still exists. Your mind may again become sensitized to the lower level of recoil impact. You could be right back where you started, flinching again. Once a behavior is learned it is hard to overcome. Flinches originate in the subconscious mind, not the conscience mind. You can tell yourself to stop flinching and flinching will stubbornly persist. Flinching cannot be unlearned, it must be corrected by solving the root cause and this is recoil, poor gun fit, surprised anticipation of the target, and shooting out of synchronization with your inner time clock. All must be dealt with to depreciate flinching. Even fear and nervousness stimulates flinches. As you can see, flinching is a complex condition and through experimentation trial and error you can learn to manage and conquer it, as long as you keep trying. One flinch is one too many. I've seen many shooters flinch, know they did, yet do nothing to deal with the problem. They simply shrug their shoulders and accept it or refuse to admit they flinch at all, as if it were an immense embarrassment to be ashamed of. The first step in solving a problem is to admit you have a problem. Denial is not a river that flows in Egypt. Talk to shooters who have had a flinch difficulty, especially the professionals, they have been there innumerable times before. Nothing new here under the sun.

SHADOW DANCING WITH THE GUN
"Pray for a miracle and you'll see one."

No great detail here, but most shooters would do themselves a world of good and improve significantly if they took a few minutes a day (or at least each week) to practice their setup and swing in front of a mirror. And practice these moves with eyes closed, visualizing breaking imaginary targets. This helps to embed "feel" into all the moves and sets up the mind to break targets. How does this work? The anxiety of hitting targets as you would on a practice trap is gone, and you are focusing all energy inwards on your moves. I can't stress enough that the setup is more important than actually pulling the trigger at a target. If the setup is sloppy so will the scores be. Get in touch with every phase of your setup and "feel" every move. With your eyes closed you will certainly feel those moves and develop fine points of repeating these moves, building muscle memory. Practice calling for the target too, tracking the target along a curve and dismounting the gun *after* the target breaks. Feel the gun in your hands with authority. Attack the target, don't chase it, just do it with smooth precision. Now if you can do this with your eyes closed, imagine what you could do with your eyes open!

CHAPTER 5

CONFIDENCE AND SKILL
"Knowledge derived from reason can't begin to compare with knowledge perceived by sense."

In this chapter we will begin to develop confidence and skill. This also is a learned event. For some it comes from pure life-long experience, for others it never arrives. So let's begin the process.

VISUALIZATION AND CONCENTRATION
"How many miles can one see with his eyes closed?"

Deep and sustained concentration is the magic to good trapshooting. Thinking is not concentration, only a segment of concentration. Thinking is setting a plan, knowing your surroundings, trap settings, weather and target environments. Visualization is concentration, an engaged focus mentally rehearsing a shot before it happens. Mix thinking, visualization and concentration and you have fragmentation. Visualization will flush the mind of needless thoughts. Try closing your eyes and visualize shooting the targets and you'll see what I mean, now do it with your eyes open. Try this before you call for a target when you practice. It's really simple but rarely easy. The big mistake is to 'try harder' to increase scores by forcing yourself to think hard, shoot faster, randomly experimenting or thinking too much to correct errors. Less thinking + visualization + concentration = broken targets. Remember the last time you ran 25 or 50 straight and it seemed so easy? You likely cannot recall the mental process. It seemed like a dream-state of mind. You weren't trying harder. You let go of your thought process and immersed yourself into yourself where your mind and body were one and the same. There was no doubt, fear, anxiety or thinking, but full confidence in tune with trust in your technique. Through visualization exercises you can once again recall and retain that smooth mode. This is the real secret professionals use to break targets, deep concentration. We all have it, we just need to practice letting it surface. Imagination is more important than knowledge. Close your eyes and imagine falling down a dark bottomless pit, watching the hole in the sky above getting smaller and smaller. That is the target! That is visualization, sustained concentration, and intense focus. Now imagine a clay target distancing itself from you in the same way, but this time, you have an imaginary gun mounted and shoot it. Try the angle targets, try each station. At practice, before mounting the gun, stop for a second and visualize breaking the three basic angled targets, and where you want to break them, then mount and call. This will help your scores leap forward after some dedicated practice.

Sometimes the game can beat us up. This is where maintaining focus and motivation with positive attitude pays off in the long and short term. You can be positive or negative on the trap line, but never both, so take your choice. A series of lost targets will test your attitude quickly. Learn to switch to a positive outlook even when all appears dismal. It may not pay dividends today, but it surely will help you on the next event or the next shoot. Positive attitude is the driving force you'll need to succeed. Any negative comment you tell yourself will supplant positivity, *"Why did you miss that you dummy?"* or *"What the heck happened?"* These self-reflecting comments actually forced you to choose to focus on the negative. Even if targets slip by unscathed, never give in to defeat; instead, use this poor day's shooting as a practice exercise to learn to turn the losses into mini-victories by hitting more targets. Okay, you had a bad day, but make the most of it, turn it to your advantage, as nothing can be gained by being negative. When you learn how to maintain a positive demeanor and remain well focused, scores rise. Never dwell on any missed target as you will certainly miss more targets if you do. Disconnect mood and attitude from scores. Focus your energy on the next target. Stay positive!

VIBRATING NERVES
"The way to overcome adversity is to try harder."

To perform well, you should relax and visualize yourself executing a perfect shot. It is a secret pros do instinctively, even when they are nervous... and yes, they do get the willies in important shootoffs, and they do miss targets! Nervousness is natural and with time, often a few seasons, nerves dissipate to acceptable levels where performance still excels. Nervousness can develop during practice sessions and more so to frightening proportions in competition. Ultimately, self-possession supplants nervousness. *"I can do it!"* is perhaps the greatest self-assurance phrase to dissipate nervousness. All trapshooters at one time or another experience symptoms of negative mood states including disappointment, anger, irritability, anxiety or headaches. Relaxation is the process of turning-off the response to demand. This is best accomplished by 15 to 20 minutes of relaxation exercise. Find a quiet place, sit or lie down, close your eyes. Try slowing down your breathing as this increases carbon dioxide (CO_2) circulation and generally decelerates the nervous system. For some people it doesn't work, so slow deep breathing is an alternative. Concentrate on each out-flowing breath as you fall deeper into a restful state of relaxation. Don't hyperventilate. The signs of hyperventilation are any of the following: tingling in hands or lips, stiffening of the fingers, wrist pain, or tightening in the throat. You can purchase books and tapes on the subject of relaxation. It is important to recharge your batteries between events. That's what most of the pros do, and for improved concentration you should too. See "Fear of Shootoff."

Many individuals experience stage fright when attending a practice shoot for the first time at the local gun club. They will watch and when asked to shoot they hold back for fear of embarrassment. This is natural and normal.

So if you are just starting out, don't be too gun shy. Everyone you see shooting so well at one time was sitting where you are today. And the cool dudes pounding the targets won't be so cool when you see them in a shootoff!

PROCURING FORMAL TRAINING
"The quickest way to accomplish something is to proceed deliberately."

Martial Art's is a sport where each city has a school. Not so with trapshooting; the principles that follow do apply. If you wish to learn self-defense, you go to school and study. You don't need lessons from the worldwide championship Karate winner to be a solid competitor and winner. That all depends on you, the student, as to how much dedication you have. Most trapshooters are not contemplative of being national champions and would just like to increase their scores, become formidable competitors, get into the shootoffs and win a fair share of option and Calcutta money. This is not an unrealistic goal and it can be had. You can earn money in trapshooting and not even have to break a hundred targets every time out on the firing line... everyone knows this. Don't they? The objective is to break 25's consistently enough and you're in the money, and sooner or later the 100's will arrive. Often, depending on the size of the shoot, running just one 25 straight (handicap targets) can refund your costs to shoot the day's event, and you'll have four chances to do it per handicap event, each day. The odds are in your favor. Second place is only the first loser! True, but you don't need to win first place to win.

Would you pick a fight with a well-trained Karate student? Would you do so even if he / she were trained by an unknown instructor with no competitive wins under his belt? Most of us would be aching fools to tackle any Karate student even from a borderline incompetent teacher. The same principle applies with trapshooting. Seek the advice and instruction of professionals as much as you can. Don't hesitate to take lessons from someone who is not a state, regional or national Champion trapshooter. I'm not affirming to take lessons from Joe Smok'em at the local club who is a notch better than you are and is just as inconsistent, too, and still learning the game. Seek out the finest shooter with a reputation in your county or state -- someone who's darn good at the game and can annihilate most shooter's into dust. If you can't, then read a lot of books and magazines and scrutinize video tapes. You must learn the basics to build a firm foundation. *"The Little Trapshooting Book"* is a good place to start, published by Further Adventures, Inc., P. O. Box 6810 Auburn, California 95604, available from Shotgun Sports Magazine (800-676-8920).

I've heard many shooters profess, *"I've never learned anything substantial from trap books and video tapes."* I agree to a point. To perfect all the variables in one hour or two is too challenging for any film producer or print publisher. Even this book will not fill all the chasms, and I need not mislead you into thinking otherwise. But holes can be filled, and filling them will ultimately result in smoking more targets. Think of a boxer, musician, race car driver or golf, bowling or baseball professionals. Do they have coaches? You bet they do. The coach is <u>not</u> the athlete! Read that again. The coach is less physically competent than the competitor. This is the real world looking right at you. If it were not true, then coaches would be the athlete winning the titles, medals and prize money. The instructor is on the outside looking in, telling you where you are making mistakes. Just as we can't see our own personality imperfections, others on the outside can, but will never tell. Find a capable mentor to help you. Later on, you may afford the best money can buy to perfect your technique, still and all, most all of us won't progress to these extremes. A drillmaster can save you thousands of hours and rounds of ammo. It's inexpensive in the long term. See "Shooting Schools & Clinics." If there is no coach available in your area or region you can attend shooting clinics or procure one to come to your gun club. Kim Little Fritz, 5 Collingdale Ct, Gaithersburg, MD 20879 (301)-417-6925 sells Frank Little's video tapes for 16 yard to handicap, doubles, including a video specifically for one-eyed shooters. Mr. Little's advice is invaluable (a Hall of Fame trapshooter). Kay Ohye International, 600 Holly Lane, North Brunswick, NJ 08902 (732)-297-0364 sells video tapes.

SHOTGUN SPORTS MAGAZINES
It wouldn't hurt to request a free-trial issue to help you gauge which magazines to subscribe to, as all are informative and well worth the subscription cost.

Clay Shooting Magazine, Thruxton Down House, Thruxton Down, Andover, Hampshire, England SP11 8PR (phone 01264-889533) The best trapshooters in the world are in Europe. Shooting tips are given.
Modern Skeet & Clays Magazine P.O. Box 98, Cumberland, RI 02864 (401)723-8202.
On Target P.O. Box 54, Grangeville, ID 83530, (208) 983-2857 (P.I.T.A. related news, etc).
Rifle & Shotgun Sport Shooting 5300 City Plex Tower, 2448 E. 81st St., Tulsa, OK 74137 (918)-491-6100.
Shotgun Sports, Inc., P.O. Box 6810 Auburn, California 95604. (800)676-8920.
Trap & Field Magazine P.O. Box 567 Indianapolis, Indiana 46206 (A.T.A. related news, etc).
USA Shooting, One Olympic Plaza, Colorado Springs, CO 80909 (US Olympic shooting team).
Women & Guns, P.O. Box 488, Station C, Buffalo, NY 14209 (206) 454-7012.

HOW TO GET THE MOST FROM MAGAZINE ARTICLES & BOOKS
"The secret of trapshooting has always been that it remained secret"

Most shooters I know subscribe to *Shotgun Sports, Trap & Field* and *Clay Shooting* Magazines for the trapshooting focus to which these magazines is dedicated. Many subscribe to other magazines, video tapes and books, too, yet never seem to progress despite the wealth of knowledge imparted. How can this be? It's quite simple. Too many shooters rely on memory, reading the articles, view tapes, reading books, yet never applying the step-outlines into actual practice. Bring the book or magazine -- or tear the page out and bring it with you -- when you practice. Read it again. If you do this, you will see improvement. It's imperative not to rely on 'study memory' as you will surely forget what you have learned unless you physically apply the knowledge. This year, make it your goal to bring one article with you whenever you practice. A reminder card is invaluable, indicating practice goals to focus on for the day. See "Practice Tips - Phase 1, 2, 3, 4, 5, 6 and 7." New trapshooting and clay target shooting books are coming on line every year. Some are never advertised, so how do you find them? Every bookstore worth its salt has the latest version of, "*Books in Print*" printed by R. R. Bowker, Inc. This huge publication lists every book in print by subject and author, and is used in the book trade for locating publishers, authors, and books. Flip through the pages and you will find the book you need.

SHOOTING SCHOOLS & CLINICS
"Try to achieve what you know you'll never achieve."

Shotgun sports magazines are excellent sources of instruction along with the books and videotapes they render. Some All-American Hall of Fame Champion shooters provide lessons. You can expect to learn visual skill development, shooting stance, gun fit, target analysis, and above all, personal instruction. Here's a few for consideration:

- Federal Wing & Clay Shooting School, 4607 NE Cedar Creek Road, Woodland, WA 98674 (800)-888-9464. Federal Cartridge Company established this school that travels to shooting facilities around the country. All essential equipment and shells are usually provided or you can bring your own. They have clinics for beginners and professionals.
- Holland & Holland Shooting School, Ducks Hill Rd., Middlesex, England.
- Kay Ohye International, 600 Holly Lane, North Brunswick, NJ 08902 (908)-297-0364. Approximately 36 scheduled clinics, at this writing, in varias states. Limited private lessons are often available by appointment.
- Les Greevy, 1460 Washington Blvd., Williamsport, PA 17701 (717)-326-6561
- Optimum Shotgun Performance Shooting School, 15020 Cutten Road, Houston, TX 77070 (713)-897-0800 They furthermore have locations in Florida, Virginia, West Virginia and California.
- Phil Kiner Trap Clinic, 3113 White Cloud, Cheyenne, WY 92001 (307)-635-1451
- Professional Trapshooting School, Daro Handy, 527 North Casa Deloma St., Sutherlin, Oregon 97479. 503-459-3409. Private on site lessons may be available.
- Remington Shooting School (315)-895-3574. Special 2-day sessions for beginners through experienced. School opens from May through mid-October in New York, Mohawk Valley at Ilion.

- Scribani Rossi Olympic Shooting School, GPO Box 1390 Sydney, Australia NSW -1043 [Phone: +61 (0)2 9555 2728] a top notch Olympic shooter with a vacation package type school.
- Thomas Bland & Sons / Woodcock Hill, Inc., P.O. Box 363, Benton, PA 17814 (714)-864-3242
- USA Shooting, One Olympic Plaza, Colorado Springs, CO 80909

Most all of us resent taking advice. It's a natural born instinct strongly embraced. Nobody takes pleasure from being fanned in the face with, *"I told you so."* Or bludgeoned by, *"What you have to do is..."* Heaven knows how many trap clubs have so called advisers who mean well, but can't shoot themselves into a shootoff. The novice trapshooter need learn one thing and it is this; *"Keep an open mind. Listen to everyone. Try it out and if it doesn't work fling it aside."* Don't ignore advice! Invariably, advice may work for you. Be a pliable shooter predisposed to try out fresh ideas. If you are not inclined to experiment, you will never understand what works and what doesn't. There is a controversy over having a coach. Yes, it is true you don't need a tutor or formal lessons. You can get out on the trap stations and shoot to learn from trial and error. There is a lot to be said in favor of veteran shooters who say, *"You don't need lessons, develop you're own technique and perfect it."* I've had top-gun money shooters tell me the same. One thing you learn in the business of trapshooting is everyone has their own opinion of employing coaches, taking lessons, etc. Incidentally, they are all right. I wish it were not so, but it is.

Shooters will tell you, *"Forget the book learning trash. Just get out there and shoot the targets."* Again, this is a double-edge sword. Yes, your scores will improve, but will they stay there? Probably not. You should absolutely forget about book learning when on station; shooting for what you learned and practiced should be imbedded as second nature, still, you can't ignore the complexity of the game. This is where books, coaches, magazines and videotapes excel. You must first know and apply the basic fundamental techniques unique to trapshooting. Then, and only then, can you let go, relax and concentrate on puffing the target. The learning curve is horrendous and oftentimes a tribulation for the new shooter. Welcome to the world of sports!

The danger of not having a coach is repeating mistakes over and over again! You must practice with a goal and a purpose. To just go out and merrily smoke targets isn't where it's at if you want to get anywhere in trapshooting. Let the festivity shooters have fun exploding shells like a pack of untamed children with firecrackers. Business before pleasure. Fun is a good thing but only when it spoils nothing better. Attend to responsibilities before enjoyment. Hook up with those who are serious about trapshooting and bounce ideas and theories off of each other. If you snare a new idea, try it, it may work. Great inventions were created by accident, hard work and perseverance. You can make anything work if you try hard enough. If someone tells you, *"You can't do that! I've never seen any professional do it,"* tell him, *"I'll try it. If it doesn't work then at least I'll know the difference why it does and doesn't work."* Never fall in a hole where you imagine improvement can't be made. For your sake, be bold to try new things. You may even invent or discover a new shooting technique!

PRACTICE TIPS - Phase 1.
"Learning without thought is labor lost."

Practice sessions should be planned in advance as well as in session. Ask yourself these questions:

1. What will I perfect today? (Use a checklist.) 2. What goal will I attain? (Must have a specific goal.) 3. Why am I'm hitting the target? (Imprint in mind what you are doing right.) 4. Why did I miss that target? (Understand what you did wrong.) 5. What did I learn? (You must learn something.) 6. Will I remember? (Write it down.) 7. Did I concentrate on my setup? (Be deliberate and precise.) 8. Did I clear my mind of cobwebs? (You can't think and shoot simultaneously.) 9. Did I get lazy? (Don't be too relaxed or overconfident the targets are easy to hit.) 10. Did I try something new? (Keep pushing to better your technique.) 11. How was my eye focus? (Learn how to see target with central vision.) 12. Did I keep my eye on the target? (If the gun hesitates, stops or jerks in the swing you took eye off the target.) 13. Why am I missing targets? (Identify and correct mistakes.) 14. Am I

focusing my eye on the proper place (top, middle or bottom) on the target depending on target angle and gun's point of impact setting? **15.** Can I say I'm a better shooter today?

The last question is vital. Don't judge yourself too harshly if you have an off day or two and nothing seems to go right. It happens to the greatest sportsmen, it will happen to you. Don't just go out and shoot without a plan, for this is not diligent practice, it is wasting money or just foolin' around. I've heard shooters who don't attend tournament shoots say, *"I shoot for fun, that's why I don't register targets."* My question is, *"How can it be fun if you never win?"* Isn't the challenge, the striving for excellence, the building of self-esteem and the joy of winning fun? Is missing targets fun? If you like to shoot for fun, it's because you like to shoot. Try registered shooting, as you'll have the opportunity to shoot a lot of targets, and that should be fun! For a trapshooter to attain an imminent degree in learning costs time, watching, hunger, dizziness in the head, weakness in the stomach, and other inconveniences. They say practice makes perfect. It's virtually a misconception. You can shoot 10,000, 20,000 or even 50,000 rounds of ammo and still not see your scores appreciate if you're just shooting for fun' n' games. Look around, there are plenty of shooters who can't win a single trap tournament in their class, yet they know it all, for they have been shooting for 15 + years. Fifteen years is a lot of practice, but are you exceptionally impressed with their shooting skills? So there it is, practice sessions should be hard work. If you don't come off the line drained of energy, then you're not learning. No pain, no gain. It takes blood, sweat and tears to excel in anything worth achieving. This doesn't mean you should shoot 100, 200 or even 300 rounds nonstop, as this isn't razor-sharp intelligent practice. The quantity of shells you shoot has no relevance to the 'quality' of your practice session. You could learn more shooting just five targets than you can with 100 targets providing you 'learned' why you hit them. Place a gun in anyone's hands and put them out there and you'll see some hits. It's amazing, since shooting is a natural ability most everyone seems to have. The mission is to hit them all -- every time! It can be learned, not through repetition alone, but through quality practice sessions. See Fig. 5-1 to review 'Practice Chart'.

On the flip side of extreme effort: Effortlessness leads to high performance, to play within your physical / mental limitations, to relax, to be comfortable with your potential. Excessive concentration and effort drains energy and performance and leads to 'burn-out'. Hard exertion is okay for practice, but lighten up in competition. Find a happy medium.

Intensity is a good thing if controlled in moderation. Novice shooters are so intense when learning they become nervous, confused, frustrated. Normal. It's a phase one must pass. In time it will fall together. Relaxation sets in with a tinge of mean determination behind the mask. Here all the learned knowledge comes into alignment with precision shooting. It won't arrive just with practice, it has to be learned, and the exclusive means to learn is through theoretical study and perfecting mechanical technique. There are no easy answers here instructing someone to practice correctly, as each individual is unique, requiring individualized visual observation. Though one common denominator shall exist whenever you practice, do so with an open frame of mind, as attending school, to master something, to learn possibilities, do the unfeasible. Everything is impossibly impossible though possible. Never again walk away from a round of trap in an intellective vacuum. Ask yourself, *"What did I learn?"* You should be able to say, *"Ah, ha! I missed that quarter angle target because I did...."* Notice the words; *"I did."* Never blame outside factors. Take responsibility for yourself in practice sessions early on. Never blame the puller for a fast or slow pull... you could have turned it down, you didn't, you missed, it's your loss. End of story.

Owing to we humans do forget what we learn, including what we wish to learn, it is important to generate a list of items you want to practice. A 3 by 5 inch ruled index card makes an excellent note card. Jot down a few reminders and review it before the practice session, then concentrate on perfecting whatever you have written down. You can retain these cards as a diary for future reflection. See Fig. 11-1 "Shoot Location Diary" and Fig. 11-2 "Average Sheet" you can also use for record keeping. Relying on your memory is not a recommended means to conduct an intellectually effective, goal-oriented practice session. You'll forget what you planned to learn once the game begins, others may distract or sidetrack your attention and you'll just be standing out there doing the same old thing over-and-over again, not actually learning anything. Those who cannot remember the past are condemned to repeat it. It is imperative to avoid repeating past mistakes, yet we all do.

Here's a list of practice tips you can use. Don't try to use them all at one time. Pick one or two and keep them in your mind each time it is your turn to shoot. This is practicing with a precise plan and a purpose. **1.** Concentrate on foot position and gun hold -- point over or on the traphouse. **2.** Feel the comb of the gun on your face at all times. **3.** Focus your eye so you see the target leave the traphouse. **4.** What angles will I get at this station? **5.** Is my eye focused directly on the target? **6.** Is the gun swinging smoothly? **7.** Is my mind wandering? **8.** Why did I hit or miss the target? **9.** Was the target angling left or right and I shot behind it?

Don't shoot yourself into a hole! Overwork leads to decreased efficiency. Shooting too much during practice sessions invents exhaustion, sloppiness and chaotic scores. Your mind, eyes, back and arms tire, along with overloading the central nervous system. It's time to stop shooting and rest, or come back another day. If you shoot to the point of deficiency, you will forget what you have learned! Rule of thumb is to shoot 50 to 100 rounds and end the day's practice session. Occasionally you can exceed this, but once targets begin slipping into the horizon, stop shooting! You'll be just throwing shot into the sky along with your money the harder you try to recover from nervous system / overexertion overload. Worse yet, you are erasing what you have learned.

Practice the right way! Practicing can be productive if you do it right. The purpose of practice is to learn techniques that can be recalled and brought out in competition. The key word is 'learn' not rehearse. Shooters restrict the learning process by shooting too many targets, then when they compete in a tournament they wonder what happened. Correcting this is simple, shoot less! Quantity diminishes quality. Excessive shooting is only a workout, a rehearsal of learned skills, an exercise of repetitive muscle toning that diminishes thought, calculation, strategy or evaluation. Obsessive trapshooting can be a trap! Going to the range is fun time, as it should be enjoyable, yet it will do you little good if you don't reserve some serious practice (learning) time. Don't shoot trap then play other games. If you must shoot hundreds of shells, then reverse the order... shoot the sporting clays, continental, skeet, and doubles if you wish, then reserve for last your serious trapshooting practice session. This way you'll retain in memory what you learned.

PRACTICE SNAPSHOOTING
"He who hesitates is lost."

Here's a diversion when the stress of practice becomes overwhelming. Practice snapshooting. That is, shooting as quick as you possibly can, substantively expeditious. Try to break the target closer and closer to the house. It's hard to do and can be merriment if you don't let the frustration build. Get tough on them targets and blow them up, right now. Don't worry about the misses, as there shall be many I assure you. The missed targets and the hit targets all serve a useful purpose. What is the purpose of snapshooting? When you finish a round or two of snapshooting, then revert to your usual timing; you will discover new talents you never realized. You'll recognize the trap game slowed down. The targets don't appear so brisk and your scores will rise. You will also be giving your eyes a workout, too. Notice how they acquire the target so easily now? Everything appears in slow motion and even the gun and your brain aren't working as hard. What snapshooting does is open your subconscious mind to subtleties you never could see with your conscience mind. Try it and you'll see improvement. Whenever you fall into a slump, snapshooting can often snap you out of it. The term snapshooting means shooting exceeds the natural time limits of your internal time clock. See "Flinching" and "Timely Flinching" which explain the internal time clock mode of shooting. It is not advisable to snapshot (shooting ultra fast) routinely, though this depends on personal preference as some shooters naturally shoot extremely fast, but to the rest of us, it appears as snap shooting. Regardless how you shoot, there really is no right or wrong way. The bottom line is broken targets. Whoever breaks the most wins! These practice exercises within will help you develop a shooting style you know is right for you. Through patient experimentation, proficiency will surface. The learning phase can be fun, as long as you try not to progress too quickly beyond your current abilities. Proceed slowly with patience by your side and you will see steady score advancement. Snapshooting is only an *exercise* and <u>not</u> to be incorporated into your style.

SETTING REALISTIC GOALS
"He who would climb the ladder must begin at the bottom."

Shoot for a purpose to achieve a specific goal over a realistic period of time. This requires you have a plan, a road map of where your competence level will be, say, within one year. Each time you step on line to shoot a round of trap, something must be learned. If you're just having fun shooting, you are probably not learning anything substantial except learning how to have fun. It's about as much learning as working at a gas station watching the cars go by. If you read a poem, it is simply read, but to memorize it takes increased mental exertion and concentration. Repetition is a key to memorization, and it takes a long time to become proficient shooting speeding deviated targets. What may seem obvious and easy should never be taken for granted, that shooting is effortless. Most shooters struggle on the line trying to hit targets. They struggle on account of they are shooting from the eye instead of the mind, or worse, from pure instinct and not from skill. Most learn trapshooting from a group at the local gun club who simply pick up a gun that does not fit them and innocently shoot targets, laughing at those they miss. Some of them are decent shots, though the majority are infinitesimally skilled for competition shoots.

A competitive shooter's mind would be racing like a computer, crunching technicalities and angles correcting the error. A missed target is no laughing matter. So this is goal #1. Why did you miss the target? The question is easy, the answer is legion and complex. Each shooting session requires a goal. Not to hit all 25 targets, but to hit only one target. One at a time. It is better to hit 18 targets and know why you hit them, and know why you missed the 7, than to hit all 25 on sheer luck of having a peculiar perfect day, or getting lucky easy-angled targets. The sole scheme to break 100 targets is to break one at a time, with each target demanding intense visual effort and mental concentration. So goal #2 is learn how to break <u>one</u> target, one at a time. The quickest way to learn this is to shoot a round of trap (25 shells or more) standing on only one station. This creates repetition, implanting memorization. Don't debate, just do it and see for yourself it works. You could lock the trap, but the fixed angles will be untrue, as trap machines oscillate in the real world. You still must learn to overcome the target exit surprise factor, so by shooting 25 shells per station you limit the angles to a manageable awareness level. For more on this see, 'Jack in the Box Syndrome'.

Here is a brief list of goals you should strive to achieve in year number one. **1.** Know why you missed the target and implement every measure so it will not happen again. At first it may take a lot of guesswork, but shooting 25 rounds on the station giving you trouble will clean up the errors fast. If you miss, realize you can't name one trapshooter who can break them all and never miss, ever. Name one Champion batter, bowler, basketball player who gets them all! **2.** Learn to treat a round of trap -- or 100 targets -- as just one target. Never think of 24 targets or 2 targets... solidly implant in your mind there is just one target and no other. **3.** Think of the hits, not the misses. Know why you missed, better yet, know why you hit the target. **4.** Make every single shot count... every single time. Pay attention! **5.** Set a realistic score goal, not 100, mid 90's would be suitable. **6.** Practice weekly at your local gun club. Join a league shoot to polish what you learn. **7.** Attend registered shoots, as this is where you'll positively learn how to shoot under pressure.

MANAGING PEER PRESSURE
"He that has a good harvest must be content with a few thistles."

You may be a good shooter at your club, then you want to try something new to see if it works. You know people are watching and you become fearful others will notice you miss targets, scoff and laugh. Let them laugh, but remember, he who laughs last, laughs best! Yes, your scores will fall when you try anything new. This is the learning curve high gun shooters had to go through too. Don't ever heed the advice of someone telling you not to try out something new. That shooter may misguide you for his own benefit. Expect to receive resistance from shooters who see you trying something different. Don't let it faze you. Learning and discovery are a string of accidental circumstances. What you try today may unlock a secret within your own technique.

CHAPTER 6

HOME ON THE RANGE
"It takes a trapshooter to teach a trapshooter."

The foremost guidance I can offer is to practice with those who shoot better than you do. If you primarily shoot with those you can beat, or come close to thrashing, you'll hardly increase your skill level. Shooting with those with higher abilities will step you up to their caliber. Haven't you heard this before? *"He shoots too good. I don't want to shoot near that guy."* Mostly the youngsters say this. The elders oftentimes remain silent, yet do the same, by unfailingly selecting a full squad of acquaintances to keep the superior shooter out of the game. Trapshooting is not a game of beating anyone! It's a game, often a lonely sport, where it's just you and the target. The only thing you are trying to beat is the target, not the other squad members. Wipe any thoughts out of your mind leading you to conclude you are competing against another shooter. It just isn't so. You are competing with yourself. When you get into a shootoff, you'll be content to remind yourself of this, otherwise you may fall to pieces reasoning you are in a neck-to-neck race with the other shooter. It's you and the target. Forget about anything else. When the final score comes in, then it's time to say, *"I won." "I lost."*

Sooner the better, challenge a shooter who is an equal or more proficient shooter to a shootoff. It's worthy practice and a lot of fun too. You will stimulate the spirit essential to win competitive shoots. The side bet could modestly be a cup of coffee or dinner for the winner. Do this, you'll strive harder to hit the targets, focus your concentration, stimulate the experience of competition. You may have to buy many a cup of coffee, but soon enough the pendulum swings to your favor. This is sound practical advice here. Attend as many Turkey Shoots as possible at various gun clubs. You'll feed your family while learning the art of competitiveness.

When you practice, keep in mind to practice concentration. It doesn't come naturally no matter how much you shoot, it must be learned. Always start shooting easy targets when learning a new system. If this means staying on post #3 for 25 rounds or more, then do so. Practice smart! Set goals and achieve them. Practice looking at the target, not just seeing the target. Looking is more intense. It is concentration, as if your eye or eyes are like telescopes zeroing in for a close snapshot (without squinting the dominant aiming eye or forcing facial muscles.) See Fig. 11-4, Fig. 11-11 and Fig. 11-12.

Breathing has deep connections to emotion. You may not have observed it, but if you alter your breathing, you can reshape your disposition. If you observe your breathing carefully, you'll notice when you are nervous you have a notable rhythm of breathing, and when relaxed a totally distinct rhythm. When you are relaxed, you breathe in a different way than when you are tense. You cannot breathe the way you do when you are relaxed and be tense at the same time. It's impossible. This means breathing is deeply related to your mental state. If you modulate your breathing you can change the state of mind. When you are in deep concentration your breathing changes, so identify how you breathe when you are shooting well. The more oxygen in the body, the more alive with awareness you become. This oxygenation creates body electricity -- bio-energy. When there is energy (electricity) in the body you can move deep within, beyond yourself. The body has its own electrical generation sources. If you apply the fuel of oxygen to these generators, with more breathing, more energy will flow. This energy is very necessary if you are to move beyond the shooting abilities you now have. Practice breathing. You may discover a well guarded secret. It is the simple techniques that develop a fine shooter, giving you the ability to reach higher scores than your current abilities say you can. Understanding sensitivity and deep inner concentration are not novice trapshooting techniques, but highly professional tuning. They are sometimes easy to do, but difficult to master. For each person is so unique only you can discover the proper 'feel' when it is done right. Shooting skill is highly individualistic. Focus on developing your own form and style, but do not ignore the fundamental rules. If possible, develop your style upon a foundation of tried and proven techniques.

PRACTICE TIPS - Phase 2.
"Learn as though you would never be able to master it."

Don't try to digest all of the following practice tips in one session. Maintain a realistic time frame and keep practicing them over time until you find what works. As we humans often forget what we learn, repetition is required so form and style can become second nature. Even then, we require refresher training every so often.

A new shooter may expect 'phases' to pass through. **Intense stage**: Where confusion is most severe. **Failure**: Forgetting what one has learned. **Success**: Putting it all together and events are won and confidence builds. **Slump**; Back to the basics to recover from learned bad habits which result from a deflective mind-set = the point where the mind averts and rejects new ideas. Experimentation of new technique is necessary to break a slump. **Let go:** The point where shooting becomes naturally instinctive, applying all learned technique consistently. Unfortunately, the majority of shooters simply have a natural aversion to formal practice discipline. It's the built-in psychological resistance to change affliction. It must be broken. Inflexibility to acquire the proper fundamentals in trapshooting is like building a house on sinking sand. Success begins with the 'willingness' to learn. You can lead a mule to water, but you can't make him drink wine. If you are now enthusiastic to learn... on each post _focus_ on and _perform_ the following:

1. Foot stance correct? Adjust if necessary. Test by swinging the gun horizontally left to right and vertically to insure no muscle strain or clothing is binding. Swing gently by the hips, not with the shoulder or pushing the gun with your arm. Your foot position is critical, as it is the foundation of how your body will swing the gun to the target. If your stance is too loose and flexible (like a forward-leaning pose) your gun will waver and track inconsistently to the target as you are using excessive muscle motion for the required move, including activating upper body muscles, arms, leg, back, knees that are not required diverting valuable energy. Your stance will be off balance, increasing instability and gun sway. If you don't swing by the hips your hand will push the gun away from your master eye and you may crossfire or no doubt misalign; eye, muzzle, sight bead, target alignment. What's more, it is an open invitation for a flinch to develop as the brain sends excessive signals to too many muscles and the nervous system overloads with cluttering, conflicting commands. If your stance is too ridged, the gun won't flow but lurch to the target, which will push your face away from the gun's comb. Missing targets by shooting over them? Check foot position and stance. Comfort is important, but make certain the body can repeatedly swing to the target smoothly each and every time. A coach or videotape will nail down this phase of the learning curve. If you still find your eye is crossing-over, try putting some tape on the non-aiming eye's shooting glasses, or force the eye to cross-back by slightly winking the non-aiming eye, or shoot with solely one eye open.

2. Look at the traphouse. Prepare for the worst angled target you will get on this station. Tell yourself, _"There is no such thing as a straight-away target."_ Identify where to hold the gun on the house when you do mount the gun. Visualize the target angles and where you plan to break the target. Visualize yourself breaking it! Calculate your lead on a hard angle. On all targets visualize the proper sight picture required to break the target. When the squad leader calls for a test target look at it. Is the target running flat? Does it have a face or is it shadowed? What about the background? Did the target emerge from its proper zone from the traphouse? How fast is it traveling? Did it behave properly?

3. Mount the gun slowly with precision. Lower face on comb in slow motion to give your eyes (iris and lens) a chance to adjust from the gun's sight plane to the traphouse and field. You should _feel_ the proper cheek pressure. If you feel no cheek pressure don't call for the bird until you do. You must 'feel the pressure' to verify your head is down. A slow deliberate pressing of the cheek to comb works best. Hug the gun... you and the gun should feel as one.

4. Look down the barrel. Are the sight beads lined up properly? Gun mounted properly? If you sense something is wrong, don't call for the bird as something _is_ wrong. You don't take chances because that's how you miss those targets that mysteriously escape. Dismount the gun immediately and remount.

5. Dismounting. If you have to dismount, then do so all the way back to where the gun was when you were waiting your turn to shoot. Don't dismount partially. You should go all the way back to the starting point just after the shell was loaded into the chamber.

6. Remounting. All feels and looks good. Is gun barrel pointed at the proper hold point on or over the house?

7. Remind yourself to shoot quickly and break that target.

8. Again, focus your eye at the proper point of view and prepare for the hardest angled target to emerge. Don't anticipate, be prepared for it. Be ready when you call for the target!

The above eight steps are the "analysis setup phase." The last steps are:

9. Stop thinking, it's time to shoot! Clear out your mind, call for the target and shoot it. The instant you think your eyes become useless. If the setup was proper, you'll be primed when hard angles or any angle target emerges. The quarter angles are easy to hit and you should have no problem with them, unless you <u>anticipated</u> a hard angle or expected a quarter angle and the target startled your nervous system and got the jump on you. When you call for the target you should not be thinking or anticipating. You should call with authority, or with inner mental aggression. A lame call is a lazy call and passivity will cause missed targets. Don't be complacent. Each target requires devoted concentration and labor to break. If you feel too at ease, too cocksure, you will likely miss one or more. Worse, complacency has a tendency to foul up the setup, cause head-lifting, lazy eye focus, etc. Know the difference between 'thinking' and 'concentration'. <u>Thinking</u> is evaluating conditions and setting a plan of action prior to shooting. <u>Concentrating</u> is clearing the mind of thought, producing central vision on the target, yet aware of only one objective... see and break the target! Keep your eye on that target and let your brain instruct your body what needs to be done. This isn't shooting without intelligence, it is shooting from memory, mental alertness learned from discerning practice sessions. Find the happy medium. Not too relaxed, not too tense. You should be ambitious with a tinge of adrenaline surge.

10. Know why you hit or missed the target. You must learn why you hit or missed. What did the sight picture look like? Recognize it! Memorize it! Don't forget it!

11. When you shot the target did you think? Thinking is like closing your eyes. Don't do it. Did you anticipate? Fail to keep eye on target? Was your head down, feeling positive cheek pressure on the comb? Did you pull the trigger within your internal time clock? Did you fail to acquire the target angle properly? Ask yourself these questions. When you ask questions you get answers.

12. Do not become so intense looking at the target you find yourself 'squinting' the eyes! If you squint you alter the focus of your eyes (distortion) and reduce light transmission. If necessity be, lift your eyebrows slightly to keep your eyelids clear and to reduce pressure on the eyeball. The added benefit is reduced eye strain = heightened focus. Precision shooters know not to aim at the bull's-eye, but to aim at the center of the bull's-eye. If you focus on the smallest detail of the target it will appear larger which gives more room for error.

13. Test your technique under stress. Offer a small wager with a higher scoring shooter. Observe if your gun mount, gun swing and trigger timing still function when the heat is on. Even if you lose the gamble, did your technique waver or was it solid? Were your moves smooth? Practice under pressure until it is perfected. This is why I say get into registered shoots as soon as you can. It's a good place to learn how to stand up under competitive pressure. It'll help dissolve nervousness over time, and perfect your game. Controlling your mental game will make it possible to relax with the physical aspects of pointing the gun with ease straight to the target. Repeated exposure to the stress of competition is the pathway to control nerves and build a winning temperament.

14. Take a moment to think when changing stations. Ask yourself, *"Are all my moves exactly the same?"* This includes all the basics of foot position/stance, gun mount, eye focus, call method, cheek pressure on comb, gun swing, timing. Trap is a game of repeating the same motions over-and-over, each and every time. Bowling is the same. To roll the ball between pin 1 and 2 (or 1 and 3) consistently, your technique must be perfectly repeatable. Repetition may be boring, but it is accurate and necessary regardless of the sport you play. When you miss a target, suspect a defect in the setup phase, identify and correct the problem (see Fig. 7-2 Missed Targets Chart). Precision shooting is the goal. Use your memory by commanding your mind to memorize how you solidly smoked each target. If technique is an obstacle, make changes, experiment, seek solutions to correct the problem. Reluctance to change styles and try new things will plainly create a perfect hit' n' miss shooter. Are you practicing the same old mistakes over-and-over again? With experimentation, you will learn what is, and what is not, a mistake.

15. Are you testing your limits? Shoot as fast as you can, then at your normal timing. Keep testing and re-testing until you know your limitations. This requires much trial and error, but you will discover when and where to shoot to build consistency and control. See *"Snap Shooting."*

16. Is your gun dragging too far behind the target? This is caused by laziness and readily apparent when you are fatigued. The gun just doesn't want to go for the target. However, it can also be a bad habit! Practice moving the gun immediately the moment you see and recognize the angle of the target, and move that gun! Be aggressive! Go for it! Don't let your guard down. Be vigilant when you call. Attack the target, don't react to it.

17. Know straight-trending targets rise and decelerate rapidly. Angle targets rise slowly, but laterally travel quickly as acceleration is sustained. Physical factors of mass, velocity and gravity cause divergence alterations. Recognize this the next time you shoot. It will help you determine timing and gun transit procedure.

18. Check your breathing rhythm. Is it consistent? Relaxing?

19. Did you take vitamins to sustain energy, endurance, and concentration?

20. Learn patience. It takes years to learn. Don't be too hard on yourself. Experience and time will reward you.

ATTEND REGISTERED TOURNAMENTS
"Well begun is half done."

As soon as possible, a new shooter should dive head-first into registered competitions. Within the first 6 to 8 months of shooting, plan to compete in your class. Why? It will enhance your skills in ways you wouldn't imagine. It breaks the initial fright (and embarrassment) of competition. It's a wonderful social outlet, BBQ's, meeting new friends... a big party. How socially limiting it can be to only shoot one gun club year-after-year. Go on out and meet some fine shooters. Put some new people in your life. Ask your club to sponsor an A.T.A., P.I.T.A., DTL, ABT or Olympic trap tournament. I hear a lot of resistance (excuses) from shooters, *"If I can't break 99 or 100 I won't go."* *"I have no interest in winning money."* Yeah, right! Cold feet, that's all it is. Understand you don't have to win to have fun. You don't have to win first-place to win money. Losing first place doesn't matter as long as the outcome is happy. Play the options and Calcutta and you play your own game, or at least you'll have a fighting chance to walk away with cash with the satisfaction it helped pay for your trip. All's well that ends well.

Before you attend a registered shoot, write to the P.I.T.A. or A.T.A and ask for the rule books. See "Competition Trapshooting Associations" for addresses. Find someone who attends or has attended competitive events at your club and shoot with him/her to learn the rules. At no time wait until you can break 100 straight targets to step into competition, because this is not the preferred means to learn competitive shooting. You learn by doing. It's an entirely new experience and each shoot location is a strange place, with new techniques to learn. For many shooters, they perform better shooting at an alternate gun club. This holds truth. So, by waiting for perfect scores you are missing out on great opportunities. It may be to your advantage to forfeit shooting singles targets and just shoot handicap events and play the options. You'll have to break 98 to 100 straight in singles, but a handicap score of 90 to 99, and even less, in the high 80's, could be a win. Most of the money is in the handicap events, anyway, at the majority of registered shoots, though larger tournaments do have sizable purses in the singles program.

Never listen to shooters at the local club who try to dissuade you from attending competitive shoots. You are never too young or too old, and it is never too late. The best place to begin is now, regardless of how competent you are with your shotgun. I didn't win my first registered shoot, but I won on my third try. I was shooting trap eight months of Sundays when I attended my first registered shoot. It was a luxuriate, though a dreaded encounter; I instantaneously became caught up in the camaraderie. It's where the action, excitement and fun is, not to mention the option money is rewarding. If you consider weekend plinking enjoyment, try competitive shooting. It'll quickly make you a meritorious shooter. You will meet professionals and learn valuable advice, that is, if you ask questions. Don't be intimidated and shy. Approach these high-gun pros to seek information. Watch how they shoot, study them. That is how to learn.

ETIQUETTE ON THE LINE

"Courtesy pays big dividends and doesn't cost a dime."

When attending registered shoots there are written and unwritten rules to know. Never disrupt the harmony of the squad is a written rule, but it doesn't explain the infractions. First, the squad leader is what it says he/she is. If the leader speaks, listen up and observe. If the squad leader is incompetent, rude, or out of line, take it to a referee or field captain to have the leader removed or excuse yourself from the squad to shoot on another. If possible, avoid shooting with anyone you can't get along with, as your scores will reveal the conflict. Competitive shoots are, for a better word, solemn affairs. Shooters are in deep concentration. Respect them. Conversation should be nil. Don't cuss, throw temper tantrums, toss shells to the ground or into the air when missing a target. Not only does it disrupt others, it sets up a whiplashing negative mind-frame and you will proceed to miss targets. The bottom of the barrel falls out. Plus you'll develop a reputation which shooters' avoid with a passion.

No emotions is the key to unlock the door to higher scores. When you miss a target, reveal no emotion. No shaking of the head, sour facial expressions, fidgeting. This is a harmful habit and must be practiced with self-discipline to eradicate. Even if you break a target but don't smoke it just right, never shake your head or twitch your face with unsatisfied expressions. This alone will hurt yourself as it sets up negative emotions the subconscious will pickup on real fast and use against you. Do this and I guarantee you'll enter a mini-slump and miss more targets. A chain reaction initiates whenever a target is missed. Recognize this chain reaction for what it is and what it can do to your scores. Discouragement encourages discouragement. It's a hard routine to break, but one way to snap to is admit it makes you appear direly unprofessional as your actions draw spectator attention to you (something you don't need right now) as the situation rapidly stumbles from bad to worse. If you miss and know why you missed, keep it to yourself. I had a habit of saying out loud during practice sessions, *"Oh, I was behind it."* It's okay to realize what you did right or wrong, but speaking out loud is counter-productive, and more so, intensely discourteous and disruptive to other shooters during practice or competition. If you desire to increase your scores, dislodge all emotional reactions. Psychologically treat a missed target as if it never happened, and setup for your next shot fully confident in your technique and level of skill. Don't dwell on the negatives. Silence is golden!

Be aware, though intentional or not, shooters may say things which will cause you to alter your shooting style or how you execute shots. It can be a simple remark such as, *"The background on trap two is horrid, you have to shoot fast or you'll miss them."* Dismiss that statement out of your mind as quickly as you can, for it will divert your concentration to the background scenery, alter your shooting timing or style, and cause missed targets. Though backgrounds are important, it's a fact of life each traphouse, and each trap club, will have differing background scenes. Concentrate your eye focus on the target, not the airplane, building, trees, weeds, flowers or bushes. In retrospect, don't comment to shooters on shooting conditions. This is no time for small talk which serves no purpose but to stimulate self-doubt in yourself and others.

Read the safety rules. Your gun must be unloaded, and action open, whenever you pick up your gun. You don't load it until you are on station, the gun is facing in safe direction, and trap setter is secure in the traphouse with no safety flag visible. Keep the gun pointed downrange. Never turn the gun toward other shooters or turn yourself completely around, or stoop to pick up spent shells. I've seen experienced shooters do this, and I'm quick to tell them the rules. I've witnessed guns discharging by accident, and so have you; fortunately, they were pointed downrange. Safety is everyone's responsibility. If you notice an infraction, speak up. Be polite about it. If it continues, tell the squad leader. If it still happens, call the referee or management and remove the person from the squad or yourself. Though accidents are rare, they are often serious. Careless shooters are dangerous.

Be professional! Be prepared! A place for everything and everything in its place. You have plenty of time to get organized before approaching the deck. Be on time. Everything should be in order, including all items in 'diaper bag' (carryall shooting bag). A disorderly shooter will ruin the mood of the shoot, and the squad will bear out your reputation precedes you whenever you attend another registered competition. Don't take forever mounting your gun and calling for the target. Try to keep a rhythm going, but don't let the rhythm accelerate or decelerate.

A good squad leader can keep the timing at a proper tempo. If the squad calls for the targets too fast, expect bad pulls and wild targets. The trap setter should be given sufficient time to load his target properly. The puller needs time to prepare for hearing the shooter's call for the bird. A squad shooting too rapidly will make the setter and puller nervous and upset, especially if the setter splits his fingernails on releasing a prematurely set target. As certain as the sun rises, future targets won't be placed on the trap's arm snugly and you'll witness peculiar U.F.O.'s. Some setters may punch a hole in the center of the target, grinning as you miss his flying rock. It is no accident pros shoot with each other. They prefer to shoot with people who break targets where they are predisposed to burst them. Slow firing shooters taking long shots disrupt professionals. If you're new to trapshooting, you won't need to fret about shooting with pros, as they build their own squads. However, you still must learn how to shoot fluently with a squad, and a good place to practice is at your home gun club.

Rest assured being disruptive ruins your game. Use quality reloads with relatively new hulls, magnum shot and the highest quality wads and powder you can afford. Better still, shoot new ammunition. You must have conviction in your ammo, including reloads. No confidence? Then trash them during practice sessions, not in competitive events. Misfires, hangfire (delayed ignition from poor quality primers and air pockets under wad) and bloopers (undercharged load) will ruin your morale and devastate your scores. Fire scrappy loads and that is precisely what the scoreboard duplicates. Garbage in, garbage out. You have heard if you mismount your gun, take the gun down, and remount it. This is good advice, still, if you find yourself doing this too often, then something is wrong... see a stockfitter to make the gun fit you. If this happens too much, it is likely you are mounting the gun too fast. Slow down your setup so your gun mounts properly the first time. Watch the pros and you'll see some good examples. Someone who is struggling on the line is disrupting the squad. Whether it's undercharged, double-charged, or blooper reloads, misfiring, gun jams, slow mounting, fast or slow calling, it all adds up to disruption. If you shoot an autoloader, use a shell catcher. Flying hulls are unspoken insults. Competition shoots are fun, even within its solemn ritual, once you get the hang of it. It all boils down to common respect for others.

If you have a problem with trap help delivering fast or slow pulls, be polite when correcting the person. I've seen angry outbursts blaming the puller for bad pulls, only to see the puller do a fine job and the angry shooter climbs the walls in frustration due to his own pent-up bitterness. It is a fact of life you will obtain slow and fast pulls, so it is the shooter's responsibility to turn them down as long as rules permit, or shoot and break them. It's unrealistic to expect every pull to be perfect. It just won't happen as long as humans push the button to release the target. If you have excessive defective pulls, it may be the way you call for them. Are you saying, "Pull" loud and clear. Or are you using a phrase that is confusing and can't be heard by the puller? If so, perhaps you should modify your call routine. If you discern a fatigued or uninitiated puller ask the referee to have the puller replaced. In any case, don't be angry with the kid as it will entirely ruin your own scores. When the fun is gone from shooting, it's time to stop shooting and take a vacation. All work and no play makes a boring day. I've seen too many disgruntled shooters take out their own frustrations on pullers when it is their own ineptitude that really demands addressing. Here's some good advice. Try pulling and scoring yourself. You can learn a lot about target release timing, squad rhythm, target placement and hearing target calls. It'll give you the edge other shooters fail to perceive.

When walking from traphouse to traphouse, don't talk to shooters who appear in deep concentration. It is common courtesy when shooters are changing houses not to joke or disrupt their mood. If they speak to you, keep it light and brief. When they have finished the event, then it's fun time, maybe, depending on the mood of the shooter. Many are tired and need to renovate equipment and prepare for the next ordeal. Respect this. There will be plenty of time to monkey around at the BBQ, social hours and fun shoots at day's end. Last but not least, read and understand the official shoot management rulebook. Knowing the A.T.A. and P.I.T.A. rules is compulsory.

CHAPTER 7

THE NEW SHOOTER'S PERILS
"Peril; for those who believe in nothing."

Woe to the neophyte learning to shoot shotgun sport games. The advice you gain is often well intended, though will totally scramble your mind in frustration. I've seen people quit the sport due to too much advice, too much peer pressure, and outright ridicule by unprofessional shooters. This is why I recommend a new shooter quickly participate in registered shoots, even if only to attend and observe. There can be animosity within the rank members of gun clubs, and from club-to-club. So much internal strife took place at one trap club in Oregon the entire trapfield was shut down! It became a meeting place for those who don't even shoot. Problems exist on golf courses, so it is not a unique adversity. It's a people problem. I believe registered shoots are the finest gatherings on the planet.

The new shooter is very sensitive and fragile, even if he's built like a brick jailhouse and can bench press 600 pounds, the ego is susceptible to embarrassment. No one wishes to make a fool of himself on the trap line. I was lucky when I joined my first trap club to find a group of mature, helpful, and friendly shooters. However, expect this to only last for a short time. As you progress, you may become a real threat to some of the 'better shooters' at the club who have shot for 15 + years. Some may be envious and toy with your mind. It can be subtle attacks, advice disguised to help you, but schemed to throw you off into missing targets. It's rare, but I've seen it happen. There is always one bad apple in a bushel. So be capable of switching from peer approval to loving the game. If you truly treasure the game, no one will have the power to derail the dream.

Don't stay put in a local gun range practicing until you can break 100 straight before attending a registered shoot. You should associate with competitive and professional shooters as soon as you can. Gun clubs cater to many disciplines, generally social gatherings, practice shooting, purely for amusement and games. Don't expect all club members will understand and support your desire to be a tournament shooter. It's not everyone's cup of brew. The more you are exposed to competition the less you'll be concerned with peer abuse, as it won't be long you'll whip the antagonist into silence with authoritative performance! Your proficiency will speak for itself. The bottom line is, don't let anyone rob you of your self-esteem because it's a killer -- a killer of potential and courage. As a new shooter you will miss a ton of targets. The average person who never fired a shotgun hits only 4 to 6 targets the first time they shoot at 25 targets. It is embarrassing to learn, as it would be with any sport. So it is meaningful to realize how wrong it is to compare yourself with others, not only when learning, but also when you become a better shooter. In the game of trapshooting you are not competing against anyone except yourself. It's just you and the target. This is all that matters. It is all the scorekeeper will record, *"Dead" or "Lost."* It is your responsibility as a fellow trapshooter to not be unprofessional yourself. You can gain many friends in this sport by having a pleasant personality. Some people shoot on account of the social outlet and personal satisfaction, others shoot for pure materialistic reasons... they shoot for money! If you shoot for score, trying to reach the perfect high score, the fun will still exist and the money will arrive, deservedly so. Too much pressure will likely create tension and you'll lose fluidity in the gun's swing to the target. Relax! It's only a game! Finding that 'right mix' of tingling adrenaline surge with a relaxed concentrated mind must to be discovered, rehearsed, controlled, and recalled at will. If you practice developing this elusive skill, other people won't be able to influence you. Developing self-awareness and confidence in your own abilities will surge your scores forward.

BEGINNERS' FATAL MISTAKES
"To learn patience, have patience. Nothing succeeds like success."

Consistently successful shooters do not win by skill alone, but by the six inches between the ears. Some of the biggest errors you can make: **1)** weak concentration, **2)** incorrect setup, **3)** inability to forget bad shots, **4)** failure to control emotions, 5) lack of patience, 6) negative thoughts, 7) fear, 8) lack of faith and loss of confidence, 9) expecting to lose or miss a target, 10) improper eye focus, 11) not looking at the target, 12) head-lifting ,13) Erratically pushing gun to target, 14) not pivoting by the hips to swing gun, 15) failure to hug the gun. Remind yourself of these things when you go out on the line to shoot. Jot them down on a memo pad to rejuvenate your memory. Learn to dream of being a good trapshooter, for without the dream there can be no realization of success. Practice with intelligence, not with feelings, thought and emotions; concentrate on hitting the target! Don't mindlessly shoot at hundreds of targets only imbedding the same mistakes over and over again into your subconscious. Do this and you'll learn how to lose with a vengeance. No good plan at all never makes a task well done. Develop a plan and stick to it, be mentally engaged on each target as if only one target matters. If you miss, don't dwell on it, move on to the next shot as if you hit the last target. Learn to be patient with yourself, as it takes years to become a good shooter. Patience develops self-discipline, so you'll be in better control of yourself. Relax and have a sense of enjoyment blended within your concentration. If you become discouraged, you are not happy, and when you are dispirited you certainly will not crunch those targets as well as if you were enjoying yourself. Serious enjoyment is how I describe the mix. Being too serious develops a slump, whereas overly joyful - serious concentration lapses. Patience readjusts attitude, which aligns outlook towards renewed awareness and focus. Patience enhances the odds of success as it changes perspective, the way you perceive situations with a positive spin. Professionals shoot with determined patience.

DEVELOPING CONFIDENCE
"Just believe."

Every cloud has a silver lining. Every misfortune has a positive aspect. An entire book could be written on this subject. Self-help books are available. Read some. The first rule to learn is when you miss a target, or lose a shootoff, you are not a loser! You may feel like one, but you are not a born loser or two-time failure. Consider for illustrative purposes two American high-gun shooters, Dan Bonnillas and Leo Harrison III, going head-to-head in a shootoff. If Dan loses, is he a loser? Of course not. If Leo loses, is he a failure? Certainly not! These men are not losers even when they do lose! Certainly only one can win a shootoff, but the word loser must be erased from your vocabulary for no one is bound to win all of the time, every season, all year, each day. Sic transit Gloria moundi: *"Thus passes away the glory of the world."* So when feelings of remorse and self-dejection befall you like a sledgehammer plunging from the sky, sidestep quickly and put life back into proper perspective... right now! Losing is part of winning! It's a process to the road to victory. Discouraging, yes. Grueling, absolutely. Heartache, tearfully so. Moreover, every top-gun experiences these feelings, too, it's just they have lost so many times before in the past they don't show any emotion. And why should they? They know they are good. Lose as if you like it; win as if you were used to it. To be a good winner you must learn how to be a gracious loser too. Some things cannot be prevented from happening. You do the best you can do with the current ability you have, today. Tomorrow is always another day. Keep on practicing so mistakes don't repeat themselves. The future is bright. See Fig. 7-1 "Confidence Chart."

There is another aspect frequently misunderstood and customarily neglected. Must you win all of the time? Is this what drives you? Is winning the exclusive goal? If so, your priorities need readjusting and quickly. If you concentrate and dedicate your game solely to winning, beating the pants off your competitor... you are not going to win. To win you should concentrate on the target, just the target, and nothing but the target. Any thoughts of winning are counterproductive equally as any thoughts of losing. Winning or losing is not the game, moreover, confidence in your skills and abilities will take you to the trophy and prize money arena. If you allow just a smidgen of thought of the prize money, trophy, belt buckle, family or friends watching you enter your mind, your concentration is destroyed. Lost targets appear and confidence disappears. Get the picture? Break the targets and you'll win! Everyone has their own formula, but keep concentrating on the task of breaking each target.

Confidence is trust. Trust in your equipment, your technique, and ability. It develops over time. The more you shoot and compete, conviction builds, slowly at first, then rapidly. It can take a few seasons to really get up to full steam. Placing small side-bets when practicing accelerates the process. Attending turkey shoots for prizes builds confidence. You compound small winnings into larger winnings. If at first you don't succeed, try, try, again. Little strokes fell great oaks. Limited strength, when persistently applied, can accomplish great feats. Nothing succeeds like success. Success breeds more success. But as you know, confidence in itself can't make you a winner, it's just one ingredient in the recipe of success. The loss of confidence is so critical it will guarantee lost targets. So, anything jeopardizing self-confidence must be dealt with, corrected, and vanquished to the graveyard to be forever buried out of sight and out of mind. The chickens will come home to roost. I call it, *"Getting your act together."*

THE CONFIDENCE BUSTERS
"Yes, Virginia, there is a Santa Claus." _{Francis Pharcellus Church (1897)}

Numerous shooters believe confidence comes from simple self-motivational suggestions such as: *"I feel like I can break 'em all today. I just know I'm going to do it. Take no survivors!"* It's a step in the wrong direction, as it does not build confidence, in fact, it sets you up for a fall. When that missed target appears, you suddenly tumble into an uncontrollable tailspin. Chaos breaks loose in your mind and the emotions and thoughts take control of the game. You know what I'm talking about. That bold, presumptuous attitude that was supposed to 'pump you up' burst your little bubble. What went wrong? You anticipated performance expectations beyond the realities of your abilities. When this happens, you are envisioning too much from yourself and simply asking for trouble to ruin a good day. Know your abilities and expect to perform at that level. If you do, you will astonish yourself as your score average will rise. Your natural learning ability will increase if you don't get in the way. It is more valuable to say; *"I'll do my best today and really concentrate to see the target. I have one target to break, just one, and I know my technique will break it."* Then after you shoot and a miss occurs? *"I only have one target to break, this one. No straight-aways. Let's go get it. The best is yet to come."* No other thoughts are in your mind. These thoughts build concentration prior to shouldering the gun. It's a mental plan of action. It's positive yet realistic and therefore attainable (reason is the emperor of all things). Prevalently, I'm so deep in concentration when the scorekeeper calls out, *"Four"* for that station's score, I'm set back a bit. That's how little attention I place on a lost target. I put all my energy into hitting the target yet to come. I never look back, not in competition. At practice it's okay to analytically evaluate missed targets, but never with registered targets. If you miss, know why you miss. Don't compound the mistake by thinking of the mistake. Think of what you do right, not what you do wrong! Squeeze big mistakes into small opportunities.

Think of confidence as the concrete foundation of an office tower. Your mind is the cement base, the corner stone and strength of the building. All the floors above are weight to bear. Someone crashes through a window, leaping from the 50th floor. The foundation doesn't move, it doesn't care, it just does what it's supposed to do. A kid 'tags' his name on the foundation defacing it. A dog sprays the wall. A city bus crashes into the building fracturing the foundation, yet the building still stands. To maintain self-assuredness you learn to disallow 'distractions'. Complications are sure to develop if you don't. Pay attention! Get tough with a motivated attitude. You should destroy the target, not just break it... you must be aggressive or you'll lose willpower, desire, motivation and concentration. Find the inner power within you and employ it.

Distractions come in many forms. It can be a bad background, a disruptive shooter, negative thoughts, and yes, even positive thoughts. Shell misfires, gun malfunctions, wind, rain, heat, cold, an itch or pain, fast and slow pulls, broken targets; bee buzzing the barrel, freeway noise, trains, airplanes, farm tractors, background conversation, you name it. Distractions are part of life and to best manage diversions is to totally ignore them. Shooting is shooting and nothing else but shooting. No thoughts other than breaking the target should enter your mind, ever. If you allowed a disruptive shooter on the squad or any of the above mentioned distractions to rattle your cage, then it's your fault for not retaining self-control. Don't grow sensitized to disruptions since there is no perfect trap club, no perfect squad, no perfect perfections. Someone once told me at the P.I.T.A. Grand, *"I couldn't concentrate with that freeway and all the vehicle noise. It just ruined everything."* I didn't watch the distant freeway, but I did see the targets. The noise of gunfire was persuasive so I don't know how he heard the cars and trucks with earplugs installed. That's a prime example of being over-sensitive. I've learned to deal with most distractions, yet one I struggle with is shooting adjacent to someone who uses a magic potion gunpowder emitting a sickening odor. It's rare, but it does happen and I have to hold my breath until the foul cloud passes. The cure I found is not to shoot with that person. To minimize distractions, don't squad up with a troublesome fumbling distractive shooter. You can usually tell who they are. Professionals usually look professional, having a confident (and often a serious) demeanor radiating from them, and are usually surrounded by a small support group. But the better shooters are reclusive and not much observed between or after events. Of course these are generalizations, yet they tend to ring true. If you have an extremely disruptive shooter on your squad change squads. You pay good money to shoot and you deserve an equal opportunity to win.

MORE CONFIDENCE-BUSTING DISTRACTIONS
"If the sky falls, hold up your hands."

Reloads. If you shoot them, ensure they are reliable. You can't have confidence in junk loads and expect good scores. If you can afford to, shoot new ammunition. Maintain your gun. If it keeps jamming or breaking, fix it once and for all, or buy a new gun. A faulty gun will get you nowhere fast. Don't be the distracter! Often shooters don't realize they are the problem. An agonizingly slow setup can drive a squad nuts. Be courteous by insuring you 'blend in' with the squad. Believe it or not, as much as you disturb the squad, you are likely disturbing yourself even more. Why? A slow setup = a reduction in concentration intensity. If your shells misfire or 'bloop' it's hurting your scores by detracting your concentration from the targets. There are shooters out there who intentionally disrupt adjacent shooters reasoning they can get the edge on them. This works only because other squad members 'allow' the disruptions to needle them. Self-control and full concentration are vital. You pay good money to shoot, so shoot. If a shooter is totally out of line and can't be tolerated, you can pull out of the squad after getting clearance from the field captain, or have the shooter removed. I've learned long ago to just play my own game and ignore everything else (except offensive gunpowder odors, but I'll still finish the event, then switch squads later).

Distractions wreck mood, and once mood is altered the game is over, unless you cancel out the negative thoughts. It's difficult to learn. One way to overcome distractions is to shoot a practice round with new shooters, or a shooter known to be disruptive and sloppy. It's a challenge, and it will educate as well as prepare you for disturbances in competition. It's no secret subtle disruptive tactics are used in shootoffs by some shooters. If you keep trying to avoid disruptions, I guarantee you'll get more than you deserve, or at least it will appear this way on account of you being sensitized to them. Not good for a trapshooter. Sensitivity must be unlearned. The best way is to ignore disruptions -- focus on total concentration and confidence in your technique. Learn to desensitize yourself to disruptions... they will always endure, so why fight it? You can run, but you can't hide. You can coexist with distractions if you practice and put your mind to it. So, folks, shooting practice sessions with the unskilled can benefit you, as they surely will force you to concentrate ever more. Family and close friends shouldn't shoot together on the same squad, as it sets up distractions, worry, and apprehensions which deviate your concentration away from the targets. For the same reasons, it is often difficult for a parent to teach a family member to shoot. These are deep psychological stumbling blocks. There are exemptions, but they are rare. Don't confuse this with appropriate squad building. It is an advantage to shoot with shooters who break the targets in the same zone, move and react to situations predictably. Shooters who you feel comfortable with will generally produce consistent shooting and high scores. Just don't fall into a habit of shooting with certain people to shoot well.

SIFTING GOLD FROM MAGNETITE
"Do not remove a fly from a friend's forehead with a hatchet."

It's not an absolute necessity to procure lessons to learn trap after you have educated yourself to sound fundamentals. Though it is difficult to undo bad habits, they can be erased. You can step on line shooting away as long as you are _learning_ something each time you shoot. If you shoot and don't come home with a new idea, you are merely having fun and not truly learning anything. Often, new ideas will come from family, friends, and gun club members. How do you know what works or won't work if you don't try it? When gold panning, a miner must sift through a ton of black sand before locating tiny flakes of gold. That is what you'll have to do if you don't have a competent instructor. A lot of trial and error. Even with a coach, there will be many trials and errors. Everyone is unique. Copy a pro's style of shooting. Try it. If it works, go for it. If it doesn't, it's time to modify the technique to your liking, or try something else that may work. There are no set rules on style, form or system; you can borrow ideas from professionals and incorporate them into your style.

Don't expect to try something just once, twice, twenty, or a hundred times to see if it works or not. Give it at least 500 to 1,000 targets, then note if something, anything, has improved. If it doesn't work, then be disposed to explain to yourself and others exactly <u>why</u> it didn't work. To just say, *"I tried it, it doesn't work,"* or *"It feels uncomfortable"* is not learning anything, it's just wasted time and ammunition and missing the train. It is laziness to do less and clearly to your disadvantage. You know you're on the right track when you can say with certainty why something didn't work. Quite a large number of shooters simply guess as to why something didn't work or make up a story for an excuse for not positively knowing what is wrong. **Example**: You try a new foot stance and you still drop too many targets. You 'discover' the gun tends to resist extending to left targets due to muscle tension in the arm, shoulder, knee, or whatever. **Example**: You try a new gun mounting position and realize your head and eye alignment to the angling target is cocked sideways giving you a false sight picture. See Fig. 11-10. It's okay to know what is wrong, but never dwell on it. It's better to know what is right than what is wrong! Imprint in your mind what smokes targets, not what misses them. The most important aspect is to learn a solid foundation of proven concepts. Video tapes and trapshooting books can teach you the basics of foot position/stance, gun hold, mount, and then some. If you are a veteran wing shooter who tries his hand at trap just to keep polished, then you have no need of any book, video tape or coach that teaches trapshooting. You need a hunting book or magazine. If you wish to be a trapshooter, you may need, at one time or another, formal instructions. Be particular to acquire guidance from a reliable source who fully understands the sport. This does not mean the instructor must be a superior shooter as long as the coach knows his stuff, has sound advice, and has helped others improve scores this may be all you need. I'm assured Evander Hollyfield's coach can't box as well as Evander can! Good advice is always good advice.

Ironically, experimentation means your scores will degenerate before they accelerate. Never judge a new technique on account of your scores dropping. Work on the approach, often for a few months before you can say it works or not. Just changing your tone of voice when calling for the target can induce targets to slip by. So, if a blip this minuscule has such powerful adverse effects, imagine what a new gun mounting or gun swing style could do to your scores. Never be too quick to judge and always be disposed to try new things. One day you'll be glad you did. Experimentation is critical if you wish to be a competitive trapshooter. You can't just pick up a shotgun, play the game, and consider no improvement needed. You may need to alter your style of shooting, perhaps a half dozen times, or more, before you find the right technique for you. Change fuels progression. Without change there can be no progress. Above all, keep an open mind. Be flexible. Listen and learn. Experiment and practice with a purpose. Set personal goals. Feel good about yourself, no matter who tells you not to deviate from a stale shooting technique, if improvement is needed. Remember, only you can make good things happen. If you like a certain method, you can make it work for you. It's okay to pilfer styles from professionals. They have no copyright or trademark to protect, and the fact is, they too borrowed ideas and knowledge from other shooters. If you are not adopting ideas and techniques from the professionals, your shooting will lag and linger, and it will take you a wee too many years to achieve proficiency. Imagine stepping into a nitro-burning funny car without instructions. Would you surely have a chance to win? Or stepping up to bat with the Red Sox? How many home runs or even base hits for that matter could you make? Would you dare step into the boxing ring with, Tyson? Winners work hard to be winners. Even so, boxers receive numerous shiners and lose many fights before they glow as professionals.

HIT AND MISS AND SLUMPS
"In the middle of difficulty lies opportunity!"

Within the first three months of weekend shooting you have already hit every angle coming out of the traphouse a multitude of times. So why do you still miss targets? Get accustomed to it, for even the pros miss targets, just not as many. When you miss a target you have experience hitting many times before, don't even think about it. If you dwell on it, you will miss again. The apprehension of missing targets causes missed targets! How often have you witnessed a squad shooting and someone misses a target then surprisingly everyone thereafter misses too? It's a subconscious phenomenon, the copycat syndrome immediately stirs apprehension in each squad member distracting their focus and concentration and the targets slip into the sky. The subconscious mind knows how to duplicate what it sees! The missed targets stop when someone hits the target. Another reason why pros prefer to shoot with pros. When someone misses a target on your squad, you shouldn't think about it. Tell yourself, *"I'm going to smokeball it."* Visualize breaking the target just before you call. If you do miss, evaluate your setup, don't deviate from the plan, just keep shooting. Of course, if wind conditions exists, you may have to deviate, but don't experiment in competition. Let your natural skill and talent go to work for you. Practice sessions are the proper place for analysis corrections. Competition is where you put all you've learned into automatic pilot.

To examine why targets are missed is much too complex for any book or video tape to fully explore. There are way too many variables, however, there is one golden rule to remember. If you miss targets, you are doing something very elementary that is wrong and easy to correct and you'll likely find something is wrong in the setup. If you slide into a slump, test fire your gun at a pattern board to insure it is shooting straight. If the gun is okay, then the problem is with you know who! When you are in a slump it is on account of your subconscious mind having convinced you (or you convinced it) you are in a decline. Or you have developed a fatal habit you are unaware of. You may likely be playing goose (lifting your head) or even losing basic eye / hand coordination, shooting behind or rushing the target shooting too fast. Confidence needs to be rebuilt. Have someone inspect your shooting to survey the problem. If your fundamentals are okay, then it's time to run a box of shells on each station to reestablish swing, sight picture, trigger control, timing, and visual focus to reactivate your winning streak. This system of staying on a station works! Try it. Like a guitarist trying to perfect a lead line for a concert, he must rehearse the lick repetitively until it sinks into his subconscious mind. Go back to the basics and practice your performance on each station until you achieve perfection. Shooting a round of trap, five shots on each post, just won't cut you out of a slump, it'll likely perpetuate the circle of confusion.

If this still fails, then explore in-depth to unwrap the riddle. It could be as simple as having your eyes examined with corrective lenses prescribed, replace worn shoes or vest, or it could be mood alterations (i.e., mild depression.) Despondency can build when you are not shooting well and becomes unstoppable as more targets are missed. This doesn't mean you'll need antidepressive medicine, it simply means you should change your disposition toward shooting, setting realistic, modest obtainable goals. Remind yourself you are a good shooter, you can hit targets, and you have wins under your belt. Often, a slump is caused by other factors. Money or family problems. These are not so easy to solve on the firing line. If the slump continues, why suffer? Seek counseling from a sports psychologist if need be. If it helps you gain self-confidence, then it's an endeavor of wisdom.

Remember, shooting must contain elements of enjoyment. If you are getting too serious too fast, a slump will materialize. Excessive shooting can induce a slump, too. Take a break from shooting. Pull or score for others. You'll detect you are not the solitary one who misses targets. You will burn out if you don't relax and enjoy the sport. This is the critical time when shooters wrongly assume they need a new gun. The bad workman always blames his tools. Our success or failure is determined not by what we have to work with but by how we employ what we have. The problem is not the gun, it is the person behind the gun. The time to buy a new gun is when you are shooting at your finest and the gun doesn't have a steep learning curve, buy it. Never blame your gun for bad scores. It's like blaming the victim for being robbed by a criminal. To deter you from buying a new gun, assume the used gun you want to buy no longer has any 100-straights left in it, that's why the guy is selling it. This parallelism makes as much sense as needing to buy 'one more' gun to aggrandize scores.

Slumps can be expected. You are not a machine. Errors of misjudgment will occur. Some say you should shoot yourself out of a slump by practicing until it hurts. Others say take a break for a couple weeks and do something else and you'll come back with a new perspective and with less apprehension. Whichever works for you is fine, but remember one thing... when you do practice, don't practice to excess. One hundred rounds of quality practice is better than 300 rounds of just shooting and hoping whatever you were doing wrong will sprout wings and fly away. You should discipline yourself to quit practicing long before you hit the wall. If you push beyond the comfort zone, fatigue arises, the eyes and mind shift to idle. False sight pictures imprint into your mind <u>canceling</u> whatever you have learned when you began the practice session. You know what happened? You wasted an opportunity to learn something, and a stack of money and ammo to boot. Observe any talented actor or musician in rehearsals or athletes in practice sessions and watch the goof-ups when they go beyond the comfort zone into physical / mental exhaustion. It's time to cut the action and lower the curtains and take scene two tomorrow. It's reckless to try to go past your comfort zone when trying to learn anything. It will set you back further and keep you in a slump, the harder you try to pull out of it. A slump can be like being captured by gravity with no hope of release. Don't fight it. Like being caught in an ocean undertow or falling in quicksand, the more you struggle the more energy you expend with disastrous results. Slumps can be resolved with patience and quality practice sessions.

Endurance is an entirely different scenario and should not be confused with a slump. A slump is basically a tired mind and very often a confused subconscious mind. Endurance is the ability to shoot for long periods of time without losing focus while maintaining physical strength. When you reach your limits of endurance, a slump occurs and missed targets become habitual. This is a temporary situation, whereas a true slump is like forgetting how to shoot targets... this is exactly what is happening too! No matter what you do, the missed targets just keep resurfacing, even with a positive attitude in your mind, the targets persistently slip away. For corrective tips on missing targets refer to Fig. 7-2 'Missed Target Chart'.

STEPS TO BREAK A SLUMP
"Where there is a will there is a way."

Slump = Serious Losing Unforgiving Mind Pressure. Slumps originate in the mind, triggered by flaws in foot position/stance and swing, shooting technique, mind-set, vision, gun fit, timing and POI. You know you're in a slump when you suddenly forget how to hit targets. It usually strikes not the novice, but highly accomplished shooters, and then one day without warning, whammo! You can't hit anything, you lose the sight pictures, lose your timing, confusion sets in and you're scratching your head wondering what happened. The shooter's first remedy is to fiddle with various shell and choke settings, but the slump persists. What can you do to break free of a slump? Try these suggestions:

1. Don't permanently quit shooting. Never believe you don't have the talent as talent can be learned. Never become discouraged with yourself. We all have good and bad days. (In the day of prosperity there is a forgetfulness of affliction, and in the day of affliction there is no more remembrance of prosperity). There is always someone out there who can shoot so well he/she could break targets with a shovel on any given day. Accept the fact you are not a 'machine' and will make mistakes, and there will always be someone who can play better. Tomorrow may be your day to pick up the shovel.
2. Take a break for a week or two. Distance your mind from the game. A good time to clean your gun, tune up trigger, etc., to prepare for the next registered shoot. There's no substitute for relaxation and no rest for the weary. If you can't get away from the gun club, then watch other shooters missing targets and evaluate why they slipped. You can learn from watching others' mistakes. You may be doing the same thing.
3. If the slump is serious, or you simply just keep missing targets here and there, shoot impulsively by speeding up your shooting, trying to break the target the moment it emerges from the traphouse. It's fast and furious and

reckless, yet it works! When you go back to your natural timing, the targets appear to be moving much slower and you'll be more relaxed. It breaks slumps! See "Snap Shooting."

4. Try an entirely new shooting system that makes sense to you. Watch a professional shooter and mimic some of his / her techniques in your style. Your scores will fall apart for at least 2 months, or more, but if the approach makes sense, it's well worth the time and strain to incorporate styles. Slumps can be caused by improper fundamentals and technique. Employing a new style of shooting rejuvenates the subconscious mind, erasing the old bad habits by replacing deficiency with new knowledge.

5. A coach can help you bust out of a slump. You are likely clutched in a groove and can't escape on your own. Attending a shooting clinic can help. Some mistakes we can't see, others we can. When you find yourself plunging into a prolonged slouch, it's time to get an instructor, at the least, someone who shoots better than you or anyone who has the unique capability to see what you are doing wrong. A trapshooting instructional videotape may help. Ask a friend to watch you shoot to see what you are doing wrong. Often, you'll have to figure it out for yourself especially if it's a timing / POI problem or you have a very knowledgeable coach.

6. Often just pure laziness induces slumps. Have you forgotten how to truly focus on the target? You may be seeing the target but truly not focusing upon it. When you see a target, it's just a target. When you focus the target appears illuminated, definitive, and lively. Try casually glancing at a flower, then really focus on it and you will see details. Do the same with a seagull or crow and you will know the difference between seeing and looking (focusing) on targets. All you should see is the flower or the bird or the target. You won't see any background. Learn to focus, not just see the target. Know where to focus on the target (top, middle or bottom, leading edge) as you are likely looking in the wrong place. See Fig. 11-4, Fig. 11-11, Fig. 11-12 and Fig. 11-14.

7. Recheck the point of impact on your gun. Know where it is shooting! The POI may have changed due to a bent barrel, dislodged sight bead, loose stock or sight rib and even the choke you replaced, or a hot barrel may be altering the point of impact. Changing the color of your sight beads may help. Shooting glasses with the proper tint may be all it takes to break the slump. Check your recoil pad and your vest pad for compression or wear. A compressed recoil pad will alter the gun's length of pull.

8. As silly as it may seem, get a lucky charm. It may be a new pair of shooting gloves, hat, shoes, vest, belt buckle, choke tubes, or whatever. It usually always works, and most shooter have one whether they know it or not. And even if they did, would they admit it? Look around and you'll see more lucky gadgets than you assumed ever existed.

9. It's time to do a recoil check. More missed targets are due to recoil flinching than shooters wish to believe. If the gun slams into your face when firing, the gun doesn't fit you, maybe the comb's contour doesn't conform to your facial structure. Discomfort in shoulder? Gun may not fit or recoil device is needed. Are you absolutely positive, without doubt, your gun fits you? Have you seen a stock fitter? You may be shooting your gun for five years and discover the gun doesn't fit you at all. No wonder targets fly away! Too many shooters are shooting guns that do not fit them. Don't be one of them. An improperly fitted gun will develop flinches, slumps, and inconsistency amidst disastrous scores.

10. Have you perceivably lost contact with your internal time clock? Are you shooting faster or slower? It's time to re-test and find out if you are still in synchronization.

11. Are you fiddling with your foot positions? Gun mount? Worrying about something prior to your turn to shoot? These tiny distraction can put you into a tailspin slump. You know how to shoot, so stop fiddling around and get back to the business of shooting.

12. Have you lost confidence? Reasonably so. Slumps have the propensity to self-inflict feelings of incompetence, insecurity and doubt. Rebuild your self-assuredness. You may have to rebuild self-confidence by shooting a box of shells on each station to reconstruct sight pictures and body moves in your mind.

13. Wear blinders to eliminate damaging peripheral vision. It helps isolate you from others. When you are not shooting well, you may grow self-conscience feeling others are watching. Blinders help dissolve these emotions. Wear a hat with a flat visor to help your eyes to focus forward and keep sunlight from refracting images within shooting glasses' lenses. Your subconscious mind will see these intrusions! You can see them, too, if you look hard; you will see reflected images imprinted on the lenses. Your brain's optical network kicks into overdrive, trying to filter out these rogue images. Mind clutter, fatigue, and a slump can materialize. The more fine-tuned you become, the more sensitive you will be to these tiny variations that to the novice seem unimportant and trivial.

You want to wear a hat and blinders to reduce peripheral vision intrusions, shade eyes from glare and increase focal concentration. Ignore this and targets will slip past the gun's muzzle all too frequently.

14. Have your eyes examined. Your vision may have changed. You may wish to try tinted shooting glasses to highlight the targets and subdue background intrusions.

15. Develop an aggressive call and one that is louder. You could be getting slow pulls and not recognizing your call is too soft to be heard, critically ever more important for those shooting the backfence (27 yard line). Once the target and your timing is out of synchronization, say good-bye to a smoked target. It's gone. Practice shooting at slow pulls, let target escape the zone then go after it. Practice turning targets down too!

16. You may have reached a peak where a transformation in shooting style is now required. It is possible to outgrow a technique to the point your mind rebels, screaming for change. Boredom is a killer that can cripple the mind. It's time to progress. Remember, if you don't learn something when you shoot, laziness sets in and so will poor scores. A new style of shooting could take you to the next level of proficiency.

17. You could be suffering from mild depression and not realize it. A good therapy is to do something else for a while, go bowling, surfing, work around the house, anything but shooting. Award yourself a break, time out to relax. Most of all, insure you are getting restful sleep and are not vitamin deficient.

18. Don't drink alcohol or party with the squad. You'll have fun until you step on station to shoot. A depressant is the atheist of alertness. A sleeping pill would be preferable to alcohol. Nothing is better than all. Don't eat huge meals, as they induce sleepiness and complacency. Get a good night of sleep.

19. In a slump? Talk to a pro. They've been there before many times and pulled through.

20. Are your eyes switching focus? You may not be concentrating and your eye is wandering or not focusing on the target. You may be seeing the target, but not really focusing on it. Worse yet, are you cross-firing? If your eyes are switching or fighting each other as to which will dominate the gun's sight beads, then you may have to wink an eye to force proper alignment, shoot with one eye, or place tape on your shooting glasses lens. Often crossover develops when you are fatigued. Fatigue materializes long before you recognize symptoms. Know when to stop shooting. Crossover and lost targets can develop into a lingering habit if you keep shooting when wearied from excessive mental exertion.

21. Relax, relax, relax! Getting too anxious, pumping adrenaline, can compound a slump into a vicious circle of never-ending fear, you'll never break out of it. Strangely, the prophesy is fulfilled the harder you try to break out of a slump, which increases inner emotional hysteria levels. Remember, it is only a game and there will always be another day. Time heals all wounds. Today is never final! As tension increases, so will muscle rigidity and a plethora a psychological apprehensions, some of which instill feelings of embarrassment, dread and despair. Realize a slump may or may not be psychological, it could be caused by just one little slip-up in technique which unknowingly became habitual. Examples: head-lifting, eye focus, foot stance, posture, etc. Any one of these can gently creep into your game if you don't pay attention to details. Be alert to any changes in technique! The better shooter you are, the more finely tuned you become and inadvertently ever more sensitive to the slightest of deviations.

22. To break a mini-slump, when suddenly breaking easy targets become futile, try doing something different to break the psychological deadlock. Try holding the gun a bit lower or hold on the traphouse, take a deep breath (which enhances your eyes' ability to focus). Lowering the gun can help you see the target, and you'll begin breaking them again. Just a temporary diversionary nudge is all that is required. This may be simplistic, but the mind is ultra sensitive to dead-locking and such diversions stimulate the brain to awaken from its sleep. A slump can be associated with damaging self-hypnosis, where you relinquish control of your shooting. A war rages within between the conscience and subconscious minds, each rebelling against the other. To understand this, you can recognize this hypnotic trance when you become mentally exhausted and can't shoot anymore. You want to continue, but your brain rebels, slowing all your muscles down, unfocusing your eyes and weakening your attention span. It's real. It exists. It is powerful. Knowing it exists and recognizing it when it happens is the first step to the cure. And the cure is easy... find a quiet place, lay down, take a nap or rest.

23. Another slump many shooters experience is so insidious it defies all methods of detection and cure. Why? Because it reveals no symptoms except for the slump itself. Everything you try simply fails. It strikes unexpectedly and very often during registered competition. You feel no pain, nevertheless you know something is wrong, for your mood has dipped for some unknown reason. You may even feel a bit on the upside, yet deep

inside your mind you still sense something is ajar. Its called the 'Silent Headache'. We all get them, but most do not realize it, owing to there are no conspicuous symptoms! Take just one buffered aspirin or acetaminophen and watch what happens... the silent headache disappears and the scores once again rise. That "something's wrong" feeling vanishes. (Don't take on an empty stomach or if you've had more than three alcoholic beverages.)

24. Slumps can be caused by a poor diet and a vitamin deficiency. It is always a good plan to take a vitamin pill each day when shooting. Stress consumes vitamins as a raging furnace burns fuel. Multivitamin supplements should be in your shell bag.

25. Physical conditioning helps break slumps, sometimes. It depends on your physiology and mental temperance. For some, pushups work and for others a nap under a cool shade tree. It is said he who is in superior physical shape wins. Somewhat true, but we've all seen unhealthy-looking people shoot like Annie Oakley in Buffalo Bill's Wild West and the Congress of Rough Riders Show. A healthier physical condition never hurts. Evaluate any recent health concerns to determine adverse affects on your shooting.

26. Unreasonable goals create terrible slumps. The goal to excel at all costs places too much emotional pressure to bear and the mind can't handle the overload. This is often caused by seeing an All-American shoot, and the desire becomes so strong to be 'that good' a crash-course mentality sets in. Never gauge yourself against shooters who have busted 20,000 registered targets a year for the last 35 years! Realize it takes a few years to become proficient in anything and everything you do. How long did it take you to learn your profession? Why be in a hurry anyway? Competitive shooting still must retain the element of fun, otherwise it becomes just another job. Simplify your plan for progress. Take time to be a skillful shooter, not a hasty one. Learn slowly. Like get rich quick schemes, crash courses never work. It's the old tortoise and the hare fable. The swift don't always finish first.

27. Here's one for you to ponder. A slump can be caused by refusing to believe you can break targets. It can paralyze the subconscious mind. You don't go on the line saying, *"I'm going to try to break them all."* You go out there with a fearless attitude, *"I can break every target that comes out of this house."* You know you can for you have done so many times. Every angle you have broken clean. So what's the problem? Self-doubt sets in, apprehension, counting the remaining targets left, wondering if you can break the last few targets, thinking too much on everything but shooting! That's what you are doing. Stop thinking. Stop tormenting yourself. Just shoot that one target, one-at-a-time. This is all you need to do. You should learn to wipe out all emotions and thoughts not associated with the business of shooting. If you don't? Expect more slumps and inconsistencies in scores. Believe. Have faith in your technique and your abilities. It is the recipe for victory, for faith is the link that overcomes our weakness.

28. Treat a slump for what it really is... it's you missing the dog-goned target, that's all it is! It's your attitude, moods and feelings dispatching deep-seated fears of missing and smashing your ego like gold ore in a stamp mill. Terror is silently consuming your mind. If you encounter this too often, then quit shooting! What I mean by quit is to discontinue fearing the target when shooting. Be aggressive, for that belligerent target will have no compassionate mercy on you if you don't get him first! It's total war out there.

29. Oftentimes, slumps are directly linked to eye focus. The eye and mind can develop a case of dullness. Try shooting sporting clays or continental trap. It's good eye training and a diversion may be all you needed. Pinball and video games do increase eye / hand coordination, highly focused central vision, fierce concentration, competition skills, quick mental-reflex training. They help build rapid and precise trigger control and eye focus training and will tune-up reflexive nerves. Shooting sporting clays targets will also build rapid eye focus.

30. Perhaps the sights on your gun need cleaning? Gun patterned-checked for accuracy? Changing the color of your sights may enhance seeing the bird / bead relationship. An experimental dab of paint will do. Red, blue or green for orange targets. Orange or gold for green or white targets. White for all colored targets. Contrast helps align bead to target. If you replace sights, don't use 'permanent' thread locking compound, as replacement later will require drilling to remove and may ruin the gun's rib.

31. Think back when the slump occurred. Did you alter settings on your gun? A new vest, hat, shoes that don't fit properly? Substitute powder, wad or shot in reloads? Change chokes or ammunition velocity? Rib, stock, POI changed?

32. Develop a winning attitude... expect to win. Losers know they will lose and usually do. A detrimental frame of mind will impose a handicap on you before the first target is launched.

33. Have you stopped learning? Only through experimentation of differing techniques is improvement made. If you're shooting same-o, same-o, odds are you're in a rut, the learning process has ceased and so have scores.

34. Check those shoes! Is your balance secure and solidly stable? Is body weight equally distributed to the middle of both feet? Close your eyes to test balance. (See "If the Shoe Fits").

35. Examine the condition of recoil pad, vest pad, vision prescriptions, weight gain or loss. You are susceptible to performance deterioration as equipment wears thin and as your body ages or changes. As you can ascertain, all the practice in the world will never compensate for worn shoes or other impaired conditions.

36. Are you shooting within your zone? Are you letting targets escape beyond the zone? Are you focusing on the target properly (top, middle or bottom, leading edge)? Fast shooting dissolves many problems.

37. Did you make adjustments on your gun? You may have to shoot 500 to as many as 1,000 targets between adjustments to see if variations are effective. Go easy whenever any settings are made. The less alterations you make the better, but don't be timid to make adjustments to insure the gun fits you and shoots where you look. It will require 5,000 to 10,000 targets to acclimate to a new gun. So think twice before buying a gun to improve your scores.

38. Recoil induces slumps by creating mini-flinches. Check gun fit, as something is wrong.

39. Are you pushing the gun with your arm to the target? You need to use your upper body and shoulders, not the arm. Put Body English back into your swing. Pivot by the hips. Pushing or shoving the gun with hand/arm destabilizes the gun for inconsistent pointing -- a common error, often unrecognized after an unexpected low score is posted.

40. Is the muzzle swinging over the top of hard-angled targets? Faulty foot position will always upset stance causing muzzle to rise (in some cases drop) on the swing. Insure position/stance posture is correct for each post. Stance is aligned to the angle targets without restricting movement to the straighter targets.

41. Refer to Fig. 7-3 'Slump Chart & Equipment Checklist' and Fig. 4-4 and 7-2.

42. See Fig. 11-16 and 11-17 to learn how to shoot off the end of the gun. This is an advanced form of shooting but it won't hurt to begin to get some exposure to it. See *"Precision Shooting"* at end of this book.

You will pull through a slump if you take curative action to pull out. A slump is often a learned habit, which is why they appear to be prolonged in nature. It is a subconscious experience revealing flaws in technique and temperament. You can't shoot your way out of a slump. You have to stop and think about it and use diversionary tactics. Laziness and complacency are the cause of many slumps. Once learned, it is hard to break. It's like learning to shoot all over again. You must investigate and sift out everything from foot position/stance, gun mount, eye focus, call tone, the whole shebang. Leave no stone unturned. Often the root cause is something foundational and rudimentary in technique, usually found in the setup. Place suspicion on the mind and eye, and don't think when shooting. You contemplate when on station as part of the setup. When it comes time to shoot, shoot! Shoot within your natural time clock, within the zone of accuracy. The slower you shoot (out of the zone of accuracy) the more problems will develop and the odds of hitting the target diminish. Perhaps it is time to readjust to your internal time clock. You may be getting to be a better shooter and not even know it, but your eye and mind are impressing you to slow down, when in reality you should be speeding up! The converse can also be true, conceivably you shoot too rapidly and could slow down a wee bit. A final word of cheer... slumps do vanish in time. You are not alone. We all get them.

SLUMP-BUSTING LOGIC
"Apathy: the disease nobody cares about."

Instead of moving directly from a goal to a solution, the mind searches in numerous directions to encounter confusion. It avoids solving problems. You can't escape a slump if you are overwhelmed. Start with the basic setup, examine each phase 'slowly'. Any problems recognized write down on a 3 by 5 index card in logical order. Putting problems on paper allows you to gain perspective and compile a reminder checklist. Progress now begins as the list relieves a whirlwind of unrecognized confusion and accompanying weight of emotions. Refer to the list at practice. Now you can discover practical solutions, which are often far easier solved than you imagined. Slumps frequently originate in the mind. This checklist communicates with the subconscious and conscience mind.

Memorization alone doesn't work. Use the list to help you visualize intellective impressions! As new problems develop, compile another list. Work on each item until it is ingrained, printed into harmonious habit.

Likely, deep problems are the cause of slumps, and it's frequently 'resisting change'. Discipline is required and without it you won't find success. Discipline is a commitment to pursue a plan of action from conception to completion. The checklist is a plan and will insure enthusiasm while canceling distraction, procrastination, doubt and confusion from your plan. Attention to details is imperative to get where you want to be. Shooters with less talent often win by virtue of having something else that more than made up for talent... they had discipline, commitment and the ability to persevere. They have skill! You'll never improve as long as you keep doing what you've always been doing. If you don't do things differently than the way you've always been doing, you'll have nothingness in the future to look forward to. Change creates excellence. Few people can change without a swift kick you-know-where, even if they are falling off track and scores are appalling. They rely on past successes; *"I used to be able to shoot better."* Today is today. Yesterday's history. Astronauts don't use rear view mirrors. Shooters outgrow style, form and routine, yet refuse to transform with growth, giving birth to slumps. *"Hey, I've fallen down and I can't get up!"* To get back on the right track, brainwash yourself with positive thinking; *"I know I can learn new things and regain my shooting skills."* Or, *"I'm good, and getting better each month."* Simple phrases with powerful mind forces. A little pat on the back can go the distance in trapshooting. Trapshooters need big feet, big hands, a short neck and a big head. Understand the entanglements of the mind. Know it is powerfully receptive to autosuggestion. To be good, you need to know you are! Learning and relearning requires serious effort, but you'll see enrichment with advancing scores. Don't fret or worry. By the time you are finished with this book you'll be one heck of a trapshooter to deal with, or very close to it. Believe me, your scores are going to rise and trapshooting is going to be a lot more fun too.

IF THE SHOE FITS
"Only the wearer knows where the shoe pinches."

Poor scores? Examine your shoes. If heels are worn, the physical foundation of your setup is radically off kilter, creating unstable balance control. You'll be shifting weight from heel-to-toe and side-to-side when swinging the gun. It'll have a similar effect as someone grabbing you from behind, yanking on your belt as you shoot. Amazingly, you'll notice more than a few tournament shooters overlooking this critical basement footing which can demolish years of technique all because of a worn or improper shoe. Wear new shoes or shoes in like-new condition. What sort of shoe should you wear? Anything comfortable is the rule; however, unventilated sneakers that cause your feet to overheat, swell, or direct strain on your back will adversely affect your game. Comfort is a prerequisite for good shooting. The slightest discomfort or pain will divert your mind away from the game and lost targets will occur. A good shooting shoe should have flat soles with solid arch support especially when shooting in the wind, to maintain solid footing and balance. Shoes that work well are quality running or walking shoes. Cowboy boots are fine, but check the heels often as they tend to wear quickly. If the heel is too high, it'll create instability, placing too much weight on the toes, stability deteriorates more so shooting on windy days.

Running shoes are inappropriate, as design entails a repetitive heel-to-toe action and no side-to-side motion. Tennis and basketball shoes share some common traits and are more suitable for trapshooting, as both have support built-in for stability in forward, reverse, and side-to-side activity. You will feel more comfortable, maintain proper balance, securing a firm foundation for your setup and stance. Regardless of the shoe you wear, comfort and stability combined with consistency is important. Switching shoes can alter your setup. If the shoe doesn't fit, scores will dip. Little attention is given to footwear by trapshooters, yet in every sport, shoes play a vital role -- golf, tennis, baseball, boxing, bowling, etc. Wearing a boot with ankle support is a viable alternative to a lightweight sports shoe. Just be certain the sole is flat, and not excessively rounded on the toe or heel. Stable support is vital to maintain accurate swing moves to the target. It is also critical for your good health not to place unnecessary strain and discomfort on your back. To test your weight distribution on both feet, close your eyes! By closing your eyes you are more able to analyze your weight distribution on your feet than if your eyes are open. Perform this test as you test-swing your gun next time you are on station.

Be aware of subtle changes which gradually degenerate your shooting. A shoe wears slowly, but wear it will, whittling away your scores over time, creating an elusive, yet insidious slump. The same holds true of your gun's recoil pad, vest pad, eye prescription changes, clothing thickness, weight gain or loss that alters gun fit. All these factors can seriously affect your shooting. Now take a look at the condition of the pros' shoes and their equipment, then compare with those who lose the shoots. You'll get the idea. Don't let the obvious bite you on the nose. If you're losing your magic touch, check those shoes!

MYTHS
"Man's mind is so formed it is far more susceptible to falsehood than to truth." Desiderius Erasmus (1509)

The sport has multifarious fables and flight of fancy tales. Everyone has opinions to share, by reason of they read it or were told by someone else. The lone real truth to believe is, *"Get behind your gun, perfect your technique, think positive, focus, and shoot to win."* Most everything else is hyperbole. You can read and practice all you wish about trapshooting, but only you can make the achievements. Some say you must have natural talent to be a good shooter. It helps, as in all endeavors in life, but trapshooting is a sport that can be learned. Professionals have been shooting relentlessly for many years, exploding tens of thousands of targets yearly. Go easy on yourself. There are five levels of proficiency: novice, apprentice, journeyman, craftsman and artist. Every top shooter was once at your level of expertise today. It requires devotion and the passage of time to achieve anything worthwhile. Can you bowl ten strikes every time? How many people do you know can? How many golfers you know can drive a hole-in-one once a month? Can a baseball hero hit a home-run all of the time? Do Hall of Fame trapshooters miss targets? Get the picture?

Believe nothing that you hear and half what you see. Optimum sources of information are directly with the manufacturers and professional trapshooters. Nothing is stopping you from writing industry customer service departments to get the lowdown on the information you need. You will be told good-hearted fables by shooters: you need an expensive gun, you need forcing cones lengthened, you need back-bored barrels, you need... All you truly need is a reliable trap gun that fits you, quality ammunition and a shooting system that works for you. Take any studio musician, say, a drummer, sit him behind a set of trash drums and he'll still play well and transform inferior drums to timbre quite decently too. Same is true with trapshooting. A good trapshooter with a wicked gun will still break more targets than someone with an exalted gun with less ability. Superior equipment can impart a slight edge, though only after you have experience behind you. How often have you seen shooters trade up to high-priced guns only to discover they can't shoot them? It's not the manufacturer's fault the shooter did not order the 'correct' gun with the 'exact' point of impact, trigger, stock and rib settings. The high-end market guns are really custom made machines... that's how you buy them. Be aware exorbitantly priced guns have very little technological improvements over quality, economical trap guns. I'm not unduly biased, it's a fact of life.

Another sophism is you don't aim a shotgun, you point it. Yes and no. Somewhat so in wing shooting, not in trap. Anyone who just points a shotgun at a 4-inch target <u>hundreds</u> of times is bound to miss many targets. The sights are important and you should use them, not like rifle aiming but for sight picture reference. After years of shooting, the shooter doesn't even realize he is using the sights. That's why they say just point the gun. What they literally mean is when your gun shoots where you are looking, you know you got it right. The sights retain a ghost-like appearance as the eye remains focused on the target. When the proper sight picture is seen in the 'minds eye' the trigger is pulled. To discern if I'm correct, the next guy that tells you to just point the gun without making a sight picture reference , check his gun. Are there sights on it? If so, he's using them, subconsciously. If not, the asphalt cowboy is a great shooter... take lessons from him.

CHAPTER 8

EYE FOCUS

"In the vast sea of nothing, you can see for miles."

A secret to hitting targets is where to focus your eye before you call *"Pull"*. You shouldn't be looking out into the trapfield or at the traphouse, but in between. Practice focusing your eye at a midway point between the traphouse and the field. If this is done correctly, you should be able to clearly see the edge of the traphouse and the field somewhere between the traphouse and the center field post. Try this. If your eye is focused properly, you won't see a comet trail or streak when the target emerges. It will appear as clear as a speeding object can be. It will appear well-defined. Another reason for focusing your eye just beyond the traphouse is in view of your eye adjusting readily from a target entering your zone of focus. It will help you acquire the target and its angle quickly. Just gazing or staring will cause the target's streak to get the jump on you and you'll react in haste, often not recognizing the target's angle. Your nervous system will be jolted and you'll become excited, a rush of adrenaline, and you won't be smooth to swing the gun, you may even flinch. This results in randomly chasing rabbits.

Study good shooters and you'll notice they take an extra quarter-second to focus the eye in a zone before they call. It may seem fast, but they all do it. When learning, it will take practice for you to learn to pause and focus. This means there should be a brief delay after you shoulder the gun. The delay may make ultra-fast rhythm shooters uncomfortable on your squad as you break the tempo a tad. Practice this before you attend registered shoots so you will be quick enough not to cause unnecessary delays. The delay, if rendered properly, will hardly be noticed as you mount the gun quickly and smoothly, delay to focus, and call. The delay is only 1/2 to 1 second duration after the gun is mounted. Remember not to take too much time, as concentration and muscle strength falls rapidly the moment you shoulder the gun. Watch the pros shoot and do what they do! When on station with gun mounted your eye should be focused from 1/3 to 1/2 out in front of the traphouse relative to the center stake. You should be prepared to acquire the meanest target angle from that station. See Fig. 4-2 (B) on where to focus eyes over the traphouse.

During eye focus, let energy within build as a battery or capacitor, call for the target with authority, focus intently on seeing the target, then unleash energy at its peak like an uncoiled spring. It's similar to a sine wave's rise and fall dynamism. This is recognizing and managing internal force. Everyone has this concentrated energy source though is often unrecognized and / or used without focus. It's difficult to explain, but you will feel it now you are aware of its existence. Martial Arts use this internal deep-concentration energy to smash bricks with bare hands, walk on coals, etc. The energy release should be focused to race right out the gun's barrel into the target, and through the eye's focus to the target. It's a blending of mind and matter. It's a real force which is often labeled deep concentration for a better description. If you pursue more aggression toward the target, you'll launch this powerful advocate.

The muzzle or sights should appear as a ghost, visible yet not well defined. When the target emerges, the gun barrel should not move, rise or drift until the target has passed into the eyes focus zone. By this time you should see the target pass by the barrel to judge its true angle, identify the flight path in which to track the target, then swing to it while your eye is zeroing-in on the target. This all takes place in microseconds and it takes intensive practice to learn. Often shooters are looking up in the sky for the target and wonder why they miss. If you don't see the target's true angle leaving the house, you will track a mirage... a target that appears to be where it is, but really isn't. You'll be lucky, but one or two targets or more will escape if you don't see the target leave the house passing by your gun barrel.

If you hold a high gun over the house, try holding the gun a bit lower than usual. You will see the flight angle of the target more accurately and be able to ride the track to the target easier with less lateral gun movement to catch the target. Try holding the gun on the house with the barrel just below the far edge of the traphouse. Here you can see the true angle as it passes by the barrel and rooftop of the traphouse. The higher you hold, the more severe the angle has already progressed and by the time you recognize it the arcing target has evolved dramatically. And there is another danger... a flipper or broken target can emerge hidden under the barrel in a blind spot, misleading you to shoot it. Ponder that for a spell! It's a good practice session to hold a low gun to see these angles. Later, you can go back to a high gun hold point if you prefer, raising the gun hold height in small increments. Now you know why 27 yard shooters are predisposed to hold a lower gun on the house than when shooting singles at 16 yard. It's not just timing as most reckon. In reality, it is target angle acquisition combined with timing, and seeing the true condition of the target as it leaves the house.

Once you focus your eye(s) at the proper depth of field, don't move your eye! You should call for the target immediately. If your eye moves, even within the focal point, billions of sensor messages in the eye flood the brain with information, and if the target emerges when the brain is processing this information, you will see a blurred target emerge from the house. By the time your eye readjusts, the target has the lead on you, the eye may lose focus as you react to chase the target. The nervous system gets a jolt and usually creates an improper or jittery move to the target. All this happens just because your eye moved! The cure? Practice your gun mount setup, eye focus, and call. The gun barrel, your eye, and your body should be still when you call for the target. A smooth and controlled setup is more important than shooting. After mounting the gun, a slight delay to focus the eye will help you see the target clearly. Each person's focusing time differs, but it shouldn't take longer than one second. Remember, this is a 'soft focus,' not an intense focus which produces eye strain.

Once the target leaves the house you'll need to focus not just on the target, but where to focus on the target. This is vitally important. A gun with a mild POI straight targets focusing on the bottom edge or middle of the target and works fine. Hard angles you may have to focus on the top leading edge. Guns with high POI straight targets focus may be an inch below. Hard angles you may need to focus on the bottom leading edge to compensate for shotstring rise, otherwise you'll shoot over the top. Every gun is unique, so you'll have to discover the proper sight picture on your own. When in doubt? Always remember that the gun may or may not be shooting where you are looking. Discover the proper place to break targets where the gun is shooting exactly where you are looking. This is called a zone. The higher the POI the gun has, the more critical it is to shoot within the zone. My Browning shoots a full pattern high at 40 yards. It doesn't shoot where I look at 40 yards, it's higher. So I have to shoot quickly and focus on the bottom edge of the targets or I'll shoot over them. If I shoot out of the zone, beyond the 40 yard point, I'll need to use a different sight picture. Understand the sight picture changes depending on distance of target, as shot speed is cut in half at 40 yards compared to 20 yards. To maintain one sight picture you need to shoot in that zone where the target breaks when you are looking at the target. High POI guns are devilish to learn how to shoot, as they are most accurate to your eye within a specific zone, designed to raise the shotstring at a certain yardage. At the 16 yard line the gun shoots relatively flat and you can aim right at the target, if you shoot quickly.

At the 27 yard you'll need to aim under or on the bottom leading edge of the target, because the shotstring is designated to rise higher relative to the increased distance. There is no formula here, it's all trial and error depending on your timing. The best all around POI setting is 80/20 (see Fig. 1-2). It shoots right where you are looking and compensates for target rise. The keys to remember: make sure the gun is shooting where you are looking and where you are looking the shotstring is present. Locate the zone of accuracy where the target breaks when you are looking at its proper leading edge (top, middle or bottom, see Fig. 11-4, Fig. 11-11, Fig. 11-12 and Fig. 11-14.) and practice shooting in that time zone and stay within that zone. Don't make the mistake of missing a target then getting too cautious by slowing down your shooting, letting targets escape the zone. Pounce on them! Be ready for the target when you call and get on it quickly. Timing is so important, as it confines the ideal zone you should be shooting in. Practice counting quickly when you call, "Pull, two, three" (fire on three). You'll be near the zone, now just find the sight picture and stay in that zone. When you leave the zone, that's when targets are missed. Watch shooters miss targets and you'll see they left the zone they normally shoot within, or they don't even have a zone to shoot in. Watch professional shooters and you'll see how tight their zone is and how fast they shoot. It's a proven method and a plan to break the targets. It builds consistency and develops synchronous eye focus on the target. You will hear shooters say not to shoot in a zone, but mostly, these are not professionals in the trap discipline. Skeet shooters shoot the zone, and sporting clays shooters try like the Dickens to identify a zone to shoot in if at all possible. *"Where is that target going to be, and where am I going to shoot it?"* Some trapshooters confuse zone shooting with snapshooting, yet both are completely different animals. Snap is shooting before the target enters your normal zone.

DOMINANT EYE
"One eye sees, the other feels."

Many shooters who are right-handed may be left-handed shooters and not even realize it. I am right handed in all things, so I shot right-handed. Then I discovered my dominant eye was my left eye, and I had to switch the gun to my left shoulder. The dominant eye dictates which shoulder the gun should be mounted to. It's a rule not to be ignored. It's not as cruel as you may think it is to switch over if you have to. Awkward at first, yes. But once you push past the initial discomfort and confusion you'll hit more targets as you are using your premium master eye for sighting the target. It is a good move to purchase a trap gun with adjustable stock and comb as it permits switching without expensive stock modifications. To test your eye for dominance see Fig. 8-1. Perform this test not once, but a few times over a one-week period to insure your eyes are stable and not playing tricks on you. Some shooters won't notice a difference and can shoot from either eye, but most will notice an eye shift in the test. The eye that does not shift is dominant. In my case it was my left eye.

If you are right-handed and your left eye is dominant you should switch over to left-handed shooting. If you can't do this for whatever reason, you can keep shooting right-handed by winking your left eye a smidgen to force focus to the right eye. It helps, but is not a substitute for shooting with the proper master eye. For those who switch, it has added benefits: you achieve superior accuracy, and your right hand holding the gun forearm has a heightened pointing ability. Right-handed people can point their right index finger at a target better than using the left hand. So, by using your left dominant eye in combination with your right hand to swing the gun you have an edge other right-handed shooters simply don't have. They have to use their left hand to point the gun.

Incredibly, I've heard shooters say left-handed shooters shoot left-handed because they are left-handed. Wrong. A left-handed person may very well be a right-handed shooter. It's the dominant eye which determines if you are a left or right-handed shooter. It has nothing to do with which hand you use to write, eat, or work. Let's assume you have been shooting for years and suddenly discover you are a left-hand shooter. You can do two things. Switch to left-handed or do nothing. Switching over is more valuable in the long run, as your scores will increase. It's no fun losing targets due to improper target sighting. The switch is made easier if you begin focusing attention on using your right hand to point the gun. Everything else then falls into place.

It requires patience and time to make the switch; however, you may be amazed how pleasant it is once you commit yourself to making it work. You are not learning to shoot all over again, so don't envision it will set you back to the days of rookie shooting. What you have learned remains with you in your mind, where shooting skill virtually takes place anyway. Nothing in your mind is being permanently altered. It is a temporary physical alteration. You'll be using muscles you haven't used before and your stance changes, but you still know how to shoot. It is just awkward, that's all it is when making the transition. Once you sense the basic feel of the new arrangement, the targets smoke even better than you did shooting right-handed. Your eye behind the sight will adjust automatically to the new switch in focus. If you find your right eye is crossing over, then "squint" or "wink" the right eye a little to push focus back to the left dominant eye. It requires a bit of practice, and most of all, determination to make it work. Your scores will temporarily drop, but this is the nature of the beast when switching technique. Initial discomfort is natural and to be expected.

I want to mention that to check your dominant eye, make certain you do so over an extended period of time -- many stockfitters and some gunsmiths can help you make further verifications. By simply standing and pointing your finger like a cowboy's quick-draw at the evaluator's nose, s/he can tell which eye is dominant. If your finger is pointed at your evaluator's right eye (evaluator's point of view) your right eye is dominant. Always seek advice from a professional as often as you can. We can't rely or trust our own evaluations, as we often can't see the errors we make... even in a mirror we can't see them. Like practicing mounting the gun to a mirror, you will make unconscious adjustments and end up with false information. Get that outside opinion from a shooting coach.

EYE CROSSOVER
"If only we could pull out our brains and use only our eyes."

It's nice to shoot with both eyes wide open, yet many can't due to severe eye crossover problems. Each eye randomly switches focus from one to the other. Some shooters use an opaque patch on the lens of shooting glasses to force the dominant eye to maintain focus along the sight plane of the gun's rib. It works, though some shooters find it distracting. A device that may help is the Nattrass Super Sight (800)-563-6185 elevated sight blades and bead (For a sight bead that glows and is only seen when the eye is looking down the rib, write to us for a brochure on the *Easy Hit* shotgun sight, or visit our web site.) Some shooters mount the gun then close one eye, call for the target and maintain this one-eye shooting until the target is broken. This will induce eye strain on the dominant eye and create 'lazy eye' symptoms as the eye muscles fatigue and focus is lost. An improved method is to keep both eyes open, call for the target, then slightly squint the opposite eye. This forces the dominant eye to maintain sight bead / rib alignment. A one-eye shooter should do the same, as he can now hold the gun over the traphouse (if desired) just as a two-eye shooter can and see the target emerge from the traphouse.

When squinting any eye, make sure you don't squint the sighting eye! This causes a change of focus, a reduction of light transmission to the eye and accentuates eye fatigue. The most effective way to reduce eye crossover is to shoot quickly. The less you swing the gun, crossover diminishes. One shooter I met claimed his eyes were crossing-over. I told him to try the 'winking' technique and I was told, *"No way, I don't want my eyes moving."* Another shooter had the same problem, tried 'winking' and popped 25 straight. The other guy is still trying to resolve his eye crossover problem by refusing to try a new style. Stubbornness and inflexibility are the enemies. Euclid once told the king of Egypt, *"There is no royal road to learning."* People prepare a smooth path for a king to move on, but no one can make it easy for a king or anyone else to learn. If we wish to learn, we must work hard for ourselves. If a method works, then use it, but above all... try new techniques! You can't find gold if you don't prospect. Necessity is the mother of invention. A need or problem demands creative efforts to meet the need or solve the problem. If you persist in not trying new techniques, you can expect nothing will come of nothing. You'll hardly improve.

ONE-EYE SHOOTING VERSUS TWO-EYE
"Out of sight, out of mind."

Some two-eye shooters would shoot better using one eye. Some one-eye shooters can only shoot with one eye. Good heavens, just shoot the way it is most comfortable for you. If you are a one-eye shooter, you can have the best of both worlds. Keep both eyes open when calling for the target, then close your other eye, or wink, as you track the target. Two-eye shooters can try this, too. It'll zero-in your sight picture to the target. Whatever works is best for you. A one-eye shooter must keep his gun pointed below the house when calling for the bird. Horse hockey! Use the wink technique and you can keep the barrel high over the house.

How high should you hold over the house? Nobody really knows. Whatever works for you. However, it is important to at least see the target leave the traphouse so you can identify its flight angle and execute a smooth transitional swing to the target. You don't want to hold your gun so far off course you have to produce an extreme angular correction playing catch-up to the clay bird. The less the gun barrel has to move, the less errors and more smoked targets. Work on a technique that requires the least gun movement. You can hold low on the house if you shoot fast. Shooting the streak, spot, or zone shooting it's called. This is difficult and often frustrating to learn and requires dedicated practice. If you can do it, do it. If you can't, keep trying. Why keep trying something that doesn't work? Because in time it will, and when you go back to your customary shooting, the game will appear much like slow-motion, and you'll hit more targets! Just remember, whatever works for you works fine. The 'know-it-alls' know nothing except what works for them. Don't heed everyone's advice as Gospel truth. The less clutter in your mind the better. *"Trapshooters have no brains. Trapshooting is easy. Anyone can stand out there and break targets."* Another deviation from truth. It is not effortless. It takes skill to break them all. One miss is one too many. Laziness is often mistaken for patience. The next guy that says it's easy let him prove it by shooting a hundred straight. If he can do it, then it's easy for him. For most it is a grueling sport with little mercy for error.

CHAPTER 9

INCLEMENT WEATHER
"Neither rain, nor sleet, hail, wind, heat or snow shall keep me from my high score."

Overcast days can be tough. Scores drop terribly for a lot of shooters. The pros have learned a few things here and it's not just tinted eye glasses. They shoot fast before the target appears narrower as it speeds away. Overcast days cede the optical illusion of the target being half or less of its size, especially with orange-colored targets under white / gray clouds. Wind is another factor where the pros shoot fast so wind has less effect on the target. Rain is a phantasm for everyone and many pros just won't shoot in a driving rain only to ruin their score averages. Cold and damp coastal weather will suppress the target's flight angle, tending to not rise into the sky, plus targets absorb moisture and are troublesome to break, so use handicap loads. In cold or damp weather use 7 1/2 lead shot 3 dram loads for cold weather lowers shell's velocity and low temperatures harden the target. Faster shooting is required, with a lower than normal gun hold over the house or on the house. Hot and dry inland conditions loftily float the target into the horizon. Here you can take a bit more time to aim before you slam the hammer. Notice I said, "aim." You still must aim a shotgun. See; "Proper Sight Picture."

HOW TO SHOOT IN THE WIND
"Whether the weather be hot, windy, wet or cold, we'll weather the weather, whatever the weather, whether we like it or not."

Wind is the biggest obstacle second to rain and there are no easy answers to deal with it. Most shooters swing the gun too hard. When it's breezy, swing easy. Whatever can go wrong is magnified when shooting in adverse weather conditions. Wind indeed has a negative effect on shooters. It is foremost to view these situations in a positive manner and simply pay more attention to the target before pulling the trigger. Keep your grip dry, stay balanced and shoot with precision. Remember, the wind bothers everyone. Here are a few tips that may help you:

1. Don't lose heart to the wind. Know it exists, but never dwell on it by trying to anticipate what the wind will do to upset the target. Just track it down and pull the trigger. Pretend you are shooting on a fine day and things couldn't be better. That's how your frame of mind should be in inclement weather... your mind and eye on the target. Nothing else should be factored into the equation of shooting, otherwise you are expending valuable mental energy on something that has nothing to do with concentration.
2. Call for the target louder, as the puller will render slow pulls if you are not heard. In addition, expect fast pulls as the wind carries other shooters' calls into your puller's ears.
3. Don't fret if you miss. The wind may take targets away from you. It's going to happen and know that it will certainly occur to everyone else, too! (Except the lucky gal on squad 32.),
4. Keep a low gun when shooting in the wind, or lower than usual if you hold a gun high over the house.
5. Use a full choke when shooting in windy conditions! A powerful 7 1/2 shot 3 dram load will help.
6. See Fig. 9-1 "Adverse Weather Chart" for how wind affects targets.
7. Wear blinders to prevent eye-watering visual distortion.
8. Resist the pressure to alter your shooting style or timing. It's much too late to change when shooting a registered shoot. Stick with what you do best and let the dice lie where they fall. As time proceeds with gained

experience you will, or at least you should, be shooting faster than when you were first learning to shoot. You can't shoot with reliability if you are in a rut zone, that is, a zone of shooting a target when the target is near its peak or is too far away. Learn to shoot a rising target. The wind must overcome a rising target's momentum energy, which is stiff to do unless you're shooting in a hurricane. Moreover, the wind will have its effect regardless of the target's velocity energy. Here is what you need to know.

HOW WIND AFFECTS TARGETS
"Trouble rides a fast horse."

LEFT WIND
Will cause left angled targets to slow down and rise. Right-angled targets accelerate and drop. You should be holding your gun lower, even way down on the traphouse, if necessary, when shooting in gusty winds. Wind forces targets to rise and fall, and changing target velocity is often too complex and unpredictable for the shooter to compensate in the small amount of time given to shoot. By lowering your gun, it will present you an edge to see what the wind is doing to the target and shoot quicker. How many times have you shot over a target as the wind suppressed it back to earth? A low gun can help you hit these inconsiderate cliff divers.

RIGHT WIND
Is the reverse of a left wind. The left-angle target will accelerate and fall quickly while the right-angled target will decelerate and rise. Gun hold and timing remains the same as a left wind.

HEAD WIND
With winds in your face, all the targets will slow down but rise quickly. Of course, if the wind is angling upward targets will rise dramatically and a down-angling wind will severely suppress the target. Regardless of wind vertical angle, the targets will decelerate. Adjusting your leads to handle wind conditions is an ever-constant game of guesswork. Experienced shooters will agree, when shooting in windy conditions don't change shooting styles, though understanding what the target may do can give you an edge. Holding a lower gun over or on the traphouse may grant you a clear visual advantage. Targets that rise like rockets? You may have to hold high over the house and shoot above the target or risk shooting underneath / behind, but be aware if you do, the wind may lull and the target unexpectedly dip or bounce. Try both gun hold points and see which works best for you, dependent on wind conditions.

TAILWIND
All targets are accelerated and suppressed. This means better to have a low gun hold on the traphouse or be nimble enough to instantly lower your gun to shoot, as these targets clip the grass, so to speak.

CROSSCURRENT WIND
Wind blowing perpendicular to the target. If the wind is blowing from left or right, front or behind, you can handle most as described above. A crosscurrent wind defies simplicity as it arrives from peculiar angles, say northeast, or southwest to the target's line of flight. The target not only is pushed off course, the wind has a tendency to undermine the high pressure zone retaining 'lift' and the target will violently flutter, jink, dip and dive sharply, shift direction or even tilt on its side. The only hope is to shoot quick. This holds true when shooting on breezy days as small gusts of wind from nowhere suddenly appear. This usually happens when it's your turn to shoot! A lower gun hold over or on the house is advised.

EDDY CURRENTS
Here we are talking ultimate disorder. Eddy currents are random atmospheric disturbances. One moment the air is still, next, a dust devil twister appears on the ground, or unseen in the air. They are formed predominately by a rippled contour of the trapfield, neighboring mountains, buildings or trees. An irrigation ditch in the trapfield will cause erratic air currents over the ditch, especially if the ditch is dry of water. Hot air will rise from the ditch like a volcano tossing the target with a jinking action. Traphouses teetering on the edge of a cliff with a descending trapfield can be an uncertainty. Crosscurrents and rising air masses can influence targets into unpredictable

mystifying flight paths. Being aware of the condition of the trapfield and watching the target motions a prior squad of shooters is experiencing is an asset -- a good reason never to be the first squad to shoot in a registered shoot, especially when in unfamiliar territory. In severe cases, it may be advantageous to re-squad, if possible, so you don't have to shoot in that particularly nasty spot. If you can't re-squad, then shoot the target before or after the eddy current takes effect. Be aware of the zone of disturbance and you'll be one-up on those who fail to recognize and compensate for the aberration.

There is no cure for eddy currents or gusty winds except to learn to shoot fast before the turbulence can affect the target. This holds true in all weather conditions. The faster you shoot, the better scores will be. A tighter shot pattern is desirable, and atmospheric conditions will have less influence on a high energy target. The wind will not affect heavy shot (lead #8 or #7 1/2) to any measurable degree. Heavy shot has more enhanced momentum, speed, and energy than the wind within the zone of shooting a still-rising target (wait any longer to shoot and the wind will absolutely disorient the target; shot energy decreases and pattern expands). A tight extra-full choke may help in windy conditions or an improved modified to open the pattern. Flip a coin. It is harder for wind to alter a tightly compact mass of shot than it is with individual pellets. This is a moot point, though, as wind has little effect on heavy shotstrings up to 40 yards. The importance lies in accuracy and speed. It is a definite advantage to use a brisk 1,200 feet-per-second handicap load. Faster is better in the wind. Haven't you shot at a target only to see the wind microseconds later step it up or down, resulting in a miss? Speed has value. Likewise, be acute to target speed variations caused by the wind. Wind is challenging.

Another factor to consider when shooting in windy conditions is how your stance affects the forces of the wind on your body, making you sway or lose balance. A firm stance and footing is required. Wear cool, ventilated flat-sole shoes to establish a solid, non-slip footing. Soft rubber soles are beneficial. Your gun, when mounted to your shoulder, will be blown about. You may need to apply more forearm pressure to counteract the wind all the way to the target. A tighter than normal grip is required. The wind will gust and shift direction, causing the target and your gun to accelerate or decelerate. Good luck if you're not holding on snugly, but not overly tight, to the gun's forearm or the gun won't swing smoothly. A good word of advice, be mindful of what wind can do to target trajectories, but overall, you may want to try altering nothing -- that is, if shooting in the wind is not much of a problem for you. Don't lose concentration, as wind is nothing more than another distraction with a twist. Focus on the target, not the wind. To determine wind direction, you can watch the tops of trees for a general indication, take a look at the flag on the flagpole, toss a tiny bit of grass in the air, or learn to feel the breezes on your neck and face and, of course, watching other shooters' targets.

SHOOTING GLASSES AND VISION
"One may have good eyes and yet see nothing."

There's little more satisfying to a trapshooter than to run all the targets straight. Still, oftentimes a shooter comes home with nothing more than a few 'near miss' chronicles, holding a bag of empty hulls. Trapshooting is a difficult sport demanding fine-tuned skills to achieve success. Of greatest importance, yet frequently overlooked by the shooter, is vision. The sport requires excellent eye / hand coordination; reflexes must be swift and the shooter's eye true to hit targets with accuracy. It is an optometrist's role to correct vision problems interfering with your shooting. It is the purpose of this book to narrowly explain the vision processes available for experimentation, in other words, the practicality of vision relative to shooting for the average person.

The vision process is complex, so much so, here's an example of what is really involved in one paragraph: Shooting - in respect to vision - requires ten functions: **Binocular Fusion** -- The ability of the brain to gather information from both eyes to form a single image. If this doesn't happen, you'll experience lazy eye syndrome. If you can't use binocular vision due to severe eye crossover, then you are a one-eye shooter. **Stereopsis** -- judging distance between two objects. **Visual Fixation** -- ability to aim eyes accurately. Requires complex split-second timing between brain and tracking a fast-moving target. **Convergence** -- ability to converge eyes toward one object. **Visual Acuity** -- ability to see objects clearly. **Field of Vision** -- all areas in view. Up, down, left, right, peripheral vision as well as center field of view. **Accommodation** -- ability to adjust focus of eyes as distance of target increases. **Form Perception** -- ability to recognize specific shapes. **Color** -- ability to see the color of the target. **Contrast** -- ability to see the color of the target standout against background interference.

There are interconnections between every area of the brain and the visual cortex -- 20% of the optical fibers do not enter the visual sectors of the brain, but go directly down to the postural centers of the body affecting control, balance and movement. The link of the eye to the muscles is the reason for eye/hand coordination. Good vision is not synonymous with good eye focus. You may be able to see well, yet still can't hit the targets. Seeing and focusing are two entirely different phenomena. Sight is the ability of the eye to see things, as focus is the ability to enhance what one sees. Without resorting to technical dullness, we will discuss balanced realistic aspects of vision as experienced in trapshooting. Be aware vision related tips are sprinkled throughout this book and not solely in one chapter. Vision is a part of shooting, not an identity to itself. It all boils down to eye / hand coordination.

We all wish to do better at the things we enjoy. But if you find yourself staring at the bottom of the score sheet crushed by the weight of faceless names piled upon yours, too often it's time to improve your vision skills. Be assured vision skills determine who wins and who loses. For trapshooters, sharpening your vision skills will improve your scores to award you the winning edge. Your vision plays a vital role. How your hands, feet and body responds to visual information is called eye / hand / body coordination. It's a vision skill that affects your overall performance as it involves timing, concentrated eye focus, and body / muscle control. If your visual information is inaccurate, it can throw off your body's timing causing missed targets. Missing too many targets and not understanding how you missed them is a sign of inaccurate vision or a combination of poor vision with improper foot position/stance and swing. It is strategic to understand the 'setup phase' is <u>more important</u> than the actual shooting of the target. Learning to coordinate your eyes with body language can be improved with practice until it is routine. In trapshooting you are <u>reacting</u> to an event.

As the target leaves the house, your mind will force any muscle it can to push the gun to the target. Observe new shooters and you'll often see them lose balance, tilting sideways, nervously jerking the gun erratically to the target. You can learn a bundle by observing the mistakes of others. Watch yourself on videotape and you may be aghast to learn you too may have these springing, nervous reactions. Proper foot position/stance and how you hold and swing your gun will place you in the most advantageous position, so when your eyes acquire the target your brain can motivate a minimum of muscles necessary to execute the move to the target. Consider your eye the trigger mechanism to the brain. If you acquire the target properly, with little surprise as it leaves the house, the swing to the target will be smooth and accurate, resulting in more broken targets. If your gun swing is jerky to the target, you likely took your eye off the target and looked back at the gun sight or muzzle. If you miss a target, you likely thought of something. Thinking diverts concentration and unfocuses the eyes!

Visualization involves picturing the target exploding in your 'mind's eye' while concentrating on seeing the target in flight. If you visualize a missed target, odds are likely you will miss. If you are distracted and your mind unfocussed or wandering, a lost target is due. You can improve your shooting by simply visualizing broken targets before you even pull the trigger. Call it confidence if you wish, but it is mind over matter nevertheless.

<u>TARGET ACQUISITION</u>
"The mind can see what the eye cannot."

One of the most difficult problems is seeing the target against a cluttered background, making the target virtually invisible, shadowed, or partially blended. The ability to distinguish a target against a distracting background requires sharp, clear vision. Visual acuity (sharpness and clarity of vision) assists in judging distances and aiming. After calling for the target, 'dynamic visual acuity' takes over to acquire the target, then 'vision pursuit' enables you to track the target in flight. Your optometrist can assist you in a vision therapy program to enhance these vision skills. There are books available on the subject. It is <u>important</u> to understand the shorter period of time you concentrate on something, the more intense concentration will be. If you miss an 'easy' target, it is likely you spent too much time concentrating and didn't concentrate intensely enough at the proper moment. The setup phase should not be longer than necessary to mount the gun, focus your eye(s) and call for the target. Not too fast, yet not too delayed. Shoot quickly, as concentration dissipates rapidly as time and target distance increases. Excessive concentrating provokes eye strain and missed targets. Relaxed focus of the mind and eye is an important visual shooting skill that must be learned. Being aware of vision timing and focus is the first phase of learning. Your scores may be good, but with sharpened vision you can achieve greater results.

EYE FOCUS
"Seeing is believing for those who open their eyes."

In addition to seeing detail clearly, you should be able to focus from the back sight of the gun to the front sight to the field within a fraction of a second. Between the ages of 40 and 50 you will gradually begin to experience difficulty in focusing on the back sight due to a condition known as presbyopia. It is a natural part of the aging process. It is recognized by having problems with reading anything closer than arm's length. It is correctable. Mascular degeneration results in a loss of color visual clarity and a dark or empty area of blurred vision in the center of the visual field. It often passes unnoticed, for it usually affects just one eye. In this case, the 'good' eye compensates for the bad eye, allowing the problem to go unnoticed by the shooter. It too is treatable.

DEPTH OF FIELD
"Look before you leap."

Determining distance between you and the target depends on your ability to see clearly. You must be able to estimate the distance and speed of the target and your eyes should be capable of adjusting quickly. If you keep missing targets it may be due to poor depth perception, howbeit depth perception is not an absolute ruling factor in trap as it is with incoming and diverging sporting clays targets. After all, one-eye shooters do exist, endure, and win without employing binocular vision depth perception. The eye functions in two basic areas, sharp and precise central vision and wide angle peripheral vision. Combined, these make up your total field of vision. Your peripheral vision first detects the target leaving the traphouse and judges the angle and speed. Once the target is acquired, your central vision kicks in to focus on muzzle alignment to break the target. Remember to maintain precise and clear central visual focus on the target before pulling the trigger. Missed targets occur on account of the shooter failing to see the target clearly, failing to focus the eye before shooting. Understanding the eye shifts from peripheral to central will up your scores. You can even practice this eye exercise just watching cars flowing down a street. Use peripheral vision to see the entire mass of traffic, then zero in on one car. Do the same by watching targets leave the traphouse. This is why I say to not be so hasty to call for the target the exact moment you mount your gun as your iris and eye lens needs time to adjust to focus. As in magic, the hand is quicker than the eye and the brain is much too fast for the muscles in the eye to respond to the will of a hasty shooter.

COLOR IDENTIFICATION
"Believe half of what you see, less than you believe and nothing of what you hear."

Some shooters can't distinguish color properly. A simple eye exam by your optometrist can help. For those who can see color, many can't see it clear enough without some assistance. Lighting conditions are a big factor in trapshooting, changing from day to day, even moment to moment. Overcast skies, bright sunlight, clouds, fog, air pollution, haze, rain, heat wave distortions, even humidity levels can alter the visual characteristics of the target (See "Lens Colors" for more on choosing proper lenses).

Shooting glasses should have the lens focus raised toward the upper frame and bridge at least on the eye that is sighting down the barrel. This can be prescribed by an optometrist or lens manufacturer. The reason being when shooting you are unlikely looking straight out in the center of the lens. Your head is down on the comb and the eye is looking in the upper area near where the bridge and frame meet. The eye has 100 million light-absorbing sensors, still most are not evenly dispersed on the back of our eye; they are packed into a small area in the center. Each eye contains 130 million rods (photo-sensitive receptors) and 7 million cones (involved in color perception).

These all interact and converge on the optic nerve, which itself contains 1 million fibers. Eyes move more than four times per second. Minute, jerky eye movements occur 30 times per second, depending on eye position and fixation of target. Since the eye can move four times per second, these sensors serve as the equivalent of half a billion sensors! Central focus produces less eye movement, reducing overloading signals to the brain. Practice starring at objects and you'll tune in central focus. Learn to control your eyes smoothly to track targets.

PRESCRIPTION GLASSES
"If you open your eyes you may be surprised."

Another item to consider is the polycarbonate plastic lens, as it is resistant to explosive mishaps. Don't wait until after you've had an accident to learn the value of eye protection. Quality impact-resistant lenses* could save your eyesight in a breech or barrel mishap or errant flying lead pellets. It is a worthy objective to take a yearly eye exam. Success in the shooting sports requires sharp, clear focus on the target. One never knows when prescription glasses are needed until symptoms arrive such as headaches, fatigue, mood changes and, yes, missed targets. Your eyes are more important than the gun you hold in your hands. The finest gun in the world won't hit targets you can't see. Most all optometrists can provide quality shooting glasses. Here's a list of manufacturers specializing in prescription shooting glasses:
Allan Lehman Optical, 3125 N. 34th Place, Phoenix, AZ 85018, (800)-255-0205.
Carl Zeiss Optical, 1015 Commerce Street, Petersburg, VA 23803, (800)-338-2984.
Cobblestone Opticians, P.O. Box 10808, Goldsboro, NC 27532, (800)-353-1511.
Decot Hy-Wyd Sport Glasses, P.O. Box 15830, Phoenix, AZ 85060, (800)-528-1901.
Dr. Frank Rively, 100 Northern Blvd., Clarks Summit, PA 18411, (717)-586-2020.
Martin Optical, 903 S. Beckham, Tyler, TX 75701, (800)-688-8466.
*Protective Optics, 1320 West Winton Ave., Hayward, CA 94535 (800)-776-7842.
William (Jack) Wills, O.D., F.A.A.O., 1823 Charles Street, Fredericksburg, VA 22401, (800)-544-9191.
Note: Write to us for a brochure on the Luca Scribani Rossi professional Olympic-class clay target shooting glasses. Our address is located on the title page of this book, or visit our web site.

ADVERSE FACTORS AFFECTING VISION
"Beauty is absolute, yet relative."

Prescription and over-the-counter medicines can adversely affect the eye's ability to focus. These include antihistamines, beta-blockers, decongestants, alcohol, sleeping medication, tranquilizers and tricyclic antidepressants, to name a few. They usually cause a condition called 'dry eye' and after age 40 dry eye problems occur in the natural aging process. Dry eye causes the eyelid to rub against the eye, causing irritation, and may lead to corneal damage.

The treatment is simple, use ordinary tear-replacement drops 30 minutes before you shoot, and by all means do wear blinders, as they tend to hold moisture within the eye area and assist eye focus and omit distracting peripheral side-vision. Dry-eye contact lenses may help. Dry eye effects often cause eye strain long before symptoms develop. If eye fatigue develops -- you'll know if you're dropping excessive targets -- use lubricating eye drops prior to an event, it just may furnish the edge you've been looking for. Dry air, wind and vitamin deficiency can cause dry eye tear film problems.

Your mood will affect vision. Most top shooters maintain an easygoing low-profile behavior pattern prior to and during a shoot. They don't overeat, drink booze and party into the late night. Even certain foods can adversely affect vision in some people. Only trial and error will discover which may be affecting your visual acuity. One small point worth mentioning. If your glasses become oiled or fogged, stop shooting. The rules allow for interruptions, so use them if necessary. I've done it myself, shot when I should have stopped to clean a condensation smudge from glasses. I've missed too many targets to boast. How often have you failed to clean your glasses, fearing upsetting the rhythm of the squad, then lost a target?

Wear a hat with suitable visor to shade eyes and block hovering peripheral vision. The combinations of a hat and blinders is as effective as a light shield on a movie camera = less reflections act on the lens for a clear picture.

DAMAGING PERIPHERAL VISION
"A husband who tries to surprise his wife is often surprised himself."

Peripheral vision is awareness of what is going on around you, and it is generally not useful in trapshooting, in fact, it can be damaging and anti-productive to the shooter. You don't see targets the same way with peripheral vision that you see a target in central vision. Peripheral vision is better described as 'awareness' than sight. This awareness of other shooters and moving objects can be devastatingly distractive to the mind, tilting concentration, ruining a good score or preventing you from obtaining one.

You have seen shooters wear 'horse blinders' on their shooting glasses. Have you tried them? If so, and you didn't like them, you should try them again until you become accustomed to wear them. They will clearly help your eyes 'focus' on targets. The predominant complaint from shooters is eyeglass fogging. There are three things you can do to reduce and perhaps eliminate fogging. **1,)** Make a pair of thin leather or fabric as these materials breathe and absorb moisture. Leather greatly dissipates fogging. The inside surface should be rough textured to suitably absorb water vapor. **2,)** You can cut the blinders to a shorter length, just enough so light can't filter through, yet allowing some air circulation. **3,)** Apply automotive windshield protectant like Rain-X® to shooting glasses' lenses, as the chemical repels condensing water vapor. The chemical makes cleaning a breeze. Test the chemical in a small area to insure it will not stain the dye, plastic or glass. I've had no problems with Rain-X.® If your glasses tend to fog even with a protective chemical, don't use cheap paper blinders. Leather absorbs water and will phase dampness through capillary action to the atmosphere. Dye the leather black to absorb radical light intrusion and reflection. Some prescription eyewear users can use contact lenses with blinders to cancel fogging. If sweat from eyebrows dripping into your eyes is a difficulty, simply wear a sweatband or use silicone rubber to glue felt on the inside frame of your glasses.

The purpose for blinders is to remove distractive peripheral vision, vision that is not essential which will severely tax the brain with unnecessary disorientation and clutter. You may not be aware of it, but your brain is working <u>twice as hard</u> in the visual center when you don't use blinders. Trapshooting requires, without exception, all of your sight capacity to focus on the target if scores are to increase and misses deleted from your game. Some shooters object to using blinders because they 'look funny'. If you're shooting for looks, you should be acting or modeling not shooting. Breaking targets <u>is</u> the game. Wear blinders and your scores should improve after you have given yourself a break-in period to become acclimated to them. Blinders have proven themselves to be effective. They block the sun from your eyes and cease reflective distortions on the inside area of glass and plastic lenses. They help you to 'ignore' what other shooters are doing on the line. The slightest distraction can create a moment of mental diversion and a lost target. Blinders help you see the angles of the targets more clearly. To not wear them is positively a disadvantage. As mentioned earlier, blinders retain moisture close to the eyes to depreciate irritation and eye fatigue, including wind-induced eye tearing which distorts and blurs visibility of target. Don't install blinders the moment you are called on deck to shoot. Put them on at least 15 minutes earlier to allow your eyes to adjust to the tunnel vision effects.

LENS COLORS
"To see means nothing, to recognize means everything."

Before we step into lens tinting, it is meaningful to perform a test. Place your hand over one eye then switch to the other. You may notice one eye appears slightly brighter, possessing more light gathering power. Most everyone has this aberration. If so, then use a slightly lighter lens tint on the weak eye. It will help to equalize your vision so you'll see the target with more clarity. A note for Cobblestone Opticians: They fashion a watermelon color lens tint suppressing green backgrounds and brightening orange targets, in fact so bright, they may alter your timing until you adjust to them. Unlike mass-produced lens dyeing, where tint variations can occur, each lens is individually dyed to maintain precision consistency. The purpose of tinted lenses is to accentuate the target and de-emphasize the background. The goal of lens tinting is to illuminate the target; dampen backgrounds, thereby increasing contrast; reduce eye fatigue; protect the eyes from ultraviolet (UV) radiation and flying objects. Acquire UV protection on all your shooting glasses. Be aware of target backgrounds, as they can be dangerous to your scores. Your eyes should always be on the target at all times, yet certain backgrounds hide the target, giving illusion of target acceleration, or obscuring the target's true flight angle. Tinted lenses for various lighting and background conditions assist immensely as a remedy.

POLARIZED LENS: Not recommended for target shooting unless shooting over highly reflective surfaces such as water, desert sand or snow. Eliminates reflective glare. If needed, have both sides of the lens coated as reflective glare will project from the inside wearing surface of the lens. A good reason to wear blinders.

CLEAR: For night shooting or late evening lighting conditions. Definitely procure anti-reflection coating on clear lenses. Anti-reflective coating is an exemplary choice for after dark shootoffs and shooting under bright night lights.

GRAY: Transmits all colors without variation in color intensity. A neutral color lens for use on intensely bright sunny days. An all-purpose tint creating a cooling effect on the eyes. Target enhancement is nil, but will reduce strong sunlight illumination, curtailing eye strain. Singly favorable for maximum sunlight blockage for shooters with ultra sensitive eyes or shooting over water, reflective desert sand or snow.

BROWN: Same as gray tint, potentially the most effective at reducing intense sunlight.

BRONZE: Same as gray and brown, but allows increased light to pass through lens. Bronze, with a slight touch of red or orange tint, will brighten orange targets. An excellent all-purpose tint for all types of backgrounds. Good for dampening bright sunlight and adding contrast. Helpful to a reasonable degree for shooters with light sensitive eyes, depending on degree of tinting.

YELLOW: Can be used on hazy, smoggy or overcast days, especially useful in early morning and late evening. Yellow is a blue-blocker and will brighten targets, but has negligible effect on enhancing the color recognition of a target. A lightly tinted lens can be used for night shooting if haze conditions persists, and performs well in nighttime shootoffs under bright lights. Use a slightly darker tint for daytime overcast conditions to reduce eye straining glare.

GOLD: Same as yellow. Brightens the target for superior target definition in low-light conditions.

AMBER GOLD: A slightly darker yellow, more soothing to the eyes on bright days. Combines the benefits of yellow and gold.

WATERMELON: Subdues green backgrounds, brightening orange targets to a large degree.

ORANGE: Excellent for dark, overcast, cloudy skies, low light conditions and partly cloudy days. A blue light blocker definitely intensifies the brightness of a orange-colored target. Most effective seeing an orange target within an open, uncluttered background. A light orange tint is good for nighttime shootoffs under artificial lighting.

VERMILION: These deep red or rose tinted lenses highlight all colored targets when the target is flying past a heavily distracting and / or solid background. Excellent to enhance orange, lime green, white and black target amid thick foliage, trees, flowers, and steep hillsides. Performance of this tint heightens target contrast, sharpens visibility of target and subdues green backgrounds, especially in low-light and shady conditions. Can be used in all background situations, though strikingly effective with a green background. Also effective on cloudy overcast days, including early morning and evenings.

PURPLE: A blend of gray and vermilion which fades green backgrounds, amplifying the color of an orange target. Good for dampening bright sunlight. Can be used for orange targets against open, uncluttered background, but works best in cluttered background conditions. Has many of the characteristics of vermilion. A dark-shaded tint is a good choice for shooters with light-sensitive eyes. Try these lenses and you may pick up a few more targets regardless of background conditions. Get a light to medium grade tint, not a dark tint.

BEFORE YOU BUY TINTED SHOOTING GLASSES

"In this world nothing is certain but death, taxes, and lost targets."

Consider polycarbonate impact-resistant lenses with a scratch-resistant hard coating. Ask your optometrist if the lens meets or exceeds FDA and ANSI standards for impact resistance. As you can surmise, you could spend a small fortune on frames and lenses, especially if you require prescription lenses. In this case, investigate frames which permit convenient lens changing. What if you only want one tint to serve your basic shooting needs? Investigate the bronze lens. It retains many of the features of target enhancement, contrast and eye comfort in most all lighting situations. It's a good choice for a multipurpose lens. Of course, each individual's needs are unique, so peer into some sample tints at your optometrist office. Vermilion (cherry color) or purple lenses are good target-enhancing choices. If you predominately shoot orange targets, bring a target with you or an orange fruit to compare lens tint color and the infinite light-to-dark custom shades of tints available. Keep in mind a dark lens may transmit 40% or less of available light, so visibility can be diminished. This is something a beach-bum may need, though anti-productive for a clay target shooter. Consider a medium, light medium or light tint, depending on the sensitivity of your eyes to sunlight. Light intensity varies; in the East, elevations are generally lower with less intense flat-angling sunlight, so a lighter lens tint is more practical. In the Western states the elevations are higher and the sunlight direct and intense, so a darker-tint lens applies.

Keep in mind the color or the target you shoot generally determines the tint of the lens. A green target will appear sharpest and brightest with a green tinted lens. The same is true with orange targets; orange lenses will prevail over any other color. The problems arise with varied backgrounds with extremes in lighting conditions. Shooting during bright sunlight, soon afterward clouds arise blocking the sun, thereupon a mixture of blue sky and white and dark clouds intermingle, virtually making lens selections a futile experience. For this reason, lighter shades of tint are more practical over darker shades, and an intermediate color (bronze or amber gold) to handle most situations satisfactorily is desired. Furthermore, each shoot location has individual background riddles, thereupon it is not practical to have every lens color mentioned here, even if you could afford the cost. Then to complicate matters, you can choose high-index aspheric lenses, no-line progressive bifocals, scratch resistant anti-reflective coatings, ultraviolet protection, blue blocker tints, etc. It seems, as with anything else on the market today, the choices are endless, confusing and expensive. Make no mistake, simplicity is the key to success, keep it that way!

EYE EXERCISES
"The eye of the master will do more work than both his hands." Benjamin Franklin

Excess tension in the muscles in and around the eyes causes poor vision. These techniques will relax the muscles in the eyes allowing you to see better. Here are some basic techniques for relaxing the eyes:
1) Shine a bright light on your closed eyes, as bright as you can stand without squinting. Focus on relaxing the eyes. In time, you can increase the intensity of the light, using the sun as a light source. Do this for no longer than 15 minutes under artificial lights, 3 minutes if using the sun. Don't rub the eyes after using this technique. 2) Now, move away from light source and cover your eyes with hands to block all light. Relax your mind and your eyes for about 8 minutes. 3) Stand indoors in center of room, eyes open and relaxed. Turn (oscillate) your body and head gently back and forth from right to left, but keep your eyes looking straight ahead of you. As you do this, focus your eye from the top of a wall slowly lowering your gaze six inches each time you turn your body. Don't stare at anything on the wall, just let your eyes gaze gently at the wall. Then reverse your gaze slowly from the floor to the ceiling. Start with 20 oscillations, later increasing to 40 or more. Don't overdue it and get dizzy or twist your back. The oscillations should be smooth and gentle. If you can't do these 3 exercises without muscular pain or eye tension just stop and don't do them. A video tape is available illustrating how to see targets quicker and determine direction of flight. Contact: Decot Hy-Wyd 800-528-1901. Another eyerobics video is available from: Kay Ohye International, 600 Holly Lane, North Burnswick, N J 08902 (908)-297-0364. Another eye exercise to increase focal concentration is to place your finger 1" from eye, close other eye and focus intensely on tip of fingerprint. Trace print lines with eye. Move finger away in 1/2" increments, retaining sharp focus at all times. This enhances eye muscle strength.

For excellent eye / hand coordination training, use a BB or pellet air rifle for practice. String a soup can to a tree branch, place a lead sinker inside for inertia and swing the target at various speeds and angles. Shoot at close and long range. Unusual, but it positively works at obvious low cost. Helping to develop eye / target acquisition, it tones muscles for smooth gun moves to the target. It builds precision accuracy as you just have one BB to plink that fast moving can. Use a long rope to create a horizontal sweeping target with a smooth vertical rise. A device that simulates throwing clay targets is available and can be used indoors, contact: Light Flyer System, Beamerline 14255 N. 79th Street, #6, Scottsdale, AZ 85260 (602)-998-4828.

To help focus concentration beyond the physical visual medium of shooting glasses, try smudging your glasses with a slight spot of sweat or thin smear of facial oil, just enough to cause a serious distraction, unusual distortion but not sufficient to totally block vision. This allows your visual center to switch over control to the subconscious mind to track the target. This is only a training exercise to increase eye focus and concentration ability. If you find yourself still hitting targets with this complication, you have effectively communicated and linked mental awareness beyond visual stimulation. Now, clean your glasses and you will find the targets much easier to hit. Seeing the target is vitally important, but your 'mind's eye' must likewise see the target. Dampening your vision forces the conscience mind to override the visual senses, much as a blind person has more sensitive awareness to events around him, though remarkably accurate in interpreting unseen predicaments. Remember, you can see a target clearly, yet still miss it clean! You need to know and see the true flight trajectory of the target. This will take much practice to learn so it arrives as second nature. It is critical not just see a target, but to train your eye to 'focus' on the target... and where to focus! This skill does not arrive by just shooting hundreds of targets, but by consciously triggering your mind-set to energize all of your mental energy into truly 'looking' at the target, not just seeing it whiz by and reacting to it, pulling the trigger and by surprise breaking it. Many trapshooters shoot this way and targets will continue to float away here and there. To "get them all" takes immense visual acuity and concentration skills. Practice this with all your might!

CHAPTER 10

CLEARING COBWEBS
PRACTICE TIPS - Phase 3.
"He who begins many things finishes but few."

1. Suitable counsel here for the beginner and the experienced shooter. Consistent shooting requires imprinting a picture in the subconscious and conscience mind of the correct sight picture to break the target. Instead of practicing on a squad, shoot alone or with someone else who wants to try the following. Start at post #3 and run a full box of 25 rounds without changing posts. Here you will hone-in and focus on minimum angles. Whenever you try a new technique, start at the easier post #3 to see if it works. Then step to station #4 and do the same. Run a box on each station thereafter. You'll be amazed at how effective this is. It's a perfect practice session and quite economical in the long and short term.
2. Another method is to lock the trap so it does not oscillate. Set it for a straight-away from station #5 and shoot at each station. Then set the trap for a straight-away from station #1 and shoot at each station. You can lock the trap at various angles like this and positively imprint in your mind the correct target / bead relationship and see the angles as they really are. I prefer the prior method of not locking the trap and just pounding away 25 targets on each station. It is less disruptive to other shooters waiting to shoot and gets the job done nicely. You can try 10 shots at each post, or as much as you wish, though 25 rounds seems (to me) the magic number. Anything less, you don't get it drilled into your head. Anything more often wastes ammo as boredom surfaces and you may not remember what you learned in the practice session. You can shoot more if you wish. Everyone has distinct tolerance levels.
3. Practice with a specific purpose and goal. Shooting a round of trap will do little good, even if you shoot ten rounds, 250 shells. You must go out there with a purpose. Not to break birds... we all want to do that! Set a goal and a plan to reach the objective. Here are some examples. First round of trap practice, perfect gun mount, timing your call to allow eyes to focus, and judging precisely each angle of target. Second round, practice hitting targets at different times in different places. Third round, practice with an extra-full choke, feeling the comb tightly on your face all the time, visualize breaking the target, call and keep your eyes on the target and smokeball each one. In this practice goal a fragmented or chipped target doesn't count, you must 'puff' the target or it is a lost target. It is a goal to build precision accuracy. Fourth round, exchange to full or improved-modified choke, shoot faster, as

quickly as you can. Following a trial and error routine with a specific goal in mind will tighten-up your game. Fifth round, just shoot the targets, not thinking of anything in particular. This will help you wind down and relax a bit so you can reflect on why you are hitting the targets so well. Know why you hit them, and know why you miss them... with more emphasis on the prior. Keep in mind practicing with an extra full choke builds accuracy by tightening up the sight picture increasing accuracy.

4. There is one way to zero-in on your aim and that is to use an 'extra-full' choke at practice. You will miss targets, believe me you will, but you'll hit them dead-on when you do, and that sight picture will be implanted into your subconscious mind to be recalled each time you see that target again. When you attend a competitive event, return to a full, light full or improved-modified choke and positively burst the targets as the shot pattern widens giving you margin for error. It's a means to fine-tune accuracy, but establish the extra full choke's point of impact is identical to the more open chokes you plan to use, otherwise it won't work by reason of the sight picture may possibly change from choke to choke. You may want to stay with your full or extra-full choke. Use the pattern board to decide which choke is best. The most pellets within the 30" circle usually, but not always, decides which choke is best to use. Understand an extra-full choke may have a tight core density, but less pellets effectively dispersed within the 30" circle. It would not be recommended or as effective as a full or light full choke for tournament shoots. The ultimate test is how the choke breaks the targets and how many you can break. Superior results (high scores) always supersede theory and technicalities.

5. Practice with shooters who shoot better than you and keep your ears open. It isn't necessary to exclusively compete, but to learn. You should walk away with new knowledge. If not, you're just shooting, having fun. That's okay, but did you learn anything? Why did you smokeball one target yet only broke the next? Why did you chip one and miss the other? You have to find the answers to these questions. You can't just go out and shoot, hit targets and be satisfied you hit them. The goal is to finely tune your shooting so you can smoke them all. This way, if your aim is off you'll likely rip a chip off the target. It will take time, but the first step is to begin observing the condition of hit targets. If you chip targets, it is in essence a missed target and you were lucky. Do the same thing and next time it may be a lost target. You should envision in your mind puffing that target into a dustball, not just breaking it. Now you are entering the finer aspect of the sport, the ability to dustball the targets at will. Reminder; never shoot behind a target, place lead on it by keeping your eye solidly focused on the leading edge of the target. The leading edge of the target can be the top, middle or bottom of the target, depending on your gun's POI and your timing, target breaking zone, and the angle of the target. You may need to focus eyes on the lower leading edge of the targets otherwise you may shoot over the top of the targets. If you keep missing targets try correcting these slips by focusing on the top, middle or bottom of the target. If this doesn't work for you, then shoot where the target will be not where it is, placing forward allowance (lead) on the target. If you find it difficult to focus on the leading edge of a target, then focus on the center of the target. Later, you'll develop the skill of identifying the leading edge with ease. Lead can be facilitated by accelerating the gun's swing. The faster the swing the more lead is generated due to inertia of the gun automatically inducing a measure of lead from muzzle follow through. Although, a point of diminishing returns can develop if the swing is so rapid you lose accuracy. In this case just calculate the leads and slip them into your memory for recall. Looking down the rib, a 1" forward allowance (perceived lead, sight picture view) will approximate a 1 foot (actual) lead ahead of the target. A miss by 1" is often a shotstring miss by 1 yard to the target. Accuracy is critical. At 40 yards the lead required is not twice that of 20 yards, but quadrupled. Why? Shot speed is halved yet distance has doubled. Now you know why targets slip by at long yardage.

6. Hold gun still on the traphouse. Shift eyes upward about 4 feet so you can no longer see the gun barrel or sight rib. Focus eyes softly to see target. Call for target. When target emerges, keep eyes on target and snap the muzzle quickly to the target, so fast you don't have time to think about anything. Just let your eye and arm do the work for you like you are not even in control. This helps speed up and tone coordination reaction. This is just a practice exercise, so don't shoot routinely this way. You want smoothness in your swing.

7. Set up a 4" stationary target 40 yards distant. Mount gun. Look at target with gun pointed at least 30 degrees horizontal (left or right) away from the target, and 10 degrees vertical (lower than target). Then practice swinging to the target. This develops pointing accuracy. You can practice with an air pistol, air rifle or a .22 caliber pistol. With a pistol, use your usual shotgunning forearm grip hand to hold the pistol, shift your eyes and safely quick-draw to the target. If you don't look at the pistol, you'll be amazed to witness the bullet hitting whatever you are

looking at. Select small targets, a spent shotgun shell, at 100 feet distant to increase fine tuning. This is a great practice session, so get your plinking 22 out of storage and put it to good use. Your scores will increase using this practice tip. But be careful as quick-drawing can be very dangerous. Don't shoot yourself in the foot. Keep the pistol pointed away from your body in a safe direction at all times. If you hold the gun at arm's length by your side, tilt the muzzle upward away from your feet before raising the gun to fire. Be safe!

8. Nothing can take the place of actually shooting clay targets from a regulation traphouse. And it is often difficult to find a trap available at the local gun club to practice shooting specific stations without a crowd of shooters wanting to sign on who will only wish to shoot five shots and move from station to station. The practice trap at registered shoots is a good place to pin down a station giving you problems, especially after the day's shoot has ended or nearly so. Clubs with automatic traps usually don't have this problem. This will also give you substantial experience to manage your rhythm, since you will likely be shooting alone without a squad. You'll have a tendency to rush your routine, throwing off your normal squad rhythm timing. Expect to miss targets until you learn to maintain your own unhurried tempo. With practice you will learn.

PATTERN MISCONCEPTIONS
"Most people aren't content with their lot...even when they get a lot more."

Trap is shooting edge-on targets where little face or skirt is normally visible, and sometimes as thin as razor blades. See Fig. 11-4, Fig. 11-11 and Fig. 11-12. You can break trap targets at any yardage (16 to 27) with any shell/choke/shot combination. This includes using light loads in wide-open modified choke with #8 shot even at the 27 yard line, but is it reliable? No. The pattern's too thin. Reliability increases with a tighter pattern, tighter than you may think! Shooters believe that using a full choke that smokes the target indicates the central core pattern is too hot and they should then use a wider, more open, choke to increase pattern size. Big mistake! Tighter core densities always produce tighter 'effective central and fringe spread' to the pattern. Core is dead center of pattern, fringe is area just beyond the dense core, annular is the outer satellite area of a 30" pattern. Tight cores increase accuracy and actually give you more room for error in aim than using a wider choke. You could miss aim as much as a foot and still smoke the target. Hard to believe but it is, in fact, a reality. An improved modified choke is less reliable and less accurate than a full choke. See Fig. 11-8 to see a hot-core pattern.

Shooters using a tight choke believe when they miss a target it is because the pattern is too tight, but in reality, using a more open choke creates pattern failure; the pattern is too wide to effectively concentrate sufficient pellets to reliably break the target. It's deceptively hit' n' miss, where more hits are made, but a miss occurs once in awhile. Hitting these lost targets can be accomplished by installing a tighter choke. Tighter chokes do increase the pattern core and do increase the 'effective central core/fringe 25" pattern and weaken the outer annular ring (26 to 30" area), but it's the 'effective central and fringe pattern,' approximately the center 25", that truly breaks the target, every time, no matter what choke size you use. Annular rings do not break targets with reliability. An open choke's effective pattern will always be more fragmented than a tighter choke, yet this is where you want more pellets, to be snug tight. So, if the open choke has a weak effective central pattern, pellet count will drop and targets will be hit, but unbroken. It takes many pellets to break the target! Rule of thumb -- the choke that produces a snug core/fringe pattern of 25" is boss. Anything over 25" is generally unreliable when shooting edge-on targets. We're not talking skeet, or sporting clays, just typical receding trapshooting targets.

So, try this on for size and see if your scores increase. Whatever choke you are now using, go to the next one or two sizes tighter and believe. If you see smoke when the target breaks, your pattern is likely right where it should be and the effective central and fringe pattern right on the dime. Remember, <u>all</u> chokes produce dense central core patterns, depending on distance to the target. At close range, say 15 yards, the central core of a modified choke will approximately be as dense as a full choke at 40 yards. Timing and distance are factors, and even a 16 yard shooter could see scores increase by using a tighter choke, because most are shooting the target more than 15 yards away, especially the hard lefts and rights that slip by. What is really deceptive, and hard to convince shooters of, is an I/M choke on the 16 yard line is better than using a modified. Why? They are shooting without precise accuracy and more on luck (with huge sloppy unreliable patterns) and they build their success over the years on the modified choke, because they seem to hit so many targets, but all along, targets are insidiously slipping away here and there, and they believe they simply missed the target by aiming error. This is deadly, as the hits they are getting are being implanted in their mind as being 'proper sight pictures' when they are in fact near misses. Then the bottom falls out of their shooting as they get punched yardage and have to switch to full chokes. The learning curve of accuracy begins all over again from the day they first lifted a shotgun to their shoulder. A tough penalty to pay! Tighten up the choke if you want reliable patterns and higher scores. Yes, your scores will go down a smidgen, or more, but they will rise dramatically as you are now learning precision shooting. Recall, Frank Little shot full choke on everything, from 16 yards to 27, and many other pros do too. Now you know why. Tighter is better! There will be disagreement for sake of argument and many theories passed about debating this, but the miracle of trapshooting is just that... a miracle. Shotgun ballistics has never been perfected, though it could be, yet hasn't been truly tested and proven. No one really knows what the shotstring is really doing. A full choke does produce a long shotstring just as it leaves the barrel, but no study has been performed to 'prove' how it behaves at longer distances. One day, I hope, we will have all the answers. For now, we must contend with conventional wisdom as we know it, based on trial and error and visual results. Enough said for our technologically enlightened space age!

HOLES IN THE PATTERN MYTH
"He who sees a louse as far away as China is unconscious of the elephant on his nose."

In a perfect pattern board there are holes you can't see. A pattern board is deceptive as it is two-dimensional, but the shotstring and the actual clay target are both three dimensional (four dimensions if time, distance within space is considered). And to make matters worse, the shotstring and target are moving, and even more complicated, at diverging angles. It doesn't hurt to pattern, still don't believe everything you see on the pattern board, for patterns only reveal a stationary or perfect linear straight-away object (height and width), not a laterally moving target or depth (length and space) of shotstring. The effective shotstring length is seven to nine feet long or more! You could have three holes in the first five feet and four holes in the last four feet and never know it! See Fig. 4-1, Fig. 10-1, Fig. 10-2 , Fig. 10-3 and Fig. 10-4 revealing shotstring holes.

It is basically a waste of time to spend hours patterning, counting hits in the 30" circle, and when using new factory loads, there isn't much you can do to alter the pattern except change the choke. The finest use of a pattern board is to check and / or adjust point of impact, where the shotstring is hitting the board. This will tell you where the gun is shooting. If it's shooting to the right or left, the barrel, sight rib, stock or comb is bent out of alignment and needs adjustment. Shooting high or low may not be much of a concern as you can compensate with gun aim, but you can have your stock or barrel bent vertically for the POI you desire, adjusting the stock and comb and retaining a gunsmith to adjust spacing or heighten / lower the sight beads to adjust impact. A good choice is an 80 / 20 POI, 80% of the shot is above, 20% below point of aim at 40 yards. You may want 60 / 40, 70 / 30, 80 / 20, 90 / 10 or 100% from 1 to as high as 12 inches above point of aim. It's a personal preference and you'll not know what you need or want until you have shot many a thousand targets, tried many guns, or you have an excellent instructor. Having an adjustable-rib gun permits you to make point of impact fine-tune adjustments for differing yardages. Another realistic use for the pattern board is to determine choke size. An improved-modified or light-full choke may actually retain more pellets within the 30" circle than a full choke, still the only way you'll find out is to pattern your gun and inspect the pattern core diameters. The choke that keeps the most pellets within the circle often wins, but this is not chiseled in stone. See "Choke Tubes and Shot".

Forget looking for holes, use the pattern board to check POI and pellet count within the central / fringe area to determine proper choke size. There is nothing you can do to correct holes in a pattern, provided you see holes or not... holes exist so accept the fact they do. Even if you don't see holes on the pattern board... there are holes! Most of the holes appear beyond 35 yards from the trap, so 23 to 27 yard handicap shooters must use a tight choke. Remember, tighter is better for any yardage. A two-dimensional pattern board won't reveal holes in a three-dimensional shotstring 7 to 12 feet long. Taking this one step further, look at a pattern board and imagine a huge 24" hole in the center. The prime means a 4" target could slip through this 'doughnut hole' is for the target to fly on a linear straight-away path (when a straight-away target reaches its apex in flight. See Fig 10-1). If you are always shooting rising targets, not at the target's apex, you'll hit the target. If the target is traveling from any angle, it will still have to cross the outer perimeter of the shotstring before it reaches the hole... so again, the target will be broken. Targets are missed occasionally, due to a hole, but generally it is a rare occurrence, otherwise shooters couldn't shoot perfect scores. Don't dwell on patterns, concentrate on your setup, POI, choke size, timing, swing technique, visual skills and your aim. Once these are solidified, then all you need do is focus your eye on the target and allow natural eye / hand coordination to take over. These are more important than patterns. It'll be to your advantage anyway, as you can't outwit the unyielding laws of physics.

If you miss targets, stop blaming the patterns, it's you, the shooter who is missing. If you visibly see holes on a pattern board, clumping and excessive flyers, correct the predicament with a quality ported extended-length full choke, use heavier 7 1/2 shot or both. You may wish to try another manufacturers ammunition (with identical velocity ratings) as the wad they use may be more effective in your gun. You may never find perfection, so don't overtax yourself detracting your attention from the achievement of shooting. Remember this...shotstrings = entropy, a state of disorder. You can't reorganize the laws of physics. That's why shotguns are called 'scatter guns,' it says what it means. Shotgun ballistics? Call it chaos theory as shotstrings are generally notoriously irregular, unpredictable, inconsistent and uncontrolled. It's another good reason to shoot fast before physical stress factors such as: radical in-flight shot collisions, distance-causing extreme shotstring elongation, peel back and expansion, including unpredictable atmospheric variables disturbing the shot (and target).

RISING PATTERNS
"Experience is not always the kindest teacher, but it is surely the best."

Unlike a rifle or pistol, a trap shotgun should shoot higher than its point of aim. If you check your point of impact on a pattern board and discover all the pellets are above the bulls-eye aim point don't panic, that's what it should do. Remember trap guns shoot high or lost targets will result. You don't want a flat shooting gun! A rising pattern allows you to see the target at all times so you won't have to cover up the target with the barrel to smoke it. You can't hit a target you can't see. The difficulty arises when we succumb to natural tendencies to touch the target with the muzzle instead of the sight beads which will result in many calls of, *"Lost."* You must discipline yourself to track and pull the trigger under the target. If you find yourself missing or chipping targets, look to see if you are indeed not shooting below the clay. The advantage of an adjustable rib gun becomes evident, as you can fine tune the sight picture, POI, and adjust the gun so it fits properly. The advantage of buying a new gun is the point of impact can be 'made to order' to your specifications. If you ask, you shall receive. If you bought a gun from a dealer's rack and later find it shoots sideways or too low, within the warranty period, return it to the factory for correction. If you bought a used gun and discover it's shooting awfully off center, take your gun to a gunsmith specializing in barrel work and have the barrel, rib or stock tweaked. Special corrective chokes can realign a minor POI offset. Everyone who buys a new gun will inevitably be required to buy another new gun in the future, not from wear and tear, but owing to discovering a gun that has a superior fit, balance, pointability, improved pattern and point of impact among other reasons. You won't need an adjustable sight rib if your gun is properly fitted by a professional, yet few shooters obtain the use of professional fitting and wonder why they miss targets.

PROPER SIGHT PICTURE
"Only when you have crossed the river can you say the crocodile has a lump on its snout."

The proper sight picture when looking down the barrel with a center and muzzle bead is a figure eight. That is, the muzzle bead rests atop the center bead. If you can't hit targets without seeing the figure eight, your gun presumably does not fit you. It's time to adjust the gun to fit so you will always see the figure eight. See Fig. 10-3. When you see the figure eight, it is a verification reference safeguarding the gun is shouldered properly. If you don't, then dismount the gun, remount, then call for the target. Never call for a target if you don't see a precise stacked-bead configuration as you will often miss the target due to a misaligned mounted gun. After verifying proper bead-stacking, lift your eyes upward away from the rib into the trapfield. Don't look back at the gun sights or muzzle, keep your eye on the target. There is an absolute, the gun must shoot where you look. The eye will see the target and your arm / body moves place the gun in the proper swing angle to hit the target. For each person, and each gun, determines the true sight picture you see at the moment of pulling the trigger. So there is no hard and fast formula to ensue. You may have to place 3" of lead (always looking ahead of the target where it will be not where it is), someone else need only place their eyes on the leading edge of the target. Your timing and point of impact will determine where to point the gun and where you should be looking at the target, but in most all cases your eye should be on the leading edge of the target. It would be better to modify your timing, style, or gun, to ensure the target breaks when you look at the forward edge of the target. This way the gun shoots wherever you are looking. Through experimentation you will discover the proper sight picture. When you check POI on a pattern board, the gun does not always shoot where you look. It may be high or low from point of aim.

This is where point of impact becomes tricky, and more than a few shooters avoid adjustable rib guns, but in reality it isn't complicated at all. Just remember, for any gun with a high point of impact, keep the target floating 'above' the sight beads. The shotstring will rise upward automatically and hit the target. Apply lead on hard left and right targets, and keep the muzzle under or slightly touch with the sight beads on straight trending targets. Each gun and shooter is different and experimentation is required to determine proper sight pictures. Your eyes should always be on the target, but your mind must still make sight bead alignment adjustments for your arm / body to execute the proper lead and bird / bead relationship. Discover what the sight picture looks like when smokeballing the targets, lock those images away deep into you memory and you'll unleash a secret professionals know all too well. See Fig. 11-4, Fig. 11-11, Fig. 11-12 and Fig. 11-14. See Fig. 11-9 on Timing Errors. Now see Fig 11-15 to see how to develop a proper sight picture using a mirror. See Fig. 11-16 and 11-17 on how to shoot off the end of the barrel.

SLOW AND FAST PULLS
"The loser is always suspicious."

More targets are lost due to slow or fast pulls than many shooters realize. Some, a minute blessed few, can shoot any target, regardless of the timing of the target's release, most can't. Just as you should learn trigger control-- when to pull the trigger -- you must learn 'turndown control'. Remember, the setup phase is critical, more so than actually shooting the target itself. When you call for the target, your mind is 'energized' and ready to go into action. If the target doesn't emerge immediately, the setup is blown and missed targets will occur if you try to 'reactivate' the mind-set. The mind will not reset itself so quickly. Also, your eyes lose focus as they 'search' for the target that isn't there. Your eyes will not re-focus and will, through searching to focus, send overload images to the brain (which is already in a state of shocked surprise) creating a mirage! That's why you miss the target and scratch your head saying, *"I don't know why I missed that!"* You saw the target, but didn't really look at it since your eyes were not focused intensely on it. The Jack in the Box Syndrome just took place. You are now reacting to the target instead of executing your move to the target. Precision is lost. It's like someone tapping you on the shoulder when no one should be in the room. It makes you jump, react, panic. The same is true with a fast pull. Freeze! Don't shoot... don't even think of shooting it! Let it go. Of the two, the slow pull is the most insidious as it knocks the entire nervous system out of kilter.

The rules say when a material delay develops you can turndown the target. What is material delay? This is for the shooter to decide as only the shooter is 'finely tuned' to know what is fast or slow in a pull. Who else can know the mind of another? I am not advocating you should turn down target after target after target. You don't want to become so sensitized if the pull isn't 'perfection' you can't shoot. However, if the target does not emerge when it should, just turn it down. Don't move. Let it float away, remount and call again. If you keep getting slow pulls increase your call voice level so the puller can clearly hear you. If it's the puller, be cordial, ask he / she be a tad quicker. Always, always, dismount the gun and start over. Don't ever keep the gun mounted and call for another target... it doesn't work! You may never be a consistent shooter unless you know when and how to turn down targets. It's something that is 'unnatural' to do and requires discipline to learn. Turning down targets is not fun. It's a drain on energy. No one relishes turning down targets, they want to break the target. Some persnickety shooters may misapply the turndown rule to extremes, but as long as the rules stand, and humans push the button, slow and fast pulls are inevitable. Learn to deal with errant pulls or they will deal you a well-deserved missed target. If an automatic voice call system is not tuned correctly, do correct the sensitivity so you can obtain proper pulls.

CHAPTER 11

THE REALITY OF REALITY
"The more we learn the more we know what we need to learn, yet know we can never know it all."

There are environmental and physical conditions that make targets appear faster and thinner than normal. These are not optical illusions but realities that can cause scores to dump. Every trapshoot you attend will have its own peculiarities. Background scene and weather variations are obvious. But what about target speed, and target angle deviations and visibility? These too are troublesome conditions of which the shooter has no control other than to compensate for the dilemma. Experience will teach you how to handle these situations, but it will pay you dividends to always remember to keep your eye solidly on the target and not to focus or divert attention to what should be oblivious. A simple tip it is, yet how often do we drop targets because we ignore or forget such simplistic mannerisms? The reality is: trapshooting is a simple sport, a simple task once learned. How often we complicate the game by overfamiliarization with the unnecessary! Focus on the important things that actually help you to hit targets with precision; mindset, setup, attitude, eye control, smoothness, trigger control.

RAZOR BLADE TARGETS
"We must make the best of those ills which cannot be avoided." Alexander Hamilton

Razor targets are optically smaller to see as they fly on a flat plane edge-on with little to no face or skirt visible. Caused singularly or by a combination of trap being improperly set in the house, throw-arm angle misalignment, trap set for speed, or sunlight facing the target's trajectory. You should walk the trap banks inspecting the conditions of the targets before you select a squad and shoot. How do you hit these targets? If a rising sun is causing the problem, don't shoot an early squad. The sun should be behind you for the best visible targets. If the sun is ahead of the target, you will shoot a flying razor blade, with only the thin edge of the target visible. If exclusively the black stripe edge is visible in a clear sky, it will be difficult to hit the target -- add a mixture of background scene and the target will disappear. You can't hit a target you can't see!

SOFT TARGETS
"Easy is ceaselessly hard to do."

Quite more than a few clubs toss soft targets to keep scores high and to entice shooters to return. Everyone likes to see their scores increase, even if they don't win a event. The term soft meaning throwing low speed targets. But all things equalize, as the better shooters also find it easy to hit soft targets. To hit soft targets, just take your time, but don't be too complacent as all targets are hard to hit. When you let your guard down, that's when the verb *"Lost"* rings loud and true.

PREDICTABLE WIND
"Nothing is predictable except the unpredictable."

Some shoot locations have a predictable wind or breeze arriving like clockwork in the afternoon. If so, shoot an early squad, but notice the sunrise location to determine the best time to shoot for maximum target visibility.

KEEPING A DIARY
"Great accomplishments are made by numerous tiny achievements."

Smart shooters keep a logbook of the conditions at each club they shoot and use it for future reference. It's more than a good idea. Professionals in all outdoor sports take diligent means to note the environmental factors that can, and have, upset their scores in the past. Fig. 11-1 is a basic logbook entry sheet you can photocopy and fill in the data you wish to note. Fig. 11-2 is a handy average sheet you can copy to keep track of your progress. You may want to slip these log sheets in this book, so all can be easily referenced when needed.

KNOW THE RULES
"He who flaunts the rules cheats himself."

You'd be appalled to discover a vast majority of shooters don't understand the rules of the game and predominately, the <u>reason</u> for the rules. Many shooters can't even distinguish a legal target from an illegal one, a slow pull, or a borderline flipper. A legal angle target is within 47° extremes. Knowing the rules and the reason for them is important. The better shooters know the rules. That should tell you something. The rules do not permit disruptions, but this does not mean you can't dismount your gun when mismounted for fear of disrupting the harmony of the squad. The rules state slow pulls can be turned down, illegal targets too, so why shoot at them? When was the last time you read the rule book? Knowledge of the rules will guard you from the disgruntled comments from discontented shooters. Losers are always confused. If you shoot at illegal targets and shoot at rule infractions you only have yourself to blame for attempting to shoot beyond the bounds of the rule book. Certainly, some rules become outdated or permit 'gray areas' which are known to cause dissension, but until the rules are changed, it's the law of the tournaments to abide by.

JACK IN THE BOX SYNDROME
"Blind wisdom is an awful surprise."

Stations 1,2,4 and 5 are the meanest for targets unexpectedly leaping out of the house, taking you by surprise. Stations 1 and 5 can be devilish. First, never call for the target until your eyes are focused and adjusted. Expect a hard angle target, left or right, depending on the station you are shooting from. Watch for it. Be ready to go after it. This is termed anticipation and it's arguably not all that good a thing to do, but it's better to expect a hard angle than be 'surprised' by it and have to play catch-up in a panic move to hit the target. Angle targets are fast and can take you by surprise. If you expect an angle and you receive a straight quarter angle target, it's easy to recover from anticipation and track it down, but the inverse is not as accommodating. Don't allow the trap machine to play Jack-in-the-box with you. On station #1 and #2 the surprise angle will be hard lefts. Station #3 just expect softer right and left angles. Station #4 and #5 expect hard rights. That's all there is to it. Trick is to remind yourself and don't forget. If you're looking down your gun sights when you call for the target, you are looking in the wrong place. Try keeping your focus where the hard angle exits the traphouse. You'll be geared when Jack leaps from the box, and you can clobber him.

Remind yourself on each station there are only three basic angles. Identify the hardest angle and call for the target expecting the hard angle target. You have little time to shoot a hard angling target before it gets away, but with a straighter target you'll have plenty of time to acquire, track and burst it. Don't focus on the straighter targets, 'be ready' for the severe angle to appear. After some practice, you won't have to anticipate but simply look for the angle to appear. If you find Jack getting the jump on you, then start expecting the angle, so he won't escape. Remember, there are essentially no straight-away targets, all are angled. Try a practice round just thinking about this. It'll open a new dimension to your game.

PRACTICE TIPS - Phase 4.
"The mountain labored and brought into existence a mouse."

Practice sessions should be hard work, still sweat alone is no substitute for learning. Take each step one-by-one, little-by-little, learn with a vengeance using the tool of patience. Neglect not the seemingly frivolous, for within trivial things lie great discoveries.

1. Stand behind shooters on the deck area and practice pointing your finger with fully extended arm at the targets as they emerge from the trap. You may discover it's not as tractable as you thought it would be, that is, to be accurate and to acquire the target quickly. This will impart rapid reflexes and exercise your master eye. Eye muscles require training just as all muscles in your body. It is these so-called trifling practice routines which forge the difference between a good shooter and a mediocre one. Try to acquire the target and imagine breaking it as close to the traphouse as possible. It's good exercise yet few do it.

2. If your handicap is 20 yards, by all means practice at that yardage, but do practice at a further distance, say 23 yards. This helps you identify target acquisition and leads, making shooting at the 20 yard line easier. Haven't you noticed after shooting handicap, shooting the 16 yard line seems effortless? That is why you should practice on your handicap, not at the 16 yard line. You are wasting time and money practicing singles. If you want to be a good singles (16 yard) shooter, start shooting handicap. All too often new shooters begin at the 16 yard line. They should be at the 20 yard line. They don't have to swing the gun as much and they can see the target better. Handicap yardage is a superior place to be to learn. Some may disagree, but try it and see for yourself. I've seen too many shooters' performance increase to doubt reality.

3. Do not practice to the point of exhaustion. Quality is superior to quantity. Shoot a couple rounds of trap and take a break. There is no requirement to shoot 150 targets in one day. Shooting 50 to 100 with frequent breaks is sufficient. Anything more and you risk shooting yourself into a tailspin. No matter how much or how little you shoot, you must <u>learn</u> something and <u>retain</u> the knowledge. Write it down if you discover something. If you don't, odds are elevated you'll forget what you have learned. Shooting 50 targets twice a week will take you to high scores faster than shooting 250 a week in one practice session. Customarily, the more you shoot, the less you'll learn if you're just shooting for the opportunity to shoot. As excess leads to disorientation, less is more. When your technique is polished, then shooting 300 targets in <u>rehearsal</u> is acceptable, but not for <u>practice</u>. Practice is learning. Rehearsal is polishing, exercising, toning, tuning-in. There's a big difference here!

4. On the last round of practice you should not think of anything you learned beyond the setup phase. Let go. Permit your subconscious mind to take control of the shooting phase. At first you may miss targets, until the subconscious learns you can expect it, but once it does learn the targets have little chance of escaping. It is important to 'connect' with the subconscious by allowing it to shoot. If you don't procure efforts to communicate, the subconscious will do its own thing, miss targets, no matter how hard you try to overcome its control. Shooters call it instinctive shooting. Some call it skill or talent. Call it as you will, but it's subconscious shooting. A musician in concert plays his instrument by 'feel' and 'inner passion.' The subconscious is playing and you can see the hypnotic trance-like state of mind, especially when soloing. A good example is watching Stevie Wonder play those keys. And other great jazz musicians. You'll observe it in bowling, baseball, tennis, including All-American, All-Stars Champion Trapshooters! How deep is your concentration? Are you too aware of your surroundings? Mind diverted on other thoughts?

5. A good phrase to remind yourself, *"Shoot fast or don't shoot at all."* I don't mean turn down targets or shoot faster than your inner time clock (snap shooting). This reminder prepares you for the fast exiting target and energizes the central nervous system. Consider any shot you shoot too slow...a lost target. Remind yourself to shoot quickly within your natural time clock. It's hard to do, so be set for a challenge; it's like learning how to shoot all over again. Alternate between fast and slow shooting. Keep experimenting. It's good eye / hand coordination training. Don't say you can't do it. You can, with practice, if you apply yourself. Fast shooting can be learned. The plan is applying item #6.

6. Never miss another target because you shot behind it. It's absolute insanity to drop a target this way, and most losses are just that... shot behind the target! Implant in your mind, *"If I'm to miss a target I'll miss because I shot too far ahead of it."* Error is a miscalculation and a belief without understanding. Most all misses = not properly seeing the target, no lead on angles, head-lifting, poor choke selection, improper timing. If you must err, do so ahead of the target so shotstring can lasso a chip. It is difficult to miss a target if you apply lead as the shotstring is well over 7 feet long. The tail end of the shotstring may rip a piece off the target. But don't rely on a long shotstring as though it may be long, it all arrives at the same time in the real world in milliseconds. If you shoot behind you don't stand a chance. Smokeballing the target is vanity, but it is ideal to increase marksmanship. Though 100 chipped targets beats 99 smokeballed targets, eventually the chip breaker's luck will run out! Always shoot ahead of the target. If you do this, it will smokeball targets if your choke / pattern is proper. Practice firing with extensive leads and see for yourself what I'm talking about here. It's hard to miss if you lead a target within 1 to 2 feet. In fact, try to intentionally miss by placing excessive lead on the target. Discover how far ahead you can shoot, with room to spare before a miss occurs. Of course, extended leads are used on hard left and right angles and if you are shooting long on a quarter angle target. Visualize and memorize where you positioned the sight bead when pulling the trigger. The optimum practice routine is to stop the gun the moment you fire so you can see the sight picture. The faster you shoot, lead is required or you venture shooting behind the target. The reason being you are shooting the target at its maximum speed. A gun with a raised point of impact can be aimed directly at the target and the shotstring will rise upward into the target.

Concentrate on what you observed when you pulled the trigger. When practicing, stop the gun barrel the moment you fire. This will help you see what you did right or wrong by (sort of) freezing the frame. There is no obligation to excessively follow through on trap targets. Swinging the muzzle through the target and pulling the trigger right at the leading edge of the target often works fine, as the muzzle will follow through perfectly without thought on your part to lead the target. This depends on your gun, swing speed and shooting form. In any case, get that barrel out on the leading edge of the target, pull the trigger and the gun's momentum will place a good measure of lead automatically. If this doesn't work, then you'll have to force yourself to lead targets. Try this, if you stop the barrel when you fire you should still hit the target hard (due to guns' forward inertia) and you'll see the sight picture close to freeze-frame! Certainly it will do no harm to swing past the target after firing (follow through) as long as you don't pull the trigger behind the bird and expect the swing to catch up to the target. Keep in mind, if you are truly looking at the target's leading edge, your head is down snug on the comb, forward allowance (lead) and trigger timing will automatically take place from instinctive shooting... it's a subconscious experience. Your mind knows when to pull the trigger when it subconsciously sees the sight bead on the leading edge of the target. Of course, you need to shoot quickly for this to work: 1 to 1 1/2 seconds from target exit before target reaches its peak. If the target sails too far away, bending into a severe arc (beyond two seconds from target exit) you will have a tough row to hoe. There will be too many sight pictures to memorize and you'll keep dropping targets here and there. Learn to shoot quick to cure heartsick scores.

7. Be aggressive, call for the target with an attitude to destroy it. Your voice need not shout, but inside you should feel a blitz of fighting instinct. Make a mental push to acquire, track, and hit that target. Be aggressively relaxed, get mean, but not angry. If you miss, display no emotion. No shaking of the head, no tossing shells to the ground, no cussing. This is reinforced negative behavior that will, I guarantee, ruin the setup phase for your next shot and cause many more missed targets. A missed target is water under the bridge. Forget it. Concentrate on the next target, for this is the one that counts. I've seen All-American Champions miss targets in handicap shootoffs and still win, and so have you. A near miss is as good as a mile, but it doesn't always mean you lost.

8. Visualize your shot pattern as a rifle bullet. Don't think of the shotstring as a long 7' long by 2 1/2' wide plow. Assume it is a bullet. Be precise when you shoot. If you want to hit more targets, hit them harder. Smoke the target into a ball of dust. If you are taking chips, then find out what is wrong. If the chips fly to the right, it means you shot to the left of the target. The chips will fly in the opposite direction of where you hit the target. Watch the chips! They tell you what you did wrong. If it smokeballs, odds are you hit it dead on, you had the proper lead on the target and the shotstring grinded it to pieces. Remember to acquire the target's true angle then lead the target. Though the shotstring can be 7 to 12 feet long, the entire pattern arrives in milliseconds, so don't rely on it.

9. Ride the track! It is vitally important to see the proper angle of the target as it leaves the traphouse. This is not just a casual glance, but to know the precise angle. Was the target 5° or 35°? Use the protractor to furnish you these estimates, then imbed them into your memory. See Fig. 3-1 - (C). Visualize the protractor in your mind. Once you identify the precise angle, you can flawlessly move your gun onto the flight path of the target. Chase the target as if both the target and gun were locked onto a slightly bent railroad track. If the target is slipping away, get that gun moving. If you shoot a high POI gun, try canting the barrel a smidgen to compensate for the target's arc and to get the jump on the retreating target with automatic lead. If you don't, you'll shoot behind or over the top of the bird, for the target is now likely curving away and dropping. Fast shooting dissolves these problems to a absolute minimum, but you still need to identify the angle of the target before you can reliably track it down and break it. Learn the angles and arcs. And remember not to move the muzzle of the gun to the target until you have actually seen the target emerge from the traphouse.

10. The bird / bead sight picture must be imprinted in memory if you are to perfect trapshooting. Your eye must <u>always</u> be on the target. If you are really seeing the target, it will appear 'bright' even if it's a cloudy day or the sun is casting shadows on it. The more you apply concentrated focus on the target, the brighter it will appear. The barrel and sight bead should also be seen, though faintly visible as a ghost. You can't forget to see the sights as some will tell you, *"Never look back at the sights or barrel."* This is true, don't look back, just be sure the ghost is where it should be when you pull the trigger. The ghost is already present as you sight down your barrel in the setup phase, all you need do is see the target and track it down. If you don't use the sights, then you are swinging the gun aimlessly. Yes, you point with a shotgun, but you have to know when to pull the trigger too! You pull that trigger when the bird / bead relationship is correct. If you don't believe this, then why do people miss targets when they lift their heads? It's because their eye is the rear sight of the gun. Lift your head and you'll miss the target regardless how intense you are looking at the target. That means aim is off! So too, you must aim a shotgun when shooting handicap. Using sight beads is required, not as shooting a rifle, but for reference to target. It's called back-sighting and shooting off the end of the muzzle, an advanced shooting technique that is explored in my other book, *"Precision Shooting."* See the back pages of this book. Shotgunning is more of a subconscious execution than a deliberate conscience act. But when learning you have to think a lot about shooting and what you are doing, and that means you have to learn how to aim a shotgun to get those correct sight pictures embedded in your mind.

11. Move your gun in concert with your eye. Don't let the eye flick to the left when tracking a hard left, then play catch-up with the gun. The gun and eye should move together as one, with your cheek locked down tight on the comb at all times. Naturally, some lagging occurs, but you can practice minimizing it. Practice moving the gun the moment the target emerges, not before it emerges. Don't play anticipation with the gun and target. You know you're doing this if you call for the target, no bird emerges and your gun moves. Correct this bad habit by asking the puller to occasionally present no birds or very late pulls. If you are looking at the forward edge of the target, the gun will move instinctively to the target, and in most cases, will automatically place the proper forward allowance (lead) on the target. Of course, proper lead depends on the angle and distance of the target, POI and your swing speed and shooting style. Lead depends on many factors and most always relates to how you swing the gun to the target. Look at the frontward rim, not the tail or body of the target. Pull the trigger when you instinctively feel it is right (which requires much practice to learn).

12. Practice turning down targets. Knowing when to turn down targets is important. How often have you shot a target and missed knowing you should have turned it down? When practicing, ask the puller to give you erratic pulls and, by golly, turn them down. You need to learn this. Ask the trapsetter to place a few misplaced targets on the trap arm so you will learn to recognize illegal targets. If you shoot at broken and illegal targets, your eyes are not properly acquiring the target. Trap is a game with boundaries and rules. Learn the rules and play by them. If you don't, be assured the better shooters will.

13. When you practice use an extra-full choke. It will do you little good to practice with a modified or improved modified choke. You may hit targets, but not all of them, as you won't particularly know why you missed owing to the central core / fringe pattern is too wide. An extra-full choke will tighten the pattern to the point you will feel you are shooting a rifle. This is fine-tuning shooting. Yes, your scores will drop and rightfully so! If you can hit targets with an extra-full choke, imagine how deadly competitive you will be when you step down to a light-full or full choke? You'll also learn to identify the proper bird / bead sight picture before pulling the trigger, to develop precise and accurate trigger control timing. Full choke = reliable patterns.

14. Take a deep breath just prior to shouldering the gun. This extra burst of oxygen opens the pupils of the eye and stimulates the brain. The advantages are obvious, yet few shooters do so. Maintain a soft eye focus with a wide field of view. A tight intense focus causes eye weariness and excessive tunnel vision where targets can slip by. But don't confuse the fact that to learn how to perform a soft focus you have to learn how to impart an intense concentrated focus. Remember, pros say use a soft focus, but they have shot so many targets they don't realize that their soft focus is really an intense focus for the rest of us! You'll find the focus that's comfortable for you after you have worked on various intensity levels.

15. Don't develop any station hang-ups. Many shooters refuse to shoot specific posts when starting a round of trap. Many disfavor being squad leader on post #1 or starting on post #5. Shoot all the posts! Don't be particular. Inevitably, you'll have to rotate turns shooting all the posts anyway. Prevalently, post one and five are

the most forbidding, so shooters avoid them. Don't do this. Tackle the hard posts, don't let any apprehensions or bad habits settle in. Be adaptable. Remember, all the posts and targets are onerous. Once you begin reasoning particular posts and specific targets are easy, you're heading for trouble and due for a lost target or two, or more. However, if you are fine tuned, tackling the hard left and right angles right away, you could start on station #5. Once you run all the targets on #5 and #1, the ensuing station angles are less severe and the odds improve you will run the entire trap. For others, starting on post #3 is easier to warm up with. Nevertheless, these are indeed hang-ups to be avoided. Which brings us to:

16. Be the squad leader during practice at your gun club. It adds responsibility and helps you deal with interruptions that naturally occur. The advantage of being squad leader is when changing posts, it gives you extra time to evaluate the trap environment and additional time to commence the setup phase when starting and changing stations, and balance the tone and rhythm of the squad.

17. Having problems with specific angles? Run a box of shells on each station that is giving you heartache. Keep in mind you mustn't just shoot lazily here, you have to pay attention. When you finish, you should have learned how to hit that target every time. The trick is not to forget what you learn (easier said than done).

18. Are you squinting? A two-eye shooter should not squint at all. A one-eye shooter should only squint the opposite eye not the sighting eye! Squinting the eyes will adversely change eye focus, reduce light transmission and intensify eye fatigue. Before calling for the target take a deep breath and raise your eyebrows slightly. You'll see the target much more clearly.

19. Get serious. It's okay to practice for thrills, but only before intensive shooting has expired. Whatever you do last you will remember. Trap is a serious game which expends enormous concentration and mental energy. There is an old adage, *"If you don't walk off the line in a sweat... you're not shooting trap."* At least not to win! If someone misses a target and a chain reaction develops, producing additional misses, pour on the heat to break the cycle to secure a dead target point. Be aggressive.

20. Evaluate setup time. Not too quick and not too slow. Maintain a consistent speed, especially in competition under pressure. Don't speed up! Play your own game at your own timing. Rapid rhythms induce a runaway train effect to the squad. Get the gun mounted, focus your eyes and call. Too quick and you're not ready. Too slow and concentration stamina dissolves. An unprepared, disorganized, unpolished, sloppy shooter is his own worst enemy, including the friends he'll forfeit for being disruptive. Watch the pros shoot and at the very least mimic their professionalism and their timing. It will help you immensely, increasing your scores. Here's an ideal setup: Your foot stance positioned at a V-angle (five past three side-stance), or 90° (square side-on) as shown in Fig. 11-6. Mount gun smoothly. Gun hold point 2 feet above traphouse, or held low on the far edge of the house. Slow deliberate cheek pressure. Cheek pressure indicates when to call for target after eyes have focused. Eye focus time after mounting gun, 2-seconds. The total setup time after last shooter fires is 6 seconds. Shoot target within 1 to 2 seconds of release. Practice performing the setup smoothly within the 6-second time limit. If you don't practice setup timing, your setup will be inconsistently disorganized, and so will your scores.

21. If you miss a target, don't be too cautious. Stay shooting within the zone. Be aggressive! Once the target leaves the zone, your timing will be totally ruined and the bottom will fall out. Have you ever run 75 straight and on the last trap hell breaks lose and targets drop by the handful? You likely became too cautious, recklessly confident letting your guard down, lost concentration and visual focus or became overly aggressive and forceful.

22. It is good to have a model, a paladin. A central character who you can rely on. Everyone has a hero, someone they admire. Pick an All-American Grand, State, or Olympic Champion you like and watch how he / she performs under pressure. Believe it or not, even they have specific shooters whom they too admire and respect. Imitation is the sincerest form of flattery. How can they help you? When the pressure is on you can visualize how they would handle the situation, then do exactly what they would do under similar circumstances. It works quite well when you get your nerves rattled in a shootoff. For example, I like to watch Daro Handy shootoff. Nerves of steel! Perfect composure! He projects an aura of serious concentration the crowd can feel. Still waters run deep. Total silence, hardly a whisper or blink of the eye so to not miss the show. Daro makes shootoffs appear easy and relaxing. Visualize what your favored shooter would do under similar conditions. Try this and you will see it will help you. It's hard to be alone in this world. You know the precept, *"Hitch your wagon to a star."*

MANAGING POINT OF IMPACT
"A good beginning makes a good ending."

Sad, but true, most shooters buy a gun, find out where it is shooting and conform themselves to the gun. This is understandable for the novice, but not for someone with shooting experience under their belt who buys a new expensive gun without full and absolute consideration of its POI setting. What often happens is the shooter can't shoot the new gun for beans! Why? Because both the POI and gun fit is in question. An experienced trapshooter knows where he wants to break the target and does so in a specific 'zone', and if the POI is improperly set the learning curve is absolutely horrendous. If he doesn't set the POI to his normal timing to hit the target in the zone he will have to do one of two things: 1) alter timing and sight picture or 2) adjust the POI so timing and sight picture is not altered. Number 2 is the preferred and least painful method. Of course, we must consider gun fit because if the gun fits it should shoot where you are looking i.e., POI will be correct or nearly so. All guns' POI can be altered by numerous means, but what is the point of impact you need? Do you know what POI your gun is shooting at 25 or 35 yards? How about 40 yards? Amazingly, not many people do know, and many uninformed shooters don't even believe POI is important at all. If you are shooting targets with no strict plan of hitting the targets in a specific area or zone, you are not taking full advantage of the 'inner secrets' of trapshooting. Ask a pro about POI and timing, you'll likely get a mind-burn on how meaningful it really is.

What does it mean when the gun shoots where you are looking? Well, the gun shoots where you are looking only when you are accustomed to breaking the target. It will not shoot where you are looking at all yardages. Assume you shoot targets reliably at its peak. If you speed up your shooting, the gun will shoot under the target. Why? Because all trap shotguns have a slightly raised POI, but the target is rising and traveling much faster and will escape. This is where the Catch-22 comes in. As you get better, you will want to shoot faster for obvious reasons of increasing target hits. Now you have to do something dreaded by all trapshooters... make an adjustment on your gun! The POI must be raised to compensate for the new timing / zone factor. POI and timing adjustments can be treacherous. You should consult a coach who fully understands POI before tinkering with any settings on your gun. What is ever more treasonous is not adjusting POI when you should! There is a vast majority who don't own guns with POI adjustments, or who have never adjusted their POI via stock or rib adjustments and shoot terribly inconsistently. In other words, the gun doesn't fit them! And the gun does not shoot where they are looking. This is something pros do not take lightly. I wonder why? Don't you? It's time to fine-tune your shooting! After all, accuracy is the name of the game. Get your gun fitted if you want to see high scores.

POINT OF IMPACT ADJUSTMENTS
"For fools rush in where angels fear to tread." Alexander Pope

First a warning: Never change POI just for the fun of it, as I can assure you it will not be a jolly experience. It will drastically destroy your shooting. You have to know what you are doing and you must have unrelenting patience to persevere the learning curve to come. Many will tell you, never touch the rib to adjust POI. True, but why is the adjustment there? It is there for increasing accuracy of the gun, taking full advantage of rising edge-on targets. Here are some tips to make the change as easy as it should be. Refer to Fig. 1-1, 1-2, 11-3 and other drawings relating to point of impact.

FIRST POI ADJUSTMENT
"The Lord deal kindly with you." 'Ruth' 1:8.

If you don't have an adjustable rib, you can change POI by adjusting stock, adding a high rib, corrective choke, adjusting sight bead spacing and height, etc. See a gunsmith / stockfitter for solid results.

1. Buying your first gun with an adjustable rib is a wise investment for the future. First, set the rib to its lowest POI setting and learn to shoot the gun. Raising the rib -- POI will rise. Some guns lower POI when rear portion

of rib is raised, read the mfg., instructions. Focus on the straighter targets on station #3. Here you should be able to place the sight bead on the target's bottom edge and burn it. If not, raise POI slightly until you can. For accuracy, use a full or extra-full choke when testing and adjusting POI. Do not vary timing lest confusion arises.
2. When adjusting POI, remember to raise or lower your comb a smidgen, too, so your eye will still see the figure-eight. If it does, your eye will be properly aligned to the rib. Remember this, it is important!
3. Shoot this gun with this setting as long as you wish, forever is okay too, depending on how fast you are shooting. Write down the setting for future reference. Now after shooting over 6 to 12 months, and you wracked up some impressive scores, don't fiddle with the rib settings if you have a bad day, week, or month of shooting. Check to insure the rib setting is okay, and pattern check POI to verify. Don't touch that rib setting! If your scores drop after much shooting with your gun, you may be experiencing a slump, not a gun or POI problem. Slump + POI adjustments = total chaos!

LAST POI ADJUSTMENT
"The road of excess leads to the palace of wisdom." William Blake

The only time to readjust the POI next is when you wish to initiate faster shooting, planning to break targets in a closer-in zone of shooting. In other words, you see the pros shooting fast and you finally realize that you too will now have to learn to shoot quicker. Why adjust POI? Well, you want the same sight picture you had before, the bead on the target. You don't want to have to adjust sight pictures and make mental corrections. Bead always on the target is the goal. Here's how to do it.

1. First, you have to experiment and find the 'spot' or general 'zone' you plan to learn where to hit the targets. Watch a pro shoot, count the seconds and you'll see an ideal zone to be in. Don't make any rib adjustments just yet. Alter the sight picture if need be just to test the 'timing' for comfort. See "Snap Shooting." With some practice, you will 'feel' the right zone for you. This will take some time to discover, maybe a few weeks. Don't confuse this with 'spot shooting' such as using a fixed maintained lead on the first target in double trap.
2. After you have a general idea of the zone, now start raising the POI no more than 1" at a time. The rib may only rise 1/8" to get a 1" rise where the target breaks. Go back to station #3 and test fire at the bottom edge of the targets. You want to smokeball that target to insure the POI is right on the mark. If the target doesn't smoke, the POI is too high or too low shooting over or under the target. Remember, for each adjustment you must readjust the comb to maintain the figure-8 sight bead alignment. Don't try setting POI without making a comb adjustment... it won't work! To get POI right, it may take many frustrating adjustments. Don't overdue the adjustments. Just keep raising or lowing the rib ever so slightly until you get it right. Confusion sets in if you set the rib and then readjust your timing to break the target (out of your zone). Don't change your timing, adjust the gun to match your timing. If targets don't smoke, then adjust the rib accordingly until it does smoke the target in the zone. Seeing a shotgun fitter will certainly help you a great deal. You should make an appointment.
3. Now that you have the POI set right, it's time to learn how to shoot fast, adjusting to the new timing and technique. Expect confusion, and frustration... more than you bargained for. It is often very difficult to make this change-over from slow shooting to fast shooting, and making gun adjustments truly puzzles the mind, making matters ever more disquieting. Believe me, you will get razzed by fellow shooters when you make the change-over, "I told you not to touch that rib! Put it back where you had it before." Of course you used to shoot better before the rib change, but know you are on the right track if you are now shooting quicker than you used to. Just remember not to snapshoot! All you are doing is speeding up your timing, and you want your shotstring to rise up and hit the target for you. The target should still be in full form floating on the top sight bead when the trigger is pulled. Once you have adjusted the POI, there is no need to fiddle with it anymore, at least on the handicap yardage you are now shooting. What if you shoot singles? You don't have to change the POI if you don't want to. Just don't shoot the target as fast and you'll be okay. If you wish, you can lower the rib for singles and maintain the same timing. If you get punched back yardage? A minor 1/2" rise in POI is normally all that would be required, if any, depending on how far you get punched -- an easy adjustment to make.

Take the shooter without a POI adjustable rib gun. When he gets punched back in yardage... the sight pictures change! He has to learn all over again the new bird / bead relationships for that yardage and apply more lead to the targets. The adjustable rib, when raised, will do this for you automatically while you maintain the same sight picture you always had. Quite an advantage to have in your favor.

ENCOURAGEMENT NEEDED
"Unless you enter the tiger's den, you cannot take the cubs."

Confidence is a trust or faith in a person or thing. A feeling of assurance, especially of self-assurance. A state or quality of being certain. Self-possession leads to confidence as you develop a feeling of emotional security ensuing from faith in oneself, resulting in composure arising from control over one's own reactions. Confidence is a firm belief in one's powers, abilities, and capacities stressing trust in one's own self-sufficiency. You gain strength, courage and self-assurance directly from experience and looking fear in the face. Trapshooting is not easy. Anyone who tells you it is, ask them to demonstrate shooting 100 - straight handicap targets! That'll set the record straight, promptly ending disagreements. Learning trapshooting is a grueling experience. At first it's just plain fun, until you begin to like the sport, then it gets wretched as targets slip away, yet you've hit them thousands of times before. Why is that? It's the nature of the beast. Ten percent of the game is equipment and 90% is mind over mater. It's all in the mind. You'll soon learn how little control we humans have over our subconscious. It's as if our minds have a mind of their own and will not do what we want them to do. This syndrome is severe in the first couple years of serious trapshooting. You must wade through the murky waters and keep swimming onward toward shore. You will have imperfect and delightful days. Moods overpower shooting performance, instituting dispositions you have little control over. All shooters have on and off days. When the off-days persist, then you have what is called a slump. This, too, is typical and is caused by myriad factors. The unequaled therapy to recover from a slump is break from shooting for a week or two. When you come back on line, don't think of anything. Just slow down your shooting to regain accuracy, shoot for amusement and you'll descry you can still shoot after all. If you are still in a slump, then it's time to retain a coach for evaluation. Odds are you are making elementary mistakes and the big seven are: **1)** Lifting your head looking for the target you expect to miss. **2)** Getting too serious, overly concentrating to the point you are not relaxed, perhaps even paranoid. **3)** Improper eye focus and gun hold to the traphouse. **4)** You lost synchronization with your inner time clock shooting too fast or too slow. **5.)** Not looking at the target's proper focal-point zone. **6.)** Foot position and stance changed swing accuracy. **7)** Somewhere, somehow, you forgot your basic setup formula or something has changed and you have no inkling of what went wrong. Insufficient memory -- an excusable excuse. It's time to shadow practice at home mounting the gun, checking foot position/stance, swing movements, eye focus, timing your call, etc. Leave no stone unturned! Check your shoes and vest pad for wear, gun rib, comb height, recoil pad, POI, chokes, loads, general health including vision exam, etc. Often the enigma is so innocent it'll make you burst into tears of laughter when you do detect the problem.

Remind yourself all athletes have slumps, bad days and good days; it's part and parcel to trapshooting. Golf professionals for example: one year they are on top of the world, and next year someone else takes their place. The same is true with basketball, bowling, baseball, etc. Trapshooters are no exemption. Don't expect miracles overnight. It takes many thousands upon thousands of rounds to be a good shooter, and it takes years. Relax, don't beat up on yourself; it's certainly not a confidence-inspiring thing to do. Slow, but steady, wins the race. Consistent, effective exertion leads to success. What the sport is all about is an individual doing his best. Be the best you can be with the skill level you currently have. Don't create overblown expectations. Yes. At times you may feel like a loser and contemplate quitting the sport, reasoning you don't have what it takes. Discouragement is trapshooting! A series of failures and self-rejections. In time, you will win, as time is on your side. Success happens. Time is the key to success. Time and determination win. Win what? The Grand American? Could happen, but is this your only goal? Set your objective a little lower and work up from there... in time! Expecting too much, too soon, creates frustration, which spirals into disarrayed, negative thought patterns. Success is a series of failures preceding success. Each failed event is a learning experience, a step up toward success. If you feel bad about your shooting performance, just think back a year or two how bad scores were then. This should give you a sense of accomplishment!

There will always be somebody who can shoot better than you, on any given day. The pros win, but not every event, they lose too! Concentrate not on matching the performance of the pros, but winning in the classification you are in. Fret about the pros when you're a back fence or All-American trapshooter. Making a living at trapshooting should not be an immediate goal, as few high gun shooters do so themselves. A realistic goal is to earn money to help pay costs. That's a reasonable and obtainable goal, though still challenging to achieve. Then what does matter? Don't leave out the fun factor. You shoot trap for enjoyment, too, don't you? Most importantly, don't burn out. If you are having down-trending or static scores know you are not alone. Thousands of trapshooters are suffering exactly as you are. Did everyone walk away with a trophy and prize money on the last shoot you attended? Okay, so you lost out. Come back another day with a new perspective and energy to boot. Losing doesn't mean you're a born loser. Losing an event is competitive birth. You'll grow out of it.

MANAGING GOALS AND FAILURE
"Those who lose today may win tomorrow."

The shooting process works only if it keeps moving from step to step. Many things can stand in the way of advanced progress. Managing your time is one. Not how many targets you break each day or week, but the quality of the learning experience takes priority. The unique way you can reach the successful completion of your plan, and your dream, is with proper time management, which means developing the discipline to do what you said you would do. Winners do it today, while losers think about doing it, someday.

Aim high; hope for great things. Set realistic obtainable goals, exceeding your grasp. If you miss the stars, you'll hit the moon. Don't give in to the easy way of saying, *"Oh, if I shot 20,000 rounds a year I too would be as good as..."* What you should say is, *"I know I'm good, I am getting better, and I'm working on my mistakes."* This builds a positive self-image, which results in enhanced performance, and develops a professional attitude, which makes you a professional on the rise. The better you feel about yourself, the better you'll do. Confidence-building is critical. Keep striving to improve and you will. Tell yourself; *"I will not quit, I'm getting better and I'll keep getting better until I achieve perfect scores."* Be sharp, quick, and eager when you call for each target. Do what pros do, just do more of it. Being committed, persistent, and disciplined will see you through. Remember these vital keys for success, COMMITMENT, PERSISTENCE, DISCIPLINE. To climb a mountain, you can't just leap to its peak; it takes perseverance, one step at a time. If you rush, you may slip and fall. Goals should have a reasonable time-frame, as a journey of a thousand miles begins with one step.

Failure plays a huge role in achieving success. Learning from mistakes (failure) builds success. As you learn from mistakes you are trying more new things. When you try new things you lose more, but in the end you win more! The glory of defeat. Here's the formula: Try more + fail more = win more! The more you try, the more you fail, but the more you fail the more you will succeed. One wins, one loses. Why? I've never been defeated in a rifle or pistol competition. Why? Because I never tried! By avoiding the above, I avoided failure but also avoided success, too. Failure and success are intimately tied together, not worlds apart as most would perceive. It is known to succeed in anything is to multiply your failures. Failure breeds success as long as you have persistence, determination, and a goal. Thomas Edison failed many times before finding the perfect filament for the light bulb. Henry Ford's engineers repeatedly told Mr. Ford, *"The V-eight engine is impossible to build."* For years Henry made them return to the lab to 'make it work'. They did! Nothing comes out right the first time we try things. Only after repeated failures is the right formula discovered.

You have to learn to live with failure to overcome failure and then success will come. Most trapshooters view failure as an end to be avoided, but an exceptionally successful shooter sees failure as a roadmap to success. The worst failure of all is avoiding failure! Babe Ruth struck-out 1,330 times, but he also hit 714 home runs! English novelist John Creasey received 753 agonizing rejection slips before he published 500 + books! Everyone loses before they win. Consider the life of a Hall of Fame baseball player. He can strike out nearly twice for each time he gets up to bat, and he's still a Hall of Famer. How can you strike out two out of three times and still be an enormous success? All you have to do it bat approximately .333 over a career and it inserts the player in the Hall of Fame. Note, that also includes lame years he had! The same is true with trapshooters, it's a numbers game. The more you play, the more you lose and the more you win. So the next time you feel like giving up, feeling it's not worth it, remind yourself slumps -- and poor performance are merely temporary frustrations and are actually opportunities to obtain knowledge. You enjoy trapshooting don't you? Yes. It can be frustrating, and your goal is often so far out of reach it might as well be on the moon, but man did eventually get to the moon.

Know your enemy. When you find yourself confronted with a seemingly impossible obstacle, seek out shooters who have had the same problem. Keep an open mind and listen to everyone, be amenable to try all things, anything, to resolve the problem. Break the problem down into small manageable steps, preferably on 3 by 5 index cards. Now go resolve each problem one-by-one. It may take a week, maybe a month or two, or more, to get it right, but the solution is there waiting for discovery. Seek progress...as progress - failure = perfection. If you can't sidestep a certain problem then go over, under or through it. You can often learn more from failures than you do from the successes. Slumps are diagnostic; they highlight problems. You'd never sprout and grow without failures. Too many shooters quit because they had a bad season or two. Often these shooters have come to a point of stagnation. The mind rebels, screaming *"I am bored"* and still the shooter fails to take on new shooting style, form or technique. Shooting is expensive. So is failure. So is success. It takes years of dedication, commitment and sacrifice. No one likes the word sacrifice, but you either work hard now for the greater prize waiting for you in the future, or take the easy road and get what you deserve afterward. Always be willing to do whatever it takes to succeed. Successful trapshooting is simply doing the right things at the right time, all of the time. Easy to say, hard to do. A slump is a temporary switch of the tracks, not a total derailment. To reset the switch may slow you down negotiating another learning curve, but a new shooting technique will point the way, and you'll soon be back on the high iron, highballing full steam to the throttle. There is a saying I coined when shooting at fun turkey shoots, *"If you want to win, you have to taste the turkey."* So it is with managing your goals, you have to know what you want and how to get it. It is not pure skill that wins, but he who wants the prize the most. How is this? Desire has a built-in reactor which can elevate your shooting talent to totally unexpected levels of accomplishment. There is no need to explain how it works, it just does. Again, mind over matter takes precedence.

THE LIGHTER SIDE OF TRAPSHOOTING
"It's obvious you won't survive with luck alone."

Stepping into the dimly-lit twilight, it's time to consider the not so obvious mysteries of kismet (a fancy word for luck and fortune). A California shooting chum was in the midst of a severe slump. I gave this shooter, as a gag, a good luck bone. I suggested having it in possession at all times when shooting, and to activate the bone's magical powers utter, *"Bad to the bone."* The shooter did and scores gradually elevated. The more this shooter believes the magic bone will help the finer shooter to be. That is the fickle mind for you. All it takes is a bit of encouragement, a small nudge of conviction and often prescribed candid humor... and the scores come back anew. The legendary rabbit foot has been encouraging thousands of years. Many people believe in it. Certainly, a foot, bone, amulet or charmstone will not impart talent. This appears from experience.

You earn your luck by consistently applying yourself to the effort, but if you need a providential charm, then by all means get one. If you don't have one, then you may need to live with the scores you are shooting until you become proficient. Which lucky charm works? Who cares! As long as they achieve results for you, then they work just fine. Remember, the mind has a disposition of its own. You can't govern it completely. Just as eye muscles can be fatigued, so shall the mind. When the gray matter gets jaded; watch out, scores plummet as stones tumble down a mine shaft. I know shooters who use lucky charms and refuse to own up to it. To their unawares, it is oftentimes a special pair of shooting glasses, a glove, a hat, their shotgun and even shotshells. If they don't use them, they can't shoot well. Think about that! Did you know the top fuel drag racers carry lucky charms with them in their cars? Ask them and you'll see they do! Positive mementos for that extra edge needed to win.

Listen to shooters' excuses for their low scores. Somewhere in the conversation, an item resembling a lucky charm will surface. *"I didn't wear my shooting vest."* Or, *"The shells I'm using are not my usual brand."* Or, *"I'm tying out this new choke."* Shooters fail to recognize when they need to buy a new gun they are searching for a magic lucky charm. They'll dispense thousands of dollars on a fashionable new gun, reasoning this will twist their luck. Most would be better off with a glorified trinket than buying a new gun. Anything, though it be a magic clam shell, feather, gold ring, foot, bone or stone, if it helps get you back on station shooting strong is worth investigating. So, the next time the wife gives you an incantation of good luck, try it... it just may work. At the least, a mite of good old-fashioned tomfoolery and humor will go the extra mile.

GETTING BACK TO THE HEAVY SIDE OF TRAPSHOOTING
"If it wasn't for bad luck, I wouldn't have no luck at all." Albert King

Luck has very little to do with shooting, other than to maintain the illusion that we are sometimes lucky, sometimes not. Excellence is not built on the foundation of luck. Many shooters engage in competitive events hoping for the best. These shooters have no expectation of winning. You don't approach tournament shoots in the same way you approach a gambling table in Reno or Las Vegas. The odds of winning are much higher in a registered shoot. You are not rolling dice! However, professionals do everything in their capacity to increase the odds in their favor. And serious people do everything in their power to increase their potential of winning. People tend to pray, wish, hope, think and dream about winning, but they seldom develop a strategy or plan of action. They spend more time and energy planning to arrive at the shoot than formulating a mental strategy of winning. Marriages are made in heaven, but winning trapshoots requires a plan. Human beings make choices. Many are poor choices, especially when it comes to relentless work and taking responsibility for decisions, in addition to mastering how to make effective choices. Genius is 1% inspiration and 99% perspiration. This is not to say digging ditches will make you a genius. But it does mean you will come closer to realizing your mind's fullest potential if you work a great deal harder building up skills.

Great accomplishments depend not so much on ingenuity but more on strategy. The point is to set up criteria, take appropriate actions, then allow for time to take its course. It's like surrounding yourself with rich, beautiful women. Eventually you'll fall in love with one of them. An intentional strategy for success can increase the odds of this happening. Winning competitions looks easy for those who win, but the many years of frustrating practice sessions, slumps, discouragement and failure are not seen behind the scene. All along the way we are collecting information and fine tuning our choices. The plan is simple, break each target, though the execution of the plan is difficult. What is the strategy? More mental stimuli, attitude adjustment, thought control, concentration, fearlessness, confidence, and a bit of fortune upon a prayer surely helps. You'll see higher scores if you act on your beliefs rather than merely talk about them. Actions speak louder than words, as people are more impressed with our sincerity if we act on our beliefs than if we merely talk about them. *"What you do sounds so loud I can't hear what you say."* Set a plan of action. Practice smart, and shoot to win! Grab your lucky charm -- you won't be the only one -- mark your calendar to attend the registered shoots.

GETTING INTO A SHOOTOFF
"Better a handful of dry dates and content therewith than to own the Gate of Peacocks and be kicked in the eye by a brooding camel."

Don't be embarrassed if you become nervous the first time or the fiftieth time. It's normal and expected. Remind yourself the other shooter is nervous too... even if he doesn't appear nervous... he is! Step one is to wipe the scene out of your mind immediately that you are shooting a race with an opponent. You are not shooting against anyone else but yourself! It's just you and the target. Never turn around and see the people watching. Just ignore them, it's time to concentrate on the target and nothing else. Don't check out the other shooter to see if he's nervous or not, or how he shoots. He doesn't exist! These are the thoughts you should have in your mind, *"Hit the target, hit the target, smoke it!"* This may all sound overly elementary and simplistic, but simplicity is the key to success. When under pressure, you have to trust in your shooting technique to carry you though the day, or should I say, the grueling tribulations of shooting off? There will be pressure on you, no doubt about it. Your knees may actually feel week and hands quiver in extreme cases. If you lose the shootoff, it will likely be to nerves, failing to see the target and inability to precisely move towards it, self-doubt, not your shooting form. A good lesson to learn is attitude is everything. In time, nervousness will decrease, but will always be present to some degree. If you're not nervous or a tad energized with apprehension something is wrong. A tinge of fear activates a heightened state of awareness and quick reflex reactions. It stimulates competitive forces to exceed your expectations. Winning always comes by surprise! Getting into shootoffs will increase self-confidence. It's like riding a roller coaster for the first time; intense fear, then after intervals of experience dispelling the fear it becomes fun. Remember, it's only a game and you likely won't win all of the time. This is a good section to read before you shootoff.

When shooting before a crowd of spectators, just remember one thing... today you are better than all, for you are here and they are yonder watching. They want to see a good shooter shoot. That's you! Alas, you have stepped into the limelight. This is where you should not be concentrating on your nervous condition. Give them a performance to applaud. People are counting on you to put on a show; actually they want you to win. They are rooting for you. It is your moment of recognition and accomplishment. Happy thoughts rejuvenate the inner spirit and will likely help you to win the match. And even if you lose, you sure did a fine job after all! Granting you win or lose, be proud of yourself; you sported the shootoff. Only the excellent players reach this stage of the game. Congratulate yourself (and the winner if you lose). You should not be thinking of the prize money or trophy. You shut everything down and concentrate only on smoking targets, especially focusing on seeing the target. Ignore the crowd's *"Ohh's"* and *"Ahh's"* and most of all ignore the other shooter. He doesn't exist! The only thing that exists is seeing and smashing the target... nothing else. And don't fret when you miss, for the odds are the other guy missed, too, or will soon miss one or two or three. It happens all the time due to tournament pressure. Don't dwell on the miss, emphasize the next target and imagine yourself hammering it into a dust cloud.

When shooting off with one or five shooters be aware of the subtle, yet effectively damaging, psychological games that can be played on you. Forewarned is forearmed. All's fair in love and war. Someone, perhaps a friend who you will shootoff with, may intentionally mention to you or within earshot how potent of a shooter his buddy is. Even well-meaning friends of yours may nudge your subconscious in reverse by saying, *"Don't miss any"* or *"Good luck."* These subtle injections can influence you, so you might remind yourself you are good, and you don't require luck, just skill and all the self-confidence you can muster through intense concentration. This is why many pros don't mingle with the crowd prior to shootoffs. If you step onto the line noticing your opponent has placed a case of shells on deck, it can be a psychological ruse to fool you into rationalizing the shooter will run them all. Don't believe it. It's never over till it's over. If you miss a target or two, don't give up too soon; there may still be a chance to win. Read these paragraphs before you answer the shootoff call.

Your opponent's friends may be shooting off with you and you may not know it. What happens here is they intentionally speed up their timing, trying to influence you to accelerate with them, knowing it will kilter your setup and timing, hoping you'll miss a target. Be very careful to maintain your own game, even if someone murmurs input about your timing or disrupting rhythm. Remember, nobody and nothing exists except you and the target. Play your own game so others will fail to influence you. Believe me, when there is money involved, people will do strange things, anything, to psyche you out. To think about the money or trophy will take your mind off the target. Before a shootoff, it is prime to spend a few minutes alone to rest and gather these thoughts of self-control to build energy and confidence. After all, you have to be good... you got into the finals! Strike when the iron is hot and use any reasonable means to reach the goal. Whether it is the psychology of a good luck charm, aspirin or a vitamin pill, this is the time to use them to seize the day. Don't forget, when answering the shootoff call, bring a lighter shade of shooting glasses as the shootoff occurs in late afternoon into the night under low light conditions. I've seen shooters overlook this simple fact and miss targets, only later discovering the problem. It is advantageous to use a reminder checklist of needed equipment. How many times have you forgotten to bring something to the shoot? Or used the wrong shells for the event? Precision requires perfection. Leave chance to memory and consistency falls.

CHAPTER 12

PSYCHOLOGY OF THE GAME
"Patience is the remedy for every trouble."

A virtue to learn is patience, patience, and more patience! Towering scores do not arrive instantaneously. It takes years of experience to excel in any sport or endeavor. Be easy on yourself and never become frustrated, as it truly is a sign of an amateur. When learning, low scores should be expected so there is no need to be embarrassed. Every high gun shooter at one time was struggling, missing targets, and kicking themselves in the seat of the pants, too... and probably a worse shooter than you were when first starting out! No one is born with a shotgun in their hands. Tournament shooting adds tremendous pressure and stress than popping a few rounds at the local gun club with the boys; it can be grueling, scary and outright embarrassing, so join the gang, you are not alone! Don't be astonished to see your score and say, *"What happened? I shoot better than this!"* You may be a good shooter at the club, yet nose-dived in the registered shoot. Welcome to the world of psychology, where mysteries abound in confusion with no clear explanation or understanding prevails!

Be prepared for the anxiety attack; it happens to shooters when tournament stress is encountered. There is a lot of pressure on you to perform and it doesn't help to be 'on stage' with a crowd behind you watching you miss targets. The first few registered shoots can be the most discouraging experience, as it instills feelings of inadequacy. When you shoot the singles event and see shooters smashing every single one of them targets and you're missing... it ain't fun! Embarrassment sets in, fear, humiliation, discouragement, anger -- the emotions just keep bombarding your mind, taking over your shooting. This is your reality wake-up call to at last confront the psychology of the game. You now know how powerful it is; it can totally ruin scores, fast! You know, you just know it, the other squad members are snickering silently as you fumble on to another lost target, but keep in mind, you may be shooting on a squad of 'Hot Dog' AA-class shooters who eat hundreds straight for breakfast! The mind floods with emotions. Expect it. It dissipates to a manageable level the more you shoot registered events, though it may never truly vanish.

Even top musicians and actors will tell you they still experience stage-fright willies before each performance, yet once they push past the first bar or dialog the fear is replaced with confidence in their abilities. Focus switches to technique. Top shooters will tell you they, too, experience uneasiness in high stake shootoff's. Fact is, that is when they are most vulnerable to miss targets; when the pressure is on. So when psychological pressure rears its ominous head and you miss a target, don't become transfixed by the error, push on past it and take your next best shot. The point I'm trying to nail down is give yourself a chance to fail before you win. Attending a competitive tournament expecting instant glory will likely disappoint you. There are many supershot shooters out there. To expect to beat them in your first year of competition should not be your goal. Too many shooters try registered shoots, get their egos trampled, and never return. It's the wrong attitude! If you can't stand the heat, get out of the kitchen is not applicable here. First of all, no one is beating anyone, and no one is truly competing against anyone. It's just you and the target, always! Break one target more than everyone else and you win! Try starting out shooting handicap events, as most everyone misses targets and you won't feel as pressured as shooting singles. Be patient as it will take a few years before your name gets around as a serious competitor. But never underestimate yourself -- you can be winning events in your assigned classification right on the first day you ever attend a registered shoot. I didn't win anything until my fourth tournament, then lost a few, then won again, lost, then won again. It's up & down, the more you lose, the more you win; this is the 'learning phase' trying to exterminate bad habits, attempting new technique and strategies, and worse, forgetting what you learned. Repetition has a way of polishing technique, including bad technique, so it's a growing and discovery phase that must be endured (it never actually ends).

Here are some tips on recognizing, experimenting, and building a shooting foundation based on psychology. There are books available on sports psychology, so we'll just touch lightly on the subject.

1. Stress: When you suffer an attack of nerves you're being attacked by the nervous system. Expect it, learn to manage it. Be totally consumed with shooting to the degree you don't know anyone is nearby. You don't even know you're in a shootoff. It's just you and the target as always. You may hear a crowd of people behind you, block it out, they are watching someone else, not you. Don't count the targets hit or missed, just keep shooting as best you can. When stress arrives along with fear, simply get down hard on that gun and concentrate just on shooting, using your proven technique, form and style. Remind yourself your system works and don't vacillate, stay with what you know works during the shootoff. Making any alteration is an open invitation for stress to take control. To beat stress fracturing, you learn to ignore stress through mental diversion. Be relaxed as possible, but be very aggressive with the eyes looking for the target and focusing hard on it when it emerges.

2. Anxiety attack: This is flinty to deal with. It can envelop you without warning and for no logical reason. It is always triggered by some event, ever so slight at times, which diverts your shooting attention toward thoughts of stress inducers, fear, embarrassment, etc. Both stress and anxiety combine to rattle your nerves. You lose control. Your hands and knees may shake, increased sweating, and fear are symptoms. It is a state of uneasiness and apprehension focused on future uncertainties and fright, resulting from anticipation of a threatening event or situation, often to a degree the natural physical and psychological functioning of the affected individual is disrupted. If you are too eager to form a good impression anxiety will often agitate your desire. Some shooters resort to alcohol to help calm the nerves, where others may resort to a mild prescription tranquilizer, while others learn to manage their stress from within their own mind. The latter is most desirable, as positive stress is beneficial to managing maximum awareness. Drugs, guns and alcohol are incompatible and counterproductive.

3. Nerves: A combination of stress and anxiety which materializes within the mind, affecting body muscles. Here is when stress gets too far out of hand, when the hands shake, pulse rises, body becomes unglued, rigid and tensed. The physical moves to the target are disrupted and no amount of concentration can overcome its disabling affects. Call it nerve-wracking, as it is intensely distressing and irritating to the nervous system and the mind. When your nerves are affected, everything falls down the proverbial rabbit hole. Every muscle is energized to overload extremes, even the oculomotor nerve muscles that move your eyes. Things get out of adjustment quickly and shooting performance disintegrates rapidly. Some shooters psyche-out their competitor in a war of nerves using subtle psychological tactics creating conflict through intimidation intended primarily to confuse his competitor and erode that person's morale. The cure is rather simple, ignore everything, everyone, and every thought that comes into your mind having nothing to do with your shooting. To combat nerves, use self-assuring thoughts, *"When the heat is on I shoot better!"* *"No fear of fear!"* *"Just shoot the target and smokeball it!"*

4. Self-confidence: What is it? Trusting or faith in a person or thing. It's a feeling of assurance, especially of self-assurance in your ability to succeed, a feeling of emotional security resulting from faith in oneself and a firm belief in one's powers, abilities, or capacities. Often, to be self-confident you must be very bold, trusting in your shooting form to take you to the top. You gain confidence through experience. You begin learning confidence on the first day you shot a clay. It comes with time and demonstrated ability. When first attending registered shoots, self-assuredness may be shattered. Your scores may even backslide to humiliating levels due to tournament stress. Negative thoughts of inability may enter your psyche. Realize we must first learn how to lose before we learn how to win. Don't quit shooting tournaments just because it was difficult or the odds seemed impossible to beat. It's a challenge! A goal to strive for! And yes, it can be fun! Of course you'll forfeit entry fees, but it won't take long before you'll receive money in the 25 and 50 options and occasionally win or place in the Calcutta and walk away with some well deserved cash. Play your own game with the options and don't concentrate on competing with high gunners or contemplate prize awards. Your day will come, believe me, it will... and likely sooner than you expect! That's how self-confidence arrives, through small victories leading to ever larger conquests.

5. Feelings of inadequacy: An entire book could be written on this subject alone. Often inadequacy is due to improper technique and bad habits. You can't shoot well if you shoot wrong! However, assuming you are shooting properly and you still feel you don't measure up, know that it is natural to have these feelings. If Mike Tyson were to lose a fight, would he say, *"Let's go celebrate!"* Of course not, but you shouldn't feel overly down in the dumps and dwell too long on failures. Failing is the path to success! Behind every success story is a

long series of failures. Failure is opportunity! It's a learning experience which motivates and eventually pays big dividends. One method of beating discouragement is to set smaller goals and to reach them one-by-one over a realistic period of time. For a new shooter the goal would be getting a 25 straight, then 50, then 75, then by that time the 100 straight is not as impossible as first presumed. Yes, still difficult, but you're real close to it now!

6. Technique is the key! Execution of movement to the target is a passport to reduce stress. It builds confidence, relaxation and concentration. This is accomplished by precision and faith in your moves. It's like watching a TV advertisement over and over, again sending messages to your subconscious mind. Your technique includes trigger control, pulling the sear off the ledge only when seeing the correct sight picture. Naturally, this similarly relates to acquiring the target rapidly so you <u>can</u> see the correct sight picture. Slow shooters experience too many sight pictures to remember. Distance traveled = increasing target arcs = impossible target sight picture combinations to reliably memorize for instant recall. Now you know one of the greater reasons why missing targets materialize. Distance is a mortal enemy to the trapshooter. Fast shooting reduces many complications and increases the odds for success.

EMOTIONAL BAGGAGE
"Men trip not on mountains; they stumble on molehills."

A small topic with enormous consequences: Emotion. Easier said than demonstrated, you put your emotional baggage where it will do you some good instead of pursuing self-defeating strategies. Emotivity induces dramatic and intense mental states where even good emotions can be as bad as displeasing feelings. This is not to say you will be a zombie on the line, but quite close to it! Rather described as being in a hypnotic state... a dreamlike state of mind where nothing can go wrong, and when a target is lost the spell isn't broken. Doesn't this describe those days when shooting seems a breeze and you're hitting all the targets with ease? If only we could latch on and retain that mood! You can, but it takes tremendous mental trial and perseverance to locate and tap into this internal energy source, but once discovered, it can be retrieved.

First, grasp there is only one advantage of emotions... to mislead! The trapshooter has no time to dedicate dispositions of joy, sorrow, disappointment, staggering shock, surprise, bewilderment, dismay, agitation, etc. There is a job to do and it's busting targets... no more, no less. It's serious business! It's also hard work! We all too often get sidetracked and open the door for emotions to wash in and thrash the mind. I associate the essence of controlling emotions as an act of war raging within our intellect. Try to control them and you'll be in for a prizefight of your life. It's a terrific learning curve to experience and a very discouraging one, at that. However, it is necessary to win the struggle to break free of the emotions holding your feet to the fire. Some shooters, and I mean many, have emotional handicaps. Most of us have strong inclinations to rely on or place too much value on emotion, believing it will help us break more targets; however, the inverse is truer in the real business of trapshooting. Imagine the consequences of a surgeon having internal emotional turmoil as he operates. If you've ever witnessed a surgery, you'd think it were a production studio's sitcom-take as jokes are passed to and fro to break tension. Imagine the potential aftermath of an airline pilot doubting with distress, wondering if he can genuinely trust his abilities to land his jet? Imagine the trapshooter's fears and apprehensions if he can break the target? See the relationship? Force of character and personality play an integral role in the world of sports, as it does in the professional disciplines of the working world.

Flip the coin. The surgeon uses positive thinking; *"I know I can do it, I know I can, I've done it a hundred times before."* This emotion may appear to be positive yet it is negative thinking. Why? The surgeon shouldn't even have to tell himself he can do it, for he already knows he can! If he's thinking, he's doubting! Confidence is jeopardized. The airline pilot: *"Maintain heading, airspeed, left rudder okay? Wind-shear could be... oh, no, jet wash could be ahead."* Bites his lower lip, *"Okay, we're drifting. Flaps! My flaps are up! Nope, they're okay."* Takes a deep breath, *"Wheels down, but are they locked? I don't trust that enunciator light, never did."* This pilot is an emotional wreck waiting for a accident to happen. He's thinking too much of what he already knows how to do as he casts unrealistic doubts on his instruments and abilities. The trapshooter: *"Another blooper! That's the fourth time now! I'll never shoot with that Bozo again, cost me a target already."* Regains his composure, *"Okay, cut the mustard now and dust that target."* He calls quickly yet gets a slow pull, fires, misses clean. *"Darn puller!"* Tries again, *"Pull."* A perfect target easy to hit, pulls trigger, misses, *"That blathering Bozo is still fiddling with his gun!"* Bozo's turn is up. He shoots, hits the target. A thought races through the shooter's mind in a micro-flash, *"Son of a...!"* Thinking can get a shooter into trouble fast. Focusing not on the target and diverting attention to placing blame for interruptions and human errors creates disaster for this shooter. His mind is raging a war within and he's losing the battle!

Emotions are deadly to the trapshooter. Get a grasp on them or they will get a grip on you. Stop thinking, as it's the passageway to self-doubt. It will surely unfocus your eyes and divert concentration away from the target. Your temperament determines your level of confidence. Mettle with emotions and be assured the following sensations will insidiously latch onto your game: inattention, carelessness, forgetfulness, neglect, oversight, omissions, indifference, unwatchfulness, unpreparedness, disregard, anger, devil-may-care attitude, recklessness, unvigilant, laziness, disorder, sloppiness, inaccuracy, disappointment, slackness, impatience, over-eagerness, over-activity, false expectation, hopelessness, resignation, lack of interest, unexpected results, fear, miscalculation, error, jack-in-the-box surprises, desperation, sorrow, jealousy, to name a few. Keep this one material fact in mind... just one negative thought can trigger a chain reaction assembling many, if not all of these elements, racing throughout your mind. As demonstrated, even a positive thought can produce identical consequences. So where should your thoughts be when shooting? Just visualize hitting the target and where you want to hit it and do just that. With uncluttered thoughts and the emotional effects they create absent, you can here and now concentrate on shooting. When your temperament is locked-in, your subconscious mind will take over eye / hand coordination and bird / bead relationships. This habit of mind does not arrive without earnest training. First, stop skipping and dodging the issue. The problem exists, so deal with it. It is an inherited characteristic. A spirit, tone, a sort of cast of mind or human defect. Call it as you will, but it's a part of personality, psychology, and psyche. Deep stuff here. Now that you are aware of the emotions and the incredible power of thought, the problems are easy to recognize when they surface. Recognition is the key to controlling emotions that can develop serious habits that adversely affect your ability to concentrate and hit targets.

Develop a predisposition and mood all winners have... the ability to <u>focus</u> on winning. Become a genius at creating tunnel vision. Losers have the expectations and frame of mind to lose, they don't expect to win even though they have tremendous physical adrenaline surges with psychological attitudes of cheerfulness, gameness, zeal, eagerness, enthusiasm, initiative, devotion, and dedication. Shooting should be spontaneous, and to shoot well the 'mind over matter' theory is utterly hard-boiled fact. Be prepared for the unexpected, unforeseen contingency and unusual occurrence. A practice session is in order. Let's try to tap into the mysterious world of emotional control. All of these conditions will 'trigger' emotional responses. Learn to control them.

PRACTICE TIPS - Phase 5
"Within silence appears inspiration."

1. Ask the puller to randomly not release a target when you call and be inconsistent, even twice in a row! This should get your thought juices steaming. Don't forget the fast pulls. You'll receive a firm education on interruption and distraction control training.
2. Ask shooters if they will participate in a 'haggle shoot' where others boldly laugh and criticize each other's shooting ability, foot position/stance, etc., all in good humor. Learn to laugh along with them, participate yourself in haggling, then turn on the juice when it's your turn to shoot, ignoring all of them. Develop mind control.
3. Shoot with a known disorderly shooter. Keep all thoughts neutral. If any thoughts come to mind, compassion should take priority, still don't let any emotion grasp on. Block <u>all</u> emotional intrusions. Turn-off conscious thoughts. Concentrate on the desired result of breaking the target! Train you subconscious mind.
4. Shoot with someone you normally avoid shooting with. It may be youngsters or treasonous shooters who talk, giggle and goof-off, or someone who misses a ton of targets. You'll learn a lot here.
5. Ask the setter to place a few 'flippers' so you'll see illegal targets. It's good to know you can handle turning down these targets without emotional intrusions.

6. Think negative thoughts; *"I'm not up to par today." "I just can't hit them all." "The game is too complex." "That shooter on post #4, I hope he misses!"* You should start dropping targets with thoughts like these. Why do it? So you'll appreciate thoughts alone can cost you targets. And if you can still hit targets, you've mastered the art of mind / emotion control, or you were just lucky.

7. If you miss a target, a thought may come to your mind, *"I'll never do that again!"* If you hit a target clean dead center, *"That was easy."* Both thoughts are harmful because now you are 'thinking,' diverting concentration towards a missed target to surely come. Don't think. Instead, visualize the error and correct it by instant replay in your mind but this time smoking the target. Some shooters talk to themselves when missing a target and for them it may just be fine, but for most it is not a good idea to flood the mind with thoughts. Learn to control emotions lest thoughts overwhelm concentration.

ASSEMBLING SKILL & KNOWLEDGE
"Who begins too much, accomplishes little."

Obviously, the key to high scores is good solid technique combined with an intelligent plan to break each target, one-by-one, and to recognize problems quickly before you drop targets. If a lost target occurs, immediately reevaluate your setup, recognize any field conditions that influenced the loss. Field conditions are effectively rectified prior to shooting by walking the trap line observing the traps, targets and backgrounds. Listen to the shooters when the squad leaves a trap. You are likely to pick up a tip or two to give you an edge. It is often said you can learn more with your ears than with your eyes. Seeing things does not always lead to accurate interpretations, though understanding the reason why a thing is done makes seeing believing. Shooters read books upon books upon legions of magazine articles, yet fail to grasp and apply what is being explained. How is that? Well, trapshooting is as difficult to explain as it would be to explain how to play golf. It's a doers sport where learning comes from doing. The next time you read a good magazine article, take it with you to practice, read it, then apply what you read. Do the same with this book and you will see great progress and rising scores!

If you find yourself making too slow progress, this is why -- we forget what we read. Take a note card with you and list specific techniques to focus on. Practical knowledge is a combination of instruction and application reinforced by hands-on doing. Knowledge without application is unusable trivia. Memorization is useless in trapshooting unless it is memorized action! Do or die. Reading without retention dislodges newly acquired knowledge. You've heard the term "muscle memory" that describes a memorization of hand / eye coordination. Muscles do not have a memory, only the brain has this capability, but by doing, the brain can recall and instruct the muscles to render remembered instructions. So if you are not refreshing and imbedding knowledge into your memory by bringing the written page with you to practice sessions, you will not progress and learn as well as you could, or not at all. The reason why I stress keeping this book with your gun or in your vehicle is so it will be available for review. Believe me, actually practicing what you have read and learned will generate a tremendous leap in your scores. Have you brought a magazine article to a practice session for the sole purpose and intent of applying the new-found knowledge? There is power in the written word.

POWER OF THE SUBCONSCIOUS
"There is an intelligence within we do not heed."

There is one aspect pros have: a presence of mind control with a strict, disciplined shooting technique. Watching them is like observing a machine. They work flawlessly. Notice the determination radiating from them as they shoot. This is attributed to many years of shooting experience, but if this were absolutely true, then the more years you shoot the better you should be, and we know that not always ring true. The secret is in the mind. The subconscious mind is so powerful it's undeniably frightening to see it in action. Go watch an entertainment hypnotist perform his trade. He will select members from the audience, talk to them, and make people do incredibly preposterous things at his command. The subjects can't say no, they unquestioningly obey no matter how much they don't wish to make morons of themselves in public, yet comply they will. The power of the subconscious is so potent, a cold spoon placed on a subject's skin and said to be red hot, causes a burn blister to appear on the skin! A less radical experiment is to close your eyes and write, *"I can hit targets."* Notice how the subconscious can write, not perfectly, but it knows what to do, guiding your hand to write letters you can not see. This is a shallow equivalent of the subconscious. Trapshooters must explore the deeper levels.

There are two ways you can tap into your subconscious mind. You can buy books and audiotapes and keep telling yourself you're a great shot (autosuggestion), or you can see a hypnotist for treatment. Many people do. Smokers have quit smoking, overweight people lost weight, depressed moods uplifted, and salespersons sell more products. Motivational hypnosis, whether self-taught or treated by a professional, will do one thing -- increase self-possessing confidence to hit more targets. Many athletes and movie stars use the services of a hypnotist or self-help program. They do work. Few ever reveal this, as it is better left a secret than risk ridicule. A coach is closely commensurate to a hypnotist, always editing errors and implanting convincing thoughts in the mind. Listen to a boxer's coach before the bell rings. Subliminal tapes can improve concentration, eliminate mental blocks, develop a winning disposition, refine consistency. *Shotgun Sports Magazine* sell them. Also, *Inner Psych Unlimited*, 3113 White Cloud, Cheyenne, Wy 82001 (307)-635-1451 (evenings). *"Championship Trapshooting"* is another cassette tape program; write to the publisher for a brochure or visit our web site. Address is on the title page of this book.

When you hear shooters tell you, *"This game is 90% mind over matter."* it's true, but it's the subconscious mind not only your conscience mind. Again, you will hear, *"The less you think, the better you'll shoot. Just go out and hit the targets,"* or *"Shooters always do well, until they start thinking."* How true it is. Once you learn the basics of shooting and have hit every varying angled target at least fifty times, then it's time to step aside and let the subconscious mind take over. It knows how to point and shoot already. It has learned. The conscience mind is forgetful, becomes confused, thinks too much, blames others, dreams up excuses, is always curious and full of mischief. It's a hindrance towards excellent shooting. The subconscious mind is like a computer. Once it learns something, it will do it over and over again without any reminders. The idea is to teach it to do the right things, not the wrong things. It is ever so important to diligently practice correct form and allow time for the subconscious to learn how to do it right. This is why coaching can be important, to insure you are not embedding improper techniques into your subconscious mind. Thankfully, any damage done is reversible as an eraser is to a blackboard, though not without shedding tears.

Notice when you have a good day hitting all the targets how easy it seemed, as if you couldn't miss! That's the subconscious mind taking over. Everything was on automatic pilot. You didn't have to think about it, you just did it -- and did it right too! Learn to tap into this valuable resource. It's residing within all of us. The intention is to recognize it is ever present. To wipe-out the 'thinking' in your shooting. Shooting should be instinctive not calculated. That's another reason shotgunner's say, *"You don't aim a shotgun, you point it."* Well, you do subjectively aim a shotgun, but the subconscious mind does it so quickly it appears aiming is not taking place. It's like pointing your finger at the target, you track it down and point at the target. You don't look at your finger first, aim along the finger, then point at the target. Even if you are looking at the target, you would know if your finger hit or missed with that ghost-like image of the finger / target sight picture. When the ghost image detects a proper sight picture, it will trigger your brain to pull the trigger automatically. Try pointing your finger at targets and you'll see how it is done. Stare at a distant object, raise your index finger at arms length, now swing your finger left and right while still focusing on the object. You will see what a sight picture looks like. Notice you don't have to look back at your finger to see if your fingertip is directly under or on the target.

Here's an approach that will positively open your eyes to the subconscious mind. Find someone who has a hand or portable target thrower and try these demonstrations. You will see for yourself how the subconscious can shoot for you -- if you step out of the way and permit it. Before trying these practice tips, realize when you mount a low gun, you don't mount it on your shoulder then call. You point and track the barrel towards the target as you mount. When the gun contacts your shoulder, you should already be on the target and nearly set to fire (depending on technique used; sustained lead, pull away, swing through). Don't mount and track the target -- a low gun is important to develop subconscious shooting. Don't delay. Focus, mount, and shoot quickly. No time for conscience thoughts to get in the way here. It's all instinctive shooting. The setter should tilt the machine so targets exit at wild angles unknown to the shooter to boost the challenge. Use a combination of these techniques. Have fun. Although you may argue trapshooting is never played this way, you will walk away a believing the subconscious mind will shoot very well if you step aside and let it take over for you. Try calling for the targets shooting fast pulls and slow pulls, too. You may surprise yourself how often you smoke the target, regardless of the timing of the pull. Try a few rounds of sporting clays or continental trap while you're at it. When you return to the trap line, you should be in for a surprise. Your scores will increase or fall apart. If they fall apart this is only temporary. What you have learned will be imbedded in the your mind. Once you roll out the kinks shooting trap, the new knowledge learned will surface, only if you remember to recall it. You must recognize and practice recalling what you have learned. If not? You will surely forget. The subconscious will never forget! It's still there waiting for recall. Practice recalling. It's an art form, and all arts are difficult to master.

PRACTICE TIPS - Phase 6.
"Be patient, always be patient."

Let's try a few fun examples, but first <u>safety</u> is a necessity. Always stand in front of the setter as you will be turning around facing the setter in some practice modes then calling for the target, spinning around rapidly to shoot - <u>away</u> from the setter. Keep the gun pointed in a safe position at all times. Check the ground surface so you don't stumble, trip or fall. Better yet, use an automatic trap so no setter is required.

1. Don't mount the gun. Use a low gun as in sporting clays. For surprise, don't call for the target, let the setter release the target at will. Keep your eyes on the target, mount the gun quickly and shoot. After a few tries, you'll be hitting them without time for thinking. If your eyes are properly tracking the forward edge (the leading rim) of the target and you shoot quickly, lead will automatically exist, in most cases. If your swing is slow, you'll need to place lead on hard-angle targets. A faster moving gun has more momentum = more follow through = more lead.
2. With gun safely pointed, turn aside so you can't see where the target is coming from and you can't see the setter. When the target is released, spin around quickly and smoke it. Use common sense not to swing gun towards trap setter. Always stand ahead of the setter. This is not a far-fetched idea, they actually do this in English Sporting Clay registered competitions. You are never shooting at, but away from the setter.
3. Now try random walking, never knowing when the target will be released, and never looking at the setter. Throw some doubles and report doubles targets, too. Again, be safe when doing this.
4. Try an unloaded gun with shell in hand. When the target is released, slip in the shell, close the breech and smokeball it. You'll get a fine education here on instinctive shooting.
5. Here's a peculiar but fun lesson. The target is released, you track, mount and aim, but you can't shoot until the setter tells you to shoot. The target may almost be on the ground, or it may be streaking out of the trap machine when the setter says, *"Shoot."* This will help you develop good eye / hand coordination, trigger control, discipline not to flinch and help you maintain intense eye focus on the target at all times during flight.
6. Use different pointing techniques. Sustained lead: Barrel always stays ahead of the target. Pull away: Muzzle aligns with target then pulls forward to compensate for lead. Swing through: Muzzle follows target flight path, gun is fired as you pull muzzle through and ahead of target.
7. Point, point, point, don't aim. You are learning how to point the gun without aiming or looking back at the sight beads. Just focus hard on seeing the target and let your body execute the moves for you. If all is right, things will happen so quickly you'll be wondering what happened. Like pointing your finger at targets, you don't think about it, you just do it. It's an instinctive natural ability everyone has. The only difference is the gun is heavier and slower to point. Try pointing at targets with a heavy stone in your outstretched hand and you'll get the feel of it. When do you pull the trigger? This will come automatically, too, without conscience thought or effort. You can try this with a standard trap. Use a low gun when calling for the targets. Later, mount your gun normally in the high gun position. Notice the game has slowed down and the targets are easier to hit. Try the above steps. It will teach you how to shoot instinctively, without thinking. But it is only the beginning.

SEIZING KNOWLEDGE
"The practical effect of a belief is the real test of its soundness." James A. Froude

If you really want to learn inside secrets to trapshooting, break away from your circle of friends and mingle with the crowd looking for 'high guns'. Talk with them, ask questions, don't be bashful. They too were once struggling to be proficient. You can learn numerous shortcuts just by talking to or standing nearby, listening to conversation. I guarantee you will pick up innumerable jewels that will salvage your time and money. And while you're at it, look around and you will recognize many new friends you haven't met yet! You can learn a ton of knowledge worth its weight in gold by speaking to the veteran shooters. You can tell by the lines on their faces they've been there! After all, they've shot more targets, practically uncountable. It is wise to seek their counsel. There's a mindful of wisdom in 30 + years of experience. Believe me, these veterans can remove many obstacles preventing you from excelling. Of course, not all advice is advisable, still much of it is. Knowledge is power. Just one tip could push your scores upward and it didn't cost you a dime! And for those who have arrived, remember, it's not easy to be the new kid on the block; remember the younger times! Think back to some of your own experiences. Make a worthy effort to welcome the novice.

Knowledge doesn't come with a bill of rights, it is earned. You have to search for knowledge, it doesn't arrive on thin air. Read books and magazines, watch video tapes, take lessons, and observe professionals shooting -- don't watch the targets, focus your attention on their setup. The setup appears simplistic, but if you watch intently you will discern intricate details in the setup. Look for foot positioning, body positioning (stance) and gun hold points on each post, cheek placement, gun grip used, type of shoes and clothing worn, shooting glasses and tints, gun mount technique, timing for eye focus before calling for target, timing of the shot, how body moves with target, if gun cants or not on hard angles, basic rhythm. The setup is way more important than the act of shooting and when you understand this and put more focus, effort, and energy into your setup, believe me, your scores will absolutely increase.

CHAIN REACTION LOSSES
"A dog in his kennel barks at his fleas; a dog hunting does not notice them."

Have you noticed when someone on the squad misses a target, often a chain reaction develops and everyone misses? That's the power of the subconscious mind at work! A lost target induces the subconscious to repeat what is seen, hence the chain reaction. A subtle microsecond of fear of missing sets into the mind-set and when that happens, you too may miss the target. The same is true with interruptions in the rhythm of the squad or a delay from a fast or slow pull. Again, a microsecond of doubt sets in, blaming the puller for the interruption. Broken targets emerging from traphouse will cause missed targets for the shooter. These must be overcome as interruptions, mechanical breakdowns and bad pulls; broken targets are a fact of life on the trap line. How did these habits form? Often when rookie shooters are interrupted, they lose their concentration and positive persuasion to hit the target. This carries over into maturity. Interestingly, to break this circle someone hits the target and everyone's confidence rises, getting back on track again. That someone should be you! To break the chain reaction, tell yourself you will break the target and focus extra hard on seeing the target! A reshaping of mood, temperament and frame of mind is essential. Never become upset with interruptions, as it is a incitement to miss targets. This is the time to maintain self-control and bank on your competence.

A positive attitude does the trick. After all, it was a negative notion that caused the chain reaction in the first place. You can behold how subtle yet powerful the subconscious mind is. If you permit it, the subconscious will exercise its authority over your own willpower. If you don't resist, it will defy every attempt you make to better yourself. It can be a friend or foe; choose which it will be. Read a textbook on the subconscious mind and you'll better understand its hidden powers and influence. Put it to good use and you'll be an excellent shooter. With autosuggestion -- telling yourself you can -- is the first psychological step to breaking targets. If you think you can win, you can win. Faith is necessary to achievement. When a prior shooter misses a target, reverse this chain reaction of losses -- pause for a moment to reset your mind, concentrate hard, focus eyes intensely to see the target, call with increased authority -- you'll break the target!

HOME PRACTICE TIPS - Phase 7
"It is not the knowing that is difficult, but the doing."

Nothing takes the place of shooting targets from a traphouse. However, there are meaningful practice sessions you can and should do at home. Of course, be careful gun is unloaded and don't swing the muzzle, striking walls and objects.

1. Practice mounting your gun. Not only does it perfect the process, it disciplines the muscles required to shoulder the gun. Remember muscle memory? Now mount the gun with both eyes closed. When you open your eyes you should be looking right down the rib, seeing the figure eight pattern of the sight beads. Doing this will ensure you are shouldering the gun properly and with ease. Now swing the gun smoothly along the wall to ceiling line. If you use a roll or slight cant technique, follow a curving arc along with straight lines. This will develop muscles and imprint a 'memory' into the conscious and subconscious mind as to which muscles are needed, and which are not used to shoot trap. Once passing through this phase of 'muscle memory,' concentrating on the target becomes natural and with less conscience thought of body coordination requirements.

2. Look at a cabinet latch, close eyes, mount gun. Open your eyes. The gun should be pointed at the latch. The subconscious mind is blind and need not see to function perfectly. If the sight beads don't line up, practice a little. If they still won't, then your gun likely does not fit you.

3. Hold a low gun. Focus eyes at an object and mount the gun, as in sporting clays, quickly to the target. Do the same, but this time look straight ahead with gun mounted, shift eyes to an object to the left or right and move muzzle quickly to where your eyes are on the target. You want to be able to instinctively swing the gun to wherever your eyes are, developing pointing skills. Don't think or aim. When the muzzle stops, then look back toward the sight rib and see if you were on the mark. Don't look back when actually shooting, this is just a practice exercise. Keep doing this and your scores will leap forward after you persevere the learning curve. If you experience problems, first point with your finger at objects, then use the gun to point. It should be as easy with the gun mounted as pointing your finger at any object. Now you'll understand the theory of pointing a shotgun. If your setup is correct, in this case mounting the gun snugly and your eye squarely situated behind the sights, wherever you look the gun will point. Since your eye is in line with the gun sights, the muzzle will naturally be aligned with the target. This takes no thought, no looking back at the gun sights, no aiming -- it just happens! The setup is more important than shooting, and now you know why! If you find you can do this well at home, but not on the range, then check POI to insure the gun is shooting where you are looking. Besides, this technique works best when shooting fast. You'll discover using this form will vastly accelerate your shooting anyway. It'll put you in touch with your natural inner time clock.

4. Now for eye /gun pointing training. Tape a flashlight on the muzzle. Shoulder the gun, pointing at the wall as you normally would over a traphouse. Shift your eye to the extreme right to an object, without moving your gun. Without moving your eye, swing the muzzle quickly to the object your eye has focused on. Now shift your eye to another object and do the same. With a tinge of practice, your gun will point to wherever you look. This is the training secret of learning how to point a shotgun. Now go to the range and do this and you'll be on your way to higher scores after you get accustomed to the method. The technique works finest when performed rapidly, instinctively, without thought. No time for thinking, just doing. If this is performed properly, things will happen so quickly it will be difficult to even see a bird / bead sight picture. You'll hit the target and wonder, *"How did I do that?"* Later, as your eye / hand coordination adapts to the speed, you'll develop the capability to see a sight picture. At first, you'll likely be shooting blind until your eye muscles adjust to speed. You'll also discover your natural internal time clock in regard to quickly dispatching targets. Remember not to stop moving your eye, tracking the target or the muzzle will stop short and you'll shoot behind. Now you know why they say not to look back at the sights or barrel, because your eye stops and so will the muzzle; the gun will always mimic the eye. Don't fidget with lead, as the gun's momentum will naturally place the proper amount of lead when you pull the trigger, inasmuch as your eye does not stop tracking the target, and as long as you are looking at the leading edge

of the target and you shoot quickly. When do you pull the trigger? When the sight picture looks right. Others say it just comes naturally. Both viewpoints are correct, as long as the targets break.

Get out of your own way and you'll learn how to shoot. Reaction shooting, impulse shooting, snap shooting, spot shooting are all practice techniques to take you to a higher level of performance to zero-in on precision shooting on a deeper level of accomplishment. Here are more in-home practice tips:

5. Have someone stand behind you to spot and swing a flashlight beam onto a wall, simulating a rising clay target. This is certainly economical and it works. Now, try randomly flashing a stationary spot on the wall and swing eye and muzzle to it. Speed up the process until you can smoothly swing the gun to the spot without looking back at the barrel or sight rib. As you progress, use a small footprint pen-type flashlight beam or laser pointer.
6. When watching TV, focus your eyes on the tip of the nose of each character as they are introduced into the frame. Ignore everything else in the scene, just keep focusing in on their nose. This will exercise the eye muscles to switch from peripheral total vision to intense focus. In action scenes, focus on a moving object. This will help you track and control central vision focus.
7. Though it may at first thought appear pointless, take the video game away from the kids and try your hand. Most shooters proclaim they are not good at these fast pace shoot em' up games. This is interesting, for shooting is eye/hand coordination and that is exactly what is taking place in these games -- shooting! You will discover with practice with these games your vision focus must tighten on the targets, eye / hand coordination must be precise, trigger control must be on the money and deep focus concentration is imperative. No wonder the kids shoot so well when you put a gun to their shoulder! I believe you will see a definite improvement in your scores as you progress with the exercises these games can give you. See #29 "Steps to Break a Slump," for what video games can do. In Europe, Top Guns are now using video games to intensify shooting skills and it's working!

FEAR OF SHOOTOFF
"The show must go on."

There is the fear we won't prove worthy in the eyes of other shooters. Panic sets in. Feelings of intimidation can demoralize the shooter, resulting in a cold sweat. A myriad of emotions set in, primarily mind numbing fright materializes. The shooter's psyche becomes alarmed to a point of being paralyzed, scared out of one's wits. The once happy face is now white as a sheet, pale as a ghost. These emotions trigger the physical body to quake, shake and tremble as the knees grow faint as a falling leaf to quivering jelly and the heart flutters as a dove's wings. For the new shooter, it's the recipe of a tailspin doomed to crash and burn. Welcome to the shootoff!

As you experience more shootoffs, you'll learn to knuckle under and get down to the business of breaking targets. Just remember the other shooter is just as worried and maybe even more fearful than you are. Take a look. I don't think he'll be laughing and leaping with joy. This should help you build courage. Some shooters develop a shootoff phobia, so much so, they won't shootoff at all as they develop intense fears triggering panic attacks. This is a real disorder and is a treatable condition through practice and counseling. There is no reason to quit shooting. All shooters in shootoffs experience some level of agitation.

For starters, it is not your job to amaze, flabbergast, confound and impress others. Subdue those thoughts. You may miss a target. Don't be ashamed or allow emotions of guilt overcome you, the best miss in shootoffs too! Fight back all thoughts of feeling inferior, inadequate, humiliated, embarrassed and hopeless. Once these defeatist emotions take root, they are hard to shake off. A lost target, or even losing the match doesn't mean you are ruined or undone, without hope of recovery or future improvement.

Shooting-off can be disquieting, and it's customary to feel emotions of impending peril. The object of dissolving disquieting feelings is to replace these emotions with happiness. Be satisfied with yourself, pleased you are in the shootoff, congratulate yourself, be cheerful and smile for it truly is a victory to be shooting with the elite of the day. Get a kick out of it and feelings of pleasure will chase the panic away. A state of euphoria displaces fear.

Look at it as having fun, taste the fancy of it all, and take no offense if you lose. A proper attitude can take you to higher levels in all walks of life. Trapshooting is no exception. Think of the finest trapshooter who you admire the most. Ask yourself how he or she would handle this situation and you'll be suitably programmed to mimic the disposition of a professional, to move or operate freely as machine parts do. Be properly prepared, have your gear, shells, ear plugs, etc., in order. And remember, you lose if you don't answer the shootoff call. You don't need any interruptions now. Remember to shoot at your own pace -- don't speed up! You may be shooting a short squad, take all the time you need, but don't slow down too much, as concentration can become blurred in the heat of battle. The mind may wander. Stay focused. If you're shooting-off in a squad, don't even consider pondering the other shooters -- they don't exist! Loud or strange audible calls from other shooters may distract you. Often, that's the plan. Mind games. It's an old trick of the trade -- to set opposing parties or interests against one another to advance one's own goals, to use disruptive tactics to play into the hands of the distracter. Don't be deceived. Best forewarning? Play your own game. Ignore the universe around you.

If you miss a target, forget about it and focus on the next target. Miss again? It's nerves getting the better of you. Do the best you can to concentrate on technique to wash out jingling nerves. Turn on a positive attitude. Use autosuggestion (suggesting to yourself you can break the targets). Be aggressive but with relaxed self-possession. Too aggressive and you'll key-up with muscle rigidity. Too relaxed and you'll fall behind the targets. Panic attacks arise in a number of ways, specifically during important events and shootoffs. The central nervous system, when stressed generates fear as the pressures are deemed threatening. Then severe, physical symptoms develop: heart palpitations, tenseness, shaking hands, weak knees, disorientation, sweating, faintness, trembling, shortness of breath, stomach distress, headache, etc. A shooter's confidence and performance can decrease as he or she fears being embarrassed by an attack. The desire is to flee to a safer place, but that's not going to happen, as you're already in the event, so here's how to deal with it.
1. Realize all shooters get nervous, particularly beginners. With time and exposure to more shootoff experience it becomes manageable. It's okay to be afraid. It's okay to lose, just as it is okay to win. Keep trying.
2. If panic attacks are frequent and severe, visit a doctor to rule out any underlying medical condition. For information, contact: Anxiety Disorders Association of America, 600 Executive Blvd., Ste., 513, Rockville, MD 20852 (301)-231-9159. Refrain from resorting to sedatives, as the cure is often worse than the disease.
3. Tell yourself to concentrate on seeing the target and rely on technique to break the target. Nerves can be unnerving, but if you step aside your subconscious mind will overrule. It's like a police officer who gets into a shoot-out, everything goes into slow motion and it is here the training automatically kicks in. Intense fear, yes. Still, the training implanted in the subconscious takes precedence.
4. Reduce breathing rate to a slow rhythm, focus your fears away by thinking of and visualizing breaking the target. Learn to relax and lighten up even if you miss a target or two or more.
5. Don't look at the crowd or other shooters. Keep focused on the targets. Don't think of anything else. When panic sets in, the mind races with thoughts. Divert these thoughts to seeing the target.

Though friends and family mean well congratulating and encouraging you, they are usually miserable comforters. Find a quiet place to rest. If you're too exited, you'll overload your nervous system (which no doubt is already keyed up). Generate a calm, relaxed state of mind. Take a vitamin pill, aspirin, energy food supplement if need be. Smile! You're where others wish they were. Reward yourself; you deserve to have arrived. If you lose? So what? Welcome to the club. Take the bitter with the sweet. Accept life's misfortunes as well as its joys. Show me a shooter who has never lost a shootoff! Exhibit one who can shoot thousands of handicap targets straight! You'll feel better knowing clay-target Hot Dog warriors do miss targets, too. If Hall of Fame Champions who have shot beyond 300,000 registered targets can miss and have an off season, so can you! Go easy on yourself. There are times you may want to turndown a shootoff. The game is not worth the candle, like playing a game of cards in which the stakes are smaller than the cost of burning a candle for light by which to play. Skip unimportant events with a trophy you don't want or shooting-off for a minor prize when you know you're in the shootoff for a major purse. The exertion put into the undertaking is vain. Why exhaust your energy and spoil a chance for the premium award? The expense may not be worth the return. Forfeit the trophy or belt buckle to the shooter who may really need a confidence boost. After all, how many belt buckles can you wear at one time?

CHAPTER 13

RESOLVING MYSTERIES
"Men in the game are blind to what men looking on see clearly."

The following subtitles are snippets worth mentioning to alleviate some of the myriad mysteries of trapshooting. All difficulties can be overcome with knowledge put into practice. Knowledge without implementation is trivia. Everything you learn in this book must be consciously tried, tested, and remembered. An impossible task, for sure using memory alone, but by the physical act of 'doing' (memory recall similar to developing a photographic memory or comprehending a picture instead of memorizing descriptive dialog) will astonish and reward your efforts. The key? It takes intelligent, patient repetitive practice sessions, and time to learn.

ELEVATIONS
"Undertake something difficult; it will do you good. Unless you try to do something beyond what you have already mastered, you will never grow." Ronald E Osborn

When shooting at high or low elevation, there can be differences in how you shoot targets. At **low elevations** the air is denser so visibility decreases. Compensate with increased eye focus and shooting glasses' lens color and pointing the gun at leading edge or ahead of the target. The target may travel faster if the trap's power setting is set for speed to reach the field stake. A faster target leaves a longer streak as it leaves the house, just wait until the steak dissolves before you shoot. Apply more lead to fast targets, just a bit more than usual, or shoot quicker. Shooting at sea level? Targets are moisture laden due to absorbing humidity in the warehouse and traphouse. You may want to switch to handicap 7 1/2 shot loads, as damp targets tend to Swiss cheese instead of breaking. At **high elevations** the air is drier and targets tend to float, due to less velocity required to reach the field stake and target weight is low as moisture content is nil. Visibility increases depending on lighting conditions. These dry targets in dry stable air -- especially out West inland from the coast -- are easiest to hit. So, using #8 shot will smokeball them with ease as the target has less tendency to perforate, that is, if the weather preceding the shoot was clear, dry, and not cold. There is less air resistance acting on the target so trap machines need not throw targets at intensified velocity to reach the field stake. Speed of the target often does increase if targets are damp and trap is set for power, but the target can actually slow down due to thin air and less lift. Depending on target speed factors, you'll likely have to shoot a tad faster and employ handicap loads with heavy shot. Changes in backgrounds can be more influential than elevation, target speed, or humidity levels. Focus on the target, apply lead, shoot quick, ignore the backgrounds, you'll have no problem. For soft, dry targets not set for speed, you can point right at the target to break them if you shoot reasonably quick.

TARGET COLOR
"Everything should be made as simple as possible, but not simpler." Albert Einstein

Solid color targets, especially white targets, appear as full moons, jumbo jets and flying trashcans. They reflect the total spectrum of light. This is not desirable, as optical misimpression occurs. The streak or comet tail is prolonged when the target leaves the house. So much light reflects from the target a 'halo' forms making the target appear larger than it really is. It's an animal within its own kingdom. They are easy to see, though what you see (a mirage) is not where the target is. It requires more lead to stay ahead of the target, to hit them due to the optical illusion. Keep this in mind when shooting white targets under lights at night. Orange with black rim targets are excellent. The color has high contrast, bright yet controlled reflection. The black rim erases comet tail streaks, though lighting conditions cast shadows, reducing the orange face of the target 50%. When this happens, focus your eyes distinctively on the black rim along with the orange, not just the orange alone. Lime green targets have similarities to white and orange. The optical illusion exist but not as severe. Black targets are not often used in trap, though virtuous for training eye focus as they are difficult to see in busy backgrounds. Some clubs do throw black targets on a blue sky, but most clubs use green or orange targets.

INTERRUPTIONS
"The closed mind, if closed long enough, can be opened by nothing short of dynamite." Gerald W Johnson

There will always be interruptions no matter who you shoot with or where. Learn to live with them. No one welcomes disturbances, particularly when the squad rhythm is steady and targets are being annihilated with ease, then without warning it happens -- everything stops! Someone's gun jams, misfires, blooper loads, disgruntled shooters acting out self-frustrations on the line, slow sloppy shooters with everlasting setups, wind gusts, rain, slow and fast pulls causing more delays, broken targets springing in succession from traphouse, trap machine failures, loud trucks or aircraft suspends shooting. The list is endless. If you don't learn to live with them and interruptions aggravate you to the verge of screaming, come to terms that this is the nature of the beast in trapshooting. Be professional and you'll shoot like a professional. No emotions! When interruptions occur, take advantage of them... they are rest breaks, a time to relax and focus. Letting emotions tamper with your thoughts and attitude will unquestionably atomize your own scores. Open your mind to the concept.

SQUAD RHYTHM
"He who hesitates is lost."

There is never any guarantee you will enjoin the right combination of shooters to form a perfect rhythm. If you can only shoot well if a squad has perfect timing, then you have a hard machine to drive. Certainly it is important, but should it be so important that if the rhythm isn't to your liking you can't score well? Learn to shoot well by playing your own game. As you know, disruptions will occur and little will modify disorder. The exclusive variable is you. Modify your philosophy and expectations. Be aware of rhythm but don't centralize on rhythm. Intensify visual focus on seeing and hitting the targets distinctively so when severe breakdowns in rhythm arise you'll perform well. Be very attentive of rhythm since rhythm can be improper as well as proper. Rhythm is tempo, a set timing, a beat, a groove. Pay attention to this tempo. Novice musicians in a jam session lose tempo as the music speeds up, principally if the drummer doesn't hold the beat down and steady. So true in trapshooting. Don't speed up and don't slow down! Keep the tempo. If the pulse of the squad increases then reset the speed by slowing down yourself. You don't have to say a word and you shouldn't talk on the line anyway. When you slow down, others will too. If they don't, it's their problem. Ever notice when targets are lost the squad rhythm tends to accelerate? Intensity pumps adrenaline and that's why squads' slam the throttle. It's not a wise thing to do. Watch the pros shoot. Notice the total self-control they each have. Their squad timing is perfect.

When rhythm speed accelerates, so will missed targets. Why? Many reasons. The trapsetter is pushed laboriously to work, he secures sloppy targets on the arm and dismembered targets see the light, inducing extended disruptions. Next, you'll earn flippers and miss them. If he gets his hand whacked by the trap arm, you can count on revenge! He'll punch a center hole or chip the rim off the target to flip a flying beast just for you! He may momentarily lock the oscillator in position to toss a hard angle as a gift. The puller may grow nervous and anticipate calls if rhythm increases fast and furious. Here come the fast and slow pulls! Who's fault is it? We are quick to blame the puller, but it's the squad. Or heaven forbid, is it me? Trapshooters forget teamwork goes beyond the squad to include the setter and the puller. Scores messed up? You've forsaken the scorekeeper! Slow down and quality targets will fly and scores will soar with less disruption. To fully grasp this reality, try setting targets, pull and score. You'll understand promptly enough.

BACKGROUND SCENE
"To reach your goal you must resolve difficulty."

Look, observe, be aware, that's all. Wipe the background out of your mind -- from windmills to fences, they don't exist! This is the finest mode to handle diverse or distracting backdrops. You should focus on the target and the target exclusively. Use properly tinted shooting glasses for the conditions in order to emphasize the target and to simultaneously blot the background. Once you allow background settings to instill concern, you'll be overwhelmed with appalling scores. After all, you can't win if you're tossing lead at the scenery; you win by dispatching targets. Shooters devote excessive attention to backgrounds, and all it achieves is anxiety and poor scores. Background recognition begins and ends before you step onto the line to shoot. You should watch the targets when the machines are being set or observe a prior squad shooting the traps you'll be assigned to. Variant backgrounds are a fact of life in trapshooting. No two shoots are analogous, as each backset will metamorphose with the seasons. Don't be sidetracked or distracted by them. Focus intently on the target. Focus is the secret! Tinted lenses will not help you if you still fail to see and intensely focus on the target together with fervently paying attention!

ADVERSE WEATHER
"If you can predict the weather, you'll predict the target" Good Luck!

Realize you have no control over weather conditions. We are at the mercy of the wind, rain, fog, hail and other elements. Take your mind off the weather and shoot the targets as best you can. As noted in this book, there are adjustments you can make when shooting in the wind or on breezy days. Ultimately, you must fully acquire the target as it leaves the traphouse and break it as soon as you possibly can before the elements obtain a foothold empowering the target to behave radically. Overcast skies exist, use tinted shooting glasses. For a sunny or partly cloudy sky, shoot ahead of or past the sun. Use blinders and tilt the visor on your hat to block direct sunlight or rain. See Fig. 9-1.

NO STRAIGHT-AWAYS
"We have to give up or destroy something to gain something."

You'll shoot better if you digest the reality there are no straight-away targets. Sure, you're supposed to see a straight-away, yet how often does it really happen? Why focus on something that may not appear and if it does is easy to hammer anyway? Some argue that on post one and five with trap set in # 2 hole you'll get a straight-away. This is fine and dandy pie in the sky dreaming. If you've shot a lot of shoots, you'll know what I'm talking about. What then do you see when the traphouse is out of alignment to the stations? Those straight-aways are now quarter angling. You'll have to reposition your gun hold (whether or not you hold on or over the house) sometimes as much as 4 inches (depending on degree of misalignment) horizontally from your typical hold point to compensate. If you don't ,you will not see the target leave the house or track it at the proper angle, or you'll entirely miscalculate the angle. In the real world targets do slip, slide, and flip off the trap arm. What looks straight likely isn't. Reasoning you will never acquire a straight target forces you to focus firmly on the target to see the angle it is traversing. That strategy alone will increase your scores!

LOOKING FOR TARGETS
"Where there is no vision, the people perish." The Bible

Don't look down the barrel or gaze too lazily out into the field. Try focusing your eye(s) about 6" softly over the far edge of the traphouse, midway from the traphouse to the field or closer in. Each shooter may encounter contrary focal points more advantageous. See Fig. 4-2. You may want to keep your eyes looking straight out as you normally would as you stand on line and allow peripheral vision to pickup the target. You'll need to experiment here to find the ideal eye hold perfect for you. Give your setup ample time for eye iris and lens to adjust and focus. Generally, use a soft focus, no squinting, but a hard focus may work for you so try both methods. If you're looking too high over the traphouse, you may lose targets by reason of surprise; they'll get the jump on you causing a surge of central nervous system activity forcing you to overreact to catch up to the target. From calm to tension within microseconds. This, too, will happen if your eye hold is too low! You'll see a speeding, streaking target. This causes hasty, reactive shooting, which causes lost targets. If eye hold is too high, your eyes will have to shift down then back up. If eye hold is too low, the eyes will flow upward without reversing direction, but the target is too 'streaky' and undefined to determine proper angulation. Both will fail to acquire the target properly, and you'll lose precision to knee-jerk reaction shooting. Your eye hold generally determines where about you will be breaking the target. Eyes nearer the house will naturally break targets sooner. No matter where eye hold or gun is held, you should see the target leave the house immediately when it emerges, judge its angle as it passes the muzzle, then track smoothly and shoot. Be certain you are looking and prepared, positively ready for the target when you call. More targets are lost due to calling and the eyes 'not prepared' to see the target than you may realize. Be ready to go when you call. You should have already set a plan to break the target even before seeing it during the setup phase. If you have not established a plan and visualized breaking the target, you are shooting on luck, not precision. When the target is in flight, are you really looking at the target or just seeing it? Are you looking at its forward edge? See Fig. 11-4, Fig. 11-11, Fig. 11-12 and Fig. 11-14. Obstacles to target sighting include 'mind drifting' prior to calling for the target, usually negative thoughts, *"I don't like this club, trap, squad, targets, weather, clouds."* etc. Don't move the gun until you see the target. Keep eyes on the target, don't look back at the gun sight beads, and keep your eyes moving with the target. If your eyes stop, so will the muzzle and you will shoot behind the target. Eye control is more important than trigger control as the eye controls the trigger.

Keep this in mind whenever you find yourself shooting behind targets. **1)** Eyes were not focused before you called. **2)** You acquired the target too late by looking too high over the house, or too low looking down the sight rib. **3)** Your swing to the target was interrupted or barrel stopped tracking the target smoothly owing to taking your eyes off the target, momentarily looking back at the sight rib or muzzle. **4)** You pulled the trigger due to 'timing' 'zone,' 'habit' or 'flinch' instead of when the sight picture looked correct. **5)** You did not lead the target. **6)** You lost concentration. **7)** You rushed the gun to the target instead of being smooth to the target. **8)** A mismounted gun can cause shooting behind, under, or over target. **9)** Ammo velocity was low. **10)** You failed to acquire the proper track and angle of target. **11)** Head-lifting usually causes shooting over or under target, but is often misdiagnosed by the shooter as shooting behind. **12)** You anticipated the target exit angle or moved the muzzle movement before the target emerged. **13)** You didn't look at the proper zone or leading edge of the target. **14)** You pushed the gun with arm to target without using body to swing. **15,)** Improper foot position/stance resulted in excessive flexibility of movement and inaccurate swing. **16)** Improper gun fit and other factors can cause loss of accuracy, though the above mentioned are primarily prevalent.

TRAPHOUSE COSMETICS
"Ugliness is the measure of imperfection."

What do you do when the traphouse is set too high off the ground? Or set too low? What about the strange appearance of the traphouse? These aberrations can cause mental shocks and mind blocks. Here are the answers of how to deal with them. **Low** house (trap machine is set high off the ground): Hold your gun on or over the house as you normally do. **High** house (trap machine is set low to the ground): Targets will leave below the edge of the traphouse, so hold a lower gun to see the target clearly. **Appearance**: Traphouses appear in dissimilar forms as diverse as snowflakes. Concrete with nasty stains, wood revealing peeling paint and blemishes, tar drippings, etc. It's not pleasant to shoot over clean, flat traphouse roofs, then suddenly on the last trap in an event come upon a grotesque corrugated metal roof filled with leaves, debris, spent wads, or a trashed roof with missing, peeled shingles. Even if it's clean, especially a corrugated roof, it absorbs attention like a clown dancing on a freeway -- things just don't look right. Elect not to shoot that house! If you must shoot it, then learn to ignore the roof (I find this hard to do). The color, shape, or materials used to build a traphouse shouldn't bother anyone; however, along the sight plane of the roof is where we are looking for the target and idiosyncratic rooftops are a nuisance, especially if it's a solitary trap highly dissimilar to other traphouses you were shooting. With inconsistent appearances of traphouses, if not recognized consciously, the subconscious will pick up on the cosmetic mutation and mysteriously targets will float away unscathed. I trust this hint to gun club managers strikes a chord to build and maintain becoming traphouses. A black painted traphouse, top, face and sides, has the highest contrast for identifying targets of any color (except black targets, which are not often thrown).

SCOUTING THE TRAPS
"Be astonished, O ye heavens, at this, and be horribly afraid."

Locate the traps you'll be assigned to shoot. Check background scene. Check if square to stations. Observe target flight behavior and illumination when trap is being set. This furthermore yields a dose of eye exercise prior to shooting. Look for unusual field slopes, ditches, wind direction. Observe target speed and distances thrown. Are the traps set properly in the house? Are targets emerging where they should be? Is the field of broken targets uneven, possibly throwing more targets to the right than to the left or center? If opportunity presents, walk the field, observe how the targets are breaking. Are they chunky? Many holes but unbroken? Switching to 3 dram 7 1/2 shot will break damp, obstinate hard targets. Overhear shooters who have just shot the trap(s). Verify what you hear by observation. Preparation gives you an edge. You may want to shoot a practice trap for warm-up at registered shoots to adjust to the unique shooting conditions.

CHOKES AND LOADS
"Remember the reason for the why."

Choke: Some shooters use a full choke for all yardages, including doubles events. A skilled shooter with a semiautomatic can't change chokes for the first and second target yet can annihilate doubles with ease. A lot of shooters use modified or improved-modified for 16 yard to mid-yardage. Do whatever works best for you. Keeps things simple. It's not necessary to keep changing chokes from 16 yard to 27 yard shooting. Foremost is still a full choke for handicap distances, and many shooters shoot full choke on all yardages only changing the shot size. Shot: #8 shot is good for the whole complex in fair weather if you shoot without unreasonable delays, and #7 1/2 shot is good for the whole shebang, but tends to hold the boundary of success in tempestuous weather conditions and long yardage handicap shooting. At the 16 yard line #8 1/2 shot may work fine for you but #9 shot is considered too 'dusty' for trapshooting, it belongs on the skeet field. Loads: Readily available factory ammunition obtainable at all gun clubs is advised in case of shootoff. Choose new shells meeting velocity standards you are accustomed to shooting. Reloads matching factory specifications with original factory components and magnum shot are recommended. Maintain standard velocities (1200 f.p.s. is fine for ATA trapshooting).

DEALING WITH KNOW IT ALL'S
"Many hands make light work, but at the same time, too many cooks spoil the broth."

Listen and learn! There is generally wisdom in much of what people say when they offer advice, though remember what works for them may only work for them. Experiment, give advice a try. If it makes sense, make it work. If not? Try anyway! In the course of experimentation, successively new discoveries are encountered. Trying new things won't forevermore disable you as a shooter. You can always recidivate to old shooting technique, yet you invariably can't progress unless you try new approaches. Of course, misinformation is to be guarded against, so it's wise to tread carefully wherever serpents lull in the meadows. There are some, few overall, who intentionally donate ill advice to inexperienced shooters. Talk and listen to professionals, read magazine interviews with Top Guns. Scrutinize how pros shoot in every detail! Also, never presume you can't learn from a lower-class short or mid-yardage shooter. You'll be thunderstruck they have remembered what you may have forgotten or taken for granted. Information sharing can help you pull out of a severe slump. We all overlook rudimentary principles! That's why we miss targets!!! Talk to professionals, for they do know it all (all meaning more than most shooters). If you are given advice, employ it. Don't expect instant, marvelous results. New techniques, like new guns, will reasonably consume 5,000 targets or more to get them down half-right. When a shooter takes lessons, the first thing that usually happens is scores decrease as bad habits are corrected. Once learned, proficiency rises. Too many shooters rely on instant results and prematurely judge a new system. If they don't witness immediate improvement, they instantly abandon it. Everyone is looking for the easy way, but the superior techniques are not easy to learn or apply. If a style makes sense, make it work! Learn from observing other shooters' mistakes. Study why they miss targets, why they hit them. This is preferred over listening to hours of advice. Better yet, purchase trapshooting video tapes, read books, take lessons. Ask your gun club's board members to stock a library of books and videos shooters can review. Members could contribute to a fund to purchase the library to keep individual costs down. A little learning is dangerous to ignorance. Keep in mind the source of advice. People who know a little do not understand how little they know and are, therefore, prone to error when giving directions. For those who must deal with argumentative types or 'know-it-alls' remember, *"He who knows all, knows nothing."* If the advisor shoots well, listen up.

EQUIPMENT
"Great oaks from little acorns grow."

If the gun you own meets the prescription of a trap gun, fits, is comfortable, shoots where you look (or shoots where you want it to, as in a high rib gun with elevated POI) then focus on the business of shooting and breaking targets. Accurate shooting is more important than gizmos, gadgets, doodads, bells, whistles and thingamajigs. The less hype, the better off you'll be in the long-term. Disappointed in your gun? If the gun shoots straight and is reliable, don't expect a new gun will increase your scores. Temporarily, it might if you regain focus in attending to the details of shooting, but the thrill is usually short-lived, and scores once again return to previous levels. Don't blame the gun if you are missing the targets! Good advice for novice shooters. It will save you a ton of cash. Shooting is 90% brain power and 10% equipment. How easily we succumb to looking for the exit when fire rages within. Put out the fires of faltering performance with quenching confidence! Rely on the certainties of self-assuredness and the trustworthiness of your technique. No gun will multiply scores in the paws of inexperience. Poor procedure, form, and Jerry-built proficiency spells, "L-O-S-T T-A-R-G-E-T-S." Good shooters shoot well owing to skill, not because they own a priceless gun.

SLOW & FAST PULLS
"Time waits for no man."

Fast and slow pulls? Turn them down! If you shoot and miss it's your fault not the puller's. Pullers will make mistakes so consider improper pulls as normal interruptions. Blame the puller and you're setting yourself up for a negative emotion to ruin your scores. It requires discipline to turn down targets. Shoot a fast pull and your eye may not be focused properly. Often you'll hit the target, but the few times you miss may steal your reward. Slow pulls are more forgiving, but the target will surprise you and that sets up a fight / flight emotional response (panic). The target should exit only when you are ready, and when you call for it.

MIND
"For all we learn, we forget, lest we do."

It's the human consciousness that originates in the brain and is manifested in thought, perception, emotion, will, memory, and imagination. The collective conscious and subconscious processes direct and influence mental and physical behavior, thinking, reasoning, acquiring and applying knowledge. Trapshooting requires great mental ability, as all sports demand, especially visual memory. It takes a lot of shooting to imprint our memories with many conceivable target behavior modes and angles. It all begins with desire, or at least the inclination to learn. Focus of thought, attention, is the name of the game. You should keep your mind on your work -- to become aware of mistakes and correct them, to set a goal or purpose, to be concerned and care about winning. Force yourself to obey mental commands which you have learned. To be careful to follow the technique you know works for you; to perfect it and make it work. Resist disliking change, changing technique that simply is wrong or needs correction. The open mind is a mind of reason predisposed to learn to take charge. It's a state of spirit within where one conquers fear -- the fear of failure, the fear of winning.

Intellect stresses the capacity for knowing, thinking, and understanding, contrasted with feeling. Opinion is ultimately determined by feelings, not by intellect. Intelligence implies the capacity for solving problems, learning from experience, and reasoning abstractly. Your success in trapshooting demands a struggle against the limitations of your intelligence. Most successful trapshooters are endowed with brains, talent, and perseverance. Reason is the capacity for rational, logical, and analytic thought. It embraces comprehension, leading to the ability to evaluate situations and draw conclusions. All can be learned. Trapshooting will teach you how little you know about yourself. Once you discover the inefficiencies causing weak concentration, you can work hard on resolving the obstacle by breaking down each problem into manageable segments.

CHALLENGE MEDIOCRITY
"Great deeds are usually wrought at great risks." Herodotus

If you watch trapshooting, it's fun. If you shoot, it's recreation, but if you work at it, it's trapshooting. More than a few don't take the sport seriously enough; it's like a joy ride taken for jest, half-heartedly and often for thrills, yielding a reckless and costly performance. Trapshooting should be engaged in for enjoyment and recreation, in contrast, it has a formal side not to be played down. Do not accept mediocrity. It's not enough to like trapshooting, you must love it! Then, and only then, can you motivate yourself to excel. It can be money-motivation to win the options -- a good place to start. Many shooters are motivated by the course of least resistance. They avoid what is difficult and unpleasant, no matter how profitable it can be to disenfranchise bad shooting habits and technique. The mind hums at peak performance when given opportunity for creativity and reaching goals. If you fall into a slump, be assured your mind is locking-up, frozen with routine boredom. The gateway to failure is listening to negative thoughts and statements. *"I'll never win those big events, as shooters there are too good,"* or *"Only talented people make it to the top."* Learn to reject the word 'impossible'. Dream of the improbable and all things become possible. To be super successful in any business, including trapshooting, you have to reinvent yourself.

If you chop wood, splinters fly, but it pays to chop wood with the sharp edge of the axe. Everyone can shoot, but not all shoot with a sharp edge. What is the difference between a Hall of Fame shooter and a mediocre shooter? Not much! To step into the Hall of Fame, you need break just one more target than everyone else. Just one target! You have to keep shooting, practicing, polishing technique every single chance you can. The difference between Hall of Famer's and others is the Hall of Famers are willing work at perfection whereas others won't. Not can't do, won't do! Successful people work toward proficiency every day until it is second nature. Even when not shooting, they are deliberating, planing, learning, evaluating new ideas, setting goals to preserve and sharpen that edge, and when they shoot -- splinters fly.

Extraordinary people are ordinary people doing extraordinary things. Successful stock market investors often do the exact opposite of what other investors do. They don't follow the 'crowd' and are known as contrarian investors. Consider all the trapshooters you have ever met -- 'the crowd' -- and distinguish their qualities from the professionals. There is a difference. Pros are determined, filled with overwhelming concentration, confidence and determination to win. They have the skills to hit targets -- and so do you! You've broken thousands of them. The sole difference between you and them is the way you think, the way you believe. A lack of resolve, zeal and accomplishment invades the mind, always comparing oneself to others. A recipe for failure is to be consumed with what is on your mind when shooting, when you should focus 100% on breaking targets. It's a responsibility many shooters can't handle, but can learn to do. To progress, a price is to be paid. To know you are stuck in a rut and refuse to learn new techniques will keep you an ordinary shooter for a very long time, perhaps forever.
To break high scores you must have an open mind, be flexible to learn new things, and visualize success. If you visualize failure, that is what you will surely earn. It's not just positive thinking, it's faith in action! Faith is believing in something you do not yet have. It is the ingredient that can make you shoot better than your skill level says you should. Faith can't be learned, it must be put into action. Start believing you can increase scores and it will happen; maybe that one target keeping you out of the money wasn't so hard after all. There really is no magic to trapshooting. You simply have to develop a plan, believe you will succeed and you will.

MIND-SET OF CONCENTRATION

"Have confidence if you have done a little thing well, you can do a bigger thing well too." Storey

Changes are always difficult. Consistency is not simply a technique. You cannot instantly learn it. It is a growth in time. You must grow towards it, hence the frustration and mental boredom. Life needs the opposite, the challenge of the opposite. Awareness is an energy phenomenon. Energy moves in a dual polarity. For energy to become dynamic, the anti-pole is essential as electricity flows with negative and positive polarities. If there is only negative polarity, electricity doesn't exist. Both poles are needed. And when both poles meet, they create electricity; a spark materializes. Wherever you look you will find the same energy moving in polarities, balancing itself. The mind moves in a simple straight line. It never moves to the opposite; it denies the opposite. A good trapshooter's mind-set appears absolutely silent. If you look closely at his face the concentration is so intense his appearance is as a dead man. Nobody can disturb him, his concentration is perfect. You cannot do anything to distract his mind; his mind is absolutely fixed. Even if the whole world goes mad, he will remain in his concentration. This silence of mind is meaningful, as concentration will have an altogether different quality to it. It will not be dull. It will be alive. It will be a subtle balance between two polarities. A good trapshooter has mastered the balance of polarities: awareness (positive pole) and emotional mind-wandering and external distractions (negative pole). A balance between these two polar opposites is concentration. Balance is important, because, like electricity, if you try to eliminate one pole, you'll end up focusing on the other pole. This is why you must practice shooting with distractions so you can learn to maintain that balance. And this balance cannot be achieved through linear efforts of self-concentration or willpower alone. It is learned exclusively by exposure to distractions and experience. Accept the negatives with the positives and you will discover the key to near-perfect concentration. Readjust your attitude. Get down-right serious, stop goofing-off, allowing emotions (negative pole) to overwhelm positive thoughts (positive pole).

DEVELOPING DEEP CONCENTRATION

"The mode by which the inevitable comes to pass is effort." Oliver Wendell Holmes

You may be able to concentrate, but not very long on the proper object, or your mind-wanders, inducing absurd mistakes. Concentration is a skill and must be practiced, too! It doesn't come naturally. These practice tips may seem trivial, but they are powerful tools to fine-tune your shooting skills.

PRACTICE TIPS - Phase 8

1. When focusing your eye(s) into the field, do not stare hard as this will certainly reduce reaction time. On the other hand, if you don't take time to focus, you will miss targets. Practice soft-focusing your eyes quickly.

2. Practice eye focus and concentration by blocking all distractions and focusing on a clay target placed on a table. Do this inside the clubhouse or near a busy area. Let no thoughts or distractions come to mind. You will find this hard to do, but you will learn how to center all your attention on a target. Place target at a distance and focus.

3. Place six quarters in an X pattern 1/4" apart on a table and selectively pick one to study. Note every detail. You may find your eyes shifting to the other quarters. Keep practicing until they don't shift. Now do the same with 6 clay targets. Sounds easy, but all thoughts must be Z-E-R-O. Each thought must be erased the moment it materializes. The key is recognition of how the mind randomly wanders and how to stop it. When obstructions do occur, repeat the command, "Focus." This will fire a decree you can later use on the trap line to lock-in on the targets. Ninety percent of shooting is mental. You are learning the 90% right now! Pure concentration is silence of mind.

4. Close your eyes and visualize the target you have studied in step #2. If you can't do this with noise, find a quiet place. Let the target hover in mid-air. Wipe any thoughts. If the picture vaporizes, open your eyes and try again to recall it. After you can recall the target at will -- picture yourself shooting the target, watch it break.

5.   Practice switching concentration on and off wherever you are each day. Pick any object, anytime. Train your mind to focus and concentrate at will. The more you do, the longer you will maintain deep levels of concentration. Relaxed concentration is desired; don't try too hard because fatigue erodes skill and technique. Be relaxed but well focused when shooting. Concentration is easy to learn, but hard to recall and maintain fixation. With practice it gets easier. Good starts win races.

DEALING WITH PRESSURE
"The greatest affliction of life is never to be afflicted."

Trapshooting is a serious and demanding business. The optimum challenge of the game is learning ways to cope and conquer high pressure shootoffs. Every shooter must contend with this punishing gauntlet. Aggression is born out of determination to win. We do require pressure to stimulate performance, but not too much. Excessive pressure diminishes learned skill profoundly. Small unnoticed defects in gun mount, swing and eye focus are greatly amplified under stress, and one fault leads to another! Knowing where this ledge is will prevent you from falling over by initializing relaxation techniques when needed. Your body will give clues: nervousness, anxiety, tense muscles, targets appear smaller, etc. For some, a sense of humor pushes them away from the edge as dead serious excessive concentration invents the deep hole. Increasing your knowledge of the game and technique places distance between you and the pit. The more you learn, the less pressure you will experience. Of course, everyone chokes and drops targets, to say otherwise means you have never experienced a tight squeeze shootoff. When pressure rises, you must leak it out before something gives. Each person should acquire their own system of stress relaxation. For starters, learn to induce moods of relaxation so you can recall them when needed. Focus 100% on your shooting technique, don't even think of anything but, or you'll become too analytical and rigid. Don't be unnerved when you miss a target, as it is a rarity the other shooters in a shootoff will run them all. Build pressure resistance by applying pressure. This means to gain experience by placing small bets with other shooters to enhance competitive stress thresholds. Shootoffs are high pressure situations with physical, mental and emotional drain. With exposure and experience you'll learn to manage pressure. Controlled breathing is a must, so force yourself to breathe deeply and with steady rhythm to stay relaxed and focused. You'll develop and sustain power, timing and precision.

Sometimes it is advisable to take a break from the game, depending on your stress level. If you are afraid you'll become too rusty, then reduce your practice sessions. Overshooting is not going to solve any problems. He who sows hurry reaps indigestion. Taking time off gives you a chance to put things back in proper perspective, a chance to evaluate, set a plan, establish a goal, rebuild your love for the game with pure and simple rest and peace of mind. Where there is love there is pain. Whoever is in a hurry shows the thing he is about to do is too big for him. Yes, you can grow stressed-out on shooting just as you can be over-stressed on a job. Don't overdue it. What will be, will be. It requires years to be a commendable trapshooter, so grant yourself a few years to arrive. When breaking from the sport for well-deserved relaxation, you can still mentally rehearse by visualizing executing perfect shots. This is time well spent and more useful than shooting for the sake of shooting out of habit. Perhaps you'll be surprised to learn after taking some time off you'll come back stronger, and that is progression replacing regression.

SAFETY
"Make haste slowly."

Besides reading the club rules, hearing protection is a must. Jet engines produce 130 dB (decibels) of sound energy but a shotgun produces even more, 154 dB. Check barrel for obstructions before loading, anything could have fallen in the barrel. Never use a stray box of shells. One never knows what evil may lurk within...hot triple charged load or steel slug? Don't take chances. It's always a good idea to mark shell boxes with your name or other identification. What if you mistakenly grab someone else's #9 reloads and you are shooting the handicap event? Imagine that! If you're switching to a release trigger, learn to set the trigger after the gun is shouldered and safely pointed. Practice with the trigger before taking the gun to the trapshoot! Be careful when trying out a gun with a standard pull trigger. You may pick up your gun and forget you're shooting a release, pull the trigger, and discharge the weapon accidentally (it happens). Don't ever turn while on station, swinging the gun toward other shooters, even if it is pointed at the ground, loaded or unloaded. Always remove shells from chamber when changing posts. Use eye protection. Bullet velocity of 200 f.p.s. is sufficient to penetrate the human skull -- it doesn't take much to ruin a life. Consider the legal liability you may face from negligence, and two lives are ruined. Accidents happen due to complacency and the unusual, seemingly impossible, unexpected mechanical failure. One is too many. Luckily, accidents are few. Let's keep it that way.

GUNS AND ALCOHOL
"Today it may be fire, tomorrow it will be ashes."

Shooters who drink alcohol at registered shoots are shooting themselves in the foot. Just as a drunk can drive better when under the influence, so will a shooter do likewise. It's not a likely means to win. This includes social gatherings after days end. Sitting around the clubhouse exchanging bull stories, drinking late into the night will ruin tomorrow's performance. If that's your game, then more power to you, just don't expect to rank high scores. You'll notice the top shooters don't party at night, play the fun-shoots, or stay up all hours of the night. You'll also note they are not strolling about with a mixed drink in their hand. If you want to drink, do so, though keep it to an absolute minimum. One or two drinks, maybe. Three, never. Abstaining is the choice policy. From a safety standpoint, the abuse of alcohol is everyone's responsibility to insure no one fires on the line while under the influence or drives a vehicle. A good night's sleep is imperative to shoot well. If you find your scores are awful, contemplate what you were doing the night before and you'll acquire the answer. Many top shooters refrain from socializing at large. They concentrate on keeping a quiet and relaxed mind-frame for the next day. They tend to reserve energy for the shoot. Life must be balanced. Too much of anything is not good, even trapshooting! This is not to say go out and get drunk, but it's okay to be human and slip up once upon a day. However, there is no room for error mixing guns and booze or drugs, for the consequences are severe and everlasting. Personal responsibility and professionalism, along with dependable associates, can keep the day safe.

CRASH AND BURN
"Some things simply can't be changed."

Shooting couldn't be better, so it seemed, then wham-o... the engine falters, sputters, flame out. We're diving nose-first racing to the ocean below. No ejection sled, no way out. A helpless, hopeless feeling, terror without end. Down we go crashing into a wall of water as unforgiving as solid concrete. Such is the trauma of a trapshooter who 'burns-out,' forgetting how to shoot, losing the sight picture. It's just one of those days we can't hit anything. The eyes and hands just refuse to cooperate, delivering the embarrassment of horrific low scores, surpassing records of a novice shooter. What a way to ruin a day! As I was writing this book, 95% finished, it happened. My practice scores tumbled to the worst I've shot in years. I couldn't believe what was happening, I mean I really couldn't fathom missing three targets on post one, two on three, four on five. Nine targets dropped on one trap! Here I'm writing a book on trapshooting and I drop nine targets? What a depressing thought. How would I ever live up to this embarrassment? And the more I tried to break out of the tailspin, the more I failed. The second round of 25 targets was equally horrific. I forgot how to shoot! All my technique vanished, sight pictures vaporized, I was lost. Every novice, and good shooters, too, at the club was watching me drop one, two, three in a row. I took a break and tried again, and with equally poor results. I was in a hole and I couldn't climb out. Feeling ill the night before, I couldn't get a good night's sleep. Moreover, I was alarmed, *"What if I shoot like this at the registered shoot next week?"* I felt like crawling in a deep dark hole and planned to wipe the shoot date from the calendar.

A few days later I felt a tad better knowing I was ill, which caused the loss of coordination, yet found it hard to blame my failure on things I had no control over, even though it was raining, I knew it wasn't the weather. Maybe it's the gun? The rain gear I wore upset the gun's length of pull -- I knew that, but I also knew it wasn't the reason solely to blame. I believed all things could be rectified. I didn't feel sick when I was shooting, just a little fatigued, but not all that bad, so I thought. The wall I hit was one I couldn't climb over or step around. So, the publishing date of this book had to wait to see if I really did forget how to shoot and how to pull out of this nose-dive. Confidence was totally shattered, and I mean the spirit within broken without mercy. Could it be the hundreds of hours working on this book burning me out? Could be. Will the reader also burn-out reading this book? Maybe. The information within is overwhelming, but I already covered this in the beginning, to learn slowly. I never crashed and burned like this before, it was a total collapse. It was surreal as I stood on line thinking I 'forgot how to shoot' and believe me, I did. I didn't know what to do, when to pull the trigger; every target was like a bullet racing away faster than my ability to visually acquire it. My gun swung like it was a fence post. By week's end I discovered how it happened and how to pull through.

The Conclusion: I discovered I was overdrawing my slumber account, experiencing a case of extreme fatigue. It appears we need a specific number of hours of sleep each night. Getting less sleep builds up a 'sleep debt' which must be repaid. This debt keeps rising for each night of sleep lost. Failure to catch up leads to degraded judgement, faulty memory and slow fixation, reaction and decision making. It turns out we can be effectively asleep with eyes open, performing all our usual activities. Unlike sleepwalking, the brain shuts down into a state of micro-sleep. Also, the brain is programmed to shut down between the hours of 3 to 5 p.m. which is why we tend to fall into a sleepy-like state. It isn't the big meal you ate that makes you groggy. Taking small naps reduces the sleep debt. In cases of extreme fatigue, the brain will go to sleep regardless of what we are doing. The event that happened to me perfectly described the research. Good to keep in mind when driving home from a shoot that social interaction, keeping radio on in car, maintaining conversation with occupants, taking frequent rest stops can prevent falling asleep at the wheel -- and on the trap field. What compounded the slump was my determination to climb out of it by using sheer brute force. Over-analysis! This intense self-evaluation compounded the problem as I became brutally fixed into forcing myself to break the target instead of focusing on the target with a relaxed attitude, smooth swing and deliberate timing. Emotions took the stage over reason. When I slowed down, the rapid searching of sight pictures, jerky gun movements, and nerves quieted. I found the book did pull me out of the slump, but for some strange reason, I forgot all that I learned, all that I knew. I think I'll keep a copy in my car, too.

DON'T QUIT FOR BAD APPLES
"I would sooner fail than not be among the greatest." John Keats 1818

At first trapshooting is fun; later it becomes work; beyond is hell. Remember the reasons why you love to shoot targets. For as time passes, skills rise and so will the frustrations, both internal and external. The internal source of frustration can be controlled by accepting the fact that it requires time to develop shooting skills. External sources of frustration are controlled by overlooking the comments of those who disappoint you. As in any sport, there are cheats, malcontents, mood destroyers, and thankfully rare but they do exist, outright wannabe bully know-it-alls that cause trouble wherever they shoot. Such is life. Gratefully, the vast majority of shooters are honest respectable people of the highest caliber. Continue shooting for the sake of the commendable, don't quit to gratify the antagonists. Attitude is crucial. Maintain the good-natured innocence you had when attending your first tournament and it will take you a long way toward enjoyment and good fortune. Cop a snobby presidential attitude and you'll live in a small world, a lonely planet with few real friends to shoot with. Promising trapshooters have quit the sport due to prolonged slumps and the embarrassment it causes; please don't quit! All great achievements require failure after failure, and often failure beyond success, to succeed again. Slumps are horrendous, but they will happen, we all have been there more than once, and one is too many. Frustration is natural too. Whether it arrives from any source, internal or external, keep a professional attitude and you'll pull through. Be aware every flower garden sprouts weeds. There are devious tricksters out there that will slyly induce a slump on shooters so they can cripple squads. **Examples**: **1)** insuring a shooter who sets-up a tad slow before a good shooter who has an aversion to slow setup shooters, **2)** causing an argument or delicately depreciate your frame of mind over some pointless trifling matter to distort your mood, **3)** purposely ignoring you, giving you the cold shoulder to demolish mindset, **4)** giving undeserved compliments to instill bewilderment and overconfidence, **5)** asking you to run an errand or do them a favor to distract you from your pre-shoot setup, **6)** jokingly embarrassing you to saturate moods of anger or self-doubt. The list is unlimited. Now you know why many top shooters are reclusive before and between events. People can disrupt your mood and concentration, often without intention, but sometimes it is deliberate. Where there is money, there will be trouble. It's a phase to learn, a mode to adapt to, a gauntlet to wear to gorge through these flames. When you survive these realities, and survive you will, a professional attitude will be yours, and when you look in the rearview mirror, you'll see the gameplayers in the background antagonizing each other. You may not be able to avoid the antagonist, but you can disregard their comments as being unprofessional and unworthy of your attention. Learn to walk away, but not leave the sport. Remember what the word trap really means: **To Really Appreciate People**. Though serious as it is, trapshooting is still a fun sport!

CHAPTER 14

GETTING DOWN TO BUSINESS
"If you strive for perfection, you're heading in the right direction."

Pleasure before profits ... for the latter is hardest to come by. Trapshooting is a money sport driving the game onward. For a few it is a self-employment business venture, for more it is fun, to a select group it is an industry, and for the diverse, a tax write-off. The above choices are yours. To maintain your practice and registered shoot averages a computer program to use is *'Shotgun Sports Enthusiast.'* You can order the software from DeSiena Digital Design, Box 364, Bearsville, NY 12409 (914)-679-2044. This program is designed for all shotgun target shooters. It's a multimedia database and tracking application with completely updateable databases for keeping track of a shooter's performance as well as inventory and expenses. You can keep average records needed for registered competitions in addition to tracking personal performance in practice, seeing score improvement, moving up in class, etc. When using the application, you will discover being more "in touch" with your records, overall performance and efficiency will increase. Included is an expense spreadsheet for keeping up with the costs of firearms, ammo, reload components, accessories and fees (registrations, memberships, range & options) plus an address book. Another program to consider is *'Lock, Stock & Barrel'* which has scoring ability with reload information encompassing rifle, pistol and shotguns. Contact; PC Proxy, 481 Timberlake Drive, Estill Springs, TN 37330.

PLAYING THE OPTIONS
"A feast is made for laughter, and wine maketh merry: but money answereth all things." So they say

Yes! money is Aladdin's lamp. It speaks with a loud voice. It's a terrible thing to chase, but a charming thing to meet. Describing the myriad option formats and pay-out schedules is not a primary subject here. The shooter's state of mind when playing the options holds more importance. I've heard frequent concerns from new -- and not so new - competition shooters worrying about option money when they shoot, *"I just can't deal with the pressure, especially when I miss a perfect 25 or 50 by one target."* Ho hum, haven't we all? Earning option money is rather like being a blonde. It is more fun but not vital. Nonetheless, for the novice this is an overwhelming and detrimental reversal, destroying scores. The suggestions I offer are simple. There is solely one target to grind up out there, just one and only one. This sets the shooter's mind away from those huge numbers 25, 50, 75, 100. The setup plan -- never think of money, prizes, winning, losing -- think of nothing but making sure you accurately see the target. The mind-set is now focused on the business at hand. Think of the option fee money you paid as a standard entry fee. Don't think of it as money lost or invested for potential gain. It's just a fee you pay to shoot. When you concentrate on the targets, the options will automatically pay off. If the pressure is too great, back off from the options until you regain technical confidence together with an easygoing psychological composure. By playing the options frequently, apprehensions dissipate. When should you begin playing the options? As soon as possible. You don't need to linger until you consistently break strings of 25s as incentive side-betting stimulates higher levels of performance. Without a mental stimulus, a goal, a desire to obtain an end result, the high scores may never materialize. Winning frequently arrives by surprise. No one is forcing you to play options. If you find it disrupts your shooting, then don't play them for now. Options raise the stakes, increase the pressure, and can win you money. That's what trapshooting is all about. You'll grow into it.

TAX DEDUCTIONS
"Money is the slavery of the free."

Tax laws fluctuate yearly, so contact the IRS 800-829-3676 and ask for the publication *"Schedule C (1040) Profit or Loss from Business."* You should comply with city, county and state law in setting up your own business. In most cases, you do not require a business license, as no physical business location exists. You simply register with the state and local tax board. There are primarily two ways to set up a small business enabling you to deduct shooting expenses.

1. As an individual trapshooter, you simply are self-employed in the business of trapshooting. Obtain a 'Dome' bookkeeping record book from any office supply store or write to *Dome Publishing Co*, Dome Building, Warwick, RI 02886. Or use a computer program specifically designed for trapshooting an updateable database for tracking inventory, performance and expenses, contact *De Siena Digital Design*, P. O. Box 364, Bearsville, NY 12409 (800) 550-7855. You can use other computer money management programs such as Quicken® to manage profit and loss bookkeeping.

2. As a business owner, you reach new customers and write off trapshooting expenses as a means of obtaining customers. This falls into the advertising expense category. Not all businesses would apply for the business deduction. For example; real estate apartment rentals, and a machine shop specializing in industrial electric motors would not qualify if the majority of potential customers attending trapshooting could not readily use your product. They don't meet a prudent marketability test. On the other hand, a service-related business, i.e. gunsmith, vehicle repair, construction-related businesses may qualify. Just be certain you <u>do</u> advertise, passing out business cards or flyers, and you are obtaining customers from these activities. You can at least write off travel and printing expenses, though you will likely still run into a problem with the IRS as the act of shooting may not establish a necessary function required to advertise. In this case, use the self-employed method in item #1 above.

Currently, tax law allows anyone to set up their own business and deduct the full cost of operating the business; however, you must show a profit within 3 years -- or the intent to show a profit. If you don't show a profit in the allotted time limit, the business may become a hobby and deductions may be limited or not allowed. In this case, it would be best to wait until your skills rise to the point you can reasonably expect to turn a modest profit within 3 years before setting up your business. You can have a primary job and still be self-employed in a trapshooting secondary side-job. Save all your expense and option money winnings receipts. That's all there is to it. There is no mystery here. Writers, artists, musicians and pro trapshooters do it, so can you. Keep in mind it is more promising to turn a profit shooting the handicap events and playing the options than playing the 16 yard singles events. It is not advisable to write off the singles events as there is little money to gain at smaller tournament shoots. If there is no potential for earning money, there would not be an honest justification to deduct these expenses on your taxes until you become proficient in winning highly competitive tournament singles events paying sizable purses. Of course, this is a matter of interpretation. You don't have to turn a profit, only the intent to profit fulfills the test. Tips on filing Schedule C: trapshooting is usually a cash business and inventory you have already (shells etc.,) are not sold so there is no inventory. You can deduct advertising, vehicle, supplies (i.e.; shells, wads, primers etc.,) repairs to gun and vehicle, travel, meals, hotel, and other business related expenses. The principal business code can be other business services # 6882, or other personal services # 7880. If you write off vehicle expenses, you must maintain a mileage log and dates of service so you can determine the business-use portion of expenses. Consult with the IRS, or a computer tax program such as *Turbo Tax*® for making tax filings easier. Tax preparation books can offer in-depth insight, too, but the tax programs are hard to beat. *Quick Books*® is a great program for all business transactions and so is *Quicken*®.

CHAPTER 15

TIME FOR REFLECTION

"Dwell on the happy days for they are secrets of greater things to come."

The last chapter is only the beginning! The tips in this book are not absolute, right-and-wrong formulas. They are ideas for experimentation, to determine what works for you and what doesn't. It will help you find and solve problems. Now that you have finished, you will need to read this book again (and probably again and again) to blend all of the elements you have learned and implant the larger picture into your mind to curtail confusion. The game can be complex, as there are so many differing guns with variant points of impact and shooting styles. No one method or means of instruction can be proclaimed to be absolute, but with experimentation with the ideas in this book, with your equipment and form, you should discover solutions to mistakes that are keeping your scores down. There are exceptions to every rule. I've seen shooters wear gloves (to reduce flinching) on trigger finger and perform just fine, which stands to reason, you can make anything work if you put your mind to it. Rules are like taxes, loopholes exist, but only after you know the rules. As to complexity, let's use one thin example; Point of Impact. With a gun with a very high POI (pattern is 100% above point of aim) timing and sight pictures look awfully different than a flat, medium, or low POI gun depending on yardage and timing. See Fig. 1-1 and 1-2.

HIGH POI: Best used when shooting long yardage targets that are accelerating rapidly and the shooter is shooting quickly. With sight bead on the target when trigger is pulled, will burn the target as the shotstring rises upward above point of aim (higher than where you were looking) to catch the rising target. Highly effective on long yardage handicap beyond 24 yards. Can be a vexatious problem at short and mid-yardage as most shooters do not shoot quick enough. Target distance and timing is tricky with the POI too high which causes the shot to pass over the top of the target if the sight bead is placed on a slower rising target (angle targets rise slower and targets slow down as distance increases). See Fig. 1-1 and 1-2. Here, the target must be floating above the sight rib at all times. I learned this the hard way. My Browning Citori Plus O&U bottom barrel's POI can shoot from 3" to 12" high, set at 8". This can be very hard to adapt to, as the gun is not shooting where you are looking with rib POI set above 6" high. At mid-yardage using the lower barrel kept missing, shooting over the targets, as it is only natural to put the sight bead on the target. It worked fine on the 27 yard line, but I couldn't hit anything at mid-yardage or on singles (shooting over the top). Speeding up the timing would cure this, but was forbidding as it was close to snap-shooting. After slipping a laser into the barrels, it verified the POI was set too high for the yardage and timing. Six inches proved to be perfect as long as targets were dispatched quickly.

LOW POI: An 80/20 - 80% of pattern high, 20% below point of aim. Switching to the top barrel which shoots relatively flat compared to the high POI lower barrel solved the problem at the 16 yard line with a rib adjustment to lower POI to 3 1/2". The gun now shoots exactly where I am looking on singles without altering timing. Adjusting POI is easier than having to adjust to sight pictures. Sight bead on the target, always! This is the most important factor in building high scores, the gun must shoot where you look. It's basic, but POI can be friend or foe depending on gun fit, yardage, timing, distance to target, shot velocity and technique. To complicate matters, POI can change with switching ammo, barrel heating, choke size, clothing worn, comb adjustments, etc. Overall, I believe reviewing this book often will isolate specific problems you may be facing through the process of elimination, boosting your scores. Confusion is a temporary state of mind. As time progresses and knowledge increases clarity displaces bewilderment. What if you're still baffled? You're not alone! Good luck, and hood shooting!

A WORD
"Show me a shooter who keeps his head still and I'll show you a shooter who can't shoot."

There is a ton of information in this book and it is important to assimilate it slowly. You may have read through this book a bit too fast, but thankfully you can start over again back to page one and begin anew. We are all too often impatient and wish to find the shortcuts towards good trapshooting. Many of the secrets have been revealed and some readers may not have even recognized the significance of the tip when given. On your second pass through this book, and perhaps at a later time when your shooting has evolved, these secrets will become more evident in importance -- extremely valuable. So don't be surprised to pick up the book a year or two from now and find some jewels of knowledge that will bail you out in the future.

The challenge facing all trapshooters is obtaining the knowledge then applying it. I can show you how, but I can't do it for you. So read the shooting tips and little secrets given in this book and do the best you can to assimilate them one-by-one, day-by-day, year-by-year and you should do just fine. The worst thing you can do is cram all this information or skip over vital sections, deeming them as irrelevant. Everything in this book was put there for a purpose.

Be very careful about making major overhauls to your shooting style all at one time. Absorb the information in this book -- the theory, the principles, the experimentation tactics, the ideas -- and make corrections one at a time. Serious corrections are like major surgery and it takes time to recover.

If you are wondering about the above quote; *"Show me a shooter who keeps his head still and I'll show you a shooter who can't shoot,"* it refers to a shooter who is not swinging the gun. This shooter fails to use his/her body as part and parcel of the swing but rather stands frozen as a statue, pushing the gun's muzzle with the forearm with brute force or snapping, stabbing action to the target. You will see this with the long-yardage shooters. Somewhere along the line of time they have *forgotten* to swing to the target, believing they don't have to because they are standing so far back from the trap. The problem is they are holding the gun too high. Most hold the gun straight-out at eye level and wonder why they miss targets. See Fig. 11-7 and Fig. 11-11 and Fig. 11-12. Are you holding your gun so high you can't see the target and you have no time to ride the target's true flight path?

Fig. 11-8 reveals the hot-core pattern, and the sooner you switch to using it, the higher-scoring shooter you will be after you adjust to the precision requirements to adapt to it. Don't worry about conventional wisdom and others who will tell you otherwise. Simply do it; and get to work and leave the others wondering how come you're getting so frustratingly difficult to beat.

Don't fall into a "timing trap" where you pull the trigger just because it "feels" like the right time. You likely have already fell victim to this bad habit and "squad timing" can induce it, so be aware of this fact. See Fig. 11-9. Be aware of timing, but not when shooting. Timing is a practice function. You learn it when practicing and when in competition it comes to you without thought. Sometimes you may have to implant a trigger word, *"Feel the shot"* to remind you of shooting the zone. Whatever problem you are having, develop a trigger word you can use to awaken the subconscious mind to get the job done.

Rib and eye alignment is not to be overlooked from gun mount to the swing to pulling the trigger. If you learn to steer the gun with your cheek, applying constant cheek pressure, your eye will not fall away from the rib. See Fig. 11-10. If you swing, using Body English, your head won't turn or rise from the comb. To steer the gun with the cheek, you allow your upper body to move so it can be accomplished.

When canting the gun, you are standing a bit sideways in the traditional trapshooting stance. At this point of body alignment you simply bow like the Japanese do, gently, to the right (bow to left for left-hand shooters). This bow is mostly from the head and neck and a tiny bit of the upper back. When you practice this bow you will see how easily the gun will flip on its side. You don't need much cant to get the job done, 8 to 10 degrees can do just fine on most targets. More cant on the extreme angles may be required.

The worst shooters are those who try to do the most. These are the "experienced shooters," shooters who have been shooting for years struggling with the game, taking all the wrong advice from other shooters who are also struggling to perfect their own game. These trapshooters know everything they do wrong and still want to know more of what they did wrong, and they become overly focused on the "wrong" and not what they do "right." Pay attention to what you do right, focus on that and the wrongs will fall by the wayside.

Excuses can be powerful detriments to shooting well. Stop making excuses when you miss a target or drop a handful on a trap. Excuses are thoughts and they have power to reproduce what you are thinking. It's imperative to know what went wrong to correct the problem, then flush the thought of the missed target out of the mind and pretend it never happened when setting up for the next shot. When multiple targets are dropped on a trap, you are thinking too much and not shooting naturally! Learning how to reset yourself like this is a great inner secret professional trapshooters know all so well. Assume you shoot a terrible low score of 80. This means you hit 80 targets and only dropped 20 -- 80 times you did something right. Concentrate on the solid hits you have produced and get your mind far away from the 20 mistakes you made. Thinking and excuses are only allowed when you practice, not when shooting a tournament. You have to learn how to think differently between practice and competition. Don't carryover thoughts from practice sessions to the match.

Now that you have just about finished this book, take another look at Fig. 11-15 and 11-16 and 11-17. These three illustrations are important, true trapshooting secrets revealed, as many things this book has, in fact, revealed. And always remember that targets never travel in straight lines but are always "bending away" from your sight bead. Now that you know what is *really* happening out there, it's a lot easier now to hit the targets.

Another secret is to feel professional when you shoot. Stand tall, call with authority, shoot with precision. Use this mindset even if the bottom is falling out and you shot a lousy 19 on a trap. The more professional you feel, the more professional you will become. It's a self-fulfilling prophesy -- mind over matter. You will become what you believe. If you would like to learn more about the power of thought and how it can help you in all areas of your life read, *"How To Change Your Life"* by Earnest Holmes, published by Science of Mind, 3251 West South Street, P.O. Box 75127, Los Angeles, CA 90075. They also have a magazine and a source of fine books you don't want to miss out on. Another book I recommend is *"The Millionaire Joshua,"* by Catherine Ponder. Can this organization improve your shooting? You bet they can! Write them right now and get started on a new life adventure that will change your life, improve your shooting and much more. Also see "The New You" subchapter.

Now that you have learned many of the inside secrets to trapshooting, do not become so mechanical you can't shoot for beans. It's like teaching someone to strike a hammer at a nail, you give the instruction of the principles of aim to the target, swing and consistency, but once learned let the rest take care of itself. You don't have to think to drive a nail or shoot a target -- but you must take dead aim at each shot. Don't take dead aim only when you remember -- remember to do it each and every time!

Your eye must remain dead-center along the center of the gun's rib, but the eyeball can move and it's okay to shift the eye up or down, left or right when setting eye hold points, just don't move your head. If you have to move your head then move the gun hold so you won't have to. See Fig. 11-10. In these drawings you will see the gun hold is adjusted so the most extreme angle target will be seen exiting the house immediately. Notice the one-eye shooter has shifted eye hold to the left to catch that hard left target. Notice the setup here. See how easy it is to see a target exit the house and how easy it will be to ride the track of the target once it emerges. Setup is everything in trapshooting. Prepare for what you are going to shoot. Know the three basic angles and setup for them on each post and your scores will rise. Setup makes the job easier to break the target. The two-eye shooter would gain visibility benefits by dropping the gun hold even lower. Look who has the better view.

Remember, you can't shoot with the eyes alone in handicap shooting. You can get away with pointing at the 16-yard line and even up to 20-yards, but beyond that pointing becomes too sloppy, and it gets real sloppy at the long-yardage areas 27-yard. Learn to hit the target hard with the eyes -- but make sure you see a 'tight' sight picture! The way to see a tight sight picture is to see the muzzle/sight bead lining up to the target.

EXTRAVAGANT PRACTICE
"More seems best to those who obsess."

It is vitally important practice be performed intelligently and in a practical manner without excess. Too much of anything is always self-destructive. You have heard it time and again to practice, practice, practice. It is true practice makes perfect, but only if performed with reasonable constructive intent. Therefore, practice for the sake of practice in itself creates a void. Even weekly Sunday practice can be too much, for some to many shooters, if they only go out of habit. A break is always required to get away from the game and allow oneself to reflect. How long of a break? Not much, perhaps skipping a practice session once every two to three months. It's difficult to do when you love the game and have nothing else to do, but time is required to distance oneself from shooting. Have you ever noticed that every Sunday you shoot you don't really get better? It's because a habit is formed over desire. Stagnation develops. By skipping, a new desire is formed to return to practice again the following week with a renewal of spirit to excel. The more you try to cram knowledge, the mind becomes overextended and falls into a slump or a state of resistance. So take breaks from shooting on occasion when you see your scores are not improving to permit that inner longing to shoot to recharge the soul. You'll come back stronger if you do. A little rest never hurts.

BE STRONG
"Weakness is the belief in it."

When you do shoot, hit hard with the utmost authority. This is not an ego thing for the crowd to observe, but an inner power within -- a total conviction within yourself to smash each target. The moment before you call for your first target, say to yourself, *"Yes. I can and I will."* This begins to release energy within and raises confidence to annihilate each target. You've heard it said trapshooting is won or lost between the ears. Well, you can't step on line with a whimsy "hope I hit them attitude." After you shoot and hit the target, again repeat a positive statement to yourself then stand with utmost authority and go to work. This may sound silly and simple, but it's so true to develop a professional mind-set. There is a power within you that must be released, and can be, if you begin the process of identification. Even when you are shooting poorly, practice building confidence for when complete confidence arises, talent emerges. Just try calling for the target with increased authority and watch what happens. If simply calling can increase target acquisition, imagine what total mental authority can do for you! Work on this as part of your practice plan and vast improvement will be yours for the taking. Watch the pros and you'll see they have it. So can you. Fact is, you already have it within -- just bring it forth and be strong about it and never look back at poor scores again (of course, you will have bad days like we all do here and there).

THE NEW YOU
"The past is the future only if you agree."

To progress in trapshooting requires knowledge applied and the ability to let one's past slide away. Your mind remembers everything, all the lousy scores, and therefore builds the future on the past, which is not good for trapshooting. You have to begin anew, forget the past and see a bright present -- now! A new life, a new beginning. You purchased this book because you are tired of the scores you are shooting. To maximize the knowledge given in these pages requires that you dare to become a new person, a new shooter, a new spirit within unleashed. It's the only way to make positive things happen in your life. And it all begins with believing in yourself and daring to believe you can. This is not a forceful thing. It's not a strain. Just simply believe in yourself and let the past slip away. God has given you the *power* of mind and free will. As Jesus said, *"The Kingdom of God is within you"* it is. Your thoughts are so powerful indeed they *will* produce external physical results. That is the *power* of mind. Professional shooters know of this power and few tell of it.

So repeat after me: *"I do not understand how the power of mind works but I will dare this day to believe good is about to happen to me. I believe I can believe and so I will. I am no longer controlled by my past. This day, I have awakened to the truth that what I think -- I will be. From this day forward I will excel in all that I do and success will come to me in unexpected ways. Never again will I believe in my past failures. Today I am a new person and I fully expect my right thinking to erase all negatives from my life. The future is bright with promise and I gladly accept this truth and give thanks to God for revealing this reality to me. Today is the day, now is the hour to believe in myself and the law of mind. As I think, so it is I shall be. I am that I am. Regardless of how bleak my external situation may be, I will believe in the good to come and never look back. From this day forward I choose to reverse my thinking and only see the good that is mine. As my simple faith is presented, I shall be rewarded immediately and know to whom I shall give thanks."*

Now if it seems a bit strange to find a prayer in a trapshooting book, let me remind you, professionals pray and ask God for help. I know many do and they are certainly not the religious-type if you know what I mean, but they do believe in the power of prayer nevertheless. The power of prayer is the *biggest secret* in trapshooting, as it is in all life endeavors. I know it works for I have seen bad things happen in my own life and turn unexpected into remarkable reversals of good fortune. Totally crushing disasters turned into marvelous blessings. It's bigger than winning trapshoots. You won't win them all, but on a grande scale of things -- incredible things happen in your life you never thought could or would. And the good news is it works for everyone!

If you really want to see a fabulous change in your life for the better where good things happen to you without extreme effort on your part simply read the following books; *"How to Change Your Life," "The Millionaire Joshua,* and *"The Science of Mind."* I suggest you read them in that order. Of all the advice I have given in this book, I will say this is the best advice of all. Write to: Science of Mind, 3251 West South Street, P.O. Box 75127, Los Angeles, CA 90075. This is not a religion, okay? It's an understanding of Biblical principles and compiled truths of all faiths and certain unmitigated laws that produce results. Regardless of your religious denomination or beliefs, these books will open your eyes to powerful life-changing truths that many of us have sought and now have found. And when you see these good things come to pass in your life, I'd enjoy hearing from you if you wish to write. Good news is always welcome news.

VIDEO SIMULATORS FOR TRAPSHOOTING
"Oh, if only I could imagine an easier way... I could win this day."

I've researched the feasibility of developing an electronic video simulator comparable to what Nintendo® would use on the television, but it won't work for numerous reasons. **1)** The screen size -- even on a household big-screen TV set -- would not enable the shooter to see a realistic depth of field. **2)** The gun you would hold or device to attach to your trap gun to transmit the signal would be an imprecise pattern and shot speed would be impaired, not reflecting the real world view and situation. **3)** The TV screen would need to be extraordinarily titanic in size to accommodate the swing angle of the shotgun to reflect real world target angles at all yardages, and would certainly do you no good on singles or handicap targets. **4)** The cost would be prohibitively high. **5)** The sensation of firing the gun would be nil to nothing, and "feel" is very important in trapshooting. With no recoil you may even begin to learn that it's safe to raise your head from the comb on a simulator. **6)** The electronic signal is so fast to the target it will seriously upset your timing and sight-pictures and that can make the simulator a serious detriment to your shooting. **7.)** You could learn terribly shot-wrecking habits if the simulator cannot simulate real-world conditions such as: pattern size and shot speed upsetting timing, target's not following realistic gravity-induced arcing flight paths, improper target speed, rise and angle settings, depth of field, etc., etc.

The bottom line, only a large-screen computerized simulator would work and it would cost beyond the reach any shooter could or would want to afford, and you wouldn't learn much, as you would only be practicing the same old mistakes over-and-over again! So we are back to square #1. Nothing will surpass imbedding into the mind actual "knowledge" and practical real world "hands-on experience" to impart that knowledge. Could you become a proficient carpenter or engineer or truly even learn how to drive a car in the 'real world' by learning from a simulator? The only benefit you could derive with a simulator would be to develop trigger control and eye/hand coordination *exercises* but that's all, and any off-the-shelf 'shoot-'em-up' video game can do that with a hand-held pushbutton controller.

Some firms have already made the large simulators, but they have not made their debut on the trapshooting circuit. They would certainly need to compete with the practice traps, and the real traps would still be the best for warm-ups. So if you see any firm offering a simulator, ask yourself if the device can measure up to the standards mentioned herein before you chuck a wad of money into the wind. There are computer games available on trapshooting, but remember -- these are novelty games not educational simulators and are designed for the fun factor only. At this time, there is only one firm that comes the closest to a real world simulator throwing targets which can be used indoors. Contact *Light Flyer System*, Beamerline 14255 N. 79th Street, #6, Scottsdale, AZ 85260 (602)-998-4828. Anything else is still a pipe dream.

PRECISION SHOOTING
"Absolutely nothing can beat precision shooting."

"Precision Shooting - The Trapshooter's Bible" is posted at the end of this book. After you have had time to learn the techniques in this book, you will then be ready for *"Precision Shooting."* This book is much larger than *Trap Shooting Secrets*, with <u>over 80 illustrations</u> and more than <u>230 questions and answers</u> to problems top shooters experience and the errors they wish to annihilate, and much more. It is written to take you to the next level in the arena where professionals reside. It is for the advanced shooter; the shooter who is dead serious about rising into the elite ranks. I believe you will be highly impressed with the results the book will impart upon your scores. You will not be disappointed!

THE LAST UNSOLVED MYSTERY
"Put the fun in dysfunctional."

You read, study, analyze, practice and still targets are lost... easy targets! It's like trying to resolve the puzzling riddle of the one lone shoe on the highway. Where's the other shoe? No one has the answer. It just happens. It's a five minute mystery, as those who place the shoe on our roads never admit to doing it. There's no secret formula or magic bullet to win at trapshooting. Learn the basic fundamentals of the game and understand the psychological aspects. Practice with an earnest goal to accomplish perfection through meaningful repetition. Get serious with hitting targets, but let your subconscious mind do the shooting once you have trained it to make all the right moves while you maintain full eye contact and concentrated focus on the target. Pull the trigger when the sight picture is right and keep your head down snug on the comb. It's all so easy, yet so hard. To compete you have to be strong. To win you need to be smart. That's life in the trapshooting arena. Do your best and your scores will reward you. Some will disagree, though generally it is not difficult to hit targets, it is easy to miss them. Humans fail to reach perfection from nonobservance, inadequacy, negligence, indifference, oblivion, carelessness, inattention, omission, disregard, avoidance, recklessness, dodging, botching, bungling, attention deficit disorder, insufficient memory. Need I say more? He who is without sin cast the first stone.

PRECISION SHOOTING BOOK

"Precision Shooting" is now available. This book is heavily illustrated and gets right down to the wire taking you into the realm of trapshooting from the moment you place the gun to your shoulder to the point of pulling the trigger. The book is for the "advanced" shooter. *"Precision Shooting"* will take you to the next level of trapshooting, into the world of deep concentration and precise accuracy. Plenty of practical "learn by doing"

exercises to develop: sharp eye focus, refined awareness, dead serious concentration, precise sight picture, deliberate shooting techniques, moving gun forms, decisive muzzle control and swing, incredible consistency, and dead-on precision shooting. When you shoot with deliberate precision, you'll outpace the competition! Inquire how you can obtain *"Precision Shooting - The Trapshooter's Bible"* wherever you purchased this book or any bookstore can order a copy for you. Order your copy today!

GUN RIGHTS

Gun Owners of America, 8001 Forbes Place, Suite 102, Springfield, VA 22151 (703)-321-8585.
National Rifle Association, 11250 Waples Hill Road, Fairfax, VA 22030 (800)-672-3888.
Second Amendment Foundation, 12500 N.E. 10th Place, Bellevue, WA 98005 (206)-454-7012.

WEB SITE

Don't miss out on the James Russell Publishing web site! There are well over 100 pages (web-size pages are twice as long as what you are reading now) all for the clay target shooter: advice, articles, answers to questions on shooting, free shooting lessons, books, tapes, videos, shotgun laser sights, and more! Our web site address is on the title page of this book. You can also use a search engine to find us under the search word, trapshooting. Come visit!

PARTING SHOT

"The happiest business in all the world is that of making friends."

Your letters, comments, recommendations, ideas and comments for future editions of trapshooting publications are welcome. I'd enjoy hearing how *'Trap Shooting Secrets'* has improved your game. Send comments to: James Russell, P.O. Box 10121, Suite 2093, Eugene, OR 97440. If you wish a reply, please do include a First Class stamped self-addressed #10 standard business-size envelope. You are always welcome to write -- and if we cross paths in this vast sea of life, please do say hello and chat for a spell.

CHAPTER 16

ILLUSTRATIONS

"A picture is a thousand words in as many languages."

Illustrations begin on following pages.

High point of impact gun.   **Flat point of impact gun.**

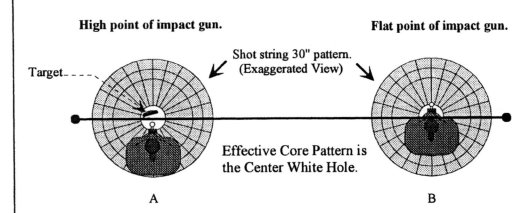

Visualize the shotstring pattern next time you practice. Notice in drawing 'A' if you pulled the trigger on the right trending target as shown, 1/2 the shot is already behind (left) of the target. More would be lost before the shot arrived, Only 20% of shot would hit the target. The importance of placing lead is critical. The target is clearly visible at all times with a gun that shoots with high point of impact and sight picture is more natural and realistic.

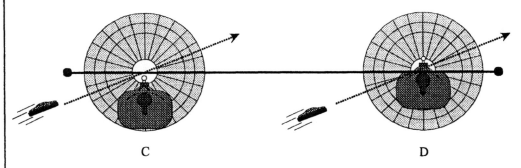

Note the natural anticipated sight picture in drawing 'C' with the high-rib gun. The flat shooting, low-rib, or low point of impact gun in drawing 'D' must cover the anticipated flight path of the target to center the shot pattern on the target's line of flight. This obscures visibility of the target and often produces a false sight picture causing missed targets. You can add a rib extension to convert your gun to a high-rib gun. Highly recommended.

Fig. 1-1

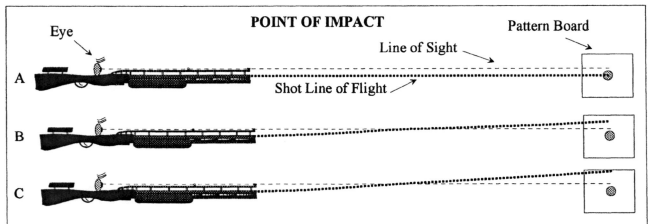

'A' shoots flat. 'B' resembles an 80/20 POI, impacting higher than point of aim. 'C' represents a full pattern high 100% POI. High POI guns are perfect for trapshooting, for all targets rise and the shot string rises to catch the target. As distance to target increases, as in handicap yardage, a higher POI is desirable to have.

Fig. 1-2

SETUP CHART

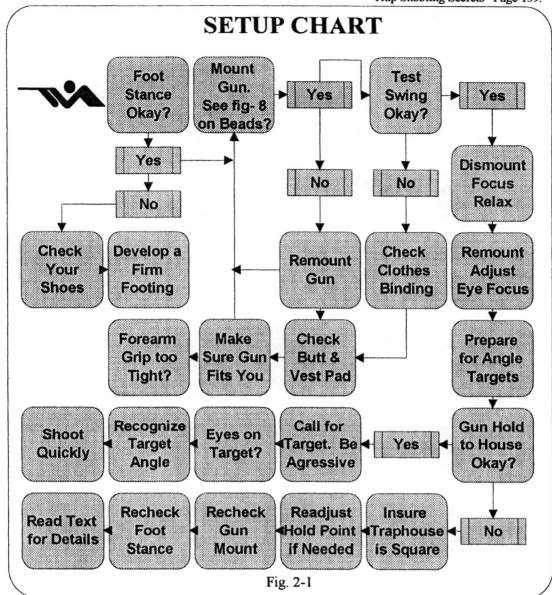

Fig. 2-1

More targets are lost to improper setup than for any other reason, yet few trapshooters truly understand the importance or apply the routine consistently. The above chart is a basic reminder. See the text for in-depth detail on each procedure.

SHOOTING VEST STABILIZES LENGTH OF PULL

 Often the most overlooked is the most important of all. Shooting glasses, blinders, billed hat, vest, glove and flat-sole shoes in good condition can make the difference between high and low scores.

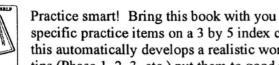 Practice smart! Bring this book with you to the practice range along with any magazine articles, or list specific practice items on a 3 by 5 index card. Relying on memory just doesn't make the grade. Doing this automatically develops a realistic workable plan of action. The text contains comprehensive practice tips (Phase 1, 2, 3, etc.) put them to good use and you will see your scores increase.

High Rib Gun - Canted Gun.

Shotstring will rise automatically so vertical gun movement is nil, cant maintains the proper lead.

Less vertical barrel movement. Smooth and rapid swing to target. Very accurate technique.

Fig. 2-2 (A)

Low Rib Gun - No Cant.

Arcing target is constantly changing direction. Gun must rise to maintain proper sight picture.

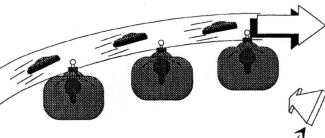

Excessive vertical barrel movement.

Fig. 2-2 (B)

Less gun movement is required with a High Rib gun, increasing precision & control. Gun easily follows the target's track with little effort and less vertical gun movement. A low rib gun will force the shooter to produce jerky gun movements as tracking arcing target with a level gun is difficult. Sporting clays shooters use the canted gun to track arcing targets. You can use this technique in trap. Most experienced shooters miss targets because they misread the target's trajectory, not because of technique. High Rib guns offer higher visibility and ease of tracking.

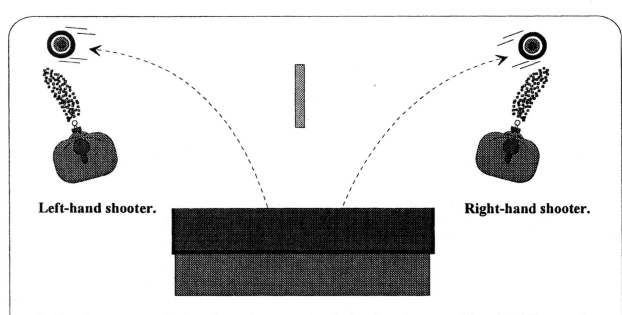

Left-hand shooter.

Right-hand shooter.

Rolling the gun muzzles into the arcing target bends the shotstring, matching the oblique angle of the target's trajectory for a head-on collision. This places more pellets directly in line with the target as opposed to shooting a gun without a slight cant on the muzzles. Attempting to hit a curving target with a straight line of shot is commonplace, but not as effective as canting. This technique is difficult to master, but it gives the shooter clear advantages. This technique is most effective with a high-rib, high point of impact shotgun. Holes in the pattern have less effect.

Fig. 2-2 (C)

SIGHT PICTURE - CANTED GUN
High Rib gun -or gun with raised point of impact.

Steep canting only works with a high point of impact gun, sending the shotstring directly ahead of the target in-line with target's trajectory. The tail end of shot will break target if lead is slightly off the mark. If your gun's POI is over 3" you can take advantage of steep cants. Using the 'bow technique' you always bow slightly, canting the gun in the same direction. Right-hand shooter bows downward to the right. Left-hand shooter bows to the left on all targets. As demonstrated, it is not easy to learn.

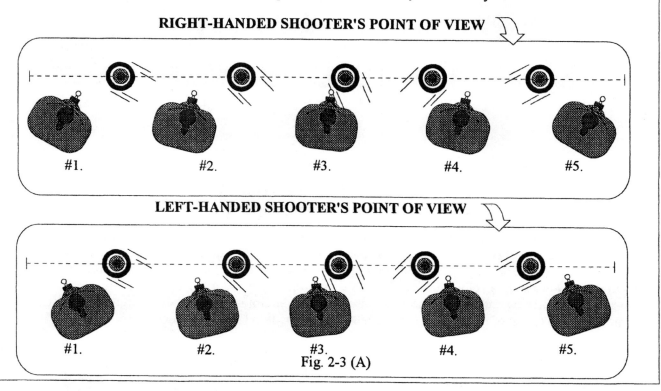

Fig. 2-3 (A)

SIGHT PICTURE
High Rib gun or gun with raised point of impact (POI).

Horizontal reference line passes through center of target not the top sight bead. Note lead on all targets as none are true straight-aways. Note 3rd gun's bead is below left center of the quarter angle target. If target is traveling right, bead would be to the right of the target. Either side will break a true straight-away target. A rising point of impact will lift shot dramatically higher directly into path of target. The target's flight path visibility is substantially enhanced with a high rib, high POI gun.

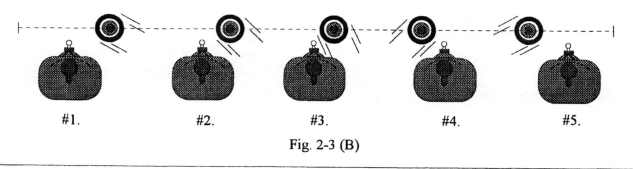

Fig. 2-3 (B)

SIGHT PICTURE
Gun with relatively flat shooting point of impact.

Horizontal reference line passes through center of target and top sight bead. Note lead on all targets as none are true straight-aways. Note 3rd gun's bead touches the left center of the quarter angle target. If target is traveling right, bead would be to the right center of target. Either side will break a true straight-away target. Muzzle rise when firing will lift shot slightly higher directly into path of target.

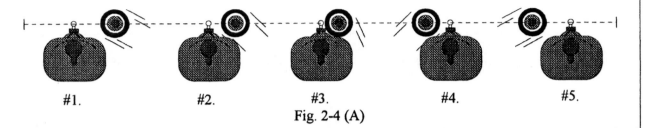

#1.   #2.   #3.   #4.   #5.

Fig. 2-4 (A)

SIGHT PICTURE - CANTED GUN.
Gun with relative flat shooting point of impact.

Cant on the gun delivers shotstring on arcing angles. Gun 1,2 & 3 sends string in line with target's line of flight. Gun 4 & 5 will curve string in opposite arc. This drawing illustrates a left-handed shooter's point of view. See Fig. 2-3 (A) for right-hand point of view. This rolling of the gun technique produces accurate dead-center hits. Note gun 1,2, 3, cants away from target and 4 & 5 cants into the target. On gun 3 you must cant to left of a left target and also cant left into a right trending target while placing sight bead to the right of target. This technique is very difficult to learn, but is deadly accurate.

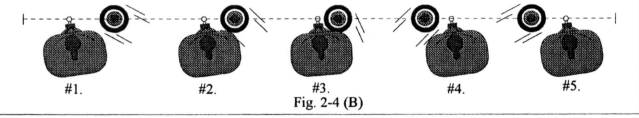

#1.   #2.   #3.   #4.   #5.

Fig. 2-4 (B)

HOLDING & POINTING THE GUN

Twist your wrist under the gun's forearm and extend index finger under or along side of the barrel's line of sight locks the gun into position, increases gun stability, enhances swing control and natural pointing ability. This simple technique pays huge dividends in rising scores.

Fig. 2-5

Is gun canting and the 'Roll Technique' for you? Only way to find out is to try it. If you like it, then make it work for you!

Everyone needs to develop their own form and style but it sure helps to first know the rules before you break them.

Watch the professionals shoot and learn. None hold a patent on their style or their techniques.

Regardless how you hold your gun, make sure it feels snug and a part of you when shouldered. You should feel it is an extension of your body so it will swing smoothly, rapidly and accurately.

TARGET ANGLES

If targets traveled in straight lines there would be less missed targets as the shot and target would intersect at precise right angles as shown.

Targets bend in a semicircular path when exiting the traphouse and continue the arced trajectory until the target hits the ground. Certainly, you can hit targets without canting the gun, as a 2 1/2 foot shot pattern is forgiving, to a degree. Angled targets are best hit with a shotstring that is in-line with the target's flight path. If you can't perfect the 'roll technique' you can pay extra attention to these diverging angles so you won't shoot behind or under the target.

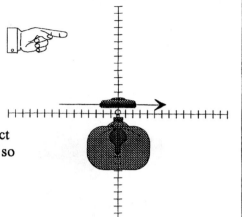

Fig. 2-6 (A)

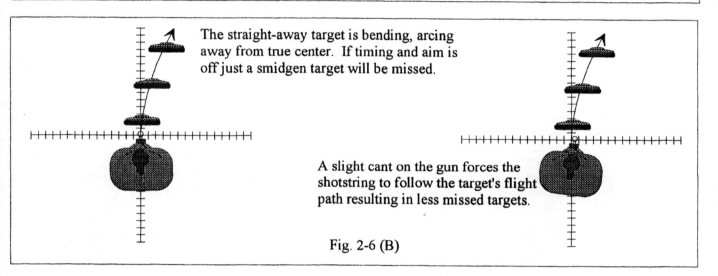

The straight-away target is bending, arcing away from true center. If timing and aim is off just a smidgen target will be missed.

A slight cant on the gun forces the shotstring to follow the target's flight path resulting in less missed targets.

Fig. 2-6 (B)

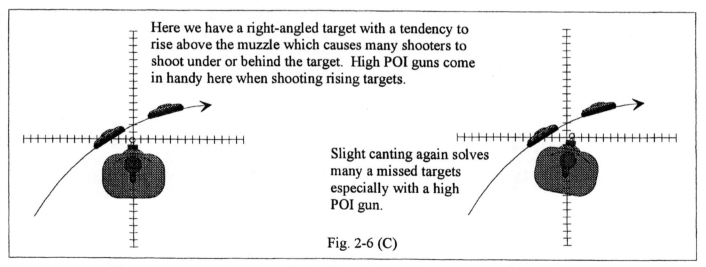

Here we have a right-angled target with a tendency to rise above the muzzle which causes many shooters to shoot under or behind the target. High POI guns come in handy here when shooting rising targets.

Slight canting again solves many a missed targets especially with a high POI gun.

Fig. 2-6 (C)

SHOOTING CIRCLES

Targets never travel in straight lines as demonstrated in Fig.3-1 (C) and 3-3. Understanding and believing you will never get a straight-away target will pump your scores upward immediately. The above drawing also demonstrates the curvature of the target's flight path. Now you know why targets are missed!

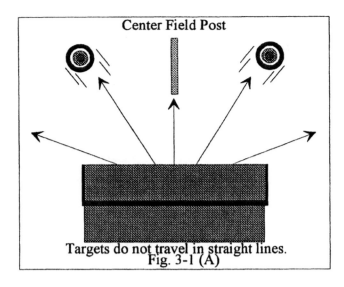

Center Field Post

Targets do not travel in straight lines.
Fig. 3-1 (A)

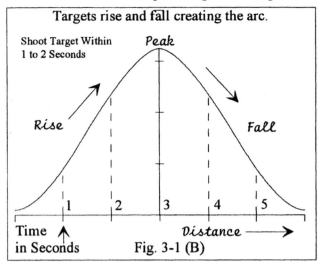

Targets rise and fall creating the arc.

Shoot Target Within 1 to 2 Seconds

Peak

Rise

Fall

1   2   3   4   5

Time in Seconds

Distance ——→

Fig. 3-1 (B)

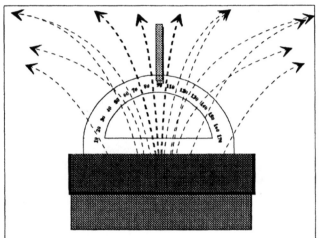

Superimpose a protractor as shown at the station you will shoot to determine the angles of target exit and arcing trajectory. Hold the protractor 1/2 of arms length or more. 90 is 0 degrees (no angle) the hard left is 35 degrees.

Fig. 3-1 (C)

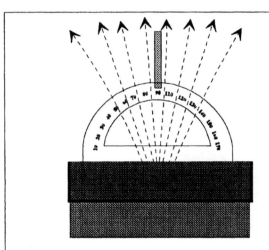

Targets do not travel in straight lines. When you hold a protractor to the traphouse you certainly will not see straight targets intersecting as shown here. Though most trapshooters assume the target is speeding away on a straight path, it is not.

Fig. 3-1 (D)

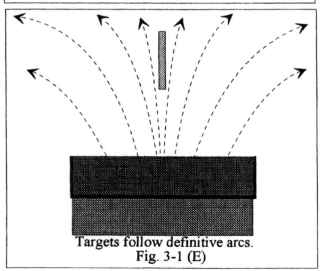

Targets follow definitive arcs.
Fig. 3-1 (E)

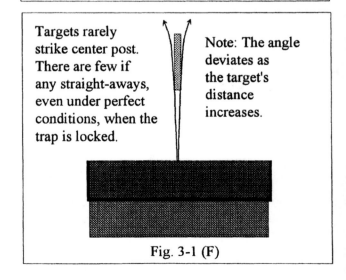

Targets rarely strike center post. There are few if any straight-aways, even under perfect conditions, when the trap is locked.

Note: The angle deviates as the target's distance increases.

Fig. 3-1 (F)

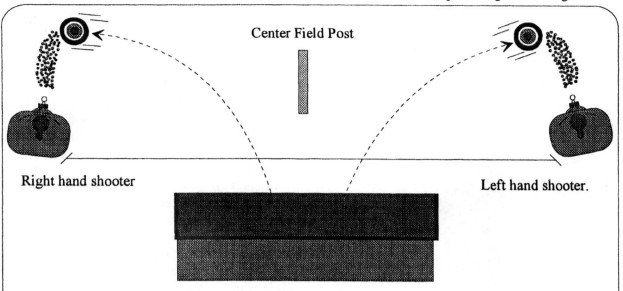

Center Field Post

Right hand shooter

Left hand shooter.

Here in the roll technique the bow and gun cant direction remains the same on both left and right targets, so a left-hand shooter will place a forward convex shot pattern to the right trending target. Right-hand shooter will cant gun to the right on all left targets. The bow technique relies heavily on using the cheek to pivot gun movement, not solely using the arm to point the gun to eliminate head-lifting and increase precision accuracy. Muzzle swing is vastly reduced. You'll need to try this to understand the concept. You'll see it does work, though it is difficult to learn.

Fig. 3-2

Gun canting is nothing new, fact is, you are canting the gun and probably don't even realize it. If you watch good shooters closely, the gun's muzzle cants slightly. Why? If your eye is truly on the target, the gun will follow the target's natural arc trajectory. Put a bit more cant on the gun and the sight picture tightens allowing shotstring to align properly to the target. You'll dead-center hit with accuracy - smoking targets with less chipping = higher scores!

SEEING TARGET ANGLES

A simple test verifying targets do not travel in straight lines, but indeed do traverse definitive arcs.

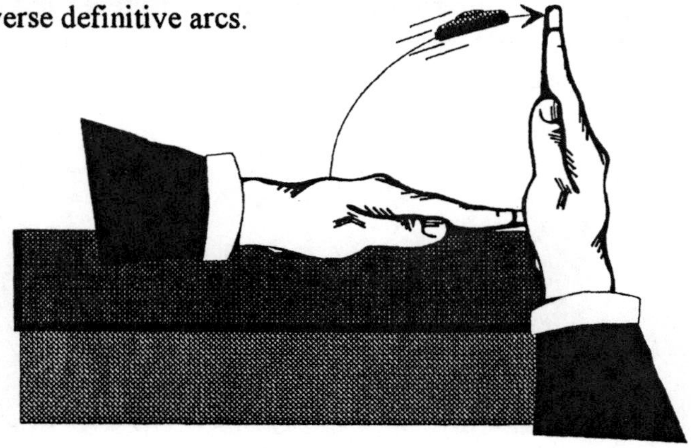

Fig. 3-3

RECOGNIZING TARGET ANGLES

There is really no mystery in deciphering target angles once you know they exist. Perform the test as shown in Fig. 3-3 and you'll recognize the angle and the arc trajectory. Also see; Fig. 3-1 (C).

Missed targets are caused by misjudging the angle and the target 'bending' away from the muzzle and shotstring. The key to high scores is to recognize these curved trajectories and shoot quickly before distance permits the arc to mature. Notice the arc is less severe closest to the traphouse, but the curved flight path still exists.

The next time you practice, watch for these bending targets. This anomaly is truly one of trapshooting's hidden secrets. Understanding target behavior makes it easier to hit more targets!

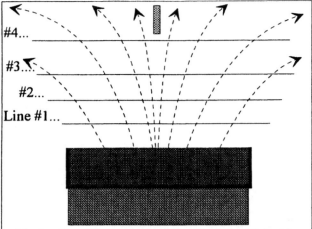

Notice line #1target angle is nil. Line #2 is 15 degrees and line #3 is 25 degrees or more. The target arc increases with distance to the trap. #4 denotes severe arcing angles beyond 40 yards. Learn to shoot targets quickly. Rapid target acquisition is the key resulting in tighter patterns and more broken targets. Shoot at lines #2 or #3 before target peaks and angle intensifies.

Fig. 3-4

SHOOTING THE CIRCLE

Fig. 3-4 reveals the basic target angles and semi-circular arc trajectories the target will follow. If you are tracking your gun on a straight line on a target traversing an oblique angle it is likely to shoot behind or over the top of the target. Take a good look the next time you miss a target and see if the target bent away from your shotstring. Odds are it did.

Remember the last time you missed the 'easy' straight-away? Take a second look at the target when it happens and you'll see the target did indeed bend away. When you miss targets it's because you did not recognize the target's true flight path.

You do not have to consciously force your gun to follow the target's arc. Once it has been implanted in your mind the target is bending, natural subconscious eye/hand coordination will compensate, as long as you <u>don't forget</u> targets do not travel in straight lines, and you shoot quickly as noted in Fig. 3-4. A smidgen of cant can always help remind you that targets do indeed bend away from straight shotstrings. Missing targets? Study the angles and arcs!

SHOT STRING EXPANSION

Shot expands as a expanding elongated cone-shaped cylinder. Density decreases to square of distance.

Notice pellet density decreases as expansion increases. Fragmentation produces gaps & holes in pattern. The use of a full choke helps, but will not cure shotstring ballistic form. An inherent defect, uncurable. Another good reason to learn to shoot quickly. It often requires more than one pellet to break a target.

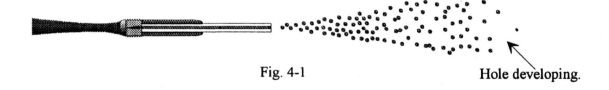

Fig. 4-1   Hole developing.

Too many shooters are quick to blame holes in the pattern for missed targets, when in reality it is the shooter who simply misjudged the angle, arc, or simply made a mistake. Two of the most common mistakes are 1) head lifting, and 2) taking your eye off the target or not following the target by stopping the eye. Once you stop your eye from following the target, the muzzles will stop! Keep your head down, feeling proper cheek pressure at all times and keep the eye on the target all of the time. These two tips will do wonders for your scores. Remember them!

The purpose of gun hold point and eye location is to prepare the gun to get on the same track as the target with ease, to hold the eye in a position to prevent blind spots, and, to prepare for seeing the most severe angle you will receive from the specific post you are standing on. Hold points vary from traphouse to traphouse.

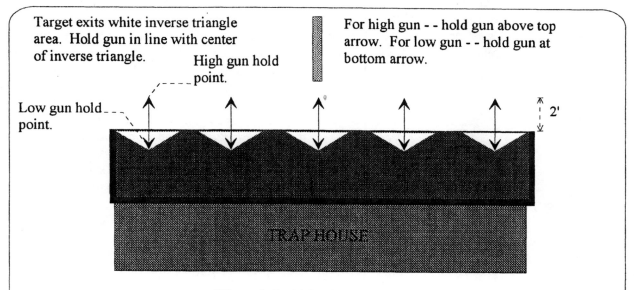

Target exits white inverse triangle area. Hold gun in line with center of inverse triangle.

High gun hold point.

Low gun hold point.

For high gun - - hold gun above top arrow. For low gun - - hold gun at bottom arrow.

TRAP HOUSE

2'

Fig. 4-2 (A) Gun Hold Points

By holding the gun in the white inverse triangle, you will pick up the target angle for proper tracking of the target. If trap is set-off to one side or another, simply readjust your gun hold to the left or right to compensate. This illustration has a centered trap set square to the house.

In Fig. 4-2 the eye hold can be higher than shown. Try holding eye straight out while standing erect, then work downward.

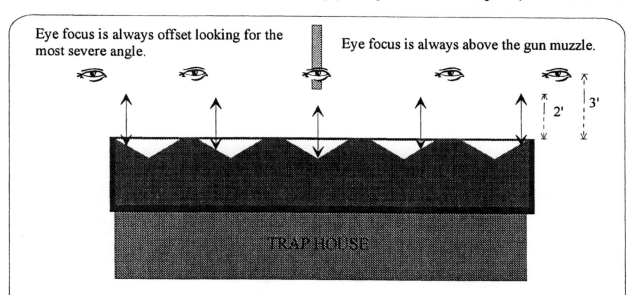

Eye focus is always offset looking for the most severe angle.

Eye focus is always above the gun muzzle.

TRAP HOUSE

2'   3'

Fig. 4-2 (B) Gun Hold Points

This illustration too has a centered trap set square to the house. The gun hold points are offset on stations #1 and #2 to the left. Stations #4 and #5 offset to the right. This is so the gun will not create a blind spot and prepare the gun's swing to the most severe angle from that specific station.

On Station #1 and #5 you can hold the gun's muzzle off the house if you wish, but make certain you can still catch the correct target angles on straighter targets emerging from the house - without zigzagging the muzzle.

HOLDING & POINTING THE GUN

This technique is for those experiencing flinching. The trigger finger is out of the trigger cage pointing directly at the target. The index finger, either below or on the side of the forearm, also extends directly to the target. This may prevent having to switch to a release trigger. Requires a steep learning curve, but it does stop the flinching.

Fig. 4-3

Riding a trigger with your index finger can actually cause a flinch for some shooters because they are feeling the trigger pull. When you feel the trigger pull to the point the hammer will fall, your mind 'anticipates' the blast and the flinch is born. The release trigger is not so well felt and has a 'surprise' factor built in so the mind can not anticipate the shockwave to come. In other words it happens so fast the mind has nottime to send nerve impulses to the body muscles to recoil into a flinch.

Keeping your finger off the trigger and 'slapping' the trigger (called slap shooting)produces anti-flinching just as a release trigger at much less cost and maintenance. Don't yank on the trigger, just smoothly pull it in one easy motion. Move your finger as you would using a release trigger, just in reverse.

TRIGGER TIPS

Place trigger on index finger first joint. There are less nerves in this area to help reduce any flinch sensitivity problems.

Place a bandage on finger to help reduce sensitivity, or, in severe cases, wear a glove.

Try 'yanking' the trigger gently instead of 'squeezing'. Don't be too gentle, it creates a flinch.

Maybe you are pulling the trigger too hard... this too will cause a flinch! Lighten-up your trigger pull. Have your trigger tuned, lubed and adjusted.

Pull the trigger, not the muzzle! The muzzles should never rise when pulling a trigger.

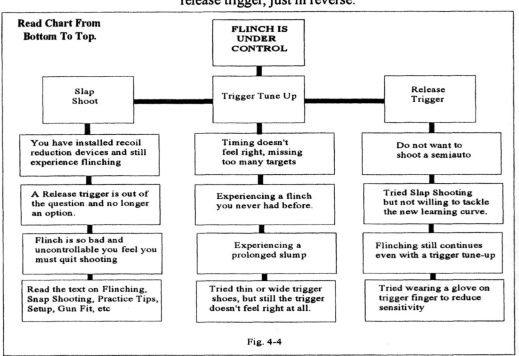

Fig. 4-4

YOU CAN BEAT A FLINCH INTO SUBMISSION

First, make sure the gun still fits you, as a gradual weight change can alter gun fit, causing the gun to rise slapping your face. Use a shooting vest, install the best recoil device money can buy (see text). Make sure you are looking for the target when you call, and don't react to the target... attack it! Use this quick reference chart (Fig. 4-4) to locate problem areas when flinching occurs.

Recoil often is not the deeper cause of flinching, it is only <u>one</u> reason shooters flinch, a symptom in search for a cure. The true cause of the most violent flinches is more often the shooter is shooting beyond the limits of his/her internal time clock - - breaking the targets in the wrong time and place (see, Flinching, Internal Time Clock Test). Other causes of flinching include squeezing-off the trigger, or relying on excessive trigger sensitivity, or too little sensitivity. Release triggers work because they reduce trigger finger sensitivity by suddenly, without warning, releasing the trigger. This prevents the brain from anticipating blast noise and recoil. Slap shooting is slapping the trigger instead of squeezing, and it will dissolve a flinch as well as a release trigger without modifications to your gun. The good news is flinching can be controlled and beaten at its own game. The text has an extensive flinch-resolving chapter, see, "Flinching."

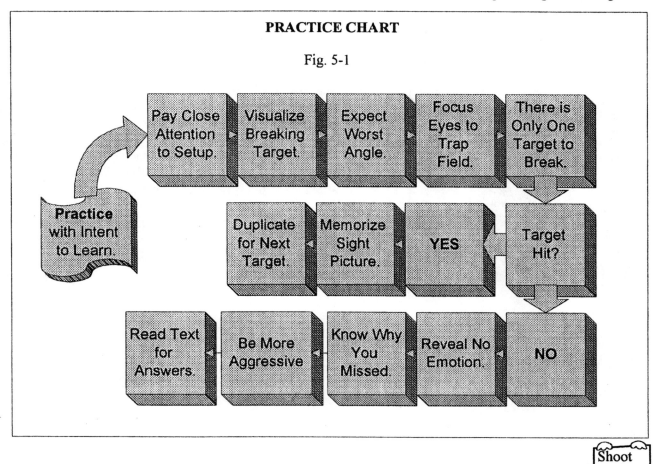

PRACTICE CHART

Fig. 5-1

THE RIGHT WAY TO PRACTICE

Read the text to understand each basic step as shown in Fig. 5-1. There's a right way and a wrong way to practice. The right way is to set an outline, a plan of action to improve your game. You have heard this time and again, but it is so true and so important, yet few shooters do so and wonder why their game goes sour.

We all try to learn everything all too fast. It's the sign of our impatient society: fast food, fast cars, fast reading, and fast learning. Trapshooting is not a mindless sport, it is a complicated game like golf, man verses machine. The learning process generates best results when each phase of the game is broken down into easy to learn steps, then later combining each phase into one form or style. Patience is the 'key' to success in trapshooting as it is in life. Persistence + Patience = Accomplishment.

Make it your resolution to jot down a list of ideas, or bring this book with you to your next practice session and select just two or three practice tips to work on for the day. Trying too many things will only lead to confusion. So much of trapshooting is mental and few minds can concentrate on several things at one time. Small steps lead to giant strides. Think of some kink to iron out or fault to correct. This is setting a plan of action, for without the plan there can be no progress. Do this and you will see much improvement in your game!

What is the most frequently asked question at registered shoots? It's, *"Well, how did you do?"* And the answer is usually, *"Not so good."* You can change that answer to *"Better than I thought I could!"* That is, if you bring a list with you to practice sessions. It's really that simple!

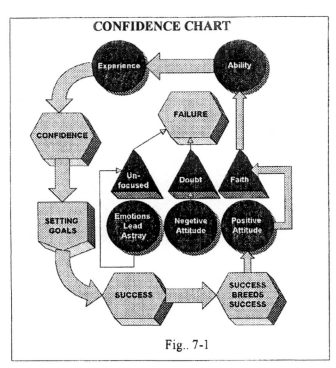

CONFIDENCE CHART

Fig.. 7-1

Confidence is often misinterpreted as positive thinking. You can think positive all you want and still end up with a disastrous score. Confidence is a blend of polished skills learned which leads to competence. In Fig. 7-1 the chart reveals the basic confidence cycle. Notice how it focuses on the mind, not equipment. Note also how the mind creates failure. It all begins with setting goals!

When you read the text in this book you will have a deeper understanding of this chart. Use this chart for a quick reference to put you back on the right track.

Remember, the key to high scores is patience! Learn and do all things with patience and not only will your trapshooting scores increase, you'll learn what the word TRAP truly is: <u>T</u>o <u>R</u>eally <u>A</u>ppreciate <u>P</u>eople. Attitude is everything!

ARE YOU MISSING TARGETS ?

Use this chart as a fast reference to decipher why you are missing. Read the text for full explanations on each problem. This chart comes in real handy at registered shoots.

As you can see, there are many reasons why targets are missed and things can get complicated quickly, resulting in confusion if you have no way to identify the problem. The professionals miss targets too, but when they do, they have the uncanny ability to 'recognize' the problem and 'correct' it immediately. This chart puts it all down visually so you can imprint it into your mind. The more you use the chart, the more you will develop the ability to quickly isolate problems and resolve them.

<u>Warning:</u> Do not flood your mind with conscious thoughts when shooting. This chart is for reference, not to be used when shooting for score. Shooting is a subconscious experience, not a thinking sport. If you miss a target, and you use this chart at <u>practice sessions,</u> the answer to the problem will come easily. Be patient. It takes time to learn.

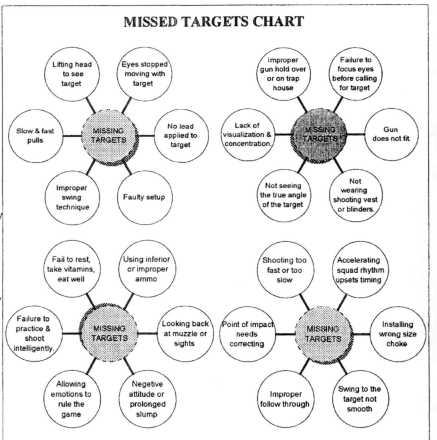

MISSED TARGETS CHART

Many complex factors are involved when trying to decipher the reason for missed targets. Use this quick reference chart to help identify the areas you feel are the root cause of missing the targets. Read the text for in-depth details to solve the problem. Take this chart with you when you practice. When you miss a target, review this chart to locate where the problem lies Once you narrow your search, you can resolve the difficulty

Fig. 7-2

SLUMP CHART & EQUIPMENT CHECKLIST

Fig. 7-3

This checklist can come in handy. Blank spaces are for your specific items to list.

✔ SLUMP	✔ SLUMP CON'T.	✔ EQUIPMENT CHECK
Gun Fits?	Comfortable Stance?	This Book in Vehicle
Sight Rib OK?	Shoes OK?	Have Gun?
Point of Impact OK?	Vest Pad OK?	Shell Bag and Shells
Choke Size OK?	Gun Grip OK?	Spare Parts & Tools
Switched Ammo?	Eye Hold Point OK?	Inspect Gun.
Dram / Velocity OK?	Shooting Too Fast?	Vitamins/Asperin
Use Proper Barrel?	Shooting Too Slow?	Shooting Glasses
Trigger OK?	Eyes Not Focused?	Blinders
Gun Hold Point OK?	Eye Exam Needed?	Wad Extractor
Length of Pull OK?	Proper Tint Lens?	Chokes & Wrench
Thinking Positive?	Thinking too Much?	Shooting Vest
Trying Too Hard?	Excessive Stress?	Shooting Glove
Eye On Target?	Take Vitamins?	Good Shoes
Head Lifting?	Too Excited?	ATA / PITA Card
Eye Drift to Sights?	Sleep Well?	Wallet/Checks/Cash
Foot Stance OK?	Lead on Targets?	Rain Gear
Smooth Setup?	Gun Moves on Call?	Lube & Gun Cleaner
Cheek Pressure OK?	Anticipating?	List Other Items Here
Comb Cast Shifted?	Snap Shooting?	
Comb Height OK?	Arm Pushing Gun?	
Call Too Soft?	Eye Crossover?	
Smooth Swing?	Silent Headache?	
Timing OK?	Visualization OK?	

MASTER EYE TEST #1.

Fig. 8-1

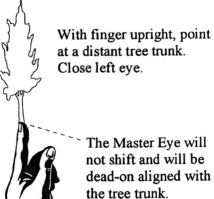

With finger upright, point at a distant tree trunk. Close left eye.

If finger shifts to the left, your left eye is the Master Eye.

The Master Eye will not shift and will be dead-on aligned with the tree trunk.

If finger shifts to the right your right eye is the Master Eye.

This basic test can be confusing due to excessive variables. Go to Test # 2 and #3 to verify results.

MASTER EYE TEST #2.

Select an object 4 feet distant. Cup hands as shown. Close left eye and see if a shift occurs. Open left eye then close right eye. Whichever eye does not shift is the Master Eye. The Master Eye determines which shoulder to place the gun. Perform all of these tests over at least a week or two before switching shoulders. The eyes will play tricks on you the more you perform these tests. Over a period of several tries the Master Eye will be discovered. Your hands should always be fully extended at arms length when performing these tests.

MASTER EYE TEST #3.

Try the open hand method using the trapfield's center post.

Cut a hole in a card to see which eye shifts.

These two tests are very precise and should be performed last to verify without doubt which eye is the Master Eye.

ADVERSE WEATHER CHART

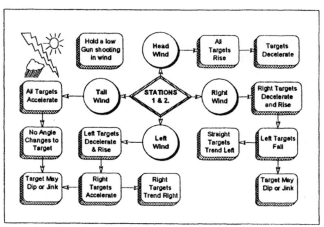

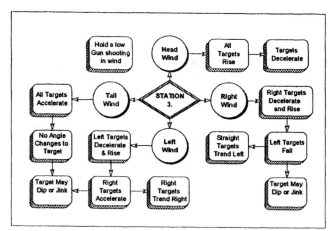

Wind Direction Determined as Standing on Station Facing Traphouse.

Remember to keep your head down snugly on the gun's comb when shooting in the wind as the eye has a tendency to search for the target and lift the head with it.

Generally, a lower gun hold should be used, especially on all targets that do not rise in the wind.

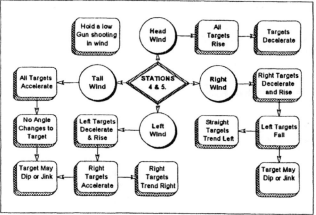

Fig. 9-1

You can hold a higher gun on targets that rise with the wind, but be aware target may dip under the barrel at any time.

You may lose targets to the wind. Don't try to out-guess the wind, just be aware how wind influences targets. Maintain a firm footing and stance and shoot quickly. The wind bothers everyone so you are not alone.

"THE WIND GROWLED AS WE RAN FOR COVER..."

Shooting in the wind generates much hot air when advisory recommendations are sought. Some adamantly advice not to change anything, while others recommend staying one step ahead of the wind. Take your pick! For those who wish to take advantage of every edge available, the above chart, Fig. 9-1, can put it all together for you. We still can't tame or outsmart Mother Nature, but we can at least understand what we see and that alone can give us the upper hand.

Many top shooters will not register targets in adverse weather conditions, and for good reason too! Call them 'fair weather shooters' if you will, but know there is reason behind the madness. Why put yourself in a situation where the odds are against high scores only to toss away option money and ruin averages? For the new shooter, it is highly advisable not to shoot in foul weather, period! Novices need all the encouragement and small victories they can get their hands on to sustain self-confidence. This self-inflicted exile should not be too prolonged as sooner or later you will need to learn how to shoot in the rain, wind, heat, and cold. Later, as experience builds, shooting in diverse weather conditions can be a barrel of fun (a.k.a. mind-searing challenge).

Do not try to anticipate what wind, eddy currents, vortexes and other atmospheric disturbances will do, just be aware of the conditions and shoot instictively. You can avoid problems through awareness. See text for details on shooting wind-blown targets, the effects of elevation, and humidity.

DOUGHNUT HOLES IN THE PATTERN

Target must pass through annular ring of pellets, even if holes exists. The target can slip through a multi-hole shotcloud, but occurs more rarely than shooters wish to believe. Regardless of pattern shape, an annular ring will always persist regardless how many holes exist, and despite all corrective efforts there is nothing you can do to stop holes from forming and / or targets occasionally slipping by. Large exaggerated holes are illustrated. Will the target still break?

Exaggerated 24" center hole and three 8" holes in annular ring.
The Target Will Still Break!

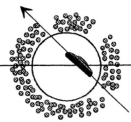

Arrow denotes target trajectory through pattern.

Fig. 10-1

SHOTSTRING SEVEN TO FIFTEEN FEET IN LENGTH

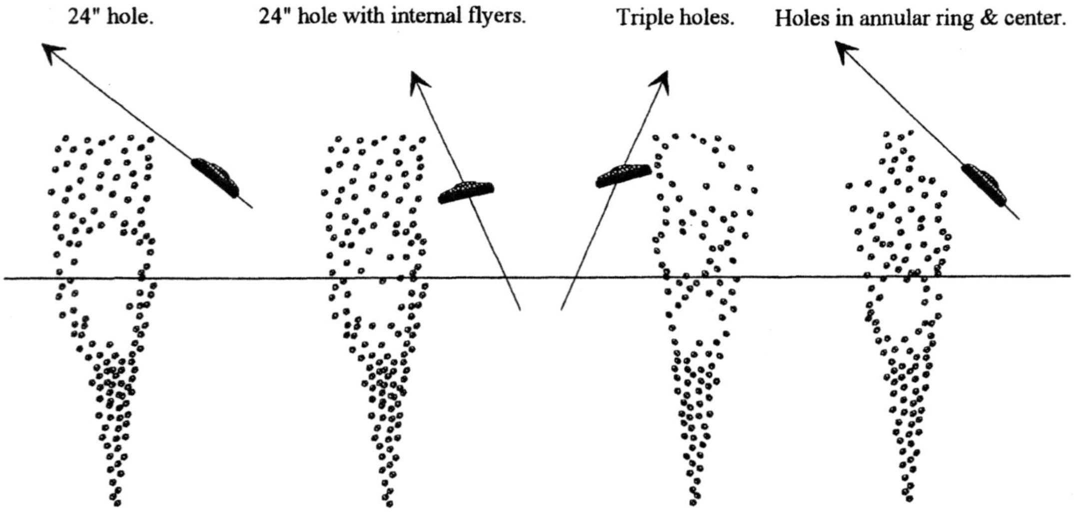

24" hole.   24" hole with internal flyers.   Triple holes.   Holes in annular ring & center.

Although huge holes exist in each of the above shotclouds, the sheer quantity of pellets overwhelms the target. Note that lead is placed on each target. Without lead it is certainly a reality the target will slip by, then, holes within the shot pattern will take full advantage of the shooter's aiming error.

Fig. 10-2

Forget about patterns and focus more on point of impact, visualization, eye / gun hold points, zone shooting and you will break more targets. It's okay to pattern check when trying a new shell, a reload or a new gun to determine optimal compatibility, just don't be caught up in thinking patterns are key to trapshooting success becausethey arenot. Way too much emphasis by shooters is given to patterns, which only misleads and diverts valuable time and energy from the real business of marksmanship. Patterns don't break targets, people do! Adjust your priorities.

SIGHT BEAD ALIGNMENT

If the gun fits, the sight beads will stack into a figure-8 and the gun should shoot exactly where you look. Point of Impact will shift whenever any adjustments are made to the gun's comb, sight rib, butt plate, etc. Match the figure-8 pattern to the Point of Impact desired, along with gun fit and you'll have a top notch accurate, competitive gun. All three criteria must be in equilibrium. #1 is correct alignment, but POI still must be adjusted, it could still be too high or too low. A stock fitter/gunsmith can perform these tricky adjustments using shims, barrel and stock bending, bead spacing, rib adjustments, etc.

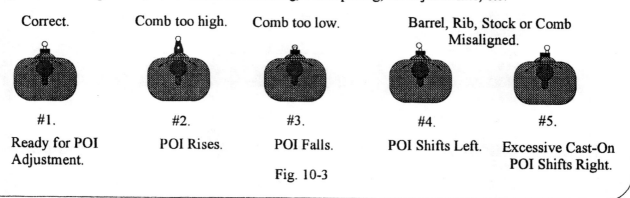

Correct.	Comb too high.	Comb too low.	Barrel, Rib, Stock or Comb Misaligned.	
#1.	#2.	#3.	#4.	#5.
Ready for POI Adjustment.	POI Rises.	POI Falls.	POI Shifts Left.	Excessive Cast-On POI Shifts Right.

Fig. 10-3

DO NOT IGNORE POINT OF IMPACT / SIGHT BEADS / LENGTH OF PULL

Sight beads are used for three primary purposes, 1) to verify proper gun mount and eye alignment, 2) For checking point of impact, 3) as a reference point for when to pull the trigger. Number 3 often creates confusion as the shotgunner points the gun at the target, not consciously aiming it (see text for explanation). Another confusing subject is Point of Impact (POI) and many shooters truly do not understand what it really is, and how it can work for or against the shooter (again, see text for explanations). Fig. 10-3 reveals proper sight bead alignment. If you are shooting a gun and the sight beads do not line-up, you are putting yourself at a major disadvantage, especially if POI has been altered. Shooting incorrectly can never be achieved correctly! Another disturbance that is quite insidious by nature, due to its inherent invisibility, is the gun's length of pull (LOP). The sight beads look perfect but the gun is out of balance, doesn't swing smoothly, and the trigger finger, well, it just doesn't feel right. It causes many lost targets and the cure is easy. Once LOP is set, be aware of the clothing you wear for it will surely deviate LOP. It is a prime reason why shooters wear shooting vests, to maintain LOP, ease of swing, recoil reduction, etc. If you don't wear a vest, you should. If you don't want to wear a vest, then be careful to verify LOP has not changed.

Once the gun is fitted properly and the POI set correctly 50% of the job of hitting targets is already done for you. The next 20% is selecting the proper ammo or components to maintain consistent velocity, and 20% is choosing the right choke and shot for realistically tight patterns. The remaining 10% is all mind over matter in the business of shooting the targets. This is not a discrepancy of the 'Golden Rule of Thumb,' but a breakdown of the importance of a properly outfitted gun. Once the gun fits, shoots where you are looking and reliably breaks targets, the Golden Rule applies; 10% of the game is equipment, 90% is between your ears!

Fig. 10-3 is an illustration of incorrect stacking of the sight beads. Example: #2 indicates the comb is set too high and the POI is high. This is not the correct way to raise POI because the sight beads are not stacked. It is workable, though as long as you can remember to stack the beads as shown in #2 consistently. Some shooters can adapt to just about anything and break many rules and still crack high scores. Nothing is impossible for those who make things happen. Most of us need too and should, stay with the rules which have proven themselves over time. As solid as giant footprints in cement, the rules are often unyielding.

The shooter who is not concerned with the above is usually an inconsistent shooter. Precision requires precision! If you want high scores, be diligent. Take the next step into fine-tuning your gun along with your technique.

SHOOT LOCATION DIARY

Fig. 11-1

SHOOT LOCATION DIARY. NAME OF CLUB____________________.

☐	Sun Location	☐	North,South East,West	☐	Shoot Late/ Early Squad
☐	Unique Weather	☐		☐	
☐	Background Scenes	☐		☐	
☐	Traphouse #___ Notes	☐		☐	
☐	Target Angles	☐		☐	
☐	Visibility of Targets	☐		☐	
☐	Trap Position in House	☐		☐	
☐	Unusual Disturbances	☐		☐	
☐	Full Face on Target?	☐		☐	
☐	Razor Blade Target	☐		☐	
☐	Target Color & Type	☐		☐	
☐	Target Speed & Height	☐		☐	
☐	Gun Hold Points	☐		☐	
☐	Field Targets Condition	☐		☐	
☐	Target Hardness	☐		☐	
☐	Shot Size to Use	☐		☐	
☐	Stations Square/Offset?	☐		☐	
☐	Best Traps to Shoot	☐		☐	
☐	Eddy Currents/Wind?	☐		☐	
☐	Names of Best Pullers	☐		☐	
☐	Squad with Who?	☐		☐	
☐			Notes:		
☐					

Blank Spacing For Your Use: Fill in criteria specific to the shoot location for memory recall. Avoid repeating mistakes made in the past. This diary may give you the edge to win tournaments!

Account Name _____

SHOOT SCORES & AVERAGE

- ☐ ATA   Acct # _____
- ☐ PITA   Acct # _____
- ☐ PRACTICE   **SCORE SHEET**

DATE	CLUB	16 YD	16 YD AVG.	HANDICAP	AVG.	DOUBLES	AVG.	PERSONAL NOTES
	TOTALS							

Note: Averages for handicap scores are not necessary, but handy for your own reference to chart progress.
This Average Sheet supplied by *"Trap Shooting Secrets"* book, availiable from any bookstore by special order.
The only book with a 100% satisfaction guarantee... Your scores rise or your money refunded!

POINT OF IMPACT ADJUSTMENT

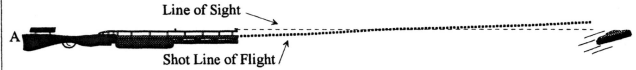

Line of Sight

A

Shot Line of Flight

Drawing 'A' is correct. Line of sight is on forward edge of target and shotstring rising to intercept target. This target will be pulverized into a cloud of smoke when hit.

B

Drawing 'B' is incorrect as POI is set too low shooting flat. Target will escape or break in large pieces Raise POI until target breaks are solidly pulverized. Remember not to alter your timing when making POI adjustments and to readjust comb height each time.

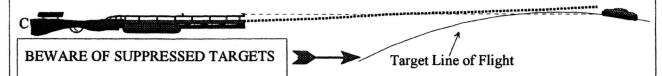

C

BEWARE OF SUPPRESSED TARGETS ▶▶▶⟶   Target Line of Flight

Drawing 'C' reveals a target that never rises due to tail wind or trap setting. High POI guns are more susceptible to miss than a lower POI gun. You'll need to shoot quicker than usual or aim under the target to break these cliff divers. Be attentive of target behavior on each station and each trap.

Fig. 11-3

SETTING THE POINT OF IMPACT AND SIGHT PICTURE
(Adjustable Rib Gun)

1. Make certain the gun fits you and when you shoulder the gun you see the stacked figure-8 sight bead. Adjust comb height, not the sight rib (POI) as you must adjust the gun to fit you, not make yourself conform to the gun.
2. Fire at pattern board to determine where the gun is shooting. See Fig. 1-2.
3. Figure out where you want to break the target as this determines your 'timing' to set POI, too.
4. Install extra-full or full choke. Stand on station #3, insure the target 'smokes' into dust when hit.
5. Adjust POI in 1/2" increments. Don't deviate from your timing or confusion will set in.
6. Move to posts #1 and #5. Mentally log the sight picture. If your timing is right on all posts, you should be able to place the sight bead directly on the target to burn the target.
7. If you find you must keep the target floating too high over the sight bead, POI is set too high or you are shooting too slow. If target must be covered up by the sight bead or muzzle, POI is set too low or you are shooting too fast.
8. You must reset comb height to see the figure-8 sight bead alignment after each adjustment; otherwise, POI will become confusing and inaccurate.
9. Once POI is set and you later miss targets, remember that you must maintain your timing. If the target leaves the zone, a different sight picture will emerge. Learn how to break targets that escape the zone, don't adjust POI.
10. Now that POI is set, lock the rib down tight, log the setting in diary and throw away the key. Inspect gun before shooting to insure settings have not changed.

The above steps are for handicap yardage shooting. You will have to test POI for shooting singles. Often, no POI adjustment is needed, just shoot a bit slower so target gains a reasonable distance. For those who have no adjustable rib/POI gun you still must visit a stockfitter to insure gun fit and POI is proper; otherwise, you may never be able to hit high scores consistently. Improper fit/POI is the reason for many shooters' inconsistency. In most cases, shooters are shooting a gun that does not fit and fails to achieve a proper POI, which ruins a shooter's timing. Shooting way too slow! Speed is king. All guns need adjustments. You can't shoot right if you're shooting wrong!

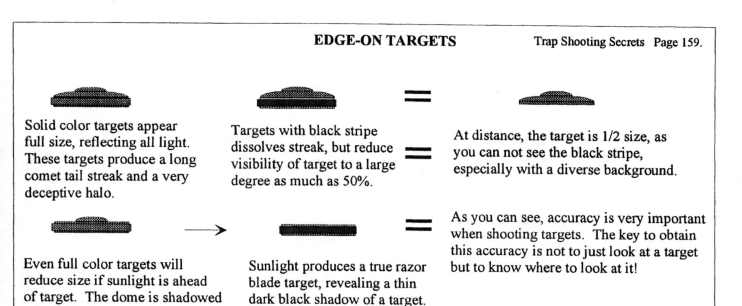

EDGE-ON TARGETS

Solid color targets appear full size, reflecting all light. These targets produce a long comet tail streak and a very deceptive halo.

Targets with black stripe dissolves streak, but reduce visibility of target to a large degree as much as 50%.

At distance, the target is 1/2 size, as you can not see the black stripe, especially with a diverse background.

Even full color targets will reduce size if sunlight is ahead of target. The dome is shadowed out of sight.

Sunlight produces a true razor blade target, revealing a thin dark black shadow of a target.

As you can see, accuracy is very important when shooting targets. The key to obtain this accuracy is not to just look at a target but to know where to look at it!

Fig. 11-4

LOOKING AT TARGETS

Many shooters see a target in their sight picture, but are truly not 'looking' at the target, which often produces many lost birds and low scores. They need to tighten-up the sight picture and increase accuracy by knowing where to look at the target. There are 4 zones on a target in which to focus on. What zone do you use? If you don't know where to focus your eyes on a target, how do you expect to hit them? By sheer luck?

THE 4 BASIC ZONES

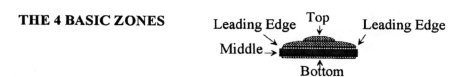

Each zone on the target is used for specific angles. By looking at these zones you will discover three jewels of knowledge, **1)** deciphering the true angle of the target in the sight picture, **2)** determining target speed and abrupt angle deviations due to air currents, etc., **3)** a tremendous increase in accuracy and higher scores. Knowing where to look is really simple. Start focusing your eye on each zone as you 'smoke' the targets. You will see these zones when you hit the target dead-on. You will not see them if you are just 'seeing' the target, you have to 'look' hard with intense visual focus. Everyone's gun is different, POI and timing varies from shooter to shooter, but you will now discover the optimum 'zone' to look at to dispatch specific targets with your gun. Use a full or extra-full choke to pinpoint these focal-point zones.

SUGGESTED FOCAL-POINT ZONES

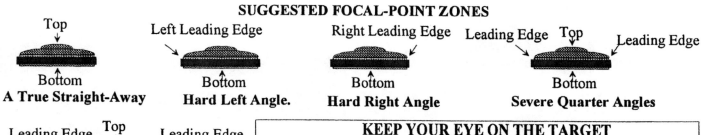

| **A True Straight-Away** | **Hard Left Angle.** | **Hard Right Angle** | **Severe Quarter Angles** |

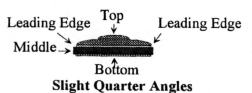

Slight Quarter Angles
May need to aim between the Top and Leading Edge on arcing Straight-aways.

KEEP YOUR EYE ON THE TARGET

It is hard to take your eyes off the target when you are 'looking' hard at a target's zone. Try focusing on target zones and see your scores rise. Those targets won't slip by so easily anymore! Why? Your eyes are becoming finely tuned on intense, centralized visual focus.

Fig. 11 - 5

If you wish to see high scores or dissolve a slump, pay special attention to the positioning of your feet. Often, what feels comfortable to you is likely an improper technique, or you have deviated from a proper foot/stance over time and it has finally surfaced, giving you a 'problem' on hitting specific targets on specific stations. Sound familiar?

It is good to experiment to find exactly what works and what doesn't, but many shooters, in the course of shooting, forget to return to the basic fundamentals and pound away, endlessly practicing the same mistakes over-and-over again. They change guns, shells, gun and eye holds, timing, etc., with little improvement. Or they improve with a lucky streak, then once again fall down into 'Slump Hell' and the process starts over again.

Shooters know how to shoot, you know how to shoot and you've shot well in the past. So when the targets are falling out of the sky intact, go back to the basics. The most critical basic tip is Foot Positioning and Stance. They are not the same. Foot Positioning is where you place your feet in relation to the traphouse. Stance is correct posture. If both are right, targets will have little chance of escaping. No matter how long you have been shooting, never, ever, underestimate Position and Stance, a reevaluation of your positioning now can deliver tremendous rewards for you.

Tip #1. Return to the traditional trap shooting stance, both feet pointed at 90 degree right-angle to traphouse. I bet your feet are now no longer in this tried and true position. Somewhere along the line you altered this position, which is causing severe consistency problems in your shooting. Go back to the basics! See top view of drawing.

Tip #2. The 'side-on' position will feel terribly uncomfortable and you will wonder, *"This doesn't feel right at all. I'll never hit targets standing so ridgid."* Try it, you'll be surprised! This foot position will straighten your stance, prevent slouching, head lifting, shoulder dipping, chin tucking, and produce smooth accurate swings to the target -- so smooth, you'll wonder why you deviated in the first place! If scores are important to you, tighten-up your stance. Be aware this stance may, or may not, run out of swing movement when shooting singles or double trap.

Tip #3. The traditional 'three past five' stance (lower drawing) 45 degree angle is not recommended to resolve problems as flexibility is too high. You need a ridgid stance to iron out kinks in shooting, reestablish precise swing mechanics, maintain vertical posture, eliminate head lifting, etc. Later, you can fine-tune to a more flexible stance, but be very careful when doing so, gun control is often lost gradually over time, producing severe slumps and inconsistent shooting. Fig. 11-6 reveals left-and right-handed shooters. **Note:** Left-hand shooter foot position is a full 90 degrees to the traphouse extreme. **You can try this to help you get on the target faster with less swing angle to contend with.** This is illustrative only, left and right-handed shooters can use either foot position technique. Simply stand facing the opposite direction as shown. The right-handed foot position reveals how most shooters pose, right in the middle of the station. Okay, as long as the trap is set square to the house. If trap is offset left, hold gun point left to compensate. You can't step off the center line to the left, as rule book may not allow for this. Foot position is the foundation of precision shooting. If it's wrong; expect inconsistent shooting and many heartache score. Once you've ironed out the kinks in the swing, then can you revert to your routine stance.

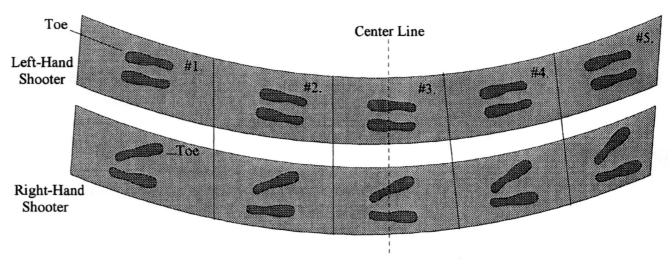

Fig. 11-6

BASIC GUN & EYE HOLDS

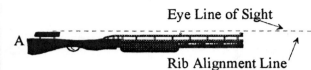

Eye Line of Sight

A

Rib Alignment Line

Traphouse

Drawing 'A' is the typical high-gun hold and surprisingly, it's often a huge mistake for most shooters to use. As you can see, the eye and gun is so high you can't see the target exit the house under the barrel. Few shooters have the quick reflexes necessary to shoot a high gun. The pros do, but many below that skill level do not shoot enough targets per year to maintain such proficiency as is required.

B

Drawing 'B' is much more recommended for the high gun hold shooter. You simply drop the gun and eye hold two to four inches or so and you'll get on the target faster. And you will ride the track of the target instead of shifting the gun left or right horizontally, which requires excessive precision to hit the targets, as the shot string can never truly line up to apply the proper angle of intersection and lead.

Fig. 11-7

 WHY YOU NEED TO DROP GUN HOLD

. In Fig. A above you are shooting "intersections" of the muzzle and target crossing each other at extreme right-angles so you have to be "dead-on" to hit the target with little room for error. How is that? If the gun is moving left and the target is moving up (as all targets do rise except the extreme lefts and rights fall as they appear to be rising) you only have a small window of opportunity to hit the target. The sight picture just doesn't last long enough to fire an accurate shot. The shotstring isn't following the target! It's only crossing past it. Also, there is no true swing in the gun anymore and that leads to "pushing" the muzzle with the forearm. Neat tip, huh?

. By lowering the gun hold as in Fig. B, you'll now have to raise the gun once the target emerges, but you will see the target sooner and you'll be able to "ride the track" to the target. You have to ride onto the target's flight path so you can swing through the target. Now the shotstring is being aligned on the same flight path as the target, and you no longer have to be "dead-on" the target to break it. Neat trick!

. If you watch the pros shoot, you will see they do in fact drop the gun a smidgen, maybe some only drop the gun 1/2" or less, but it's enough for them to aquire and ride that target's flight path.

. The mistake most shooters fall into is seeing the pros hold the gun straight out at eye level and thinking this is the proper way, since the pros "appear" to do it. Now you know they don't. Watch them and you will see they do, in fact, ride that target and the gun does not just move left to right on a flat plane... there is a small "swing" even at the 27 yard line. Look closely, you'll see it and learn.

. Now some will argue that now you will have more room for error, having to add vertical rise to the gun swing and this will create more chances of error in swing / pointing, but all this is canceled as the benefits truly outweigh any extra measure of swing. Remember, there is more room for error with a higher gun hold than there is a slightly lower gun hold -- hands down! Fact:The low-gun shooter raises the odds of more targets hit. Just try this technique. Generally, you'll see your scores rise the lower you hold your gun. **Tip**: If the gun is held too high, there is no more swing to the target and you'll end up pushing the muzzle left or right with your forearm and that is a huge mistake way too many shooters make. Drop your gun hold and ride up on the target and you'll soon believe.

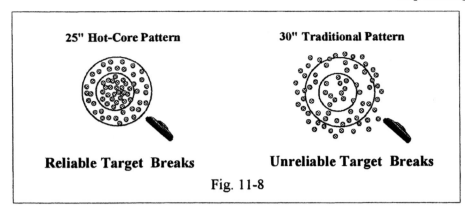

25" Hot-Core Pattern   **30" Traditional Pattern**

Reliable Target Breaks   **Unreliable Target Breaks**

Fig. 11-8

You can see the advantage of the 25" hot-core pattern as the target breaks will not be fragmented but dusted into smoke. The 30" pattern is too wide and too loose for "reliable" target breaks and targets will be left unbroken even though you were dead-on the target, as the pellets are too dispersed and not of enough of them are available to break the target 100% of the time. Of course, these are two-dimensional views, but the hot-core pattern will perform very reliably in the "real world" three & fourth dimension conditions; height, width, length & time.

With a hot-core pattern you will need to be more accurate in your shooting aim, but that is what you want. If you are shooting with a wide pattern and sloppiness is present in your point/aim, then you are shooting on luck and too many targets will slip by. You can try a 28" pattern if you prefer, but steer clear of the 30.

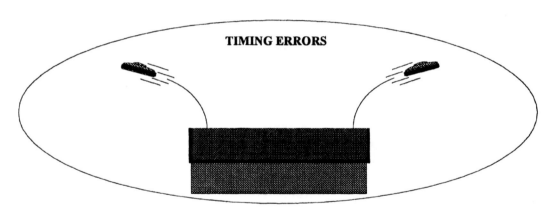

TIMING ERRORS

Fig. 11-9.

Here you can see a "zone" where you tend to break the targets. You should shoot in a zone, but you must be careful not to fall into a "timing trap." You know what this is -- it's when you pull the trigger because you feel that's the time to do so. You'll miss too many targets if you shoot on timing alone. Timing sets the zone (target distance from traphouse where you plan to shoot targets) but you must learn that timing does not tell you when to pull the trigger -- only the sight picture tells you when to pull that trigger.

It may seem confusing, but just think of timing as part and parcel of the swing to get the muzzle to the target, then pull the trigger when the sight picture is dead-on. Keep these two elements separate from each other for now. Later, you'll be able to blend the forms when you become a better shooter. Certainly, eye and gun hold points absolutely affect and adjust the zone and timing. Experiment with various eye and gun holds on each post to find what works best for you. Be smooth in your swing and only pull the trigger when the sight picture is dead-on --forget about timing as it comes naturally to you as you work on it.

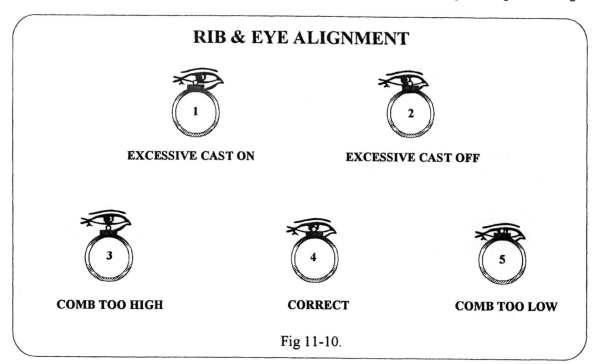

RIB & EYE ALIGNMENT

EXCESSIVE CAST ON

EXCESSIVE CAST OFF

COMB TOO HIGH

CORRECT

COMB TOO LOW

Fig 11-10.

Gun fit is critical, so it has to be right, and once fit is established you must insure you are mounting the gun properly so the eye lines up concentric to the sight bead... each and every time. This alignment must remain rock steady during the swing to the target.

This is why you should learn how to steer the gun with your cheek, not with arm or body motion alone. Body English is important, for if it does not exist you will tend to push the muzzle away from your eye as in #1 and #2, even if your gun mount and fit is perfect as in #4.

#1 Reveals a right-hand shooter with excessive cast on... meaning the gun's comb is set towards the shooter's cheek, pushing the bead to the right from the shooter's point of view (left muzzle view).
#2 Reveals too much cast off... the comb allows the cheek to move past the rib/bead.
#3 The comb is set too high allowing the eye to float above the sight bead.
#4 Is correct and right on the money.
#5 The comb is set too low, allowing the eye to sink deeply into the rib obscuring vision.

You can check this by looking in the mirror, but it's unreliable, as you will make fidgeting adjustments to make it look right. Then when you go out to shoot you will return to the same old habit and not be able to recognize you are in fact messing up again. This is why you must visit a stockfitter to have the gun checked. You need that person on the outside looking in. Once the gun is fit, eye/rib alignment is easily verified by stacking the sight beads to a figure-8 configuration.

You can see where "feel" comes into play here. You must feel the gun mount process and embed that feeling in your mind so you are not always diverting your eyes to the sight beads. That feeling will always place the gun on your shoulder in the proper place, like clockwork.

Cheek pressure is critical and it must be felt. You can see what can happen if cheek pressure is not used to steer the gun to maintain consistent pressure. See #3 and #5.

HIT HARD WITH THE EYES

DUAL EYE HOLD

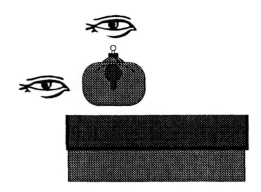

SINGLE EYE HOLD

**TWO-EYE RIGHT HANDSHOOTER
HIGH GUN HOLD**

**ONE-EYE LEFT-HANDED SHOOTER
LOW GUN HOLD**

Fig. 11-11

Keep in mind the above examples are not static. There are variations on the theme you can use, such as changing the gun and eye hold positions. In the high gun drawing, the master eye along the gun's rib can be lifted upward, not by lifting your head off the comb but by simply looking up. The opposite eye is looking for the most severe angle of the target in peripheral vision.

The one eye shooter's eye is also looking for the extreme angle by shifting the eye to the left. The gun hold can be as shown, off the house to the left a smidgen or held a bit higher so the sight bead floats a tad above the far end of the traphouse. Move the gun if the eye must shift too far off from the rib. You don't want your eye to be too distant, left or right, from the center line of the rib.

Before calling for the target, always have your mind made up you are going to hit the target. You need this positive affirmation to trigger the unconscious mind into correct action. You shouldn't think when shooting, but positive trigger words are always acceptable and welcome.

One of the secrets in good trapshooting is, one shooter gets more hits because s/he uses the eyes and mind for power while the other person tries to get hits by using brute force. If there is to be any aggression, it must be mental, not physical, and controlled.

The above drawings reveal a segment of the setup. You can see that by setting up your gun and eye holds you are definitely taking full advantage of the scientific realities of the game. A shooter who does not use these secrets has little chance of beating a shooter who has mastered gun and eye holds. That's why pros shoot so fast and it appears so easy --they got it all figured out. You can too!

Once the gun is mounted and the eye and gun hold set, develop the ability to "feel the shot." That's one of the secrets of trapshooting for when you feel all your moves, targets get annihilated with less effort. Sure it's still hard work, but not as hard as it would be without feeling.   Trapshooting is conditioned and controlled by feel, not by thoughts or brute physical or mental force.

SIGHT PICTURES ON EACH POST

Fig. 11-12

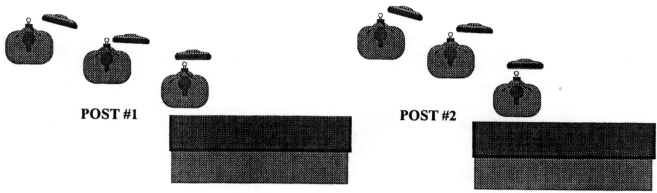

POST #1   POST #2

NO STRAIGHT-AWAY TARGETS

Any target that looks straight --look again, then
shoot to the left or the right of the target. If the
target truly is straight, you will hit it anyway.

These lead sight pictures will no doubt need to
be altered to adjust to your timing, but these are
good pictures to strive for as lead is minimal.

Note: Post three the straight target point of aim
is shifted to the right edge, but you may need to
shift to the left if target exits left.

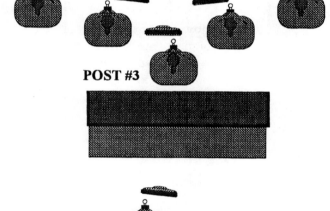

POST #3

POST #4

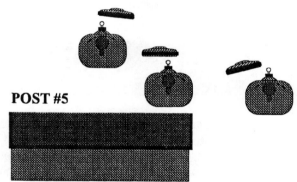

POST #5

TIP

Note: Be aware on post #4 & #5 the odds are
heavy in your favor you will receive a hard right
angle target or left targets... straight targets don't
appear very often as a general rule, so always setup
for the hardest angle target on each post. This holds
true on posts #1 & #2 just that left targets will be
dominant.

DICIPLINE REMINDER

Sight pictures are extremely critical for they
tell you "when" to pull the trigger. Learn to
only pull the trigger when the picture is
right. This has to be "learned" or you will
pull the trigger based on "timing" alone.
Timing, sight pictures and trigger control
are separate entities and each must be incorporated. Requires serious practice!

CHECK YOUR GUN MOUNT

Fig. 11-13

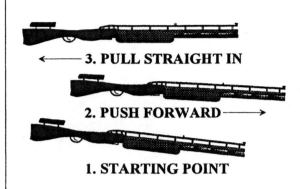

3. PULL STRAIGHT IN

2. PUSH FORWARD ⟶

1. STARTING POINT

3-POINT CIRCULAR MOUNT

Uncomplicate your gun mount and you will increase consistent shouldering eye/rib alignment. **1)** With the gun in the down position push the gun outward **2)** and begin to level the gun horizontally. The gun should be perfectly horizontal as the gun reaches the end of the forward thrust. **3)** Draw the gun straight back into your shoulder. It is performed in a smooth circular unhurried motion. Never "rush" your gun mount or you'll make mistakes galore... many shooters rush and gain low scores.

 THINK PRECISION... BE CONSISTENT... BE A WINNER!

Every move you make, insert precision into it.   Feel everything and develop a sense of purpose in all you do. This is the prime method of building a repeatable, mechanical nature into your game. Simply slapping the gun to your shoulder, calling for the target and chasing it down with a devil-may-care attitude will get you nowhere fast. It will get you to the 27-yard line where you will get your rear whipped time-and-time again by the better shooters who know what precision shooting is all about.

 Such is the fate of those who shoot with no precise purpose!

... A WORD OF ADVICE ...

When you are learning to apply these tricks and secrets, your scores may lag for a time and other shooters may seem to be beating you back to the back-fence while you're still stuck on the 22, or you may be on the 27 and not beating the scores of other club members. That's okay, it won't last long. When you finally get a handle on just 10% of this book and apply it, you will see precision scores inching higher and higher, and it's not luck, but skill at work. So, don't be "pressurized" by peer pressure or "nagged" by the jeers. Every professional shooter had to walk this learning gauntlet and look where they are today! They are tough to beat. And believe me, you will be hard to beat, too! Get serious and ignore the crowd.

So don't be in such a great hurry to get to the back-fence because it's a hellish place to be for a shooter who has no concept of precision shooting techniques. It's not the getting there, but the staying there, that counts and "winning" once you do arrive. What good will it do you to be on the back line and can't win?
Earn your yardage at the bigger shoots. If you get punched at smaller shoots where competition is nil, you will earn yardage, but you won't win at the 27... until you learn how to shoot... precisely.

SLOW, STEADY AND <u>SURE</u> TO WIN !

WHERE TO SHOOT THE TARGET

THE 4 BASIC ZONES

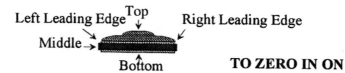

Left Leading Edge ↘ Top ↓ Right Leading Edge ↙
Middle →
Bottom ↑   **TO ZERO IN ON**

Straight-trending Target

Depending on your gun's POI setting, your timing and zone, you may have to put the bead on the target on top or the bottom. You may want to test if the bead is on the outer or inner edges, too, as shown. You still have to look closely to see if the target is "bending" to the left or right. Never put the sight bead on the middle area of the target or you'll lose too many of them.

Severe Quarter Left

Here most shooters will use the bottom leading edge on high POI guns. You should make a small chart where the sight bead is best to be placed for your gun and refer to it until it sinks in. If you have never done this with your gun the best time is... now! It will help you to a high degree knowing exactly where to sight in that target.

Slight Quarter Left

As you can see here, you don't just see a target, you have to look at it, then you have to really look hard again to see where that sight bead is lining up to the target's zone. It takes practice to see targets this well, but just by trying you begin to learn how to do it. Of course, it helps to shoot in slow-motion mode so you can do it --this means intense eye focus when calling.

Extreme Left Angle

Get that sight bead way ahead of the target... don't be afraid to shoot too far ahead of it, as shooting behind and over the top of these devils is the biggest blunder shooters make. Also, keep the gun held down low, under the target on high POI guns as the target drops in elevation even though it "*appears*" it is rising. Watch them closely and you 'll see them drop!

No need for duplication as the right-trending targets require the same sight pictures as the left except for one variation. You may find the sight pictures must be altered due to swing dynamics. The right-hand shooter may be slower to swing to the right and may even tend to raise the muzzle during the swing. The opposite may be true with the left-handed shooter shooting left-trending targets. The point here is to discover if there is a difference between sight pictures on the left and right targets. Now that you know a difference exists, you can make the appropriate corrections into memory.

Only you can determine what sight pictures are right for you depending on your style and speed of shooting and the gun you use. You can find them and that's what this illustration is all about, to help you find those sight pictures. Precision shooting requires using the sight pictures and this, too, requires using the gun's sights -- not just pointing. Pointing is too inaccurate for handicap targets. Backsighting the sight beads is the key to shooting off the end of your barrel. Practice looking in the mirror with your finger wavering in front of your eye so you can adapt to what sight pictures are.

Keep in mind those **X** marks are where you can lock your eye onto the target... look deep and you'll build precision into your shooting.

Fig. 11-14

GETTING THE SIGHT PICTURE RIGHT

Stand in front of a mirror, close one eye and stare with your eye into the mirror's eye. Now wave your thumb or index finger side to side slowly. Can you see your finger clearly? Yet you are still staring into the mirror at your eye at all times without wavering?

Now you've got it! That is a sight picture. Now stare at the tip of your nose, pretending it is a target and bring your finger, which is your gun's sight bead, to your nose. Mystery solved!

Do practice this often and recall this when actually shooting, and you will start seeing very clear and precise sight pictures.

When shooting, seeing the sight bead coming on to the target like you see in the mirror is called, "back-sighting." It is a critical technique to learn to aim the gun. It's not aiming like rifle shooting but it is aiming a shotgun and it's the only way to aim a trapgun. You will need to back-sight when shooting handicap events. Pointing alone won't cut it; you can't just shoot with your eyes alone. You have to aim for precision shooting to occur. The sight picture controls the trigger finger!

Fig. 11-15

SHOOTING OFF THE END OF THE BARREL
The Secret Revealed

TYPICAL VIEW

This is how most shooters see a sight picture. It's okay but it causes missed targets, as the view is so linear and flat and controlling the gun, getting it to the target, requires more body moves, increased swing and it is just too slow to get a heavy trap gun to the target.

This is not to say you can't shoot this way and win, but to shoot with much increased precision it is better to shoot with the end of your barrel. The drawing below isn't the best rendering, but it will give you the view of how it's done.

Fig. 11-16

SHOOTING AT THE END OF MUZZLE VIEW

By simply raising the end of the muzzle a smidgen, you can see the sight bead is now floating in the air. The gun becomes more lively and moves quickly to the target. Using your cheek to press down on the comb and to steer the gun to the target allows you to shoot off the end of the gun. Now the gun is truly "pointing," yet precise "aim" can still be performed.

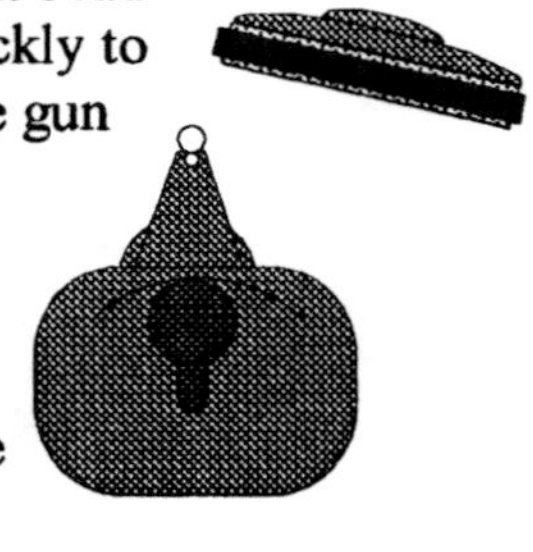

Try to keep the end of the muzzle up so it pin points the target. It will require a bit of practice, but it's great when you finally get it down. The targets break great.

Fig. 11-17

BEWARE OF SHALLOW TARGETS

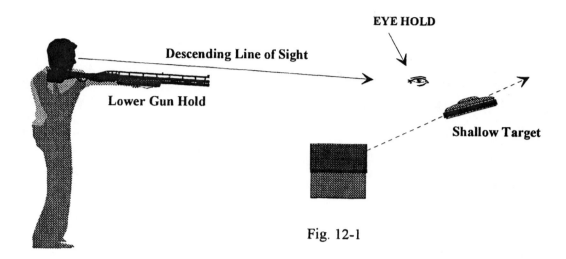

Fig. 12-1

There is a lot to learn here in Fig. 12-1. The handicap shooter should drop the gun hold downward at least one inch when holding a high gun position. This is so you can see and move to the target sooner and catch a ride on the target's true flight path so you will not be crossing over shooting left-to-right. This will assist to eliminate "pushing" or "shoving" the muzzle to the target. You still have to swing to the target even at the 27-yard line. If you do not drop the gun hold? You will react and shoot too fast and the shot string will work against you as the muzzle is not following the target's flight line. You will always see the target too late and this creates a "hurry-up" mentality where smoothness and precise repeatable timing is lost.

Notice the eye hold is also lowered so you can see the target sooner especially so when shooting shallow targets as shown above! You can see the target is resisting to follow the typical flight angle. It is flying at a shallow angle. What is deceptive here is the target appears normal when it leaves the house with a full face, but the moment it rises into the air where you will shoot, it flattens to a razor blade. That is how the shooter perceives the optical illusion as the target does not actually tilt in midair, but it appears to do so because you are standing and the target is rising. First you see a bright full-face target and suddenly it is a tiny sliver of a razor blade slipping away. You shoot and you miss clean. The next time you attend a tournament and shoot terrible scores way below your average the shallow target is likely to be the culprit.

The practice trap at competitive shoots are often the blame for poor handicap scores. How? Many clubs fail to set the practice traps precisely as the tournament traps. The shooter practices on nice soft (slow) targets rising with a full face and performs quite well score wise, then falls apart terribly in the actual competition event. What went wrong? The shooter's eye and gun hold and timing was firmly embedded in the warm up fully expecting the same targets in the competition event, but instead received "fast" and "shallow" targets upsetting the entire setup and execution of the shot. A terrific low score is the result. Be aware that some shooters have been known to intentionally do this with the practice traps to give them a huge advantage. Educate club management to make sure they set the practice traps too! I saw 20-trailers pull out of a State-level shoot because of this... they were shooting so poorly it was no use staying.

So what is the solution to shooting shallow targets? 1.) Drop the gun hold a bit more so you will not shoot over the target. 2.) Lower your eye hold so you can see the target sooner. 3.) Wait, wait, wait, for the target to rise up beyond the muzzle before you move to the target. You need a small time delay here so your eye can see the target's transition from full face to razor blade. 4.) You will have to force yourself to shoot under the target at all times by keeping an "air gap" between the sight bead and the target. If you put the bead on the target you will certainly shoot over the top and miss. Extra work is required. It will not feel so natural shooting this way at all as the target's are shallow. Set legal? Yes, but right on the edge! 5.) A lighter shade of eyeglass lens color will help you to see these thin targets. 6.) Good luck! It takes a lot of energy and exceptionally good eyes to shoot these targets. 7.) If you have an adjustable point of impact gun? Simply lower the POI and you will be right back to normal. 7.) You may need to apply vertical separation. See Fig. 12-2.

Which Is Better #7 1/2 Shot or #8?   You Be The Judge!

Beyond the 24 yard line #7 1/2 is the rule. But try this to increase your odds of picking up targets if the targets are warm, soft and dry as in desert conditions. Use #8 to increase your odds of breaking the targets. How? There are 64 more pellets in each 1 1/8oz shell. In a 100-bird handicap event you will be throwing 6,400 more pellets at the targets than you would with 7 1/2. Do the math. The more pellets you can throw at a target the higher the odds you will hit just a few more targets. Make sure your gun can shoot and pattern #8 shot and the targets are not cold, damp or of a hard composition. Keep in mind that #7 1/2 shot is still King of the Handicap under all conditions as the energy level is approximately 20% higher for reliable target breaks and will pattern tighter than #8 in most guns.

VERTICAL SEPERATION

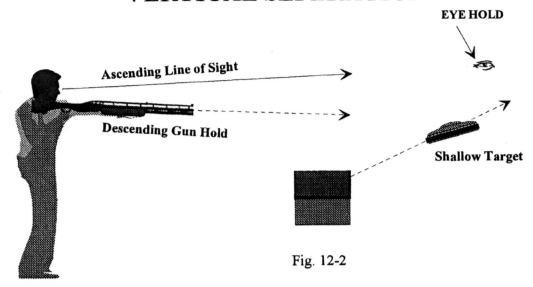

Fig. 12-2

Many shooters will find scores rising if vertical separation is used. Here the eye hold is raised and the gun hold is lowered to form a "V" configuration. You should start like this. 1.) As you stand look straight out. This is the neutral eye hold position. You can always use the neutral eye hold position. 2.) Place the gun hold straight out as you normally do. This is the neutral gun hold position. 3. Drop the gun hold only about 1-inch and shoot. See if this helps you hit more targets. Give it some time so you can adapt to the new form. 4. Now begin to raise your eye hold upward in small increments 1/2 inch at a time. See if this helps you hit more targets.

The separation method performs many things. It will absolutely stop you from "rushing" the targets and prevent pushing and shoving the muzzle to the target... a major problem with handicap shooters! You will feel way more relaxed and at ease to swing to the target. You will allow the target to be seen with peripheral vision exiting the house instead of centralized vision. This will prevent an eye flinch called, "eye flicker" which defocuses the eyes and causes the eye to "search" for the target when it exits the house. Once the eye searches like this the target is lost. You may get lucky a few times, but more missed targets are due to eye flickering than most shooter's realize! I spoke with Daro Handy about this and his advice was, "Forget about trigger control. Focus on eye control!" Correct he is. For it is the eye that tells the trigger finger when to pull the trigger.

PRACTICE TRACKING TARGETS AT HOME

Cieling Line

Fig. 12-3

The old method to track targets was to shoulder the gun and follow a horizontal ceiling line. While this method does work it lacks realism as no target will be shot traveling on a straight line moving left to right as shown in Fig. 12-3. Also targets are rising and curving in flight so you accomplish little with this method in the practical sense.

Light Beam
Flashlight

A better method is to attach a small penlight flashlight with tape to the rib of your gun and shine it on a wall. You can now place a target on the wall and practice swinging to it. You may want to draw lines from the targets so you can follow the flight path of the target. You will get a much better feel for shooting and with a safety snap-cap installed you can pull the trigger when the light illuminates the target. Try this and you'll be mimicking trapshooting to a high degree of efficiency.

Fig. 12-4

When you draw slightly curved lines you will be mimicking the swing angle required to track targets on a higher level of reality. Targets do not travel in straight lines... they bend due to gravity and air mass variations along with weather conditions.

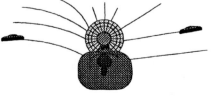

Fig. 12-5

You can draw straight lines on the wall if you wish. The novice shooter should start with straight lines then progress to bent lines. One or the other will work best for you.

DOUBLE TRAP TIPS
DOUBLE TROUBLE -TWICE THE FUN!

OFF HOUSE   **ON HOUSE**

Fig. 12-6

TAKING THE FIRST SHOT

You <u>can</u> hold the gun off the house to take out the first target, but only if you shoot the angle target first. Hold the gun on the house when shooting the straight target first. Most shooters prefer the later, but some Olympic double-trap pros always shoot the angle target first. You may want to try it to see how it works for you. The point is; you get the hard target out of the way first, so you have 'plenty of time' to swing and hit the straight-away target. You need to be a bit reckless when shooting the first target, but less so when shooting the angle target first, as time is no longer a critical moment when shooting an angle target first.

LOW GUN   **HIGH GUN**

Fig. 12-7

GUN & EYE HOLD

Time is very critical when shooting doubles. By holding a lower gun, even just 1" lower than normal, you can see the target sooner and shoot it quicker. The lower you hold the gun, the faster you can shoot, but keep your eye hold up high! This will prevent seeing a strong comet-tail streak and allow you to better see the bird/bead sight picture for an accurate first shot hit. Hold the gun where you 'know' the target will exit so when you see the "flash" of the target, you can pull the trigger quickly and get the eye moving immediately over to the second target. Get the eye moving, not the gun. The gun will follow the eye, but you must work on moving the eyes quickly.

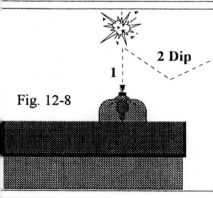

3 On Track

2 Dip

1

Fig. 12-8

V-DIP SWING

Many shooters attempt to cross-over the gun from left-to-right in a straight horizontal line to catch the second target, but this can create many errors in aim and missed second-angled targets. By simply dipping the gun one inch downward you can catch the true track of the target and rise up into it for a solid follow-through hit. Targets will still be broken, as shown, quite close in line, once your speed is perfected. The straight-line cross-over technique does work, but the V-dip method can be a lifesaver for those who just keep on missing those nasty second-angled targets. Veteran shooters will benefit.

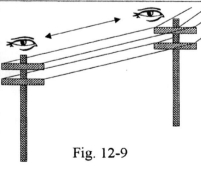

Fig. 12-9

EYE CONTROL

This exercise is so simple it defies reason, but it works so well. You have to learn how to switch your eyes from one target to the other very quickly and with dead-on focus. Try switching your eyes from one telephone pole to another--real telephone poles, that is. Doing this you will begin to get the feel of controlling the speed of your eyes to locate and lock-on to targets. Now, remember to switch your eyes to the target without moving your gun. The eyes must switch first, lock-on, then the gun follows, as the eye continues to track the target. Shooters who shoot poorly in double trap fail to use eye control!

If you begin hitting the second targets, and then find yourself dropping the first targets, it's because you are rushing or getting too nervous to hit the first target. Be ready, but relaxed. Know that you do have plenty of time to hit the distancing second target, if you practice moving your eyes away from the first target the moment you pull the trigger. Do not wait to see the target explode or sail away unburned. Get the eyes moving and be smooth about it.

DOUBLE TRAP TIPS
DOUBLE TROUBLE -TWICE THE FUN!

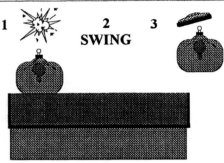

Fig. 13-1

1-2-3 TIMING

Number 1 time count begins not when you call for the target, but when you pull the trigger on the first target. Don't make the mistake of starting the count when you call or it will force you to shoot too fast and you will drop too many targets being in a rush-mode. The eyes swing to the target on count #2 and the gun is allowed to follow naturally. Do not swing as your eyes are still looking for the second target! This timing structure allows you to catch the second-angle target with little to no lead in the sight picture. You rush the first straight-away shot and 'glide' smoothly over to the second-angle target. Be precise on the second target.

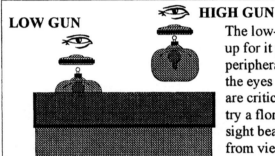

FLASH SHOOTING

The low-gun need not rise by much to catch the first straight target, if you set up for it properly, knowing where it will exit the top of the trap house. Use peripheral vision to see the "flash" of the target, then pull the trigger and get the eyes away quickly to the second-angle target. Gun and eye hold points are critical here to establish the timing and accuracy of the shot. You should try a florescent gun sight, as they work great on double targets, since white sight beads tend to blend with the scene causing many missed targets and fade from view due to gun and target speed. See Fig.13-9 advertisement. Timing is way less important than accuracy, yet proper timing creates accuracy.

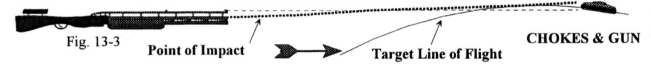

Fig. 13-3   **Point of Impact**   **Target Line of Flight**   **CHOKES & GUN**

Many pro trap shooter know how important point of impact is, and more so with doubles. If you are shooting with an autoloader at double targets, you are at a disadvantage because you only have one POI. The Over & Under shotgun has the advantage of the bottom barrel shooting a high POI, to grab the fast-rising #1 target, and the lower POI in the upper barrel shoots flatter, to hit the flatter flight angle #2 target. Is your doubles gun shooting properly? It must comply with the above barrel setting pertaining to POI. Pattern check to insure the lower barrel is higher in POI than the upper barell. Are you shooting your first shot with the lower barrel?

TECHNIQUE

Don't use the same stance and shooting techniques as you do with single target trap. Revamp your mindset strongly that this is a 'different' game and set up accordingly. Readjust your gun and eye hold and timing and swing velocity to compensate. You can lean into the gun a little bit more in doubles than you should in singles, as shown in the illustration at left. Also, if you decide to shoot the angle target first, you do so on all posts -- you do not switch-over. That is another advantage, since there is no confusion of which target should be shot first from post to post. You can shoot the straight or the angle target first, it is a personal preference -- not a rule! Each method has advantages. Try both and see which one works best for you.

Fig. 13-4

If your double-rise (double-trap) scores are falling, or not rising at all, it's time to change things. Doubles usually are shot after shooting single target events. You may fall into the habit of shooting the same way; same stance, san eye & gun holds, same timing, etc., when shooting double-trap. It's an entirely different game with its own set of rules. Change your technique. Take lessons to make the learning experience easier and more enjoyable.

Fig. 13-5   # TWO MORE BOOKS BY JAMES RUSSELL

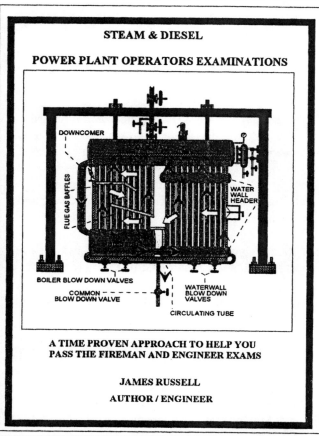
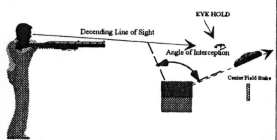

Fig. 13-6   Trap Shooting Secrets   Page 174.

"SHOOTING IS FUN... ESPECIALLY WHEN YOU WIN!"

Visit our web site: http://www.powernet.net/~scrnplay

James Russell

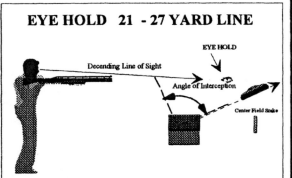

Fig. 13-7

Trap Shooting Secrets   Page 175.

Fig. 13-8

Trap Shooting Secrets   Page 176.

NOTES

NOTES

"SHOOTING IS FUN... ESPECIALLY WHEN YOU WIN!"

Visit our web site:www.powernet.net/~scrnplay

James Russell

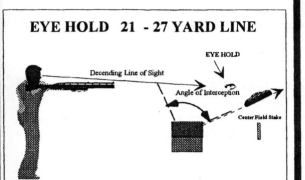
You shoot to win, that's why you compete, that's why you love trapshooting, but it sure isn't fun losing. Fact is, it can be quite depressing to see your name scratched from the option pay-out list making everyone else a tad bit richer.

Okay, you had a bad day. But how many more *bad day's* are still to come? Wouldn't you like to turn that situation around and insure you take home *your* share of purse money and prizes?

Precision Shooting will help you do just that by polishing you into a finely-tuned competitor, increasing your scores, and hammering those targets that now slip into the horizon.

You're a good shooter - you wouldn't shoot if you weren't -- but too many targets slipped away today, just like yesterday, last month and last year too. Something is wrong, and you can't seem to identify the problem to resolve the difficulty. The same mistakes keep repeating themselves and targets are *"Lost."*

SEEING TARGET ANGLES
A simple test verifying targets do not travel in straight lines, but indeed do traverse definitive arcs

Targets 'bend' away causing many low scores.

WHY DID YOU MISS THOSE TARGETS?

Not by mistake, but through miscalculation of target angle and the target *bending* away from shotstring. Problem is, you'll keep on missing targets like a <u>bad habit</u>! Sound familiar? Once you understand target angularity and behavior... it'll be hard to miss! *Precision Shooting* will absolutely tighten-up your sight picture to a micron. You'll be shooting with fine-tuned accurate precision smokeballing targets dead-on. And if you do miss,you'll likely rip a piece off the target so you won't be hearing *"Lost"* ringing in your ears. Figure left, reveals a hidden secret as how targets *bend*. Did targets bend away from you today? They sure did, but do you know how to hit them?

 YOU CAN RAISE YOUR SCORES !
ORDER YOUR COPY... TODAY!

Everyone drops a target now and then, even professionals do, but maybe you're dropping too many which is keeping you out of the money. One thing *Precision Shooting* will do for you is develop precise shooting, especially in handicap events; because this book is focused on mid/long yardage shooting. The bottom line is your scores will increase when you <u>stop missing</u> those flying beasts that slip and slide far into the horizon all too often. Those are the 'hard' targets and you'll learn how to not let them escape. Professional shooting techniques you've never read in any book or magazine. We don't talk about trapshooting like other books, we do it... like having a professional trapshooting coach by your side telling you what to do! This book is much larger than *Trap Shooting Secrets* with over 85 drawings and 190 + pages of text with over 230 questions & answers given to tough shooting conditions. You absolutely will not be disappointed. Satisfaction guaranteed or purchase price refunded. No publisher offers a warrantee like this! $34.95 James Russell, P.O. Box 10121, Suite 2093, Eugene Oregon 97440   You're going to like Precision Shooting!

VISIT JAMES RUSSELL'S WEB SITE
www.powernet.net/~scrnplay

NO COMPUTER OR INTERNET? NO PROBLEM...
VISIT YOUR LOCAL LIBRARY AND THEY WILL GET YOU ON-LINE FOR FREE !

- **FREE SHOOTING TIPS - OVER 500! GET ANSWERS TO YOUR SHOOTING PROBLEMS! LEARN HOW TO SHOOT WAY BETTER THAN YOU DO NOW... AND IT'S ALL FREE!**

- **INFORMATIVE DETAILED ARTICLES! EVERYTHING FROM WHAT TO LOOK FOR WHEN BUYING A NEW GUN TO BEING A GOOD SQUAD LEADER... TIPS ON HOW TO MANAGE CONCENTRATION, SEE TARGETS, ETC.**

- **COMEDY - TRAP SHOOTING JOKES. MEET CLARANCE BAGASAND III, AND LEARN HOW YOU TOO CAN BE A PROFESSIONAL SANDBAGGER! FUNNY INTERVIEWS... SEE THE LIGHTER SIDE OF TRAPSHOOTING !**

- **LOOKING FOR A GUN PART? A NEW GUN? NEED A SHOOTING INSTRUCTOR TO LIFT YOUR SCORES? WANT TO TAKE A CLAY TARGET SHOOTING VACATION? SEE OUR "LINKS" SECTION.**

- **THIS WEB SITE IS HUGE... OVER 120-LONG FORMAT PAGES OF TRAPSHOOTING TIPS, ADVICE, PROBLEM SOLVING INSTRUCTIONS. THIS IS THE WORLD'S LARGEST TRAPSHOOTING WEB SITE. DON'T MISS IT !**

- **YOU WILL LEARN TRAPSHOOTING TECHNIQUES YOU HAVE NEVER READ BEFORE IN ANY MAGAZINE, BOOK OR SAW IN ANY VIDEOTAPE. TIPS THE TOP OLYMPIC & ATA PROFESSIONALS USE... GUARANTEED!**

- **NEW PRODUCTS ARE REVIEWED WITH ADVICE ON HOW TO USE THE PRODUCT TO INCREASE YOUR SCORES! CHECK OUT THE 'EASYHIT' SHOTGUN SIGHT THAT CAN HAMMER TARGETS AND SHOW YOU WHAT YOU DID WRONG INSTANTLY IF YOU MISS, SO YOU WON'T MISS AGAIN! WE CALL IT THE $40 MIRACLE !**

THE MORE YOU LEARN... THE MORE YOU EARN...
AND THE MORE FUN YOU'LL HAVE TRAP SHOOTING !

... NEW ...   ... NEW ...   ... NEW ...   ... NEW ...   ... NEW ...   ... NEW ...

TRAP SHOOTING BOOKS

WHO ENDORSES THESE TEXTBOOKS?

DARO HANDY - ATA Top Gun in USA & Shooting Instructor
PHIL KINER - ATA All-American & Shooting Instructor
LUCA SCRIBANI ROSSI - Olympic Gold Medallist & Team Coach.
Shotgun Sports Magazine - USA
Clay Shooting Magazine - Europe
Gun Web Magazine - USA

> **"Number 1 of the top-10 books Trap Shooting Secrets by James Russell!"**
> Clay Shooting Magazine

100's of Competition Trapshooters reading these books see an immediate pick up in scores. Like having a shooting coach by your side telling you exactly what to do!

These are the first technical trap shooting books ever published. They don't just talk about trap shooting... they tell you how to shoot!

You will learn many of the inside secrets professional trapshooters use to annhilate targets... and it's quite easy to learn too!

WHERE TO GET YOUR COPY
Barnes & Noble bookstores
Amazon.com & Varsity.com internet bookstore
BooksAMillion bookstores
Walden Books bookstores
Borders bookstores
Shotgun Sports Magazine call 800-676-8920
ATA Trap & Field Magazine
Clay Shooting Magazine
Any Bookstore can order the books!

> **BORED? TRY TRAP SHOOTING**
> Visit our Web Site. URL Address is listed above.

TESTIMONIAL EDORSEMENTS

DARO HANDY
Top Gun Hall of Fame Shooter

There is a lot of constructive information in Trap Shooting Secrets and Precision Shooting - The Trapshooter's Bible. The concepts in these two books are strongly presented, understandable and easily applied. If you would like to step into the world where professional trapshooter's reside, these books can reveal valuable technical information to improve your shooting. And, in conjunction with a qualified shooting instructor, these two books should give the trapshooter a high measure of success. *Daro Handy.*

LUCA SCRIBANI ROSSI
Olympic Medallist - Twice World Champion

I strongly recommend shotgun competition shooters to read both, Trap Shooting Secrets, and Precision Shooting - The Trapshooter's Bible. If you read these books you simply can 't go wrong. Just follow the steps outlined and you'll leap ahead in the rankings of any competition you'll attend. That's my recommendation. *Luca Scribani Rossi.*

PHIL KINER
ATA All-American Shooter

I have reviewed both of James Russell's new trapshooting books and I have found them to be full of useful trapshooting tips. These books will be an excellent edition to every trapshooter's library. *Phil Kiner.*

DOZEN'S MORE ON OUR WEB SITE !

FREE TRAPSHOOTING LESSONS ON THE WEB SITE --HUNDREDS OF TRAP SHOOTING TIPS AND ADVICE

WWW.POWERNET.NET/~SCRNPLAY

No computer or Internet access? No problem. Go to your public library or college and they will connect you. Many trap shooting articles await you with answers to your shooting questions, how to select a trap gun, product reviews and much more!.

<u>Note</u>: If the web site address fails to work, use a search engine and type in the word; trapshooting and look for JR Publishing or James Russell Publishing. We are linked on most all the major trapshooting site link pages. You'll find us!

Printed in the United Kingdom
by Lightning Source UK Ltd.
135652UK00001B/68/A

9 780916 367091